# The Intrepid Arkansas Traveler

Michael Reisig

Clear Creek Press

Clear Creek Publishing
P.O. Box 1081
Mena, Arkansas 71953
(501) 394-4992

ISBN 0-9651240-0-2



Cover art by Peter Bradley

**Acknowledgments**

We must first extend our appreciation to the Arkansas Department of Parks and Tourism, Cranford Johnson Robinson Woods and the National Forestry Service for the material they so generously provided.

A special thanks to Ms. Tiffany Lane for her invaluable assistance in final typing, design and proofing.

Thanks also to August House Publishers and W. K. McNeil for their "Ozark Mountain Humor" inserts.

Last but not least, my love and gratitude to my lady and my editor, Bonnie Lee.

# ARKANSAS

I cannot tell what makes me pine
For those dear native hills of mine,
Nor can I tell why clearer gleams
The water of my mountain streams,
Nor why the earth and sky and air
Seems kindlier there than anywhere.
It must be that by Nature's law
They all belong in Arkansas.

- George L. Stockard

# THE INTREPID ARKANSAS TRAVELER

The original Intrepid Arkansas Traveler was one Ignatius Bartholomew Benton. He was the product of an Eastern school teacher and a Mississippi gambler, and as he grew into manhood, Ignatius came to embody the attributes of both. He cherished the written word, reading and writing well, and he possessed a wonderful imagination. But he liked the feel of a deck of cards in his hand, and whiskey, though a close companion, was more often a foe than a friend.

In the early months of 1868, having survived the Civil War in which he served the Southern cause, Ignatius journeyed to Arkansas for the first time. He fell in love with the lush green rolling hills, the springtime dogwood colors and the clear, cool creeks and rivers. He traveled from town to town, gambling a bit, working when he had to, and writing stories of the colorful people and the wonderful country he encountered. Once in a while he sold a story to a local newspaper for whiskey money, but most of his tales ended up in a notebook which he kept in his saddlebag, and were not widely read until after his death.

His untimely departure from this world was a combination of poor judgment and bad luck. He was caught with another man's woman. That alone could have hastened his exit; the fact that the lady was the sheriff's wife added a goodly amount of fuel to the fires of fate.

That night, in the resulting confusion, an oil lamp was quickly extinguished; flashes of gunfire creased a darkened room accompanied by angry shouts and the screams of a thoroughly frightened lady. Somehow Ignatius managed to stumble out the window onto the balcony and jump to the ground. However, being slightly drunk and completely unnerved, he grabbed the wrong horse from the hitching rail. Sad to say, it was also the sheriff's horse.

The next morning, the sheriff, on a borrowed mount accompanied by a hastily gathered posse, caught up with the writer/philanderer turned inadvertent horsethief, and under the spreading limbs of an Arkansas oak, Ignatius Bartholomew Benton was unceremoniously hanged.

Remarkably enough his writings were salvaged by none other than the sheriff's wife, who, without the constable's knowledge, sent them to a publisher friend back East. The following year a book of his stories was published.

The Intrepid Arkansas Traveler told of the land, the politics and the people of Arkansas. He sought to find the heart of those courageous souls who had braved the wilderness and carved a future from the great oaks and the rocky soil of that new land.

Ignatius wrote with warmth and humor, and a touch of acerbic wit. He told of fishing and hunting trips, and took an occasional stab at the newly entrenched bureaucracy, its politicians and some of their policies he thought less than beneficial. He acknowledged the trials of everyday life, but recognized the strengths and the pride of the Arkansans, discovering their unique sense of humor and the optimism they shared for the future.

It is in keeping with this tradition that I have picked up his torch and his namesake and offer you the adventures of the new Intrepid Arkansas Traveler. I hope you'll come along and share with me my travels and my observations, as I explore the heartland of America.

The Intrepid Arkansas Traveler

**Some characters and circumstances in the Traveler's writings may be fictitious.*

# CONTENTS

# POINTS of INTEREST ENTERTAINMENT/ RECREATION

Ah, to set out on bright morn toward new adventure, wending crooked road in gay anticipation, searching out virgin sights and sounds and smells like gypsies on a Roman holiday.

Onward we trek, all the while forging crystal memories that we hold in soft cocoons of passing time, recollections tucked away like tiny treasures, to be drawn out at leisure and mulled with a gentle smile.

The Traveler

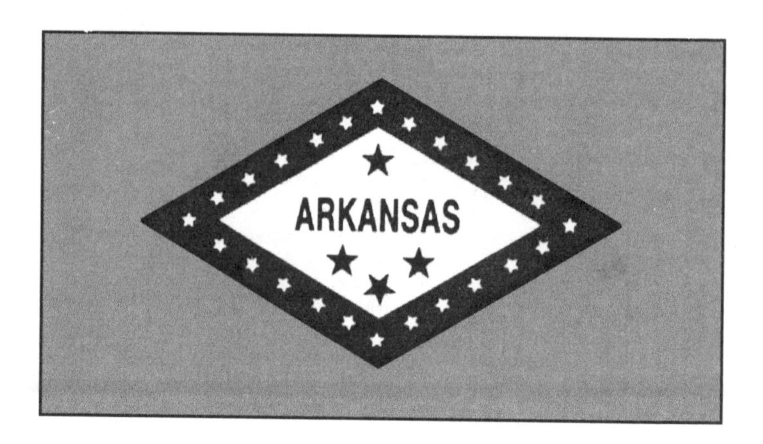


Arkansas means "downstream people." It is from the name of an Indian tribe called Quapaw or Oo-gaq-pa. Algonquin Indians pronounced it o-ka-na-sa. French explorers had their own versions. Marquette wrote Arkansoa. LaSalle wrote Arkensa. DeTonti's was Arkancas. And LaHarpe wrote Arkansas. The state was spelled Arkansas when it was admitted to the Union in 1836. The pronunciation "Ark-an-saw" was settled upon by a legislative committee in 1881.

**VITAL STATISTICS**

* Population - 2.4 million
* Area - 53,187 square miles
* Extreme Length - 240 miles
* Capital - Little Rock
* Time Zone - Central
* Extreme Width - 275 miles
* Climate - Average annual temperature: 61.4 degrees F.

**STATE SYMBOLS**

* State Bird - Mockingbird
* State Flower - Apple blossom
* State Fruit/Vegetable - Pink tomato
* State Musical Instrument - Fiddle
* State Tree - Pine
* State Insect - Honeybee
* State Beverage - Milk
* State Gem - Diamond
* State Motto - Regnat Populus (The People Rule)
* State Nicknames - "The Land of Opportunity", "The Natural State"
* State Historical Song - "The Arkansas Traveler" (folk song)
* There are 600,000 acres of lakes, 9,700 miles of streams of rivers, and 2.4 million acres of national forestland in Arkansas.

## *Northwest Ozarks Entertainment, Recreation and Attractions*

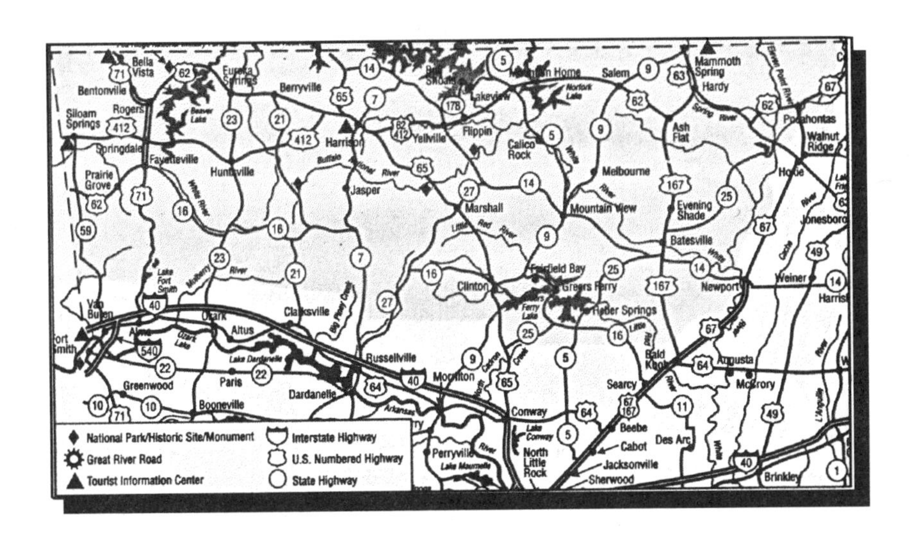


1. ***Abundant Memories Heritage Village*** *(501) 253-6764*
   Ark. 23 N., Eureka Springs. Living history programs and authentic antiques from Revolutionary War through Civil War times. Includes 26 picturesque buildings and thousands of antiques, guns, tools, carriages and furniture.
2. ***Arkansas and Missouri Railroad*** *(501) 751-8600 / 800-687-8600*
   107 N. Commercial St., Springdale. Travel through the Boston Mountains from Springdale to historic Van Buren and back. Restored railway cars cross trestles and 1882 Winslow tunnel.
3. ***Artist Point*** *(501) 369-2226*
   U.S. 71, north of Mountainburg. Views of Ozarks and river valley. Museum of Native American artifacts and arts and crafts store with locally made crafts including woodcarvings.
4. ***Arts Center of the Ozarks*** *(501) 751-5441*
   216 W. Grove, Springdale. Drama, outdoor musicals, gallery showings, classes, cultural events, 425-seat theater.
5. ***Belle of the Ozarks*** *(501) 253-6200*
   Starkey Marina, off U.S. 62 W., Eureka Springs. Beaver Lake excursion cruises.
6. ***Cosmic Cavern*** *(501) 749-2298*
   Ark. 21 N., Berryville. Site of the Ozarks' largest underground lake. One hour guided tour through subterranean rooms, across an underground bridge.

Gemstone mining.

7. ***Dinosaur World - Land of Kong*** *(501) 253-8113*
   Ark. 187, Eureka Springs. More than 100 life-sized dinosaur replicas, four-story King Kong statue. Camping.

8. ***Elna N. Smith Foundation Site*** *(501) 253-9200 / 800-882-PLAY*
   Statue Rd. Off U.S. 62 E., Eureka Springs. Location of The Great Passion Play, plus the seven-story-high Christ of the Ozarks statue; the Sacred Arts Center, with more than 1,000 exhibits; the Bible Museum, the New Holy Land, re-creations of Biblical sites including Moses' Tabernacle in the Wilderness; the Smith Memorial Chapel; a 10-foot section of Berlin Wall; shops and more.
9. ***Eureka Springs and North Arkansas Railway*** *(501) 253-9623*
   Scenic Ark. 23 N., Eureka Springs. Restored steam engine and passenger car rides. Lunch and dinner served aboard Eurekan Dining Car. Historic depot, gift shop.
10. ***Eureka Springs Art Galleries*** *(501) 253-8737*
    Eureka Springs gained a reputation as an artists' colony in the 1930s and 1940s, and has since emerged as one of the respected fine arts centers of the mid-South. Fine art galleries and other outlets showcase their talent. The city's May Fine Arts Festival is a highlight. Some galleries are now staying open until 9 p.m. on Saturdays through December for the convenience of visitors.
11. ***Eureka Springs Gardens*** *(501) 253-9244 / 800-333-1599 / (501) 253-9256 (for recorded color and seasonal display information)*
    U.S. 62 W., Eureka Springs. 33 acres of hardwood trees, select native plants, thousand of annuals and perennials, high bluffs. Blue Spring, one of the Ozarks' largest, is within the grounds. Wooden ramps provide barrier-free access. Gift shop.
12. ***Frog Fantasies*** *(501) 253-7227*
    151 Spring St., Eureka Springs. Frogs in every shape, color, size, material collected over 50 years.
13. ***Indian Paintbrush Gallery*** *(501) 524-6920*

U.S. 412 W., Siloam Springs. Native American paintings, limited edition prints, weavings, pottery, baskets.

14. ***The Last Precinct Police Museum*** *(501) 253-4948*
U.S. 62 W., Eureka Springs. Police cars, uniforms, weapons. Hollywood memorabilia.

The Lost Spur Ranch - Harrison

15. ***The Lost Spur Guest Ranch*** *(501) 743-SPUR*
Be a cowboy or a cowgirl for a few days. Ride the range, fish, explore or just relax in comfortable cabins. Outside Harrison off Highway 47.

16. ***Music Shows***
Pine Mountain Jamboree and Ozark Mountain Hoe-Down, Eureka Springs. Sugar Creek Country, Lowell. Little O' Oprey, West Fork.

17. ***Newton County Ecotours*** *(501) 446-5898*
Jasper. Explore the unspoiled wilderness of Newton County in small groups, visiting the Buffalo River, Boxley or other sites. Tours include historical walks, wildlife and craft workshops.

18. ***Onyx Cave*** *(501) 253-9321*
Off U.S. 62 E., Eureka Springs. Radio-guided tours of underground rooms, unique formations, ramp access to cave, museum.

19. ***Opera of the Ozarks/Inspiration Point Fine Arts Colony*** *(501) 253-8595*
U.S. 62 W., Eureka Springs. Summer opera presentations. Outdoor theater. Classical music and dance. Undergoing expansion.

20. ***Ozark Native Craft Shop*** *(501) 634-3791*
U.S. 71, near Winslow. Features the handiwork of more than 300 mountain craftspeople.

21. ***Pendergraft's*** *(501) 446-5267*
Scenic 7 Byway, near Jasper. An art gallery with craft exhibits.

22. ***Pine Mountain Village*** *(501) 253-9156*
U.S. 62 E., Eureka Springs. Craftspeople, horse-drawn buggies, shops, in this re-creation of a Victorian-era village.

23. ***Quigley's Castle*** *(501) 253-8311*

Ark. 23 S., Eureka Springs. Extensive collections of butterflies, moths, rocks, arrowheads and flowers.

24. ***Red Bud Valley Chuckwagon*** *(501) 253-2000 or (501) 253-9028*
U.S. 62 E., Eureka Springs. Covered wagon ride to mountain ridge. Barbecue dinner, entertainment.

25. ***Sager Creek Arts Center*** *(501) 524-4000*
West Twin Springs, Siloam Springs. Drama, works by area artists showcased in an old church.

26. ***Terra Studios*** *(501) 643-3185 / 800-255-8995*
Ark. 16, Durham. Handmade glassworks and pottery. Demonstrations. Gardens, picnic area.

27. ***The Great Passion Play*** *(501) 253-9200 / 800-882-PLAY*
Statue Rd., off U.S. 62 E., Eureka Springs. Outdoor drama depicting the last week of Christ's life on Earth has drawn more than five million visitors in 26 seasons. Late April through October. Nightly except Monday, Thursday.

28. ***Vene's Native American Art Gallery*** *(501) 751-6489*
3041 N. Oak St., Springdale. Original paintings, prints, dolls, patchwork, baskets, jewelry, pottery, sculpture and other artworks.

29. ***Walton Arts Center*** *(501) 443-9216 (office) / (501) 443-5600 (box office)*
495 W. Dickson St., Fayetteville. Theaters, galleries, performing areas and more. Home of the North Arkansas Symphony, the center draws Broadway touring shows and other top attractions.

30. ***War Eagle Cavern*** *(501) 789-2909 / (501) 756-0913*
Scenic Ark. 12, Rogers. Guided tours through underground formations, including onyx, rimstone and crinoid fossils.

31. ***Wild Wilderness Safari*** *(501) 736-8383*
Located on Safari Rd. Off Hwy. 59, Gentry. Drive through to see about 20 species of animals. Petting zoo.

## *Northwest Ozarks Festivals*

Famed for its crafters, Northwest Arkansas hosts a number of arts and crafts fairs from spring right on into December. The biggest of them all is the War Eagle Fair, the third weekend of October, centerpiece of more than two dozen shows spread all over the landscape. The region welcomes spring with events like the Dogwood Festival at Siloam Springs in April, the May Fine Arts Festival in Eureka Springs and Sugar Creek Arts and Crafts Fair at Bentonville. Summer events include the Rodeo of the Ozarks at Springdale on the Fourth of July and Brumley Gospel Sing in Springdale in August and Tontitown's annual Grape Festival the same month. Celebrating music is a natural pastime in Arkansas. Among the celebrations are the Music Festival of Arkansas at Fayetteville and the Eureka Springs Blues Festival in June, and the Eureka Springs Jazz Festival and Frisco Days in Rogers each September. Other autumn festivals include the huge Clothesline Fair at Prairie Grove Battlefield State Park on

Labor Day Weekend, Autumnfest at Fayetteville, and Arkansas Apple Festival at Lincoln and Ozark Folk Festival in October. In December, the region glows with decorations, especially at Eureka Springs and Fayetteville.

## *Historic Sites, Museums*

1. ***Arkansas Air Museum*** *(501) 521-4947*
   Drake Field, U.S. 71S., Fayetteville. Vintage aircraft, including pre-World War II racing planes in flying condition, aeronautical memorabilia, gift shop in historic white frame hangar.
2. ***Bank of Eureka Springs*** *(501) 253-8241*
   70 S. Main, Eureka Springs. This working bank re-creates the turn of the century, with brass tellers' cages and old-style equipment.
3. ***Boone County Historical Museum*** *(501) 741-3312*
   Central and Cherry Sts., Harrison. Railroad artifacts, antiques, Indian artifacts, Civil War memorabilia.
4. ***Carroll County Heritage Center*** *(501) 423-6312*
   On the Square, Berryville. Artifacts from Berryville and Carroll County are housed in historic building. Moonshine still, funeral parlor and one-room school among exhibits.
5. ***Daisy International Air Gun Museum*** *(501) 636-1200*
   U.S. 71B, Rogers. On the grounds of Daisy Manufacturing Co., extensive collection of antique and contemporary air guns, rifles.
6. ***Eureka Springs Historical Museum*** *(501) 253-9417*
   95 S. Main, Eureka Springs. Relics from Eureka Springs' historic past are collected here. See documents, clothing, mementos, photographs, furniture.
7. ***Gay Nineties Button and Doll Museum*** *(501) 253-9321*
   Onyx Cave, U.S. 62 E., Eureka Springs. Button Mosaics and dolls collected over many years.
8. ***Hammond Museum of Bells*** *(501) 253-7411*
   Spring and Pine Sts., Eureka Springs. More than 1,000 bells of every size, age and description.

9. ***Headquarters House and Grounds*** *(501) 521-2970*
118 E. Dickson St., Fayetteville. Both Union and Confederate troops used this 1853 home as headquarters during the Civil War. Civil War artifacts. Grounds with period landscaping.

10. ***John Brown University*** *(501) 524-3131*
Siloam Springs. Founded in 1919, this liberal arts college has log cabin home of pioneer settler Simon Sager on its grounds.

11. ***Miles Musical Museum*** *(501) 253-8961*
U.S. 62 W., Eureka Springs. Musical instruments of every sort: calliope, nickelodeons, band organs, music boxes, player pianos and much more. Featured in April 1995 issue of the *Smithsonian Magazine.*

12. ***Pea Ridge National Military Park*** *(501) 451-8122*
400 S. Walton Blvd., Bentonville. An Italianate villa built in 1875 by Col. Sam Peel, a prominent early figure in Bentonville history. Restored mansion and gardens are open to the public.

13. ***Poor Richard's Gift and Confectionary Shop*** *(501) 631-7687*
116 S. First St., Rogers. Listed on National Register, 1907 restored drugstore has the original soda fountain, tile floors, gifts.

14. ***Prairie Grove Battlefield State Park*** *(501) 846-2990*
U.S. 62, Prairie Grove. Site commemorates Civil War battle in 1862. Park contains 130 acres, including battlefields, monuments, museum, historic homes, park store. Battle re-enacted every other year in December, other living history programs. Self-guided driving tour which includes sites outside the park.

15. ***Queen Anne Mansion and Wings*** *(501) 253-8825*
U.S. 62 W., Eureka Springs. Built in Carthage, MO in 1891, magnificent home was taken apart and moved to Eureka Springs, then reassembled, piece by piece. Handcrafted woodwork, seven fireplaces.

16. ***Rogers Historical Museum*** *(501) 621-1154*
322 S. Second, Rogers. Newly renovated. Exhibits on local history housed in 1895 Hawkins House and addition. Antique quilts, Christmas decor, a series of room facades, Will Rogers artifacts.

17. ***Saunders Memorial Museum*** *(501) 423-2563*
113-115 Madison, Berryville. Extensive collection of firearms, including antique and unusual pieces. Also knives, Victorian clothing, accessories, textiles, furniture.

18. ***Shiloh Museum*** *(501) 750-8165*
118 W. Johnson, Springdale. Collections from Ozarks region, including extensive photographic images, pioneer artifacts, agriculture, clothing. Pioneer cabin, other historic buildings, wildflower exhibit on grounds.

19. ***Siloam Springs Museum*** *(501) 524-4011*
112 N. Maxwell, Siloam Springs. Pioneer artifacts, documents, vintage clothing.

20. ***St. Elizabeth's Catholic Church*** *(501) 253-9853*
Crescent Dr., Eureka Springs. Enter through the bell tower to see this historic church. Listed in Ripley's "Believe It or Not."

21. ***University Museum*** *(501) 575-3466*

Garland Ave., University of Arkansas, Fayetteville. Extensive collection of exhibits is not limited to Arkansas. Contains displays on anthropology, geology, dinosaurs, glassware, flora, fauna, astronomy and more. Gift shop.

22. ***University of Arkansas Campus*** *(501) 575-2000*
    Fayetteville. The twin towers of Old Main, completed in 1875, preside over this scenic campus. Completely renovated and rededicated in 1991, the building once again houses classrooms. Other sites: University Museum; the Chi Omega Greek Amphitheater, built in 1930; and Senior Walk, inscribed with the names of every graduating senior since 1876.
23. ***University of Arkansas Sports Museums***
    University of Arkansas Campus, Fayetteville. The Tommy Boyer Hall of Champions Museum in Bud Walton Arena treats visitors to great moments of Razorback basketball, track and field, baseball, tennis and golf. One display is the 1994 national championship basketball trophy, plus trophies earned by Razorback cross country, indoor and outdoor track teams for the 22 consecutive national championship titles they have won. The Jerry Jones/Jim Lindsey Hall of champions Museum in the newly renovated Frank Broyles Center displays a century of Arkansas football memories. Both museums are open to the public at no charge during regular business hours.
24. ***Wal-Mart Visitors Center*** *(501) 273-1329*
    105 N. Main, Bentonville. Contains exhibits tracing formation and growth of Wal-Mart stores, the giant discount chain. More than 35 electronic displays, founder Sam Walton's desk.
25. ***War Eagle Mill*** *(501) 789-5343*
    Scenic Ark. 12, Rogers. Contains a working water-powered grist mill, restaurant, gift shop.

## *North-Central/Eastern Ozarks Entertainment, Recreation and Attractions*

1. ***Arts Centers, Theater Productions*** *(501) 362-7971*
   At Heber Springs, the Cleburne County Arts Center at 719 W. Main offers a new art exhibit each month. Local and touring theater groups perform throughout the region. Contact chambers of commerce for schedules in Fairfield Bay, Cherokee Village, Mountain Home, Pocahontas and Batesville.
2. ***Brickshy's Showboat Theater and Resort*** *800-794-2226*
   Mountain View's little piece of Nashville. Music shows, country comedy, great family fun.
3. ***Cash's White River Hoedown*** *800-759-6474*
   Mountain View. For the last eleven years the "Hoedown" has been attracting people from all parts of the country. A great family show with country music and comedy.

The "Ghost Room"

Flowstone

*4.* ***Caverns Tours***

Off Ark. 14, north of Mountain View. Blanchard Springs Caverns, ranked among the 10 most outstanding in North America, is the only cave system in the nation developed and operated by the U.S. Forest Service. Open year-round, the massive underground spectacle offers two guided tours during the warm seasons and one in winter. Visitors center with exhibits, movie theater and book store. Camping nearby. *(501) 757-2211.* In addition, the central Ozarks region also has several privately-owned caverns that are spectacular. Bull Shoals Caverns, off Ark. 178 in the Bull Shoals community, claims formations millions of years in the making. The site has been used by prehistoric natives, Civil War soldiers and moonshiners. *800-445-7177.* Hurricane River Cave, off U.S. 65 south of Harrison, is known for its 45-foot waterfall at the entrance. The remains of prehistoric bears and a saber-toothed tiger have been found among the cavern's ancient calcite formations. *800-245-2282.* Mystic Caverns, south of Harrison on Ark. Scenic 7 Byway, has two beautiful caves featuring guided tours, plus a mineral museum and gift shop. *(501) 743-1739.*

*5.* ***Concert Vineyard*** *(501) 431-9463*

Off Ark. 178, Old Ferry Road, Lakeview. Open to visitors during the warm seasons and by appointment throughout the year.

*6.* ***Corps of Engineers Tours***

Two of the state's largest concrete dams are open for public tours during the summer. Bull Shoals Dam, built immediately after World War II, and Greers Ferry Dam, completed in 1963, are hydroelectric power dams. Free tours include the generator and power control rooms, plus sections of the "caverns" beneath the massive dams. Bull Shoals offers tours in June and July; visitors center open year-round.

7. ***Crafts and Antiques Shopping***
   One of the oldest guilds in the mid-South is headquartered at Mountain View. Arkansas Craft Galleries has the work of over 300 quality craftspersons with outlets in Little Rock, Hot Springs, Eureka Springs and Mountain View. *(501) 269-3897.* Independently-owned craft shops -- such as Ferguson's Country Store on U.S. 65 at St. Joe -- and excellent antique and collectibles outlets are found in the region. Some favorite shopping areas include Hardy, Mountain Home, Mammoth Springs, Batesville, Heber Springs, Clinton, Newark, Harrison, Marshall, Leslie, and Mountain View.
8. ***Evening Shade*** *(501) 266-3833*
   U.S. 167 N. Made famous by the CBS series, this little community has attracted thousands of visitors since the sit-com hit the airwaves. Fame has led to the opening of a visitors center.
9. ***Garner Visitor Center*** *(501) 362-9067*
   Ark. 25, north of Heber Springs. A museum, exhibition hall and theater for the Greers Ferry Lake region. Information center and homebase for tours of the massive dam and hikers bound for Mossy Bluff Trail. Free weekend entertainment in season.
10. ***Hardy Old Town*** *(501) 856-3210*
    U.S. 62-63, Hardy. Virtually unchanged from the 1920s, this little village is a preserve for antique shops, gift nooks, specialty stores, cafes and craft shops overlooking the famous Spring River. Musical shows and special celebrations are presented in season.
11. ***Imperial Theater*** *(501) 892-7200*
    N. Marr St., one block off court square in Pocahontas. Refurbished 1940 movie house converted into dinner theater with musical productions throughout the year.
12. ***Jimmy Driftwood Barn and Folk Museum*** *(501) 269-8042*
    Come by Friday and Sunday evenings in Mountain View, for free down-home entertainment.
13. ***Mammoth Spring State Park*** *(501) 625-7364*
    U.S. 63, Mammoth Spring. One of the great natural wonders of the mid-South, Mammoth Spring flows at an average hourly rate of almost 10 million gallons of 58-degree water. The pour-off crates Spring River, popular for canoeing and trout fishing. 1883 Frisco Depot Museum, picnic sites, pavilion, nature trails and early hydroelectric power dam.
14. ***Mountain Village 1890/Bull Shoals Caverns*** *(501) 445-7177*
    Off Ark. 178, Bull Shoals. A working village from the last century, complete with authentic structures and frontier characters. Craftsmen demonstrations and guided tours of village.
15. ***Musical Shows***
    Folk, country/western, bluegrass, gospel, big band and classic rock are among the possibilities when choosing a music theater in the Ozarks. Mountain View, home of traditional folk music, has the Folk Center State Park, Mountain View and Rackensack Folklore Societies, plus several privately-owned shows offering a wide range of folk and country entertainment. Other towns with musical offerings

include Salem, Walnut Ridge, Hardy and Fairfield Bay.

***16. National Fish Hatcheries***

Trout are produced at facilities below Norfork Dam, east of Mountain Home *(501) 499-5255,* and below Greers Ferry Dam, near Heber Springs *(501) 362-3615.* Tours available. A federal hatchery at Mammoth Spring, adjacent to the state park, produces bass and other native species. *(501) 625-3912.*

***17. Ozark Folk Center** (501) 269-3851 (information); (501) 269-3871 or 800-264-3655 (lodge reservations).*

Off Ark. 5-9-14, Mountain View. This "living museum" state park takes visitors back in time o re-create the music and skills of the last century. Quilting, furniture making, blacksmithing, pottery, woodworking and 20 other frontier skills are demonstrated in the park's large crafts forum. Concerts, performed in the traditional mountain style, are staged from April through October in the center's 1,064-seat auditorium. Restaurant, lodge, conference center, folkways library, gift shop, visitors center.

***18. Peel Ferry***

Along Ark. 125, at the Arkansas-Missouri border. The last public ferryboat operating in the Arkansas Ozarks. Peel Ferry transports vehicles and passengers across a section of Bull Shoals Lake. Open daily from 7 a.m. to 6 p.m.

***19. Scott Valley Resort and Guest Ranch** (501) 425-5136*

Fishing, boating, swimming pool and excellent family accomodations await you at this ranch. Mountain Home, AR.

***20. Searcy's Christmas Lights** (501) 268-2458*

Searcy. This White County city was among the first to use clear Christmas lights to decorate its downtown area and courthouse.

***21. Top O' the Ozarks Tower** (501) 425-5121*

Ark. 178, Bull Shoals. One of the most panoramic views in the state overlooks the White River Valley from atop Bull Mountain. The elevator-equipped tower is 20 stories tall.

The Old Fashioned

# SODA FOUNTAIN

Mountain View, Arkansas

HISTORICAL DOWNTOWN,
MOUNTAIN VIEW,
ARKANSAS
( 501 ) 269-8304

This early 1900's antique soda fountain, restored for your dining pleasure specializes in deli sandwiches and old fashioned ice cream treats. It is located in Woods Pharmacy, one block west of the square on main street.

# RESORT

*"Home Of The World Record Brown Trout"*

**RAINBOW TROUT FISHING AT ITS BEST**

CABINS
BOATS
MOTORS

CAMPSITES
GUIDES
TACKLE

**3 Miles East Of**
**Heber Springs, AR**
**Paved State Highway 110**

**100 Swinging Bridge Drive**
**Heber Springs, AR 72543**
**(501) 362-3327**

*George and Joan Heine, Owners*

22. ***Tyler Bend Visitor Center*** *(501) 741-5443*
Off U.S. 65, north of Marshall. Operated by the National Park Service, a native stone structure with a museum, greeting area, theater and book store overlooking the Buffalo National River.

23. ***White River Railway Excursion*** *800-305-6527*
100 N. Main Pl., Flippin. 1940s-era passenger cars travel along the famous White River for 90-mile round trips between Flippin and Calico Rock. Near Cotter, the train passes through a 1,000-ft. tunnel and bridges the river. Scenic limestone bluffs and historic old rivertowns along the way.

24. ***Wood's Old-Fashioned Soda Fountain*** *(501) 269-8304*
Step back in time, to a real old-fashioned soda shop, near the town square of Mountain View.

## *North-Central/Eastern Ozarks Festivals*

Celebrations are a natural part of living in the highlands. Here's just a sampling: In January, Bull Shoals State Park hosts Eagle Awareness Weekend, complete with barge tours. March brings the Arkansas Fiddlers Jamboree to Harrison; April features the Ozark Scottish Festival at Lyon College in Batesville, Spring Arts Fest at Fairfield Bay, the Buffalo National Canoe Race at Yellville and the famous Arkansas Folk Festival at Mountain View. In May, Bald Knob and Salem stage homecoming celebrations, while Melbourne conducts its Pioneer Day, and Harrison holds Crooked Creek Crawdad Days. June brings the Spring River Canoe Races at Hardy, Buffalo River Days at Marshall, and PortFest at Jacksonport State Park. July starts with a bang with Independence Day fireworks at Bull Shoals and the Cardboard Boat Race at Greers Ferry Lake later in the month, followed by the White River Water Carnival in early August. The Greers Ferry Lake Water Festival happens in mid-August; plus there's the Northwest Arkansas Blue Grass Festival in Harrison. In September, the award-winning Greers Ferry Lake and Little Red River cleanup is a festive event. Clinton holds its Championship Chuck Wagon Races, and the Ozark Folk Center stages the State Old Time Fiddle Contest. October brings fiery fall colors and arts and crafts festivals at Mountain Home, Hardy, Heber Springs and Mountain View. In addition, Yellville hold the National Turkey Calling Championship, and Mountain View's Bean Fest and Great Arkansas Outhouse Race is a favorite. November debuts the "Constellation of Lights" from Thanksgiving through New Year's as Searcy, Heber Springs, Newport, Mountain View, Batesville, Beebe, and other towns present their downtown holiday light displays. The Ozark Folk Center and Batesville also conduct Christmas craft shows in early December.

## *Historic Sites, Museums*

1. ***Cotter Bridge***
   Along U.S. 62-B, Cotter. Built in 1930, this rainbow-arched bridge is ranked among the most beautiful spans in mid-America. Listed on the National Register.
2. ***Gilbert General Store*** *(501) 439-2888*
   Ark. 333, off U.S. 65, Gilbert. Built in 1900, this traditional country store continues to serve this tiny community on the banks of the Buffalo National River.
3. ***Indian Rock House*** *(501) 884-3490*
   Off Ark. 16, Fairfield Bay. Nestled under a hillside at Indian Hills Golf Course, this natural sandstone grotto was the home of prehistoric cave dwellers and is still used today as an outdoor theater. The community's Log Cabin Museum is nearby with exhibits of local and national interest. Other Indian rock houses may be found at Blanchard Springs Caverns public use area and at Buffalo Point on the Buffalo National River.
4. ***Jacksonport Courthouse Museum*** *(501) 523-2143*
   Ark. 69, north of Newport. The 1869 courthouse houses historical artifacts from every era of Arkansas history. The last paddlewheeler to ply the White River, Mary Woods II, is moored nearby to provide a glimpse of life on the river during the last century. Picnic sites, pavilions, camping.
5. ***Living Farm Museum*** *(501) 892-9545*
   Ark. 166, south of Pocahontas. Spring planting and fall harvest festivals are held at the E. Sloan Heritage Farm adjacent to Old Davidsonville State Park. Horse-drawn plows, steam thrashers, other old-fashioned homestead methods are demonstrated.
6. ***Mammoth Spring Depot Museum*** *(501) 625-7364*
   U.S. 63, at the Arkansas-Missouri border. Restored in the early 1970s, this 110-year-old station museum houses railroad memorabilia from the days of steam. Part of Mammoth Spring State Park.
7. ***Maynard Pioneer Museum*** *(501) 647-2701*
   Off Ark. 115, north of Pocahontas. Housed in a century-old log house, exhibits depict a typical rural home of the late 1800s. Park surrounds museum.
8. ***Old Davidsonville*** *(501) 892-4708*
   Ark. 166, south of Pocahontas. Once a vital outpost on the Old Southwest Trail, Davidsonville is one of the state's oldest townsites. A state park surrounds the historic old riverport offering camping, lake and river fishing, trails, playground and museum.
9. ***Old Mill***
   Main St., Mountain View. Built in 1914, the mill once supplied residents with fresh cornmeal and flour. Restored in 1983, the original equipment is still demonstrated for visitors to the adjoining pioneer museum.
10. ***Ozark Heritage Arts Center and Museum*** *(501) 447-2500*
    Oak St., Leslie. Housed in a restored 1938 building near historic old downtown. It features a 400-seat theater and an art gallery. Relics from the world's largest whiskey barrel factory. Documents, clothing, mementos, photographs and

furniture from Leslie's colorful past.

***11. Powhatan Courthouse Museum** (501) 878-6794*

Ark. 25, south of Black Rock. This 1888 Victorian brick structure housed the Lawrence County government for almost a century. Now a state park museum with local historical displays. The 1873 county jail has also been restored and opened.

***12. Resettlement Village***

Off U.S. 67, south of Walnut Ridge. Clover Bend's glory years were during the Depression when displaced farmers were given a fresh start on new homesteads. Several original buildings are preserved and one serves as a local museum.

***13. Rush Historic District** (501) 741-5443*

Eight miles off Ark. 14, south of Yellville. Along the lower reaches of the Buffalo National River, the town of Rush was created after the discovery of zinc during the 1880s. Remains of homes and ore smelter make up the "ghost town", now under the protection of the National Park Service.

***14. Searcy County Museum***

Off U.S. 65, Marshall. Housed in a 1902 jailhouse with local memorabilia and old photographs.

***15. Sylamore Swinging Bridge***

Off Ark. 14, six miles north of Mountain View. Built in 1914, this historic landmark has survived floods, time and progress. Once part of major highway, the main road bypassed the picturesque swinging bridge 30 years ago.

***16. Veteran's Military Museum***

U.S. 62-63, Hardy. Museum houses thousands of items from every American conflict from the Revolutionary War to Desert Storm. Photographs, weapons, uniforms, G.I. equipment and vehicles.

## *Entertainment, Recreation and Attractions*

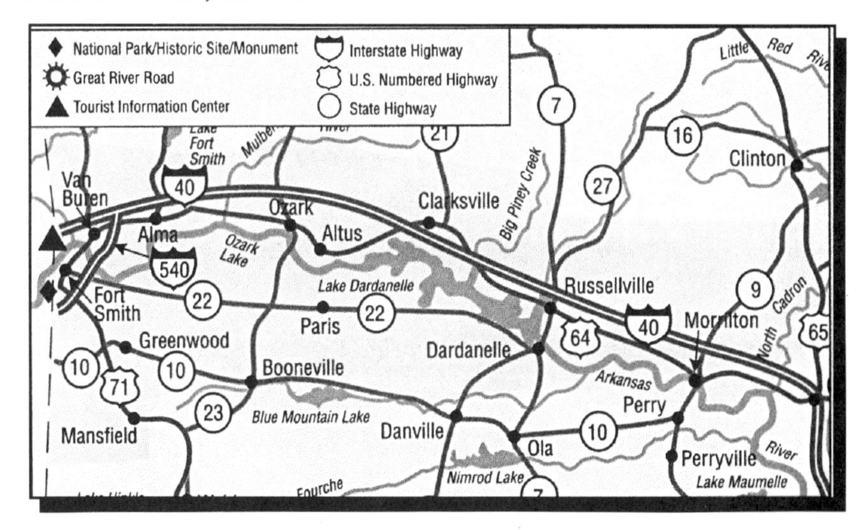


1. ***Alma, "Spinach Capital of the World"***
   Tons of spinach are packed here each year for the Popeye brand. A statue of the cartoon character stands downtown. City celebrates its crop with an April festival.
2. ***Antique Mall*** *(501) 968-3449*
   1712 N. Arkansas Ave., Russellville. Largest antique mall in the Arkansas River Valley area; collector items, furniture, chandeliers, paintings, jewelry, primitives.
3. ***"Antiquing"***
   Opportunities abound in the River Valley for great finds in antiques. Fort Smith, Van Buren, Russellville and Dardanelle all boast numerous shops and malls. Quaint shops are also located in Morrilton, Casa, Danville, Paris and Mulberry.
4. ***Arkansas-Oklahoma State Fair***
   Kay Rodgers Park on Midland Blvd, Fort Smith. Featuring the "world's largest and richest" barrel race futurity. Nightly entertainment, livestock shows and much more.
5. ***Booger Hollow Trading Post*** *(501) 468-2611*
   Scenic 7 Byway, north of Dover. Gift shop that boasts "population 7, countin' one coon dog"; features hot ham sandwiches, crafts, smoked meats.
6. ***Cowie Wine Cellars*** *(501) 963-3990*
   Ark. 22, Paris. A family-owned and operated winery with tours and tastings; the Gallery of Barrels features scenes depicting the history of the Cowie family and winemaking.
7. ***Crescent S-T Ranch*** *(501) 754-7089 or (501) 754-2388*
   Off Ark. 292, Clarksville. 1-hr. to overnight pleasure rides, evening picnic

carriage rides, and evening and moonlight hay rides; farrier and general store on premises.

8. ***Frontier Belle*** *(501) 471-5441*
   Mike Meyer Riverfront Park, Van Buren. Sightseeing excursions, luncheon and dinner cruises daily with historical narration about the area.
9. ***Hanging Judge Chuckwagon/Hayride*** *(501) 674-2865*
   Clayton Expressway behind Miss Laura's, Fort Smith. Groups can experience the Old West on a haywagon, complete with desperados, dancing Native Americans, a beautiful songstress, a sheriff and a meal at trail's end.
10. ***Historic Downtown Van Buren Shopping District*** *800-332-5889*
    Six blocks of art galleries, antique shops, Victoriana, restaurants and historical attractions. Often used for film location.
11. ***International Learning & Livestock Center*** *(501) 889-5124*
    Ark. 9, Perryville. Educational and retreat facility developed by Heifer Project Intl.; a Global Village depicts how HPI helps underdeveloped countries become self-sustaining; guided tours and gift shop/information center.
12. ***Jimmy Lile Custom Knives*** *(501) 968-2011*
    Scenic 7 Byway S., Russellville. Home of knives made by the "Arkansas Knifemaker"; included are the knives used in the "Rambo" movie series.
13. ***John Paul McConnell Memorabilia Room***
    City Library, Booneville. Medals, photos, souvenirs and other mementos of native son John Paul McConnell, U. S. Air Force Chief of Staff from 1965 to 1969.
14. ***Morrilton Historic District***
    Church and Broadway Sts. See the Carnegie Library, the classic revival courthouse, handsome churches and homes, downtown shopping.
15. ***Mount Bethel Winery*** *(501) 468-2444*
    U. S. 64, Altus. Historic cellar offers over 100-year-old tradition of wine making, bottling and tasting, plus tours.
16. ***National Scenic 7 Byway***
    Lofty mountain peaks, breathtaking vistas, exciting attractions and entertainment - it's all a part of the Scenic 7 Byway adventure. From the state's northern border through the heart of the River Valley, you won't find a more beautiful route. *Car and Driver* magazine named part of Scenic 7 Byway as one of the top 10 driving experiences in the country. It is the state's first official scenic byway.
17. ***Original Ozark Mural*** *(501) 667-2181*
    600 W. Commercial, Ozark. 56-foot sand-carved historic mural in Bank of Ozark.
18. ***Ozark Bridge***
    Ozark. Spanning Scenic Ark. 23, this structure is considered to be one of the most beautiful bridges in the U. S.
19. ***Ozark Crafts & Market Place*** *(501) 667-5664*
    Exit 37, I-40 to Airport Rd. (Ark. 96), Ozark. Handmade crafts by artisans in the Arkansas River Valley; Ark. juices, jams, jellies and other fine food; fresh in-season berries, grapes and other fruit.

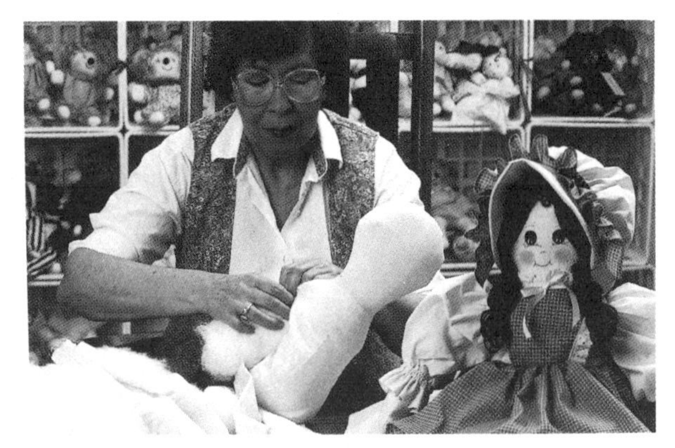

***20. Ozark Heritage Crafts** (501) 967-3232*
Scenic 7 Byway, north at Russellville. Features handmade items of over 200 crafters. Woodcarving shop with demonstrations.

***21. Ozark Scenic Railway** 800-687-8600*
813 Main, Van Buren. A 70-mile scenic rail excursion through the Boston Mountains that departs from the Fresco Depot for round-trip to Winslow.

***22. Post Familie Winery** (501) 468-2740*
Ark. 186, Altus. A fifth-generation family-operated vineyard and winery since 1880 offers tours that include wine and juice tastings, grape-related gift shop.

***23. St. Mary's Catholic Church***
Altus. Beautiful 1902 Roman Basilical style church is known for its paintings and ornate goldleaf work. It's listed on the National Register.

***24. University of the Ozarks** (501) 754-3839*
415 College Ave., Clarksville. A private liberal arts university affiliated with the Presbyterian Church. The Gothic 1932 Raymond Munger Memorial Chapel is listed on the National Register.

***25. Walton Fine Arts Center** (501) 754-3839*
University of the Ozarks campus, Clarksville. Features Stephens Art Gallery, with glass and ivory carvings collections, and numerous original oil paintings. Theater.

***26. West Garrison Avenue Historic District***
Fort Smith. Restaurants, craft malls and antique shops. Listed on the National Register of Historic Places.

***27. Whitetail World** (501) 754-8620*
Ark. 103 and Porter Industrial Road, Clarksville. 10,000-square-foot showroom displays over 70 replicas of world-renowned buck deer, plus wildlife art, photography and sculpture. Gift shop.

***28. Wiederkehr Wine Cellars** (501) 468-WINE*
Ark. 186 S., Altus. Swiss-German heritage, vineyard tours and wine tastings, restaurant, gift shop; family-owned since 1880.

***29. Wye Mountain** (501) 330-2268*

Ark. 113, north of Ark. 10. Seven acres of blazing yellow daffodils are celebrated with the Daffodil Festival in early March.

Whitetail World, Clarksville

## *Festivals*

In April, Alma celebrates its famous crop with the Spinach Festival and Russellville holds Taste of the Valley. Early May brings the Free State of Yell Fest to Dardanelle and the Picklefest to Atkins, Arkansas's pickle capital. Van Buren's Old Timers Day also takes place in May. Car buffs flock to the top of Petit Jean Mountain each June for the Antique Auto Show and Swap Meet at the Museum of Automobiles. Fort Smith hosts the Old Fort Days Rodeo and Old Fort Days River Festival in June. A summer tradition for politicians and visitors is the Mount Nebo Chicken Fry held in mid-July at Mount Nebo State Park. This is also the time for the Johnson County Peach Festival at Clarksville and the Grape Festival at Altus. Food is the focus of the Great Arkansas Pig-Out in early August in Morrilton. In late August, there's the Hang-In at Mount Nebo State Park, while a celebration of the grape is held in Paris at the Arkansas Championship Grape Stomp and Wine Festival. Wiederkehr Winery at Wiederkehr Village hosts an annual Weinfest the last weekend of September. The Arkansas/Oklahoma State Fair is held in Fort Smith during late September and early October. Mount Magazine Frontier Day comes in early October at Paris, while Van Buren honors the season with its Fall Festival. In time for the holidays, Russellville hosts the Arkansas River Valley Arts and Crafts Show in early November.

## *Historic Sites, Museums*

1. ***Altus Heritage House Museum*** *(501) 468-4684*
   106 N. Franklin. Original German-American State Bank, circa 1800s, with early coal mining equipment, local history.
2. ***Arkansas River Valley Arts Center*** *(501) 968-2452*
   Knoxville and B Sts., Russellville. Visual art displays by well-known artists; a local artists gallery, theater productions.
3. ***Arkansas River Visitor Center*** *(501) 968-5008*
   Old Post Road Park, Russellville. "Renaissance of a River" interpretive exhibits chronicle the development of the river.
4. ***Arkansas Tech University Museum of Pre-History and History*** *(501) 968-3941*
   ATU campus, Russellville. Exhibits on the people and events of the Arkansas Ozarks and the Arkansas River Valley.
5. ***Belle Grove Historic District*** *(501) 783-8888*
   Downtown Fort Smith. A 22-block area of restored homes and buildings showcasing Romanesque Revival, Queen Anne, Eastlake Victorian Renaissance, Gothic Revival and Neo-Classical.
6. ***Bob Burns Exhibit*** *800-332-5889*
   Old Fresco Depot, 813 Main St., Van Buren. A radio and motion picture star of the 30s and 40s is remembered; studio photos, items from his Van Buren childhood and Hollywood days, and an original Bazooka, used by Burns on his radio show.
7. ***Bonneville House*** *(501) 782-7854*
   318 N. 7th St., Fort Smith. An 1860s Victorian Renaissance home with period antiques.
8. ***Clayton House*** *(501) 783-3000*
   514 N. 6th, Fort Smith. An excellent example of Classic Revival Victorian architecture, this museum home belonged to the district attorney under Judge Isaac C. Parker.
9. ***Council Oak***
   Council Oaks City Park, Dardanelle. A massive 400- to 500-year-old white oak tree where a Cherokee Indian chief signed a treaty giving all land south of the Arkansas River to the territory in 1820.
10. ***Crawford County Art Center***
    104 N. 13th St., Van Buren. Housed in the Old St. Michael's Catholic Church, built in 1912, the center offers shows, workshops, lessons, gifts and special events.
11. ***Crawford County Bank Building*** *(501) 474-4202*
    633 Main St., Van Buren. Built in 1889; now the Old Van Buren Inn Restaurant and Bed and Breakfast.
12. ***Crawford County Courthouse***
    5th and Main, Van Buren. The oldest active county courthouse west of the Mississippi; has the original Seth Thomas tower clock.
13. ***Darby House*** *(501) 782-3388*

311 General Darby St., Fort Smith. The boyhood home of General William O. Darby, leader of Darby's Rangers in World War II; contains tributes to Darby and artifacts from Cisterna, Italy, Fort Smith's sister city.

**14. *Dardanelle Rock*** *(501) 229-3328*
Dardanelle. This large rock formation rises near the Arkansas River bank and was used as a lookout point by the Indians and later by Confederate soldiers.

**15. *Fort Smith Art Center*** *(501) 782-1156*
423 N. 6th St., Fort Smith. Housed in the Vaughn-Schaap House, a Victorian Second Empire structure, the center presents changing exhibits and permanent collections.

Old Fort Museum, Fort Smith

**16. *Fort Smith National Historic Site*** *(501) 783-3961*
3rd and Rogers, Fort Smith. Features the remains of two frontier garrisons, the Federal Court for the Western District of Arkansas, "Hangin' Judge" Isaac C. Parker's courtroom, a reproduction of the 1886 gallows, the "Hell on the Border" jail, the 1846 Commissary Storehouse and re-creation of the old fort's flagpole.

**17. *Fort Smith Trolley Museum*** *(501) 783-0205*
100 S. 4th, Fort Smith. Take a ride between Old Fort and Trolley Museums on a 1926 Birney electric streetcar which is listed on the National Register. Also on display at the museum is a collection of railroad and transportation memorabilia.

**18. *King Opera House*** *800-332-5889*
427 Main St., Van Buren. Restored 1880s structure that once played host to Jenny Lind and William Jennings Bryan still has theatre and musical productions.

**19. *Logan County Museum*** *(501) 963-3936*
414 N. Elm, Paris. Small museum of local history is housed in the old jail where the last hanging in the state took place; listed on the National Register.

**20. *Miss Laura's Visitor Center*** *(501) 783-8888 / 800-637-1477*

2 N. B St., Fort Smith. A restored turn-of-the-century brothel that now serves as the city's visitor center. Interpretive tours are given; self-guided driving/walking brochure available; the only bordello listed on the National Register.

**21. *Mount Olive United Methodist Church***
Knox and Lafayette Sts., Van Buren. Constructed in 1889, this church is said to consist of the oldest Black congregation of the UMC system west of the Mississippi.

**22. *Museum of Automobiles*** *(501)727-5427*
Ark. 154, Petit Jean Mountain, Morrilton. A collection of 50 regularly rotated vintage vehicles. On display is President Bill Clinton's 1967 Mustang convertible.

**23. *Old Fort Museum*** *(501) 783-7841*
320 Rogers Ave., Fort Smith. Artifacts depict the history and culture of the area from Native Americans to present, military activity, notable personalities; also has revolving exhibits, old-time soda fountain and gift shop.

**24. *Old Fresco Depot*** *800-332-5889*
813 Main St., Van Buren. Built in 1901, the restored depot serves as the chamber of commerce office.

**25. *Patent Model Museum*** *(501) 782-9014*
400 N. 8th, Fort Smith. Housed in the Rogers-Tilles House, the oldest residence in Fort Smith; features 85 working patent models dating from 1836 to the 1870s; also has 17 drawings of models dating from 1810 to 1836.

**26. *Potts Inn Museum*** *(501) 968-1877*
Ark. 247, Pottsville. Once a major stop on the Butterfield Overland Stage route, this restored antebellum home now showcases antiques and a hat museum.

**27. *Subiaco Abbey Academy*** *(501) 934-4291 / (501) 934-4295*
Scenic Ark. 22, Subiaco. Established in 1878 as a Benedictine Monastery, now serves as a private preparatory school for boys. Tours available.

**28. *U. S. National Cemetery***
522 Garland and 6th Sts., Fort Smith. Established in 1818 as part of the original post, the cemetery includes interments that date to 1812 and include Judge Parker, many of his deputies and World War II hero, Gen. W. O. Darby.

## *Entertainment, Recreation and Attractions*

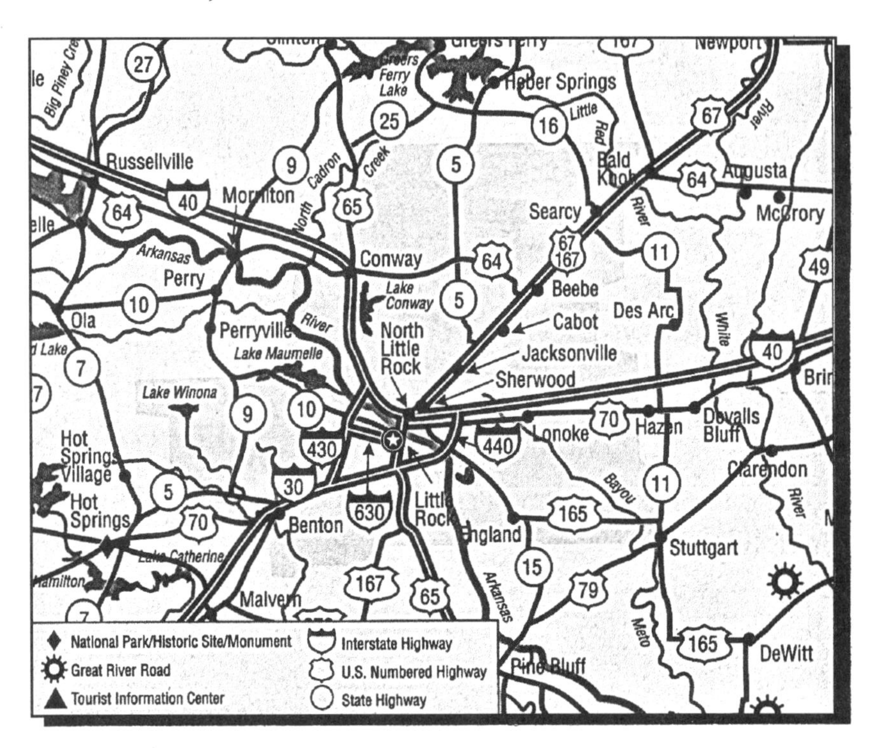


1. ***Aerospace Education Center*** *(501) 371-0331*
   3301 E. Roosevelt at Bond St., Little Rock. 250-seat IMAX® Theater delivers "like you're really there" experiences from films shown on six-story screen. Exhibits of Russian/U. S. space hardware, Aerospace Library, antique aircraft, gift shop.
2. ***Arkansas Repertory Theatre*** *(501) 378-0405*
   Main and 6th Sts., Little Rock. Classics and contemporary dramas, comedies and musicals.
3. ***Arkansas Riverboat Co., "The Spirit"*** *(501) 376-4150*
   Riverfront Park, North Little Rock. 150-passenger excursion boat makes regularly scheduled cruises.
4. ***Arkansas State Fair*** *(501) 372-8341*
   State Fairgrounds, Little Rock. Ten days of top entertainment featuring some of the hottest names in country music, plus championship PRCA rodeo, livestock judging, arts and crafts, exhibits and the state's biggest midway with exciting rides. Arkansas State Fair dates for 1996 are October 6-15.

5. ***Grayhawk Frontier Town** (501) 843-8829*
   Ark. 5, Cabot. Re-creation of a pioneer town of Old West fans.
6. ***Joe Hogan State Fish Hatchery** (501) 676-6963*
   U. S. 70, near Lonoke. One of the largest in the U. S. Tours available.
7. ***Little Rock Air Force Base** (501) 988-3601*
   U. S. 67-167, Jacksonville. Largest training and maintenance facilities for C-130s. Group tours available.
8. ***Little Rock Zoo** (501) 666-2406*
   One Jonesboro Dr., War Memorial Park, Little Rock. A 40-acre zoological park which houses over 600 mammals, birds, reptiles and amphibians. Restaurant.
9. ***Murry's Dinner Playhouse** (501) 562-3131*
   6323 Asher Ave., Little Rock. Contemporary comedies and musicals follow buffet dinner.
10. ***Pickles Gap Village** (501) 329-9049*
    U. S. 65, north of Conway. Crafts, antique shops, flea market, covered bridge, water wheel, zoo, tourist information, restaurant.
11. ***Robinson Center Music Hall** (501) 376-4781 / 800-844-4781*
    W. Markham and Broadway, Little Rock. Principal performing arts auditorium for Central Arkansas and home of Arkansas Symphony Orchestra, Broadway Theatre Series, Ballet Arkansas.
12. ***Safaripark** (501) 679-3455*
    Ark. 285 and U. S. 65 N. Greenbrier. Lions, tigers and more are at home to visitors at this exotic animal conservatory.
13. ***University of Arkansas at Little Rock***
    2801 S. University, Little Rock. The Planetarium boasts a Minolta star projector which simulates night skies from any location on Earth and any time frame. (501) 569-3259. The Fine Arts Building includes galleries where the works of students, faculty and guest artists are displayed. (501) 569-3182. Theatre Auditorium stages classical and contemporary productions. (501) 569-3291.
14. ***Wildwood Park for the Performing Arts** (501) 821-7275*
    Denny Rd., 1.6 miles off Kanis Road, west of Little Rock. A 105-acre forested performing arts complex where several major music and crafts festivals are held each year.
15. ***Wild River Country** (501) 753-8600*
    I-40 and Crystal Hill Rd., North Little Rock. A 23-acre water theme park featuring the "Arkansas Ocean" and a collection of slides, swings, chutes and pools.

## *Festivals*

There are plenty of good times to be found in Central Arkansas. March brings the Spring Motocross Races to North Little Rock, followed by a Wildflower Weekend and Earth Day observances at Pinnacle Mountain State Park in April. The Quapaw

Quarter Tour of Historic Homes in Little Rock is an early May event with the city's big Memorial Day Weekend Riverfest rounding out the month. Also in May, Conway hold its uniquely named Toad Suck Daze. In June, Toltec Mounds State Park has an Archeological Mystery Tour, and Des Arc holds its Steamboat Days Festival. In July, Pops on the River marks the Independence Day Weekend in Little Rock.

August brings Zoo Days to Little Rock. September features the International Children's Festival at Wildwood Park for the Performing Arts, and in October, Benton holds Festival of the Scots, while Cabot stages Cabotfest and England its Fluff 'N Feather Fest.

Special holiday celebrations are plentiful throughout the area in November and December.

## *Historic Sites, Museums*

1. ***Argenta Historic District***
   Contains many of North Little Rock's earliest structures, including City Hall.
2. ***Arkansas Arts Center*** *(501) 372-4000*
   MacArthur Park, Little Rock. Nationally recognized collection of drawings and prints; also traveling exhibits. Includes gift shop, Arkansas Children's Theatre, restaurant.
3. ***Arkansas Carousel Restoration Studio*** *(501) 375-5556*
   107 Main, Little Rock. This is the only remaining Herschell-Spillman track carousel today.
4. ***Arkansas Governor's Mansion***
   81th and Center Sts., Little Rock. Home of all Arkansas Governors since its completion in 1950, including Bill and Hillary Clinton, who lived there during the 12 years he was Governor. Bust of Clinton on display.
5. ***Arkansas Museum of Science and History***
   MacArthur Park, Little Rock. Displays of historic and scientific collections in the 1841 Headquarters Building of former Little Rock Arsenal. General Douglas MacArthur was born here in 1880.
6. ***Arkansas State Capitol*** *(501) 682-5080*
   Woodlane and Capitol Ave., Little Rock. Construction began in 1899, legislature first met here in 1911. Guided or audio tours available. Vietnam Memorial, Liberty Bell Pavilion, gardens.
7. ***Arkansas Territorial Restoration*** *(501) 324-9351*
   3rd and Scott Sts., Little Rock. Oldest structures in Little Rock are preserved in this handsomely maintained restoration. Arkansas crafts shop, Arkansas artists exhibits, Cromwell Exhibition Hall, history wall, authentically furnished museum houses and outbuildings. Guided tours.
8. ***Bauxite Museum*** *(501) 557-5318 / (501) 557-2997*
   Just off Ark. 183 behind post office, Bauxite. Displays from early days of mining town, once the center of U. S. Aluminum production.

9. ***Camp Nelson Cemetery***
Ark. 89 S., Cabot. Historic monument to unknown Texas and Arkansas Confederate soldiers.

10. ***Children's Museum of Arkansas*** *(501) 374-6655*
Union Station, W. Markham and Victory Sts., Little Rock. Includes simulated farmer's market, Victorian house, interactive exhibits, changing exhibits on life in other lands.

11. ***Daniel Greathouse Home*** *(501) 327-7788*
Courthouse grounds, Conway. Restored early 19th-century structure with dogtrot. Antiques.

12. ***Decorative Arts Museum*** *(501) 372-4000*
E. 7th and Rock Sts., Little Rock. Occupying the historic Pike-Fletcher-Terry House, this adjunct to the Arkansas Arts Center displays permanent collection and traveling exhibits.

13. ***Gann Museum*** *(501) 778-5513*
218 S. Market St., Benton. Built in 1893, this is the world's only structure constructed of bauxite.

14. ***Hillcrest Historic District***
Little Rock. National Register listed collection of city's early residential areas.

15. ***Little Rock Central High School*** *(501) 324-2300*
14th and Park Sts., Little Rock. The integration of this school in 1957 was a landmark in U. S. desegregation efforts.

16. ***Marlsgate Plantation*** *(501) 961-1307 / (501) 961-1515*
Off U. S. 165 at Bearskin Lake, Scott. A turn-of-the-century plantation home restored with vintage furnishings and accessories. Open to groups and for special occasions by appointment.

17. ***Mosaic Templars of America Headquarters***
900 Broadway, Little Rock. Constructed in 1911, this was the headquarters for one of the largest African-American fraternal organizations in the country.

18. ***Mount Holly Cemetery***
14th and Broadway Sts., Little Rock. "The Westminister of Arkansas" is listed on the National Register. Burial site for notable Arkansans.

19. ***National Cemetery*** *(501) 324-6401*
2523 Confederate Blvd., Little Rock. Established in 1866, this final resting place has over 22,000 graves of veterans from Civil War to Desert Storm.

20. ***Old Mill*** *(501) 758-2400*
Lakeshore Dr. and Fairway, North Little Rock. Re-creation of a water-powered grist mill, which achieved fame in the opening credits of "Gone With The Wind."

21. ***Old State House*** *(501) 324-9685*
300 W. Markham, Little Rock. One of the finest examples of Greek Revival architecture in the South, this historic building houses a museum of state history and served as the setting for President Clinton's election night triumph in 1992. A special exhibit on Clinton and a Wilderness Gallery are of interest.

22. ***Plantation Agriculture Museum*** *(501) 961-1409*
Jct. U. S. 165 and Ark. 161, Scott. Tells the story of cotton and its role in the

fortunes of the South.

23. ***Prairie County Museum*** *(501) 256-3711*
W. Main St., Des Arc. Interprets history of Arkansas's navigable rivers and their impact on her people, emphasizing lower White River.

24. ***Quapaw Quarter Historic District*** *(501) 371-0075*
Historic downtown area, Little Rock. Restored Antebellum and Victorian structures. Driving/walking tours are available.

25. ***Shoppach House*** *(501) 778-2729*
503 N. Main, Benton. Occupied by both sides during Civil War, this 1853 house contains collections of period furnishings. By appointment.

26. ***Taborian Hall***
9th and State Sts., Little Rock. Constructed in 1916 as headquarters for the Arkansas Chapter of the Knights and Daughters of Tabor, a national Black fraternity, the building was one of the anchors of 9th Street which served as the center of Black business and culture until the 1950s.

27. ***Toltec Mounds Archeological State Park*** *(501) 961-9442*
490 Toltec Mounds Rd., off U. S. 165, Scott. One of the largest Mound Builders sites remaining in the Lower Mississippi River Valley. A visitor center contains displays, and there are guided ours of the mounds area. Occasional archeological digs are of interest.

28. ***Villa Marre*** *(501) 371-0075 / (501) 374-9979*
1321 S. Scott St., Little Rock. The Villa is open for tours of its authentically decorated rooms. The house served as location for the action on the CBS comedy "Designing Women."

29. ***Wagon Yard Museum*** *(501) 842-2222*
South Allis, one block from U. S. 165, England. A collection of early wagons and stagecoaches, farm equipment.

## In Business for Himself

There was an Arkansas farmer in the Depression who got very discouraged by the fact that it always seemed to cost more to grow things than you made on them. So he decided to go into business for himself--he decided to sell axe handles. He went into the hardware store and bought one dozen and went out and peddled them. He came back for another dozen axe handles and went out and peddled them. When he showed up for the third dozen the hardware store owner asked what he was doing with them. The man replied that he was out peddling them. The dealer asked how much he was getting for them. He replied, "Twenty-five cents apiece." The hardware man said, "You can't make a profit that way. You pay me thirty cents; you're losing a nickel on each one." The man replied, "Sure beats the hell out of farming."

"Quality Lodging in the Heart of the Ouachitas"

1308 Hwy. 71 North
Mena, Arkansas 71953
(501) 394-7477

• Choice Steaks • Prime Ribs •
Seafood • Chicken

Large Salad Bar & Buffet
*Full Service Menu*
Breakfast • Lunch • Dinner
Seafood Buffet
( Friday / Saturday )
Two Private Dining rooms for Banquets & Bus tours

## *Entertainment, Recreation and Attractions*

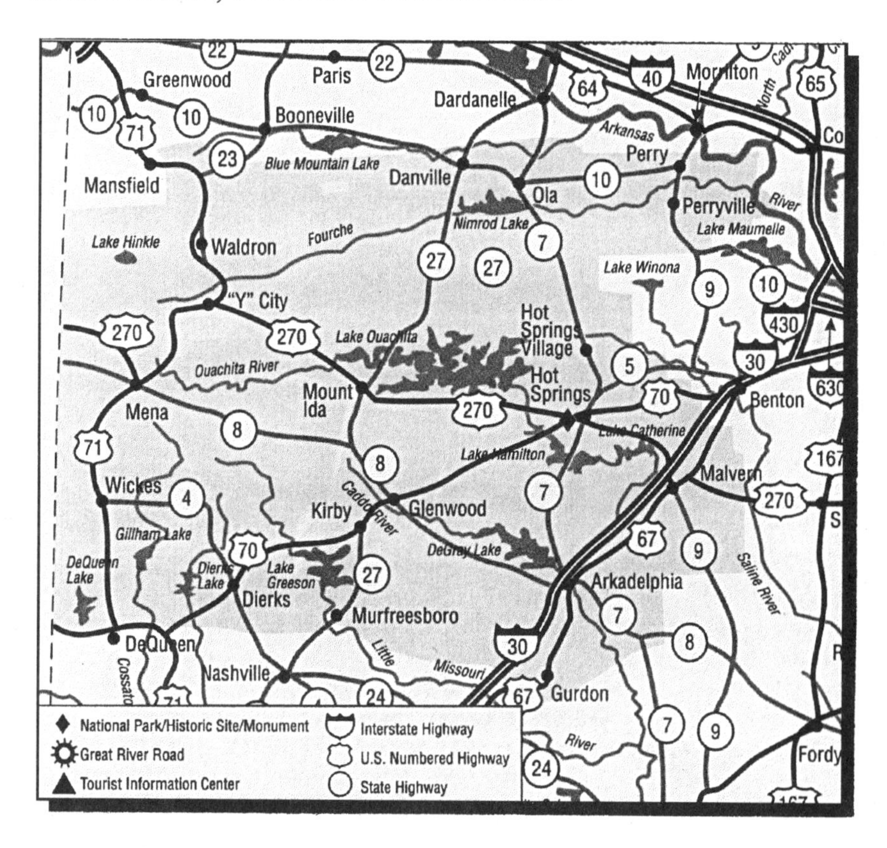


1. ***Ansata Arabian Stud Farm*** *(501) 394-5288*
   Off Ark. 8, Mena. See Egyptian Arabian horses. Tours by appointment.
2. ***Antiques and Crafts***
   Numerous antique and craft shops are located here including, in Hot Springs: outlets at the Morris Antique Mall (501) 623-4249, Sellers Showcase (501) 525-2098, the Arkansas Craft Gallery (501) 321-1640, which features handmade crafts by Arkansas artisans, and the Basket House (501) 525-2652. In Mena: Mena Street Antique Mall (501) 394-3231 and Bird's Nest Antiques and Crafts (501) 394-3003.
3. ***Arkansas Alligator Farm and Petting Zoo*** *(501) 623-6172*
   847 Whittington Ave., Hot Springs. See more than 100 alligators ranging from six inches to six feet long. Deer, ostriches, llamas and pygmy goats. Souvenir shop.

4. ***Arkansas House of Reptiles*** *(501) 623-8516*
   420 Central Ave., Hot Springs. Sixty-seven displays with reptiles from six continents. Cobras, 18-foot python, tortoises and more.
5. ***Arlington Mall*** *(501) 623-7771*
   Central Ave. and Fountain St., Hot Springs. Located in the lower level of the Arlington Resort Hotel and Spa. Specialty shops featuring gifts, collectibles, clothing and accessories. Beauty salon.

6. ***Belle of Hot Springs*** *(501) 525-4438*
   5200 Central Ave., Hot Springs. Take a cruise on beautiful Lake Hamilton on this 400-passenger riverboat. Sightseeing, lunch, dinner and dance cruises.
7. ***Brady Mountain Riding Stables*** *(501) 767-3422*
   4120 Brady Mountain Rd., Royal. Trail rides (½ hour, 1 hour or 2 hours) through the scenic Ouachita National Forest. Riding pen for children.
8. ***Castleberry Riding Stables*** *(501) 623-6609 / (501) 624-7291*
   537 Walnut Valley Rd., Hot Springs. Ride horseback on beautiful mountain trails. Hayrides, overnight camping, riding lessons.
9. ***Central Country Music Theater*** *(501) 624-2268*
   1008 Central Ave., Hot Springs. Family-oriented country music show with comedy. Gift shop.
10. ***Crater of Diamonds State Park*** *(501) 285-3113*
    Ark. 301, Murfreesboro. Search for diamonds at the only diamond-bearing field on the North American continent which is open to the public. Keep any you find. Campsites, picnic sites, gift shop, exhibits.
11. ***Dryden Potteries*** *(501) 623-4201*
    341 Whittington Ave., Hot Springs. Demonstrations on potter's wheels, gift shop.
12. ***Ducks in the Park Tours*** *(501) 321-9667*
    316 Central Ave., Hot Springs. Sightseeing on land and water.
13. ***Educated Animal Zoo*** *(501) 623-4311*
    380 Whittington Ave., Hot Springs. Stage shows starring trained animals.

21176

**14. *Feathered Nest*** *(501) 332-3563*
U. S. 67, south of Malvern. A wildlife farm featuring exotic birds, deer, miniature donkeys, goats. Gift shop has decorative eggs, crafts.

**15. *Fun Trackers Go-Karts*** *(501) 767-8140*
U. S. 270 W., Hot Springs. Ride go-karts on a pro-style track. Kiddie track, game room.

**16. *Gator Golf*** *(501) 767-8601*
U. S. 270 W., Hot Springs. 18-hole mini-golf course features a mountain, waterfall and life-size exotic animals.

**17. *Hot Springs Art Center*** *(501) 624-0489*
405 Park Ave., Hot Springs. Art exhibits, workshops.

**18. *Hot Springs Factory Outlet Stores*** *(501) 525-0888*
Scenic 7 Byway, Hot Springs. Great shopping for brand-name men's and women's clothing, footwear, home accessories, cosmetics, books.

**19. *Hot Springs Mall*** *(501) 525-3254*
Scenic 7 Byway, Hot Springs. Major department stores and more than 70 shops and restaurants.

**20. *Hot Springs Mountain Tower*** *(501) 623-6035*
Hot Springs Mountain Dr., Hot Springs. A 216-foot observation tower atop Hot Springs Mountain. Two viewing levels. Spectacular view of Hot Springs National Park and the Ouachita Mountains and National Forest.

**21. *Hot Springs Mule Trolley*** *(501) 624-2202*
264 Central Ave., Hot Springs. Take a ride on a mule-drawn trolley - a replica of ones used in 1870.

**22. *Hot Springs Trolleys*** *(501) 321-2020*
Hill Wheatley Plaza, Central Ave., Hot Springs. Catch a ride on a trolley to see the city's historic district, the mountain tower and outlying areas.

"Little Caesar" of Hot Springs Zoological Park

23. ***Hot Springs Zoological Park*** *(501) 767-0478*
2179 Old Bear Rd., Royal. Ninety-acre park features lions, tigers, bears, wolves and petting zoo with goats and sheep in wooded setting.
24. ***Iron Mountain Railroad*** *(501) 246-7594*
Ark. 7, Caddo Valley. Miniature train rides for all ages. Miniature village, picnic area, snacks.
25. ***Jones Performing Arts Center*** *(501) 245-5000*
Off U. S. 67, Ouachita Baptist University, Arkadelphia. State-of-the-art facility is the site of numerous productions, including appearances by Arkansas Symphony Orchestra and Arkansas Repertory Theatre.
26. ***Kartland*** *(501) 321-2430*
3500 Central Ave., Hot Springs. Go-karts, video games.
27. ***Magic Springs Theme Park*** *(501) 624-5411*
1701 E. Grand Ave., Hot Springs. Thrilling rides including the "Arkansas Twister" roller coaster, Black Lightning. Live concerts featuring national recording artists.
28. ***Mountain Harbor Riding Stable*** *(501) 867-3022*
U. S. Hwy. 270, west of Hot Springs. Scenic trail rides through the Ouachita Mountains and along Lake Ouachita atop expertly groomed and trained horses.
29. ***Music Mountain Jamboree*** *(501) 767-3841*
U. S. 270 W., Hot Springs. Live country music and comedy show featuring the Mullenix family. Country-western, bluegrass, gospel and patriotic music. Gift shop, restaurant.
30. ***National Park Aquarium*** *(501) 624-3474*
209 Central Ave., Hot Springs. Native Arkansas fish and exotic saltwater species displayed in their natural habitat. Gift shop.
31. ***National Park Duck Tours*** *(501) 321-2911*
418 Central Ave., Hot Springs. Amphibious vehicles known as "ducks" take visitors on tours of the city and Lake Hamilton.
32. ***Oaklawn Park*** *(501) 623-4411 / 800-OAKLAWN*
2705 Central Ave., Hot Springs. One of the top thoroughbred race tracks in the country. Live meet held January 12 - April 13, 1996. Simulcasting of Triple Crown races and more during summer and fall. Oaklawn's new Signals satellite racing room boasts the finest in customer service and amenities for the dedicated horseplayer and serious handicapper.
33. ***Outdoor Adventure Tours*** *(501) 525-4457 / 800-489-TOUR (out of state)*
300 Long Island Dr., Hot Springs. Canoeing, mountain biking, hiking excursions. Vacation packages available.
34. ***Panther Valley Ranch*** *(501) 623-5556*
1942 Mill Creek Rd., Hot Springs. Authentic western horse ranch offering scenic, guided horseback rides and hayrides. Overnight camping, barn dinners, bunkhouse.
35. ***Pirate's Cove Adventure Golf*** *(501) 525-9311*
4612 Central Ave., Hot Springs. Miniature golf.
36. ***Putt-N-Win Mini Golf*** *(501) 525-2652*

- Located on Scenic Talimena Dr. Hwy. 88 W - Mena, AR
- A special place for special people.
- Newly redecorated living/bedroom combo with full bath & kitchen.
- Fully furnished
- Complimentary continental breakfast
- Private driveway & carport
- Waiting for YOU!
- Weekly or Night Rates

**FOR RESERVATIONS OR INFORMATION CALL:**
**(501) 394-6310 JOHNIE STALCUP - PROP.**
**512 GRANDVIEW HEIGHTS**

3818 Central Ave., Hot Springs. Eighteen holes featuring motorized hazards and the ABC Satellite Slide for the kids.

37. ***Quartz Crystal Mines/Rock Shops*** *(501) 867-2723*
Mount Ida/Hot Springs/Jessieville. Several mines in the Mount Ida and Jessieville areas allow people to dig for quartz crystal for a fee. Numerous rock shops in the area also have quartz and a wide variety of other rocks for sale.

38. ***Queen Wilhelmina State Park*** *(501) 394-2863 / 800-264-2477 for lodge reservations.*
Ark. 88, west of Mena. Located atop Rich Mountain along the Talimena National Scenic Byway. Features a 36-room lodge, restaurant, campsites, picnic areas, trails, miniature scenic railroad, animal park, miniature golf course.

39. ***Talimena National Scenic Byway*** *(501) 321-5202*
Ark. 88, Mena. Beginning at Mena, this 54-mile scenic byway stretches across the crests of the forested Ouachita Mountains to Talihina, Oklahoma. Spectacular vistas.

40. ***The Art of Hot Springs***
The arts have become a major attraction for Hot Springs. Works of artists from across the nation and beyond are displayed in a dozen or more galleries. Many artists and gallery owners have purchased and restored historic buildings. Monthly Gallery Walks are held which coincide with the openings of new exhibits at the galleries. Each month, internationally-known artists' works are previewed in the city. Several of these artists are in residence in Hot Springs.

41. ***The Bath House Show*** *(501) 623-1415*
701 Central Ave., Hot Springs. Live show featuring the history of Hot Springs told through the music of the last six decades. Comedy.

42. ***The Original White and Yellow Ducks Sightseeing Tours*** *(501) 623-1111*
406 Central Ave., Hot Springs. Amphibious vehicles known as "ducks" take visitors on tours of the city and Lake Hamilton.

43. ***The Witness*** *(501) 623-9781*
Mid-America Amphitheater off U. S. 270 W., Hot Springs. Contemporary Christian musical drama. Summer and October.

44. ***Thermal Bathing*** *(501) 321-2277 / 800-SPA-CITY*
Various locations, Hot Springs. Enjoy a relaxing bath at one of six locations. The Buckstaff Bathhouse is the only operating bathhouse on famous Bathhouse Row. Others available in city hotels and private facilities.

45. ***Tiny Town*** *(501) 624-4742*
374 Whittington Ave., Hot Springs. Fascinating miniature village, billed as the world's greatest indoor mechanical display.

46. ***Twentieth Century Gardens*** *(501) 623-7871*
Lake Hamilton, Hot Springs. Features 230 acres of woodland gardens on the shores of Lake Hamilton. Group tours (minimum of 20 people) offered by appointment. Public tours offered twice yearly.

## *Festivals*

In the Ouachitas, festivals are big drawing cards. Waldron hold its Lakeview and Turkey Track Bluegrass Festivals in April and September. Each April and May, visitors head for Arkadelphia for the Festival of Two Rivers and to Murfreesboro for the Diamond Festival. The fun continues in June as Malvern celebrates with Brickfest, and Mena honors a famous 1940s radio team during Lum and Abner Days. In August, Mountainfest is celebrated atop Rich Mountain at Queen Wilhelmina State Park and in September, Caddo River Sawmill Days in Glenwood is held. The activity picks up in October with the World's Championship Quartz Crystal Dig/Quartz, Quiltz and Craftz Festival at Mount Ida, Forest Festival in Gurdon and Oktoberfest in Hot Springs. In November, get in shape with Healthfest at Hot Springs, shop for Christmas at Holiday Arts and Crafts Fair in Malvern or enjoy the Arkansas Celebration of the Arts/Documentary Film Festival at Hot Springs. And in December, Hot Springs celebrates Christmas with a variety of events during Holiday in the Park, while many other towns in the region stage special lighting for the season.

## *Historic Sites, Museums*

1. ***Arkadelphia's Historic Homes Tour*** *(501) 246-5542*
   Arkadelphia. Take a driving tour to see several homes listed on the National Register, some of which date to the 1840s. Brochures available at chamber of commerce, 6th and Caddo Sts.
2. ***Bathhouse Row*** *(501) 623-1433*
   Central Ave., Hot Springs National Park. Named a National Historic Landmark in 1987, the Row consists of eight bathhouses built around the turn of the century. The Fordyce serves as a visitor center/museum; the Buckstaff is the only working bathhouse on the Row.
3. ***Blythe's Museum*** *(501) 637-3730*
   635 N. Main, Waldron. Large collection of Indian artifacts found in the area. Local history exhibits.
4. ***Central Avenue Historic District*** *(501) 321-2277 / 800-SPA-CITY*
   Central Ave. (Prospect Ave. to Park Ave.), Downtown Hot Springs. Restored buildings dating from the late 1800s and early 1900s now house art galleries, coffee houses, restaurants, shops.
5. ***Clinton Sites*** *(501) 321-2277 / 800-SPA-CITY*
   Various locations, Hot Springs. Visit the sites related to President Bill Clinton, who grew up here. See his boyhood home, his high school, his favorite hamburger hangout and more. For self-guided brochures, call.
6. ***Conway Hotel*** *(501) 285-3131*
   Off Ark. 24, Murfreesboro. Hotel listed on the National Register features handmade crafts, tourist information. Free entertainment on Friday nights during

the summer.

7. ***Fordyce Bathhouse Visitor Center*** *(501) 623-1433*
   369 Central Ave., Hot Springs National Park. This restored bathhouse now serves as the visitor center for Hot Springs National Park and as a museum for the thermal bathing industry. Stained glass windows and the DeSoto Fountain grace the interior. Bookstore, orientation film.
8. ***Henderson State University Museum*** *(501) 246-7311*
   Off U. S. 67, Henderson State University, Arkadelphia. Located in a home built in 1892. Interesting collection of Indian artifacts, college memorabilia.
9. ***Historic National Park Tour*** *(501) 525-4457*
   300 Long Island Dr., Hot Springs. See the hot springs, historic sties and places related to President Clinton who grew up here. Curbside service from local hotels with reservations.
10. ***Hot Spring County Museum/The Boyle House*** *(501) 332-5441*
    302 E. 3rd St., Malvern. Artifacts and memorabilia relating to local history.
11. ***Janssen Park*** *(501) 394-2912*
    Off 7th St., Mena. Features an 1800s log cabin, two small lakes.
12. ***Josephine Tussaud Wax Museum*** *(501) 623-5836*
    250 Central Ave., Hot Springs. More than 100 wax figures and 27 scenes, including President and Mrs. Clinton.
13. ***Lum and Abner Museum and Jot 'Em Down Store*** *(501) 326-4442*
    Ark. 88, Pine Ridge. Features memorabilia relating to the popular 1940s radio team, Lum and Abner, and local history. Gift shop.

Photo by T. C. Masters

14. ***Mena Depot Center*** *(501) 394-2912*
    524 Sherwood, Mena. Located in a restored train depot. Visitor information, local history museum, art gallery featuring works of local artists in a restored train depot.

**15. Mid-America Science Museum** *(501) 767-3461 / 800-632-0583 inside Arkansas*
500 Mid-America Blvd., off U. S. 270 W., Hot Springs. "Hands-on" museum featuring exhibits explaining scientific principles. Also features a laser show.

**16. Mountain Valley Spring Co.** *(501) 623-6671*
150 Central Ave., Hot Springs. Home of the famous Mountain Valley Water. Visitor center located on the main floor of this historic building. Collection of antique bottles, hydroponic gardens, "Hall of Fame." Enjoy free samples.

**17. Museum of Hot Springs** *(501) 624-5545*
201 Central Ave., Hot Springs. Located in the historic 1920 Howe Hotel Building, the museum chronicles Spa City history from 1850 to 1950.

**18. Ocus Stanley and Son Rock and Mineral Museum** *(501) 867-3556*
U. S. 270 and Ark. 27, Mount Ida. Numerous crystals and other rocks and minerals on display.

**19. Short-Dodson House** *(501) 624-9555*
755 Park Ave., Hot Springs. Tour this Victorian home which is listed on the National Register. Period furnishings.

## There's One in Every Crowd

The politician was campaigning through the South and stopped at one cabin. "My, you have a fine family -- eighteen boys!" he told the man in the cabin. "All good Democrats, I suppose?"

"Well," the man said, "I tried to bring 'em up right, and they're all good Christians, and all but Sam is Democrats -- that ornery cuss, he got to readin'."

## He's For Sure

A Republican canvasser was trying to persuade a voter to support his party. "I'm sorry," the voter said, "but my father was a Democrat and his father before him, so I won't vote anything but the Democratic ticket."

"That's a poor argument," said the canvasser. "Suppose your father and grandfather had been horse thieves -- would that make you a horse thief?"

"No," the voter replied, "that would make me a Republican."

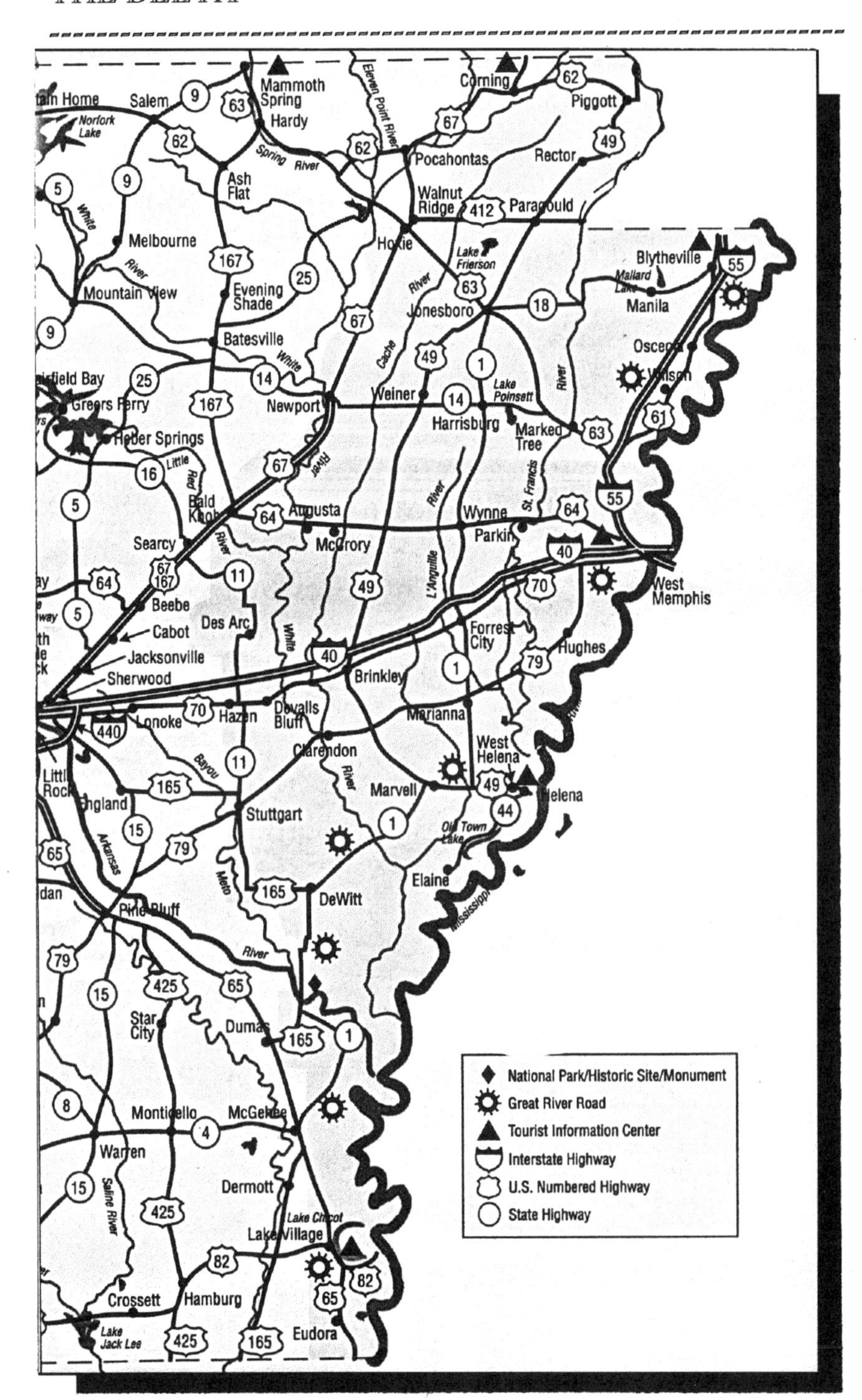
Mammoth Spring
Hardy
Salem
Norfork Lake
Spring River
Eleven Point River
Corning
Piggott
Rector
Pocahontas
Walnut Ridge
Paragould
Ash Flat
Hoxie
Melbourne
White River
Mountain View
Evening Shade
Lake Frierson
Blytheville
Mallard Lake
Manila
Jonesboro
Batesville
Cache River
Osceola
Wilson
Greers Ferry
Heber Springs
Newport
Weiner
Harrisburg
Lake Poinsett
Marked Tree
Little Red River
Bald Knob
Augusta
Wynne
St. Francis River
Parkin
Searcy
McCrory
L'Anguille River
West Memphis
Beebe
Cabot
Des Arc
Jacksonville
Sherwood
Forrest City
Hughes
Brinkley
Lonoke
Hazen
Devalls Bluff
Marianna
Clarendon
West Helena
Helena
Little Rock
England
Bayou
Stuttgart
Marvell
Old Town Lake
Arkansas River
Meto
Elaine
DeWitt
Mississippi
Pine Bluff
Star City
Dumas
Monticello
McGehee
Warren
Saline River
Dermott
Lake Chicot
Lake Village
Crossett
Hamburg
Lake Jack Lee
Eudora
National Park/Historic Site/Monument
Great River Road
Tourist Information Center
Interstate Highway
U.S. Numbered Highway
State Highway

## *Entertainment, Recreation and Attractions*

1. ***Anderson House*** *(501) 355-8443*
   185 S. Main, off U. S. 65, Eudora. Restored 1901 house is the town's visitors center.
2. ***Arkansas State University Convocation Center*** *(501) 972-3870*
   217 Olympic Dr., ASU campus, Jonesboro. State-of-the-art sports and entertainment complex.
3. ***Blues Corner*** *(501) 338-3501*
   105 Cherry St., Helena. Complete collection of recordings and sheet music featuring classic Delta blues.
4. ***Forrest City Municipal Sports Complex***
   Facilities for softball, baseball, basketball, soccer and football.
5. ***Forum Civic Center*** *(501) 935-2726*
   115 E. Monroe, Jonesboro. A restored former movie theater now serves as a performing arts center.
6. ***Heart of Arkansas Farm Tours*** *(501) 673-2202*
   1908 S. Oak St., Stuttgart. Visits to rice and soybean farming operations, Stuttgart Agricultural Museum and prairie lands.
7. ***Lephiew Cotton Gin*** *(501) 538-5288*
   Ark. 35, Dermott. Operated since 1886, the gin is open for tours during fall harvest season.
8. ***Old Almer Store*** *(501) 338-6060*
   Columbia and Miller Sts., Helena. Dating from 1872, this simple plantation store was restored for the Bicentennial and now houses Delta arts and crafts.
9. ***Paragould Mural***
   Between Court and Emerson Sts. off Main, Paragould. A 200-foot mural depicts early transportation in a town that was built by the railroads.
10. ***Quality Gladiolas Gardens*** *(501) 932-4533*
    Ark. 1 B S., Jonesboro. Walking and van tours available by appointment for this 50-acre site.
11. ***Ritz Civic Center*** *(501) 762-1744*
    306 W. Main, Blytheville. Local and touring stage productions are showcased in this renovated former movie palace.
12. ***Sea Wall Mural***
    100 Cherry St., Helena. Mural depicts blues history and early Helena culture.
13. ***Southland Greyhound Park*** *(501) 735-3670 / 800-467-6182*
    1550 N. Ingram Blvd., West Memphis. One of the largest greyhound racing facilities in the country, Southland plays to packed houses year-round.
14. ***That Bookstore in Blytheville*** *(501) 763-3333*
    The storefront is a folk art celebration of books. The book selection features many autographed works by the best contemporary authors - John Grisham included.

## *Festivals*

February blows in strong at Jonesboro with the Rotary Sports Show, while Lake Chicot State Park holds a Winter Wings Weekend for Birdwatchers. The Warfield Concert Series is a major cultural event in Helena in March. April is greeted with Ding Dong Days at Dumas and Blytheville's Springtime on the Mall Festival. In May, Dermott stages its Crawfish Festival and Paragould celebrates with its Loose Caboose Festival. Summer is heralded by the Lake Chicot Water Festival at Lake Village in June, while Jacksonport State Park hosts the Portfest Rollin' on the River Festival. Then, in July, Corning and Piggott both stage major Homecomings and Picnics on the Fourth. Also in July is the Mighty Mite Triathlon at Forrest City and the Farm Fest at Wynne. In August, Gould holds its popular Turtle Derby and West Memphis, its Livin' on the Levee, and, in September, Septembirds is celebrated at Lake Chicot State Park. September and October mean the big, big King Biscuit Blues Festival at Helena, Harvest Festival at Forrest City and Weiner's Arkansas Rice Festival. November's biggest event is the Wings Over the Prairie Festival at Stuttgart featuring the World's Championship Duck Calling Contest. And in December, Christmas parades, holiday open houses and special lightings characterize cities and towns throughout the region. Jonesboro hold its Lights on the Ridge throughout December.

Sunset over Lake Chicot

## *Historic Sites, Museums*

1. ***Arkansas County Museum*** *(501) 548-2634*
   Ark. 169, off U. S. 165, south of Gillett. A collection of authentic structures from the Delta, including an exhibit of farm equipment.
2. ***Arkansas Post National Memorial*** *(501) 548-2207*
   Ark. 169, off U. S. 165, south of Gillett. Commemorates site of first permanent settlement in lower Mississippi River Valley, established by de Tonti in 1686. Visitor center, barrier-free trails, fishing areas.
3. ***Arkansas State University Fine Arts Gallery, Museum*** *(501) 972-3050 (Gallery) (501) 972-2074 (Museum)*
   Caraway Road, ASU campus, Jonesboro. Changing exhibits of local and regional art; over 100 museum exhibits ranging from prehistory to present including major collection of Carroll Cloar's work.
4. ***Centennial Baptist Church*** *(501) 338-7550*
   York and Columbia Sts., Helena. Black church designed by a Black architect. The church grew from 23 members in 1879 to over 1,000 in 1922. Listed on the National Register.
5. ***Chalk Bluff Park***
   North of St. Francis. Site of a Civil War battle and listed on the National Register.
6. ***Confederate Cemetery*** *(501) 338-8327*
   1801 Holly St., Helena. Historic cemetery laid out on the upsurge of Crowley's Ridge at northern edge of town. Includes Confederate burial ground with sweeping views of Mississippi River.
7. ***Crittenden County Museum*** *(501) 792-7374*
   Main St., Earle. A collection of artifacts, including an exhibit on rural physicians, is contained in the Missouri Pacific train depot.
8. ***Delta Cultural Center*** *(501) 338-8919*
   Missouri and Natchez Sts., Helena. "The Arkansas Delta: Landscape of Change" is the title of detailed look at the life and times of the Delta housed in a 1912 train depot.
9. ***Desha County Museum*** *(501) 382-4222*
   165 S. Main, Dumas. Five restored buildings contain artifacts that re-create life in a typical south Arkansas farming community.
10. ***Fargo Agricultural School Museum*** *(501) 734-1140*
    Fargo (U. S. 49, just north of Brinkley). The school was started in 1919 to provide a quality high school education to Black students by its founder Floyd Brown. The school, operated for 30 years, is now a museum.
11. ***Hampson Museum*** *(501) 655-8622*
    U. S. 61 and Lake Dr., Wilson. Prehistoric Indian artifacts dating from 1350 to 1700 collected by a local doctor at the nearby Nodena site are on display at this state park museum.
12. ***Herman Davis Memorial***
    Ark. 18, Manila. A one-acre state park and monument commemorate one of

World War I's greatest heroes.

13. ***Historic Homes***
Helena is noted for its rich collection of antebellum and Victorian homes. The chamber of commerce publishes driving tours of the city, and Beauchamp by the River Tours at (501) 338-3607 offers guided tours. Beech Street and Perry Street Historic Districts are listed on the National Register.

14. ***Lindbergh Marker***
Lakeshore Dr., Lake Village. Marks the area where Col. Charles A. Lindbergh made his first night flight over Lake Chicot in 1923.

15. ***Louisiana Purchase State Park*** *(501) 734-4965*
Ark. 362, off U. S. 49, between Brinkley and Marvell. A monument marks the starting point of 1815 surveys for the Louisiana Purchase. A Boardwalk leads to the marker.

16. ***Magnolia Cemetery***
Off Springdale Rd., on Wire Rd., Helena. Final resting place of William H. Grey, one of the first African-Americans elected to the Arkansas General Assembly in 1869. Dates from 1850

17. ***Marianna/Lee County Museum*** *(501) 295-2469*
67 W. Main, Marianna. Exhibits include general store, parlor and kitchen, cotton farming. Also Civil War and World War II artifacts.

18. ***Museum Lepanto USA*** *(501) 475-6215 / (501) 475-6166*
Main St., Lepanto. Quaint displays of Delta history in replicas of old-time stores.

19. ***Parkin Archeological State Park*** *(501) 755-2500*
Jct. Of U. S. 64 and Ark. 184, Parkin. Preserves the site of a Mississippian Period Indian Village, 1350 to 1550. Research station, museum, interpretive center.

20. ***Phillips County Museum*** *(501) 338-7790*
623 Pecan St., Helena. Historical items including Civil War memorabilia.

21. ***Rohwer Historic Marker***
Ark. 1, Rohwer. Site of Japanese internment camp during World War II. A cemetery and several monuments remain.

22. ***Rubye and Henry Connerly Museum*** *(501) 355-4633*
431 S. Cherry St., Eudora. Artifacts of the area in an old grocery store.

23. ***Sonny Boy's Place*** *(501) 338-8719*
301 Cherry St., Helena. Periodic live blues performances sponsored by "Sonny Boy" Williamson Blues Society.

24. ***Stuttgart Agricultural Museum*** *(501) 673-7001*
4th and Park, Stuttgart. Depicts the history of farming and early lifestyles on the Grand Prairie.

## *Entertainment, Recreation and Attractions*

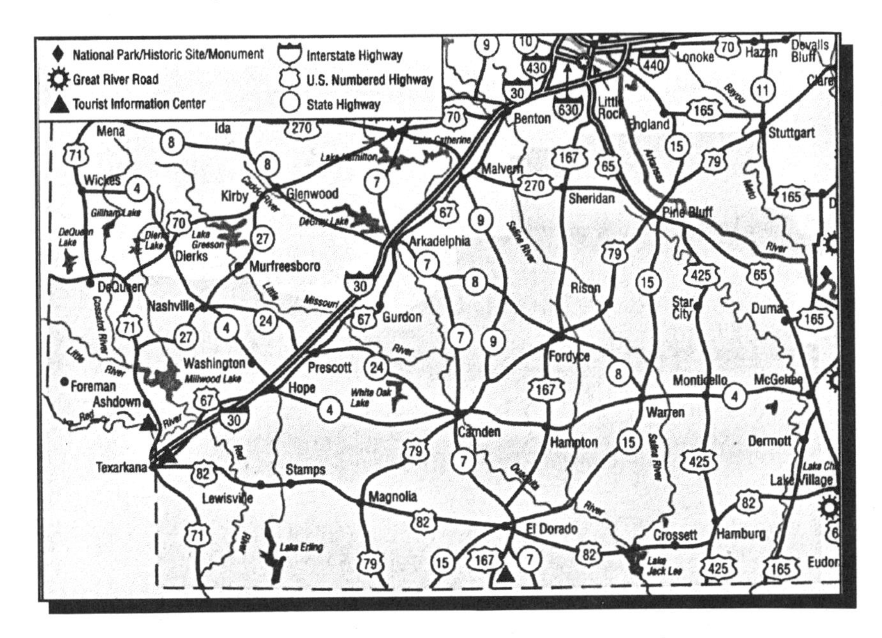


1. ***Antiques and Crafts***
   Try downtown Antique Mall (Camden), Imperial Antique Mall (Magnolia), Main Street Antique Mall (El Dorado). In Pine Bluff: Sissy's Log Cabin, Jo-Be's Antiques and Collectibles, Texarkana has M. M. Fabrics and Mini Mall, Treasure Hunter's Paradise, Twin City Craft and Antique Mall.
2. ***Artificial Marsh Tour*** *(501) 234-6122 / 800-237-6122*
   420 E. Main, Magnolia. Albemarle Corp's artificial marsh designed to be a natural water purification system. Lots of wildlife, aquatic plants.
3. ***Arts and Science Center for Southeast Arkansas*** *(501) 536-3375*
   710 Main St., Pine Bluff. Exhibits in the visual arts and sciences. Theater performances.
4. ***Bladesmithing School*** *(501) 983-2684 / (903) 838-4541, ext. 237*
   Water St., Old Washington Historic State Park. The knifemaking tradition that started the first Bowie knife.
5. ***Camden Driving Tours*** *(501) 836-6426*
   141 Jackson S. W., Chamber of commerce, Camden. Antebellum homes and Civil War landmarks on self-guided driving tours.
6. ***Farm and Home Tours*** *(501) 234-6122 / 800-237-6122*
   420 E. Main, Magnolia. Guided tour of Southern Arkansas University's 658-acre farm. Home tours available including historic Magnolia Place B&B.

The Arts & Science Center for Southeast Arkansas, Pine Bluff

7. ***Fordyce Civic Center*** *(501) 352-3000*
   Off U. S. 79, Fordyce. New 22,000-square-foot center for special events, concerts. Softball fields. Tennis courts. Nature trails.
8. ***Japanese Garden***
   Civic Center Complex, 8th and State, Pine Bluff. Authentic Japanese garden.
9. ***Klappenbach Bakery*** *(501) 352-7771*
   108 W. 4th, Fordyce. Popular bakery has become an attraction.
10. ***Perot Theatre*** *(903) 792-4992 / 800-333-0927*
    221 Main, Texarkana. Theater hosts top performing artists and touring Broadway shows.
11. ***Photographer's Island***
    State Line Avenue, Texarkana. Stand at the Post Office and be photographed with one foot in Texas, the other in Arkansas.
12. ***South Arkansas Arts Center*** *(501) 862-5474*
    110 E. 5th, El Dorado. Gallery, theater, performing arts, workshops.
13. ***Texarkana Regional Arts Center*** *(903) 792-8681*
    321 W. 4th, Texarkana. Exhibits, lectures, classes, programs.
14. ***Union Street Station*** *(501) 234-6010*
    406 W. Union St., Magnolia. KVMA Columbia County Hayride show with down-home country music, third Saturday of each month. Gospel shows.

## *Festivals*

In the Timberlands, festival season gets under way in March with the Jonquil Festival at Old Washington Historic State Park and Pioneer Crafts Festival/Arkansas

Dutch Oven Cook-Off at Rison. It continues in April as Fordyce celebrates with Fordyce on the Cotton Belt Festival. In May, Hamburg hosts Armadillo Days, and Magnolia goes all out for the Magnolia Blossom Festival/World's Championship Steak Cook-Off. The Oil Town Festival at Smackover, the Purple Hull Pea Festival at Emerson and the Pink Tomato Festival at Warren are June favorites. In August, you can beat the heat with the Watermelon Festival in Hope and, in September, there's the Tate Barn Sale in Camden and the Quadrangle Festival in Texarkana. October offers MusicFest in El Dorado, the Wiggins Cabin Festival in Crossett and Frontier Days in Fountain Hill. Christmas events include the Christmas Flotilla and Festival on Lake Enterprise at Wilmot, Texarkana's "Twice As Bright Festival," the "Holiday Land O' Lights" in Ashdown and the "Lights Fantastic Festival" in Magnolia.

## *Historic Sites, Museums*

1. ***Ace of Clubs House** (903) 793-4831*
   420 Pine, Texarkana. Floor plan in the shape of a playing card "club." Original furnishings.
2. ***Arkansas Oil and Brine Museum** (501) 725-2877*
   Ark. 7, Smackover. See exhibits chronicling the 1920s oil boom in south Arkansas. Outdoors are an oil well, pumping rig and three derricks. New permanent indoor exhibits. See "The Land and People of a President."
3. ***Arkansas Railroad Museum** (501) 541-1819*
   Off U. S. 65 on E. Barraque, Pine Bluff. Engine 819, passenger and freight cars, railroad memorabilia.
4. ***Ashley County Museum** (501) 853-2433 / (501) 853-5796*
   302 N. Cherry, Hamburg. Items pertaining to local history.
5. ***Band Museum** (501) 534-4676*
   423-425 Main St., Pine Bluff. Antique band instruments, some dating to the early 1700s. Old-time soda fountain.
6. ***Bradley County Historical Museum** (501) 226-7166*
   Walnut and Ash Sts., Warren. Located in a National Register-listed home built in the 1850s.
7. ***Charlotte Street Historic District** (501) 352-3520*
   Charlotte St., Fordyce. Take a driving tour of about 19 homes dating from 1920 to 1930.
8. ***City of Murals** (501) 536-8742*
   Downtown Pine Bluff. Colorful murals depicting city's past.
9. ***Civil War Battlegrounds State Parks** (501) 682-1191*
   Poison Spring (Ark. 76, west of Camden), Marks' Mills (Ark. 97 and 8, east of Fordyce) and Jenkins' Ferry (Ark. 46, south of Sheridan) preserve the battle sites of Union Army's "Red River Campaign."
10. ***Clinton Birthplace/Boyhood Homes** (501) 777-7500 / 800-223-HOPE*
    Various locations, Hope. Stop by the new visitors center/museum at the restored

Hope Depot in downtown to get a map outlining sites relating to President Clinton including his first boyhood home (opening in 1996). Guided tours available.

11. ***Community Theatre Museum*** *(501) 534-8880*
    207 W. 2nd, Pine Bluff. Showings of classic westerns and local history films for groups by appointment. Also, films and live music each Wednesday at noon. Movie memorabilia.
12. ***Conway Cemetery State Park*** *(501) 682-1191*
    Off Ark. 160, west of Bradley. The state's first governor, James Sevier Conway, is buried here. No camping or visitors services.
13. ***Dexter Harding House/ Historic Home Tours*** *(501) 536-7606*
    U. S. 65 and Pine St., Pine Bluff. Historic home has tourist information. Tours of city's historic homes and Trinity Episcopal Church, oldest Episcopal church in Arkansas, can also be arranged with advance notice.
14. ***Discovery Place*** *(903) 793-4831*
    215 Pine, Texarkana. Hands-on exhibits of science and history.
15. ***Drew County Historical Museum*** *(501) 367-7446*
    404 S. Main, Monticello. Artifacts, antiques in a home built in 1909. Two 1800s log cabins.
16. ***Ethnic Minority Memorabilia Association Museum*** *(501) 983-2891 / (501) 983-2684*
    Ark. 4 and Franklin St., Old Washington Historic State Park. Museum focusing on Black Arkansas. By appointment.
17. ***Grant County Museum / Heritage Village*** *(501) 942-4496*
    Off Ark. 46, Sheridan. A new exhibit building has artifacts relating to the county's history. Also a collection of restored buildings.
18. ***Howard County Museum*** *(501) 845-4590*
    Hempstead and 2nd St., Nashville. Local history exhibits. Open on Sundays by appointment.
19. ***Hudson-Grace-Pearson Home*** *(501) 535-0463*
    716 W. Barraque, Pine Bluff. French Provincial home restored by Ben Pearson, world-famous archer. Group tours.
20. ***Magnolia Murals***
    Downtown Magnolia. See colorful murals in the historic square.
21. ***McCollum-Chidester House*** *(501) 836-9243*
    926 Washington, Camden. Served as headquarters for Union General Frederick Steele in the Civil War.
22. ***Nevada County Depot Museum*** *(501) 887-5821*
    400 W. 1st St., Prescott. Tour an old-fashioned railroad depot.
23. ***New Rocky Comfort Museum*** *(501) 542-7887*
    3rd and Schuman, Foreman. Restored 1902 jail contains local artifacts, documents.
24. ***North Main Historic District***
    Main Street area, Monticello. Fifty homes, buildings on the National Register.
25. ***Old Washington Historic State Park*** *(501) 983-2684*

Ark. 4, northwest of Hope. Guided tours of a preserved 19th-century town that was once a popular stop for pioneers traveling to Texas. Arkansas's Confederate Capitol, antebellum homes, re-created tavern inn, blacksmith shop, weapons museum.

26. ***Phil's Antique Barn*** *(501) 798-2244*
County Road 153, off U. S. 167, Hampton. Old barn filled with local artifacts and memorabilia. By appointment.

27. ***Pine Bluff/Jefferson County Historical Museum*** *(501) 541-5402*
201 E. 4th, Pine Bluff. History of the city and region plus railroad memorabilia.

28. ***Pioneer Village*** *(501) 325-7444*
Off Ark. 35, Cleveland County Fairgrounds, Rison. Re-created 19th-century village with a blacksmith shop, log cabins.

29. ***Scott Joplin Mural***
3rd and Main Sts., Texarkana. Depicts life of Black composer Scott Joplin, a Texarkana native.

30. ***Sevier County Museum*** *(501) 642-6642*
717 N. Maple, DeQueen. Museum featuring items relating to the county's history. Also, tours (by appointment) of 1840 home at the site of Paraclifta, once a thriving town.

31. ***Texarkana Historical Museum*** *(903) 793-4831*
219 State Line Ave., Texarkana. Caddo Indian artifacts and much more.

32. ***White Hall Museum*** *(501) 247-9406 / (501) 247-3092*
9011 Dollarway Rd., White Hall. Local historical artifacts. Antique doll collection. Restored caboose.

33. ***Wiggins Cabin/Old Company House*** *(501) 364-6591*
Crossett City Park, Crossett. A log cabin and "shotgun" mill house, fishing pond, hiking trail, zoo. Tours by appointment.

Texarkana Historical Museum

Ace of Clubs House

## TOURISTS, CHIGGERS, AND OTHER INDIGENOUS INSECTS

Having come from South Florida to Arkansas, I was immediately aware of several of the more obvious differences between the two states. Take tourists, for instance. In Florida there is a love-hate relationship with tourists: nobody really likes them, but everybody needs their money. Here, in typical Arkansas fashion, tourists are made to feel quite welcome. Oh, there are a few glances and a chuckle or two when they ask directions to the Wa-chita River, or when they come back from walking in the woods and they're doing the Arkansas Chigger Dance: take one step forward and scratch your ____, take two steps back and itch your ____. (You can fill in the blanks.)

Chiggers, now those are one of Mother Nature's most contrary creatures. They sort of remind me of Arkansas's version of the Yeti or Sasquatch; everybody talks about them but nobody's really sure what they look like, and one encounter with them is generally enough to satisfy a person's curiosity.

This reminds me of a friend of mine who lives north of DeQueen, just off Highway 71, in Southwestern Arkansas. You could say he was taken more than most by this Yeti/Sasquatch thing. One day he drove to Little Rock and bought a gorilla suit at a costume store. Every once in a while, late at night, he used to get drunk, put the suit on and wait in the woods by the highway near his house. When he saw a pair of lights approaching, he'd lumber out onto the road, hands swinging by his knees, then stop in front of the car and raise his arms menacingly. About the time the wide-eyed driver began to slam on his brakes, my drunken buddy would lurch into the woods laughing like a hyena! On occasion, one or two of the more observant victims would question what a Sasquatch was doing carrying a bottle of Jack Daniels, but even so, the phenomenon began to gain notoriety.

Eventually he had to give up his little late night charade; the Sasquatch investigators showed up with infra-red cameras and tranquilizer dart guns, trying to capture what the local press had labeled as the ArkaMan, the Southwest's missing link!

Those of us that knew hadn't the heart to tell them they were dealing with a sotted local wearing a monkey suit and a Tina Turner wig.

You know what else I like about Arkansas? I like the mosquitos here. That is to say I like the fact that they look like mosquitos, and there aren't clouds of them like in Florida. In Southern Florida the mosquitos are bigger than Arkansas hummingbirds. They laugh at bug repellent; in fact, I think they developed a taste for it. They're so big, the only way to stop them is with a 410 shotgun and #8 shot. (Floridians have learned, however, that it is better to use this method of repulsion outside their homes.)

Speaking of guns, that's another one of the big differences between rural Arkansas and South Florida. You're not allowed to carry a gun in your car in Florida, but you need one. In rural Arkansas nobody needs a gun, but everybody's got one in the window of their pickup. I love this place.

In closing this little piece today, I'd like to tell you what I really appreciate about Arkansas as opposed to Florida. The genuine Arkansans that I have met here have not forgotten the value of integrity, both personally and on a community level.

The best example I can give you is the guy that owns the fruit stand in front of his house, on Highway 88. He leaves his fruit in the stand, day and night. He leaves $20.00 in change in a tin can on the counter. There's a note on the can that reads, "If I'm not here, help yourself and put your money in the can. Make your own change." I told him, "If this was Miami, the first night you left that stand alone, the fruit would be gone, the money would be gone, and the next time anyone saw that stand it would be painted a garish yellow and somebody would be selling burritos out of it on Biscayne Boulevard!"

Twenty dollars in a tin can, for goodness sake, on a well-traveled road. . . . He told me that in all the years he's been selling fruit, he's never had a dime stolen.

At the risk of sounding like a Burger King commercial, I just gotta tell you, "I love this place!"

The Intrepid Arkansas Traveler

## THE DOUGHBOY BISCUIT FIASCO

Every once in a while something happens that is just so much better than anything I could invent, that I just have to shake my head in wonder and smile in appreciation of the devil's sense of humor. Now this story is true, I swear. It may however, have been embellished somewhat by the time it reached me, but it was so good by then that it required little artistic license on my part. This is the tale as I heard it. . . .

A woman went grocery shopping at one of the stores in Polk County, one of the large stores--a super-sized store you might say. When she finished her shopping, she returned to the car, put her groceries in the back, got in behind the wheel and relaxed for a moment while waiting for her son who was still in the store. Time passed, it was a hot day. . . .

A little while later, a fellow who had just left the big store was walking through the parking lot when he heard someone cry out. He looked over and observed the lady behind the wheel of her car, writhing and moaning loudly, holding the back of her head with her hands. He rushed over and knocked on her window, asking if he could be of assistance. She--or he--(the story's a little fuzzy here) managed to get the door open, but at that point the lady was nearing hysterics. "Help me! Help me!" she cried, "Call 911! I've been shot in the back of the head!" The man's first response was to reach forward to examine the wound, but the lady pulled back screaming, "No! No! Don't touch me! I'm holding my brains in with my hands! Please, call 911 now!"

Who would have ever thought? An innocent soul shot while waiting at a store in our quiet little county! What is this world coming to? The man, quite unnerved, dashed off to the pay phone and called for an ambulance. Within minutes the ambulance and the police arrived, prepared for the worst, searching for the sniper, the point of entry, and looking for the blood . . . but there wasn't any. Nope, no crazed gunman, no shattered windows or rendered flesh, no gore. When they calmed the woman down enough to examine her, they discovered that while she waited for her son, a package of refrigerated biscuits in the backseat had warmed to critical mass and exploded, the contents of which striking her in the back of the head. Yes, you heard right, struck down in her prime by a biscuit-bullet, a gooey projectile of Pillsbury's best that had smacked her hard enough to jiggle her eyeballs. (I swear I'm not making this up!) Those precious brains she was attempting to keep from draining out of her cranium were nothing more than the Doughboy's buttermilks!

Now I have to wonder what was going through the lady's mind (or what was left of it, as she perceived it) as she attempted to squeeze the biscuit/brains back into her head. Did it occur to her at any time that she was remarkably lucid for having the better part of her grey matter oozing through her fingers and dripping down the headrest? Did she notice at all that her brains seemed a little chilled? Well, these questions and many more we'll probably never have answers to, disappointing as it is. But I felt the tale itself was worth the telling.

In closing, let me leave you with the moral of this little story. It just goes to show you that you have to be careful out there, because calamity can rise up at anytime and strike you when you yeast expect it. . . .

The Intrepid Arkansas Traveler

## A DAY AT THE ZOO

As we travel the backroads of Arkansas on weekend excursions, my lady and I are always tickled at how many people smile and wave at us, or just nod and lift a finger from the steering wheel in hello--people we've never seen before in our lives. It was such a novelty when we first arrived here from South Florida. We had a wonderful time as I practiced different waves, developing my own personal style, pleased beyond belief that we had found a place so genuinely middle-American.

Where we came from if anybody waved at you on the road, usually four of their five fingers were tucked in the palm of their hand, and you didn't return the gesture unless you were feeling lucky and had lots of ammunition.

In all seriousness though, that wave, the nod and the small smile that Arkansans give each other on the road is a precious part of the tradition of this area, a genuine example of the Arkansan's warmth and innately friendly nature. I say to all of you, don't lose that. Teach it to your children, display it to your new neighbors so that they too may adopt your values rather than applying their own. When you've traveled as much as I have, you are given perspective; you realize much of the world out there is cold and wary, and unforgiving. It is up to us to avoid becoming one of the places we read about and sadly shake our heads.

This column came to me last Saturday, as we wove our way along a rural highway headed for Hot Springs, smiling and waving at strangers; we were on our way to the Zoo.

The Hot Springs Zoo is located on Hwy. 88 just east of the city. The main habitat cages for the larger animals are not yet finished, but the petting zoo is open. You can buy a bag of bread crumbs for 50 cents and can get your fingers nibbled on by an assortment of animals from Llamas to exotic deer. (One slightly exuberant goat managed three cuff buttons off my shirt sleeve before I got away, but I figured I got the better of him. They were large metal buttons, and he would remember the exchange in a day or so.)

In the small lake next to the petting zoo, you can feed the fish, and the flock of geese and ducks that are as thoroughly voracious as any self-respecting school of piranha. When you've finished the initial tour, which often includes the feeding of their baby Bengal tiger, the owner will take you up the hill to where the big cats and bears are temporarily caged. Though it lacks much in the way of aesthetics, this tour is still incredible. There are huge Bengal tigers, black panthers and jaguars, mountain lions and African lions and leopards, all no more than a few feet from you. You have no idea how awesome an 800-pound tiger is when he's close enough for you to see the flecks of last night's dinner on his canines. Or how intimidating a black leopard can be when his cold yellow eyes rivet you, and he throws his head back and hisses like a freight train, near enough for you to feel the heat from his breath. Needless to say, children are strongly required to maintain attachment to their parents at all times during this little sojourn. The owner actually pets some of the cats through the bars, scratching their heads and ears, but I'll tell you right now, after observing the glacial stares of those creatures, you couldn't get my hand in there if you promised me lifetime tickets to the Razorback games and threw in Christie Brinkley to boot.

Watching those huge creatures I realized something about cats and dogs, probably the biggest difference between the two. If your favorite hound weighed 500 pounds and you came home drunk in the wee hours of the night, he might bark at first, but when he recognized you he'd sidle over, tail wagging and you'd have to push him away, tell him to go lay down--and he would. But if your wife's cat weighed 500 pounds and you came home drunk in the middle of the night--well, my guess is all they'd find would be a few scraps of clothing and a hairball or two the size of a basketball. That, my friends, is the difference between felines and canines. If you don't think I'm right, take the tour at the Hot Springs Zoo. And while you're headed that way, be sure to wave at your neighbors.

The Intrepid Arkansas Traveler

# STATE PARKS of ARKANSAS

Whisper quiet praise to those who came before us, men of vision whose wisdom preserved these, nature's mansions, of which there are too few these days.

The Traveler

# STATE PARKS

The State Parks of Arkansas are statewide gems showcasing the rich natural and cultural diversity of The Natural State. You'll find parks on scenic mountaintops ... and along quiet streams. In the lush Mississippi Delta lands ... and beside leisurely lakes. Snuggled in secluded mountain valleys ... and preserving settings that are among the state's most historic sites.

For vacation getaways, weekend retreats, group tours and conferences, the 47 state parks are naturals for enjoying the year-round opportunities and seasonal beauty of Arkansas. Call (501) 682-1191 (V/TT) for more information.

## ARKANSAS OIL AND BRINE MUSEUM

3853 Smackover Highway / Smackover, AR 71762 (501) 725-2877

The museum collects, preserves and exhibits examples of Arkansas' changing oil technology and brine industry, and focuses on the 1920s oil boom in south Arkansas. Working outdoor exhibits include an oil well, pumping rig and three derricks. Temporary and traveling exhibits are displayed inside the museum and two video presentations depict the discovery of oil and brine in Arkansas. Admission is free.

The museum is on Ark. 7 one mile south of Smackover.

**Meeting Room** (100 person capacity)
$100/use; Cleanup deposit - $50/use
**Education Building**
$50/use; Cleanup deposit - $25/use

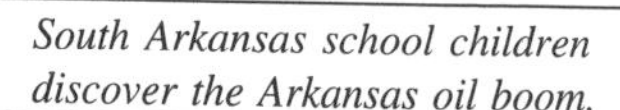

*South Arkansas school children discover the Arkansas oil boom.*

**Hours of Operation**

Open—8 a.m.-5 p.m. (Monday-Saturday)
1 p.m.-5 p.m. (Sunday)

Closed—New Year's Day, Thanksgiving Day, Christmas Eve and Christmas Day

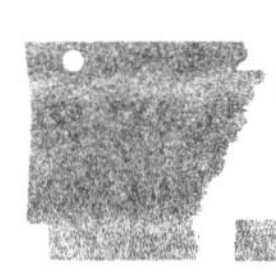

## BEAVER LAKE STATE PARK

20344 East Highway 12 / Rogers, AR 72756 (501) 789-2380

The 11,646-acre Hobbs State Management Area (HSMA) is open for limited outdoor recreation and nature study, and offers undeveloped access to 28,000-acre Beaver Lake. Arkansas State Parks, the Arkansas Natural Heritage Commission, and the Arkansas Game and Fish Commission jointly manage the HSMA property.

The Management Area includes an all-weather public firing range and regulated seasonal hunting opportunities. Two trails offer 10 miles of hiking and five remote, primitive campsites.

Beaver Lake State Park, within HSMA, is in its initial development. Approximately 2,400 acres are planned for future park development including camping, cabins, picnicking and educational opportunities. A park superintendent is on site.

HSMA lies on the southern shores of Beaver Lake and north of the War Eagle River. The Management Area is located 10 miles east of Rogers on State Highway 12.

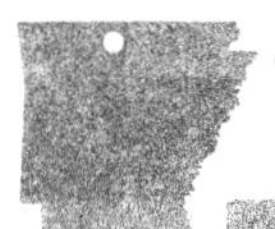

## BULL SHOALS STATE PARK

P.O. Box 205 / Bull Shoals, AR 72619 (501) 431-5521

In the Ozark Mountains, you'll discover one of the nation's finest fishing and boating combinations: the White River and Bull Shoals Lake. The two form a much-touted "fishing paradise." The White River, one of mid-America's premier trout streams, is famous for record rainbow and brown trout. A dam forms the 45,440-acre lake where anglers enjoy lunker bass, trout, catfish, crappie and bream-filled waters.

*Rent-A-Camp at Bull Shoals, Lake Catherine and Petit Jean gives everyone a chance to "rough it" in style.*

Situated below the dam, Bull Shoals State Park shares the lakeshore and riverside. **The park features 105 campsites along the river—85 Preferred Class A sites and 20 with no hookups.**

Park facilities include picnic areas, standard pavilions, playgrounds and trails. A trout dock offers boat, motor and canoe rentals; supplies and equipment; and gifts.

From Mountain Home, travel six miles north on Ark. 5, then eight miles west on Ark. 178 to the park.

**SEE PAGE 2-4 FOR CAMPING FEES, DISCOUNTS AND WINTER RATES.**

**Trout Dock**

| | |
|---|---|
| Johnboat—20 ft. | $15/one-half day; $20/day |
| Johnboat w/Motor | $35/one-half day; $50/day |
| (Fuel extra on all motor rentals) | |
| Canoe (for floating the river/haul back included) | $30/day |
| Canoe (for use in immediate park area) | $15/one-half day; $20/day |
| Haul Back Service (for a private canoe) | $25/day |

**Interpretive Services**

Johnboat Scenic Float Trip on White River
1-1 1/2 hour—2 persons/boat--$14/hr; 3 persons/boat--$21/hr [plus fuel]

Guided Canoe Trip on White River [1 mile] $4/person

Party Barge Scenic Tour on Bull Shoals Lake [1 1/2 hour]
Adult—$4 each; Child (6-12)—$2 each

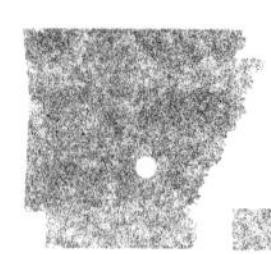

# CANE CREEK STATE PARK

P.O. Box 96 / Star City, AR 71667 (501) 628-4714

Developed by Arkansas State Parks and the Soil Conservation Service, this 2,053-acre park is situated on timber-filled, 1,675-acre Cane Creek Lake where two of Arkansas' physiographic regions come together. The Mississippi Delta flatlands and the rolling hills of south Arkansas' Gulf Coastal Plain blend into a recreational haven rich in flora, fauna and outdoor opportunities.

Facilities include **30 Class A campsites including Preferred sites**, picnic sites, a standard pavilion, visitor center with exhibits and gift shop, launch ramp, barrier-free fishing piers, trail, a bathhouse and rest room.

From Star City, go five miles east on Ark. 293 to the park.

**SEE PAGE 2-4 FOR CAMPING FEES, DISCOUNTS AND WINTER RATES.**

*Exhibits welcome you to the beauty of Cane Creek State Park.*

## Conway Cemetery State Park

When Arkansas was admitted to the Union as the 25th state on June 15, 1836, James Sevier Conway took office as Arkansas' first governor. This 11-acre historic site preserves Conway's final resting place. The cemetery is the family plot of the former Conway homesite and cotton plantation, Walnut Hill. Forty-three graves lie within the graveyard. [NOTE: There are no camping or visitor services available.]

From Bradley, travel two miles west on Ark. 160 to the community of Walnut Hill. Then turn south on the county road and go 1/2 mile to the park.

## Cossatot River State Park-Natural Area

960 Highway 4 East / Wickes, AR 71973 (501) 385-2201

This park-natural area extends 11 miles along one of Arkansas' wildest streams. The river forms Cossatot Falls, a rugged and rocky canyon challenging the most experienced canoeists and kayakers (Class IV rapids). Floatable river levels are usually limited to fall, winter and spring. For river stage information (in feet) from the Highway 246 access, call: (501) 387-3141.

Development at this primitive area is limited to the Brushy Creek Recreation Area adjacent to the Highway 246 bridge. Day-use facilities include picnic sites, a nature trail, rest rooms, and a river access point for floating. A pedestrian walkway crosses the river and offers barrier-free access on the west side.

Now owned by the state of Arkansas, the Cossatot River State Park-Natural Area's (CRSPNA) 5,233 acres emphasize outdoor recreation, river preservation and environmental education. The state park-natural area is managed by Arkansas State Parks and the Arkansas Natural Heritage Commission. A park superintendent is on site.

CRSPNA is south of Mena in west central Arkansas. The northern route is via Ark. 246 between Vandervoort and Athens. The southern route is via Ark. 4 between Wickes and Umpire. Weyerhaeuser Company roads provide access to the river.

*Cossatot Falls, a favorite of serious kayakers, is one of Arkansas' most dramatic settings.*

## Crater of Diamonds State Park

Route 1, Box 364 / Murfreesboro, AR 71958 (501) 285-3113

Crater of Diamonds offers a one-of-a-kind adventure—the chance to hunt for and keep real diamonds. Search a 35-acre field [the eroded surface of an ancient, gem-bearing volcanic pipe], the world's only diamond site where you can prospect for and keep any gems you find. Prospectors enter the field through the park visitor center which includes exhibits and an A/V program explaining the area's geology and tips on recognizing diamonds in the rough.

Diamonds were first discovered here in 1906, and since then over 70,000 have been found including the 40.23-carat "Uncle Sam," the 16.37-carat "Amarillo Starlight," and the 15.33-carat "Star of Arkansas." Since Crater became a park in 1972, over 18,000 diamonds have been carried home by visitors. Amethyst, garnet, jasper, agate, quartz and more can also be found. Digging tools are available for rent and the park staff provides free identification and certification of diamonds.

*Nowhere else can you dig for diamonds and keep what you find.*

The park offers **60 Class A campsites,** picnic sites, a short-order restaurant, laundry, gift shop, trail and interpretive programs. The park is two miles southeast of Murfreesboro on Ark. 301.

**Admission to Mine Area/day**

Adult—$4 each; Child (6-12)—$1.50 each

Group Rates (20 or more with advance notice)—1/2 above fees.

## Crowley's Ridge State Park

P.O. Box 97 / Walcott, AR 72474-0097
PARK/CAMPSITE RESERVATIONS: (501) 573-6751
CABIN RESERVATIONS: 1-800-264-2405

This popular recreational retreat lies atop a narrow arc of rolling, forested hills called Crowley's Ridge. The park occupies the former homestead of Benjamin Crowley, whose family first settled the area.

Cozy log and stone structures constructed by the Civilian Conservation Corps set the mood for the park's rustic warmth. Facilities include four fully-equipped modern cabins with kitchens; group cabin area with rental kitchen and dining hall; **26 campsites—18 Class A, 8 tent sites**; picnic areas; snack bar; trails; standard pavilions; baseball field; 30-acre fishing lake (electric motors only); fishing boats and canoes; and swimming lake.

The park is 15 miles north of Jonesboro on Ark. 141; or nine miles west of Paragould on U.S. 412, then two miles south on Ark. 168.

| | | |
|---|---|---|
| **Cabins (with kitchens)** | | |
| Two double beds (fireplace): | Sun.-Thurs. | $50/two persons/day |
| | Fri.-Sat. | $55/two persons/day |
| One double bed (fireplace): | Sun.-Thurs. | $45/two persons/day |
| | Fri.-Sat. | $50/two persons/day |
| Each additional person | | $5/day |
| **Group Facilities (deposits required)** | | |
| For 1 to 20 persons (bunk cabins only) | | $110/day (Sun.-Thurs.); $125/day (Fri.-Sat.) |
| For 21 to 60 persons (bunk cabins only) | | $4/person/day |
| Kitchen/Dining Hall (w/bunk cabin rental) | | $25/day |
| Kitchen/Dining Hall (to others) | | $65/day |
| **Swimming Beach** | | $1.75/person/day |
| **Pedal Boat** | | $2.50/one-half hour; $3.75/hour |
| **Fishing Boat** | | $4/one-half day; $6/day |
| **Canoe** | | $3.25/hour; $5.50/one-half day; $11/day |

## Daisy State Park

HC-71, Box 66 / Kirby, AR 71950-8105 (501) 398-4487

Lake Greeson, the Little Missouri River and Daisy State Park make a winning combination in the Ouachita foothills. Greeson—7,000 acres of clear water and mountain scenery—delights water enthusiasts with black and white bass, stripers, crappie, catfish and bluegill accounting for the lake's fishing popularity. The Little Missouri joins four other popular float streams that offer challenging spring and early summer trout fishing.

On Lake Greeson, Daisy State Park offers a base camp for enjoying these outdoor recreational opportunities. Facilities include **118 campsites—97 Class A, 21 tent sites;** picnic areas, a standard pavilion, launch ramps, hiking trails and a motorcycle/ mountain bike trail. [Many visitors to Crater of Diamonds, just 23 miles south, enjoy camping at Daisy's lakeshore campsites.]

The park is 1/4 mile south of Daisy off U.S. 70.

| | |
|---|---|
| **Bicycle Rental** | $1.50/hour; $8/day |

# DeGray Lake Resort State Park

Route 3, Box 490 / Bismarck, AR 71929-8194
PARK/CAMPSITE RESERVATIONS: (501) 865-2801
LODGE: 1-800-737-8355 (V/TT) or (501) 865-2851

Arkansas' premier resort park lies on the north shore of a 13,800-acre fishing and water sport paradise. A 96-room lodge, camping **(113 sites: Preferred and Class A),** swimming, tennis, golf, hiking, bicycling and more are available at this "you can have it all" state park. The park's full-service marina (open year-round) offers tackle, dock space, fuel and boat rentals of all kinds.

*Better Homes and Gardens magazine named DeGray one of America's 30 favorite family resorts for 1993.*

*You can have it all at DeGray Lake Resort State Park.*

A causeway takes you from the mainland to the island lodge and convention center offering scenic views of the lake and Ouachita foothills. The Shoreline Restaurant overlooking the lake and pool offers a full menu, plus banquet catering services. Meeting rooms and a 500-seat convention center are also available. **Group Rates/Package Plans available.**

The park has an 18-hole, public championship golf course (7,200 yards) and driving range. The Pro Shop offers refreshments, golf equipment and apparel, as well as cart and club rentals. A store, pavilion, trails, tennis courts and laundry round out DeGray Lake Resort.

Interpreters offer scenic boat tours, slide presentations, movies and outdoor workshops. The park offers a host of year-round special events [lodging package plans available]. Each January, the popular Eagles Et Cetera Weekend celebrates the migration of bald eagles to DeGray Lake.

Take Exit #78 off I-30 at Caddo Valley/Arkadelphia and travel seven miles north on Scenic Ark. 7 to the park.

**Lodge (96 rooms)**

| | |
|---|---|
| Lake view | $70/two persons/day |
| Woods view | $60/two persons/day |
| Each additional person | $5/day |
| Rollaway | $5/day |
| Bicycle Rental: Regular bicycle | $2/hour; $8/day |
| Bicycle for two | $3/hour; $10/day |

**Lodge Conference Center**

**Individual Conference Rooms:**

| | |
|---|---|
| Lodge occupancy (36-96 rooms) | No charge |
| Lodge occupancy (11-35 rooms) | $75/use |
| Outside groups (or 1-10 rooms) | $150/use |

**Total Conference Center:**

| | |
|---|---|
| Lodge occupancy (72-96 rooms) | No charge |
| Lodge occupancy (36-71 rooms) | $125/use |
| Lodge occupancy (11-35 rooms) | $200/use |
| Lodge occupancy (1-10 rooms) | $300/use |
| Outside groups | $350/use |

**Lodge Meeting Rooms:**

| | |
|---|---|
| Lodge occupancy (25 rooms or more) | No charge |
| Lodge occupancy (Less than 25 rooms) | $50/use |
| Outside groups (Non-lodge guests) | $100/use |

**Golf Course:** Call Pro Shop for tee times: (501) 865-2807.

| | **9 holes** | **18 holes** |
|---|---|---|
| Weekday Greens Fee | $8 | $10 |
| Weekend/Holiday Greens Fee | $9 | $11 |
| Senior Citizen Greens Fee [Age 65 and above] (Mon.-Fri.) | $6 | $8 |
| Annual Greens Fee: | | $400/person<br>$525/family |

| | **9 holes** | **18 holes** |
|---|---|---|
| Power Cart | $9 | $16 |
| Pull Cart | | $3/use |
| Clubs (Starter Set) | | $5/use |
| Driver Rental | | $1/use |
| Driving Range | | $1.50/half bucket; $2.50/bucket |

**Lakeside Vista Area** $50/use

**Marina**

The Service Dock has fuel, bait, tackle, ice and refreshments year-round.

Large Craft-Covered Slip (Oct. - Feb.)--$75/month; (Mar. - Sept.)--$100/month

| | |
|---|---|
| Small Craft-Covered Slip | $50/month |
| Party Barge-Uncovered Slip | $55/month |
| Houseboat-Covered Slip | $115/month |
| Houseboat-Uncovered Slip | $70/month |
| Transient Slip | $8/day; $30/week |
| Mooring Buoy | $35/month |
| Battery Charge | $2.50/charge |
| Towing/Service Charge: | $15/hour (one-hour minimum) For registered guests: $7.50 (one hour minimum) |
| Houseboat Dump Station Use | $5/use |
| Fishing Boat—14-16 ft. | $6/one-half day; $10/day |
| Boat w/Motor | $20/one-half day; $30/day |
| Boat w/Electric Motor | $10/one-half day; $14/day |
| Deluxe Fishing Package (includes boat and motor, trolling motor and seats): | $30/one-half day; $45/day |
| Party Barge: | $105/one-half day; $150/day (May - Oct.) $45/one-half day; $75/day (Nov. - April) |

(Fuel extra on all motor rentals)

Canoe $3.25/hour

Sailboats—Catamaran—16 ft.:
$40/one-half day; 55/day
(during season)
$20/one-half day; $35/day
(during off-season)

Sailboats—Sunfish
$7/hour; $15/one-half day; $20/day

Houseboat—32 ft.
[Houseboat Rental (Mem. Day to Labor Day) min. 2 nights rental on weekends, min. 3 nights rental on holiday weekends]
Call marina for reservations (501)865-2811

May - Oct. Rates:
$160/weeknight, or
$290/weekend, or
$275/2 weeknights, or
$425/3 weeknights, or
$525/4 weeknights, or
$625/5 weeknights, or
$775/7 nights

Nov - April Rates:
$100/night, or
$175/weekend, or
$250/3 weeknights, or
$400/5 weeknights, or
$500/7 nights

(Fuel/security dep. extra)

*DeGray is a water sport paradise.*

| | |
|---|---|
| Tube Skis | $7/one-half day; $10/day |
| Water Skis | $7/one-half day; $13/day |
| Wave Runner | $25/one-half hour; $35/hour; $95/one-half day; $175/day; Deposit required |
| Rod and Reel Rental | $3/one-half day; $5/day |
| Life Jacket Rental | $3/one-half day; $5/day; Deposit—$10/use |

**Interpretive Services**

Party Barge Scenic Tour on DeGray Lake
Adult - $4 each; Child (6-12) - $2 each

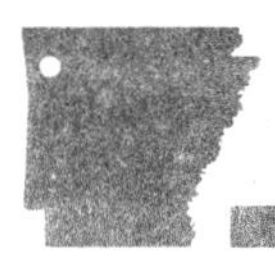

## DEVIL'S DEN STATE PARK

11333 West Arkansas Highway 74 / West Fork, AR 72774
PARK/CAMPSITE RESERVATIONS: (501) 761-3325
CABIN RESERVATIONS: 1-800-264-2417

At Devil's Den, in a picturesque Ozark valley, you can explore caves, crevices and bluff overlooks. Selected as a park site in the 1930s, Lee Creek Valley provided materials for the Civilian Conservation Corps to build the park's Rustic-style wood and stone structures which today offer modern conveniences. The mountain stream forms a small 8-acre lake before cascading over a magnificent native stone dam. Hiking and backpacking trails access backcountry areas of this nature park.

Thirteen fully-equipped cabins with kitchens and fireplaces (fireplaces open October 1 - April 30) are nestled in the natural beauty of this enchanting park. A cafe and pool (both open in summer only) overlook the lake. Groceries, gifts and snacks are available at the park store. Campsites **(154 sites: 57 Class A including Preferred sites; 15 Class B; 32 tent; 44 horse with hookups)** are spaced along the valley, and a horse camp area and riding trails are also available. The park includes a group camp, a standard pavilion and mountain bike trails.

Interpreters provide hikes [along several miles of trails including the 14-mile Butterfield Hiking Trail], games and programs daily during summer. Programming is available year-round by request.

To reach the park, travel eight miles south of Fayetteville on U.S. 71 to West Fork, then go 18 miles southwest on Ark. 170; or exit U.S. 71 at Winslow and go 13 miles west on Ark. 74 (TRAILERS LONGER THAN 26 FT. SHOULD USE CAUTION WHEN USING **ARK. 74** DUE TO MOUNTAINOUS ROAD.)

*Bicycling, backpacking and bat watching are popular at Devil's Den.*

| | |
|---|---|
| **Cabins (with kitchens)** | |
| Rustic-style/One bedroom (fireplace): | $55/two persons/day |
| Rustic-style/Two bedrooms (fireplace): | $65/two persons/day |
| Rustic-style/Three bedrooms (fireplace): | $75/two persons/day |
| Each additional person (no rollaways available) | $5/day |
| **Camping** | |
| Group Camp Area: | |
| $1/person/day [$25 minimum/10 person minimum/75 person maximum) | |
| Rent-A-Backpack Equipment (deposit req.)/24 hour period: | |
| Partial Set—$7; Tent—$7; Backpack—$10.50; Full Set—$21 | |
| **Swimming Pool** | $2/person/day; Pool Pass (20 admissions) - $33 |
| **Pedal Boat** | $2.50/one-half hour; $3.75/hour |
| **Canoe** | $3.75/hour |
| **Mountain Bike Rental** | $5/hour; $15/one-half day; $25/day |
| **Visitor Center Meeting Room** | $25/use; $40/day; Cleanup deposit—$20/use |

## HAMPSON MUSEUM STATE PARK

P.O. Box 156 / Wilson, AR 72395 (501) 655-8622

*See an outstanding collection of Late Mississippian pottery on display at Hampson Museum.*

Hampson Museum exhibits a remarkable collection of artifacts from the Nodena site, a Late Mississippi Period culture. The Nodena were farmers who developed a complex civilization of art, religion, political structure and trading networks. The remarkable collection owes its preservation to Dr. James K. Hampson. He and his family meticulously excavated, studied and inventoried the mounds and subsurface remains of this complex civilization which inhabited the area from A.D. 1350 to 1700. The collection was donated to the State of Arkansas in the 1950s. Adjacent to the museum are picnic sites and a playground.

Hampson Museum is in the community of Wilson at the junction of U.S. 61 and Lake Drive (seven miles east of I-55).

**Museum Entrance Fee**
Adult—$2 each; Child (6-12)—$1 each
Group Rates (20 or more with advance notice)—$.25 off above fees
Bona Fide School Groups (with advance notice)—$.65 per person
**Hours of Operation**
Open—8 a.m.-5 p.m. (Tuesday-Saturday)
1 p.m.-5 p.m. (Sunday)
Closed—Mondays (except Monday holidays), New Year's Day, Thanksgiving Day, Christmas Eve and Christmas Day

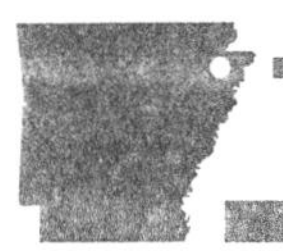

## Herman Davis State Park

This one-acre park surrounds the monument to Private Herman Davis, an Arkansas farm boy and World War I hero. Fourth on General John J. Pershing's list of World War I's 100 greatest heroes, he received the Distinguished Service Cross, the Croix de Guere, and the Medaulle Militaire awards from the American and French governments.

The monument is at the community of Manila on Ark. 18 (16 miles west of Blytheville).

## Jacksonport State Park

P.O. Box 8 / Jacksonport, AR 72075 (501) 523-2143

During the 1800s, steamboats made Jacksonport a thriving river port. In the Civil War, the town was occupied by both Confederate and Union forces because of its crucial locale. Jacksonport became county seat in 1854, and in 1869 a two-story brick courthouse was constructed. The town began to decline in the 1870s when bypassed by the railroad. In 1891 the county seat was moved and the stores, wharves and saloons vanished.

The park is dominated by the restored 1869 courthouse which includes exhibits of Jackson County's rich history. The landscaped court-house square leads to the river's edge where the Mary Woods II, a recon-structed White River paddlewheeler, is available for walking

*Go on board one of the last sternwheelers in America, the Mary Woods II, at Jacksonport State Park.*

tours. The park offers **20 Class A campsites**, a swimming beach on the White River, a standard pavilion and picnic sites. The park is on Ark. 69 at Jacksonport, just three miles north of Newport off U.S. 67.

**Courthouse Museum or Mary Woods II Riverboat Museum**
Adult—$2 each; Child (6-12)—$1 each
Combo Ticket (Courthouse & Riverboat): Adult-$3.50 each; Child (6-12)-$1.50 each
Group Rates (20 or more with advance notice)—$.25 off above fees
Bona Fide School Groups (with advance notice)—$.65 per person
**Gazebo** $20/use

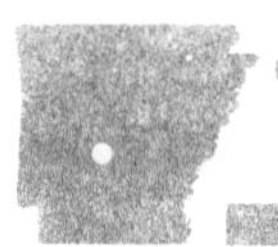

## Lake Catherine State Park

1200 Catherine Park Road / Hot Springs, AR 71913
PARK/CAMPSITE RESERVATIONS: (501) 844-4176
CABIN RESERVATIONS: 1-800-264-2422

A popular recreation destination between Malvern and Hot Springs, this park covers 2,180 acres of Ouachita Mountain beauty on the shores of Lake Catherine. Shades of the past are seen in wood and stone facilities constructed by the Civilian Conservation Corps that today combine rustic warmth and modern conveniences. The park offers rental boats (year-round), a marina offering bait and fuel (summer only), a launch ramp, standard pavilion, picnic sites, playground, laundry and trails. Groceries, gifts and ice are available at the store/restaurant (summer) which overlooks the swimming area and nature center (summer). Nestled along the shore are 17 fully-equipped cabins with kitchens (some with fireplaces) and a boat dock. **Seventy Class A campsites including Preferred sites and** a Rent-A-Camp site dot the lakeshore and secluded woodlands. Interpreters provide guided hikes, boat tours, programs and workshops during summer or by advance request year-round.

*Trails overlook the beautiful lake and lead to an enchanting waterfall.*

Take Exit #97 off I-30 at Malvern and travel 12 miles north on Ark. 171 to the park.

**Cabins (with kitchens)**

| | |
|---|---|
| Rustic-style (fireplace) | $65/two persons/day |
| Duplex (fireplace) | $65/two persons/day |
| Duplex | $60/two persons/day |
| Each additional person | $5/day |
| Rollaway | $5/day |

**Marina**

| | |
|---|---|
| Fishing Boat | $9/one-half day; $12/day |
| Boat w/Motor (fuel extra) | $18/one-half day; $25/day |
| Transient Slip | $7/day |
| Party Barge | $45/one-half day; $65/day (Nov. - Apr.)<br>$75/one-half day; $115/day (May - Oct.) |
| Pedal Boat | $2.50/one-half hour; $3.75/hour |

Canoe
$4.50/hour;
$8/one-half day;
$15/day

Rowboat
$3/one-half hour;
$4/hour;
$9/one-half day;
$12/day

Rod and Reel Rental
$2.50/one-half day; $5/day

**Interpretive Services**

Party Barge Scenic Lake Tour
Adult--$4 each;
Child (6-12)--
$2 each

*The nature cabin, evening programs, boat tours and hikes introduce you to beautiful Lake Catherine State Park.*

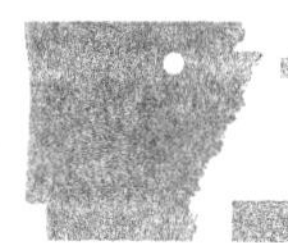

# Lake Charles State Park

3705 Highway 25 / Powhatan, AR 72458 (501) 878-6595

Lake Charles, 645 acres of spring-fed waters in the Ozark foothills, offers fine catches of bass, crappie, bream and catfish. The park includes **93 campsites (Class A including Preferred sites and Class B; 10 no hookups),** picnic sites, a standard pavilion, launch ramp, hiking trails and sandy swimming beach.

This park is a perfect camp for exploring the area's historical and natural attractions [see Old Davidsonville and Powhatan Courthouse]. Springtime float-fishing on area rivers is popular, and hunting is available in nearby wildlife management areas.

From Hoxie, travel eight miles northwest on U.S. 63, then go six miles south on Ark. 25 to the park.

# Lake Chicot State Park

Route 1, Box 1555 / Lake Village, AR 71653
PARK/CAMPSITE RESERVATIONS: (501) 265-5480
CABIN RESERVATIONS: 1-800-264-2430

The Mississippi Delta's quiet beauty and abundant recreational opportunities come together on Arkansas' largest natural lake. A 20-mile long oxbow lake, cut off centuries ago when the mighty Mississippi changed course, is a peaceful site for fishing and boating. Fishing for crappie, bass and bream is popular, especially on the upper end of the lake during spring and fall. Fishing for catfish is outstanding year-round.

*Birding, fishing and sunsets hold your attention at Lake Chicot.*

Nestled in a pecan grove, the park offers **127 campsites (Preferred with sewer, Preferred and Class A),** 14 fully-equipped cabins with kitchens (many with lake view patio and fishing dock), pool (summer), picnicking, standard pavilions, laundry and playground. You'll find food and gifts at the store/marina plus boats, motors, fuel, bait and a launch ramp. A visitor center presents the area's history and natural resources through exhibits and programs. Located in the Mississippi Flyway, the park offers outstanding bird watching. Each September the park hosts party barge tours of the lake, levee tours and programs for viewing rare storks, ibis, egrets and ducks.

The park is eight miles northeast of Lake Village on Ark. 144.

**Cabins (with kitchens)**

| | | |
|---|---|---|
| Lake view | | $55/two persons/day |
| Woods view | | $50/two persons/day |
| Special Rates: | Sun. - Wed. (four days for the price of three) | |
| | Lake view | $165 |
| | Woods view | $150 |
| | Sun. - Thurs. (five days for the price of four) | |
| | Lake view | $220 |
| | Woods view | $200 |
| Each additional person (rollaway included) | | $5/day |
| **Swimming Pool** | | $2/person/day |
| **Marina** | | |
| Fishing Boat | | $5/one-half day; $10/day |
| Boat w/Motor | | $7/hour; $15/one-half day; $25/day |
| (Fuel extra on all motor rentals) | | |
| Pedal Boat | | $2.50/one-half hour; $3.75/hour |

**Bicycle Rental:** Regular bicycle $1.50/hour, $8/day; Bicycle for two $2.50/hour, $10/day

**Interpretive Services**

Party Barge Scenic Tour on Lake Chicot -- Adult-$5 each; Child (6-12)-$2.50 each

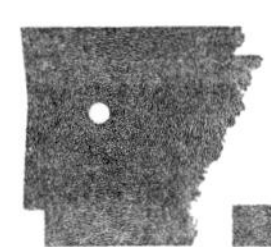

# Lake Dardanelle State Park

2428 Marina Road / Russellville, AR 72801 (501) 967-5516

This park offers three lakeside areas on Lake Dardanelle, a 34,000-acre lake on the Arkansas River. The Russellville (main park), and Dardanelle locations offer **camping (82 sites: Russellville - Preferred and Class A; Dardanelle - Class A;),** launch ramps, standard pavilions, picnicking, rest rooms and bathhouses with hot showers. A visitor center, marina (Dardanelle also), barrier-free fishing pier, miniature golf course and hiking trail are part of the Russellville Area. Ouita offers picnic sites, rest rooms and a launch ramp.

To reach each area: 1) **Russellville Area**—Take Exit #81 (Ark. Hwy. 7) off I-40 at Russellville. Turn south, then immediately turn west on Ark. 326 and go four miles. 2) **Dardanelle Area**—Four miles west of Dardanelle on Ark. 22. 3) **Ouita Area**—Take Exit #81 (Ark. Hwy. 7) off I-40 at Russellville. Turn south, then immediately turn west on Ark. 326 and go 3/4 mile.

| | | |
|---|---|---|
| **Bicycle Rental:** | Regular bicycle | $1.50/hour; $8/day |
| | Bicycle for two | $2.50/hour; $10/day |

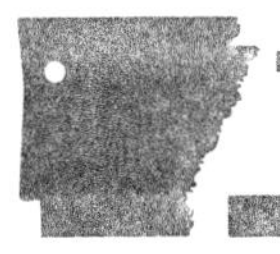

# Lake Fort Smith State Park

P.O. Box 4 / Mountainburg, AR 72946
PARK/CAMPSITE RESERVATIONS: (501) 369-2469
CABIN RESERVATIONS: 1-800-264-2435

Nestled in an Ozark valley adjacent to the Ozark National Forest, this park offers some of Arkansas' most beautiful scenery, facilities and backpacking opportunities [the 178-mile Ozark Highlands Trail begins here]. The park's scenic beauty is enhanced during spring and fall rains with a cascading spillway created by the Lake Fort Smith dam.

Facilities include **12 Class A campsites** (no sanitary trailer station), picnic sites, a standard pavilion, olympic-sized pool, tennis courts (unlighted), trails, a launch ramp and eight fully-equipped cabins with kitchens. The visitor center offers rental canoes, fishing boats and motors. A group dormitory with kitchen and dining hall is also available for rent.

The park is at the northern edge of Mountainburg. Watch for the park access sign on U.S. 71, then travel 1/2 mile east to the park.

**Cabins (with kitchens)**

| | |
|---|---|
| Rustic-style/Spillway View-Two bedrooms (fireplace): | $70/two persons/day |
| Rustic-style/Two bedrooms (no fireplace): | $60/two persons/day |

| | |
|---|---|
| Rustic-style/Spillway View -One bedroom (fireplace): | $55/two persons/day |
| Rustic-style/Woods View - One bedroom (fireplace): | $45/two persons/day |
| Each additional person (no rollaways available) | $5/day |

**Group Facilities (deposits required)**

[2 night minimum on weekends]

For 1 to 30 persons (dorm and kitchen)
$225/day

For 31 to 110 persons (dormitory only)
$7.50/person/day

Kitchen (to others if available 30 days in advance)
$100/use

**Swimming Pool**

$2/person/day

**Bicycle Rental**

$1.50/hour; $8/day

**Tennis Racquet Rental**

$1.50/hour;
Deposit—$5/use

**Volleyball and Net**

Deposit—$5/use

*A snug cabin and a light snow make wonderful weekends in Arkansas State Parks.*

**Boat Rentals**

| | |
|---|---|
| Fishing Boat | $6/day |
| Boat w/Motor (fuel extra) | $12/one-half day; $20/day |
| Canoe | $3.75/hour; $8/one-half day; $15/day |

(A deposit of $10/use is required for each boat rental.)

## LAKE FRIERSON STATE PARK

7904 Highway 141 / Jonesboro, AR 72401 (501) 932-2615

On Crowley's Ridge in northeast Arkansas, this park is known for its year-round fishing and springtime blaze of wild dogwoods. The lake's 335-acres provides fine catches of bass, bream, crappie and catfish. Park facilities include **seven Class B campsites,** tables and grills, rest rooms, picnic sites, a playground, self-guided trail, boat rentals, launch ramp, barrier-free fishing pier and visitor center.
The park is 10 miles north of Jonesboro on Ark. 141.

**Boat Rentals**

| | |
|---|---|
| Fishing Boat—14 ft. | $7/day; Deposit—$7/use |

# Lake Ouachita State Park

5451 Mountain Pine Road / Mountain Pine, AR 71956
PARK/CAMPSITE RESERVATIONS: (501) 767-9366
CABIN RESERVATIONS: 1-800-264-2441

Known for the clarity of its water, Arkansas' largest man-made lake stretches across 48,000 acres and has 975 miles of impressive mountainous shoreline. Swimming, skiing, scuba diving, boating and fishing for bream, crappie, catfish, stripers, and trout can be enjoyed in open waters and quiet coves. At the lake's eastern tip, the state park includes historic Three Sisters' Springs [accessible through a modern springhouse], once thought to have curative powers. The park offers **112 campsites (Preferred, Class A and Class B),** picnic areas, a marina (with boat, motor and slip rentals; bait and supplies), swimming area and trails. A store and snack bar are located in the visitor center. Fully-equipped cabins with kitchens overlook the lake.

From Hot Springs, travel three miles west on U.S. 270, then go 12 miles north on Ark. 227 to the park.

**Cabins (with kitchens)**

| | |
|---|---|
| Three bedrooms: | $85/two persons/day |
| Two bedrooms: | $70/two persons/day |
| Each additional person (no rollaways available) | $5/day |

**Marina**

| | |
|---|---|
| Covered Slip —8'x16' | $60/month |
| Covered Slip —9'x18' | $65/month |
| Covered Slip —10'x22' (elec.) | $90/month |
| —10'x22' (no elec.) | $70/month |
| Uncovered Slip —10'x20' | $60/month |
| Transient Slip | $10/day |
| Mooring Buoy | $45/month |
| Battery Charge | $3/charge |

Service Charge: $15/hour (NOTE: Service is free for registered park guests.)

| | |
|---|---|
| Fishing Boats: 16 ft. | $17.50/day |
| 16 ft. w/Motor | $25/one-half day; $40/day; Deposit—$50/use |

Party Barges:
- 29 ft. $100/one-half day; $150/day; Deposit-$100/use
- 28 ft. $70/one-half day; $125/day; Deposit-$100/use

(Fuel extra on all motor rentals)

*Lake Ouachita creates special experiences everyday.*

Pedal Boat $2.50/one-half hour; $3.75/hour
Canoe $3.75/hour; $15/day

**Interpretive Services**
Party Barge Scenic Tour on Lake Ouachita
Adult—$5/each; Child (6-12)—$2.50/each
Extended Party Barge Tours
Adult—$3.75/hour; Child (6-12)—$2/hour

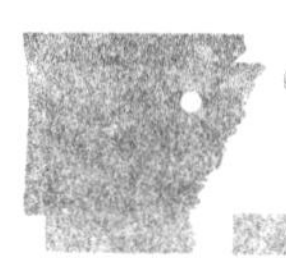

## Lake Poinsett State Park

5752 State Park Lane / Harrisburg, AR 72432-9571 (501) 578-2064

Anglers find shallow 640-acre Lake Poinsett, nestled atop Crowley's Ridge in northeast Arkansas, a special getaway for bass, bream, catfish and crappie fishing. The park offers **30 campsites (Class A & B),** picnic areas, a screened-in standard pavilion (with a special $10 per hour weekday rate), playground, hiking trail, launch ramp and boat rentals.

From Harrisburg, travel one mile east on Ark. 14, then go three miles south on Ark. 163 to the park.

**Boat Rentals**
Fishing Boat—14 ft. $7/day; Deposit—$7/use

## Logoly State Park

P.O. Box 245 / McNeil, AR 71752 (501) 695-3561

At Arkansas' first environmental education state park, interpreters present workshops on ecological and environmental topics. The park's natural resources provide a living laboratory for students and nature lovers. Most of Logoly's 368 acres comprise a State Natural Area with unique plant life and numerous mineral springs. Facilities include **six group tent sites (no hookups),** a bathhouse with hot showers, standard pavilion (free to educational groups), picnic sites, trails and a visitor center with an exhibit area and indoor classroom. [NOTE: Educational groups have preference and may make reservations. Individuals may use campsites on a first-come basis, but must vacate for scheduled groups.]

From U.S. 79 at McNeil, go one mile on County Road 47 (Logoly Road) to the park.

**Camping**
Group Camp (6 tent sites—no hookups) $1/person/day
Minimum daily charge $6.50/site

**Visitor Center Meeting Room** $25/use; Cleanup deposit—$25/use
(NOTE: Public schools, educational groups and State agencies conducting environmental education or park-related meetings may use the meeting room at no charge.)

## Louisiana Purchase State Park

At the junction of Lee, Monroe and Phillips Counties, this park preserves the initial point from which all surveys of property acquired through the Louisiana Purchase of 1815 initiated. The park includes 36 acres within a headwater swamp, a fast-disappearing ecological setting in eastern Arkansas. A boardwalk with exhibits provides access to a monument in the swamp's interior marking the survey's initial point.

From I-40 at Brinkley, take U.S. 49 and travel 21 miles south, then go two miles east on Ark. 362 to the park.

*The Louisiana Purchase monument is just one of Arkansas' unique historic sites.*

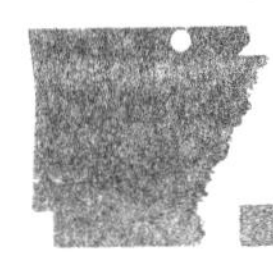

## Mammoth Spring State Park

P.O. Box 36 / Mammoth Spring, AR 72554 (501) 625-7364

Mammoth Spring, Arkansas' largest spring, flows nine million gallons of water hourly. Forming a scenic 10-acre lake, it then flows south as the Spring River, a popular trout and float stream. Near the spring, a beautifully-restored 1886 Frisco depot houses a collection of railroad memorabilia. The baggage room displays local history exhibits, and outside is a Frisco caboose. Park facilities include an information center with exhibits on the area's rich history and natural resources, picnic sites, a standard pavilion, trail and ball field.

The park is on U.S. 63 at the community of Mammoth Spring.

**Depot and Caboose**
Adult-$1 each;
Child (6-12)-$.50 each

*Visitors to Mammoth Spring can learn history and geology, explore a train station and a hydroelectric power plant, and see a spring large enough to start a river.*

# Millwood State Park

Route 1, Box 37AB / Ashdown, AR 71822 (501) 898-2800

*Millwood is famous for many types of freshwater fishing.*

One of the South's hottest fishing areas is 29,500-acre Millwood Lake. A series of boat lanes lead anglers among timber to marshes and oxbow cutoffs—a "tree-filled" fishing paradise. Famous for bass tournaments, the lake abounds in largemouth, white and hybrid bass, and in spring and fall offers some of Arkansas' best crappie fishing. Summer provides easy catches of catfish and bream. Bird watching is popular with a wintering bald eagle population, flocks of migrating pelicans and ducks in the fall, and a variety of year-round inhabitants. Facilities include **117 campsites (114 Class A; 3 tent)**, picnic sites, a standard pavilion, and self-guided trail.

A marina offers souvenirs, gift items, groceries, bait and gas. Fishing boats, pedal boats and "free" fishing advice are available. Fishing boats and slip rentals are available year round. [Marina: (501) 898-5334]

From junction I-30 and U.S. 71 at Texarkana, travel 16 miles north on U.S. 71 to Ashdown, then nine miles east on Ark. 32 to the park.

| | |
|---|---|
| **Group Pavilion** (Standard) | $15/use; $25/day |
| **Marina** | |
| Covered Slip—12'x16' | $40/month |
| Covered Slip—6'x16' | $30/month |
| Covered Transient Slip—6'x16' | $5/day |
| Fishing Boat—14 ft. | $8/one-half day; $15/day |
| Boat w/Motor (fuel & deposit extra) | $17.50/one-half day; $30/day |
| Pedal Boat | $2.50/one-half hour; $3.75/hour |

# Moro Bay State Park

6071 Highway 15 South / Jersey, AR 71651 (501) 463-8555

You'll find one of the most popular fishing and water sport areas in south central Arkansas where Moro Bay and Raymond Lake join the Ouachita River. Park facilities include **20 Class A campsites,** picnic sites, a store, marina, standard pavilion, playground and trail.

The park is 29 miles southwest of Warren on Ark. 15; or 23 miles northeast of El Dorado on Ark. 15.

| | |
|---|---|
| **Indoor Group Facility** (cleanup deposit required) | $50/use; $75/day |
| **Boat Rentals** | |
| Fishing Boat—14 ft. | $7/day |
| Boat w/Motor (fuel extra) | $12/one-half day; $20/day |
| Large Craft Uncovered Slip—16'x20' | $60/month |
| Small Craft Covered Slip—8'x20' | $50/month (Mar. - Sept.); $37.50/month (Oct. - Feb.) |
| Small Craft Uncovered Slip—8'x20' | $45/month |
| Transient Slip | $5/day |

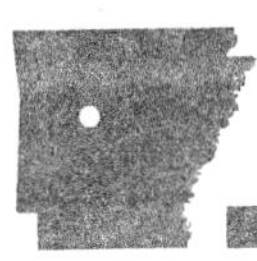

# MOUNT NEBO STATE PARK

Route 3, Box 374 / Dardanelle, AR 72834
PARK/CAMPSITE RESERVATIONS: (501) 229-3655
CABIN RESERVATIONS: 1-800-264-2458

Rising 1,350 feet above the Arkansas River Valley, Mount Nebo offers spectacular views. The mountain has been attracting travelers and settlers for over 100 years when a resort hostelry was operated on the mountaintop for steamboat travelers. In 1933, a portion of the mountain was chosen as a park site, and logs and stones from Mount Nebo were used by the Civilian Conservation Corps to construct many of the park's bridges, trails, charming Rustic-style cabins and pavilions. The park offers **35 campsites (Class B; 10 hike-in** - no trailer dump station) and 15 fully-equipped cabins with kitchens. Fourteen miles of trails encircle Mount Nebo. A pool, tennis courts, picnic areas, playgrounds, extra large enclosed and small open pavilions, and a ball field are available. The visitor center houses exhibits and a store. Please note that many private homes are also on the mountain.

The park is seven miles west of Dardanelle on Ark. 155. [NOTE: Highway 155 zigzags up the mountain and includes hairpin curves. Trailers over 24 feet should not attempt the climb.]

| | |
|---|---|
| **Cabins (with kitchens)** | |
| A-Frame/Two bedrooms (fireplace): | $75/two persons/day |
| Rustic-style/Two double beds (fireplace): | $70/two persons/day |
| Rustic-style/One double bed (fireplace): | $65/two persons/day |
| Rustic-style/One double bed (no fireplace): | $60/two persons/day |
| Each additional person | $5/day |
| Rollaway | $5/day |
| Television Rental (Available from the visitor center for cabin use.) | $5/day |
| **Tent (30'x90'):** First day | $300 |
| Each additional day | $75 (Put-up & take-down included) |
| **Tennis Racquet Rental** | $1.50/hour; Deposit—$5/use |
| **Bicycle Rental** | $2/hour; $10/day |
| **Mountain Bike Rental** | $5/hour; $15/one-half day; $25/day |
| **Swimming (Pool)** | $2/person/day |

## OLD DAVIDSONVILLE STATE PARK

7953 Hwy. 166 South / Pocahontas, AR 72455 (501) 892-4708

The park preserves the locale of historic Davidsonville established in 1815, the site of the Arkansas Territory's first post office, courthouse, and land office. Bypassed by the Old Military Road, an overland route from St. Louis southward, the river port's days as a major trade center faded by the 1830s. Indoor and outdoor exhibits provide information on this important frontier town.

Fishing is the major activity at Old Davidsonville today. The park borders the Black River (boat launch ramp) and an 11-acre fishing lake (no launch ramp) offering a boat dock, barrier-free fishing pier, fishing boat (trolling motors only) and pedal boat rentals plus a bait shop. Using the park as a base camp, anglers may choose from the nearby Spring and Eleven Point Rivers. Park facilities include **50 campsites (25 Class A; 25 tent sites);** picnic areas; a standard pavilion; playground and trails.

From Pocahontas, travel two miles west on U.S. 62, then go nine miles south on Ark. 166 to the park. Or from Black Rock take U.S. Highway 63 to State Highway 361, then go 6 miles north.

**Boat Rentals**

| | |
|---|---|
| Fishing Boat | $7/day |
| Pedal Boat | $2.50/one-half hour; $3.75/hour |

## OLD WASHINGTON HISTORIC STATE PARK

P.O. Box 98 / Washington, AR 71862 (501) 983-2684

Washington is a unique, historic Arkansas community conserved and interpreted by Arkansas State Parks in conjunction with the Pioneer Washington Restoration Foundation. From its establishment in 1824, Washington was an important stop on the rugged Southwest Trail for pioneers traveling to Texas. James Bowie, Sam Houston and Davy Crockett traveled through Washington and James Black, a local blacksmith, is credited with creating the legendary Bowie Knife here. Later, the town became a major service center for area planters, merchants and professionals, and was the Confederate Capital of Arkansas from 1863-1865.

*Southern specialties are always on the menu at William's Tavern Restaurant.*

Established in 1973, the state park interprets Washington from 1824-1875. Tours include visits to the Confederate Capitol, Tavern Inn, Blacksmith Shop, Weapons Museum and several residences. The 19th-century restoration town includes a print museum, steam-powered cotton gin and dining at the Williams Tavern Restaurant. The 1874 Courthouse serves as the visitor center. The park also houses the Southwest Arkansas Regional Archives, a resource center for historical and genealogical research.

Take Exit #30 off I-30 at Hope and travel nine miles northwest on Ark. 4 to Washington.

**Guided Walking Tours:**

"The Old Town Tour: Pioneers, Planters and Merchants Bring Life to Old Washington 1820-1865"

Adult—$5.95 each; Child (6-12)—$2.95 each (1 1/2-2 hours)

"Living in Town: The Washington Community Matures 1840-1875" (1 1/2-2 hours)

Adult—$5.95 each; Child (6-12)—$2.95 each

**Day Pass** (Includes "Old Town," "Living in Town" and Weapons Museum)

Adult—$10 each; Child (6-12)—$5 each

**One Day Family Pass** (Includes "Old Town," "Living in Town" and Weapons Museum)

Family—$25/day

**Old Washington Museum Experience:**

Enjoy the village at your own pace. Visit the Blacksmith Shop, Print Museum, Weapons Museum and special exhibits when available.

Adult—$3.50 each; Child (6-12)—$1.75 each

[Note: Passes are valid for State Park-sponsored tours and facilities only.]

**Guided Motor Coach Tour** (Driving tour of Old Washington)

"Old Washington Narrative Experience"--$20/tour

**Group Rates:**

(20 or more with advance notice)—$1 off above rates

**Bona Fide School Groups:**

(With advance notice)—$1.50 per student

**Special Events Parking**

$2/car/day

**Hours:**

Open—8 a.m.-5 p.m. daily (year-round)

Closed—New Year's Day, Thanksgiving Day and Christmas Day

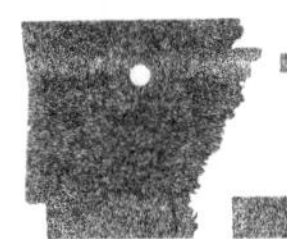

## OZARK FOLK CENTER

P.O. Box 500 / Mountain View, AR 72560
PARK: (501) 269-3851; LODGE: 1-800-264-3655 (V/TT) or (501) 269-3871

Sample the rich heritage of Ozark life through music, crafts and dance in the unique mountain setting of the Ozark Folk Center. During the season [first two weekends in April; daily April 14-November 5] artisans demonstrate over 20 homestead skills and crafts from 10 a.m. to 5 p.m. The comfortable, climate-controlled auditorium hosts live entertainment at 7:30 p.m., six nights a week with Sunday Gospel Concerts, during the season. Special musical performances and craft fairs celebrate Thanksgiving and Christmas. Music is played as it was before 1940; acoustic instruments only.

*You'll enjoy authentic Ozark music . . .*

The Homespun Gift Shop offers handmade items including toys, rocking chairs, pottery, shuck dolls, quilts, white oak baskets, peach and apple butter. Comfortable lodging, delicious meals in the scenic, full-service Iron Skillet Restaurant and Smokehouse Sandwich Buffet Restaurant, free tram service, and the Heritage Herb Gardens add to your enjoyment.

Festivals highlight the spring and fall seasons, and special music shows, contests, workshops and craft exhibitions are held throughout the year. **Check with the Center for a complete schedule of events.**

The Ozark Folk Center is one mile north of Mountain View on Spur 382 off Highways 5, 9 and 14.

**Dry Creek Lodge (60 rooms)** [Open year-round]
Standard Room: Sun.-Wed. $45/two persons/day; Thurs.-Sat. $50/two persons/day
Each additional person (no rollaways available) $5/day
Special rates for groups of 20 or more. Conference packages available.

**Admission to Music Auditorium**
Adult—$7 each; Child (6-12)—$4.50 each; Child under 6—No charge;
Family—$17.25

**Admission to Craft Forum**
Adult—$6.50 each;
Child (6-12)—$3.75 each;
Child under 6—No charge;
Family—$17.25

**Combination Ticket (Crafts & Music):**
Adult—$12.25 each;
Child (6-12)—$6.50 each;
Child under 6—No charge;
Family—$31.25

*. . . and a variety of Ozark crafts.*

**Three-Day Combination Ticket—any 3 consecutive days (Crafts & Music)**
Adult—$27.50 each; Child (6-12)—$14.25 each; Child under 6—No charge
**Individual Season Ticket (Crafts & Music):**
Adult—$37.50 each; Child (6-12)—$20 each
Special rates for groups of 20 or more.
Craft Forum tickets purchased after 3 p.m. good for following day.

**Conference Rooms & Facility Rates:**

**3 Small Conference Rooms (Administration Building)** $45 each/day
Lodge occupancy (21-40 rooms)— 1 conference room free
Lodge occupancy (41-60 rooms)— 2 conference rooms free; or free use of lodge rec. room (off-season only), or auditorium conference center, or restaurant "dry hole"

**Lodge Recreation Room (Off-season only)** $60/day
Lodge occupancy (21-40 rooms)— $35/day
Lodge occupancy (41-60 rooms)— No charge; or free use of two small conference rooms, or auditorium conference center, or restaurant "dry hole"

**Small Auditorium Conference Center (167 seats)** $85/day
Lodge occupancy (21-40 rooms)— $50/day
Lodge occupancy (41-60 rooms)— No charge; or free use of two small conference rooms, or lodge rec. room (off-season only), or restaurant "dry hole"

**Restaurant "Dry Hole"** $50/use (or free with $100 food purchase)
**Large Auditorium (1,025-seats):** $500/day
[NOTE: The off-season (Dec. 4-Mar. 30) charge for groups with a lodge occupancy of 41-60 rooms will be a $300 base rate plus the additional charges listed below.]
Sound Technician—$15/hour Cleaning Deposit—$100/day
Tram Service (Off-season, December 4-March 30): $100/day

## PARKIN ARCHEOLOGICAL STATE PARK

P.O. Box 1110 / Parkin, AR 72373-1110 (501) 755-2500

Parkin represents a turning point in American history. This park interprets the Mississippi Period Native American village located here from A.D. 1000 to 1550 and visited by the Hernando de Soto expedition in 1541. Arkansas State Parks and the Arkansas Archeological Survey manage the site as a research station, museum and interpretive center. Archeological excavations are conducted each July thru October. The park is in the community of Parkin at the junction of U.S. 64 and Ark. 184.

**Hours of Operation**
Open—8 a.m.-5 p.m. (Tuesday-Saturday); Noon-5 p.m. (Sunday)
Closed—Monday (except Monday holidays), New Year's Day, Thanksgiving Day, Christmas Eve and Christmas Day

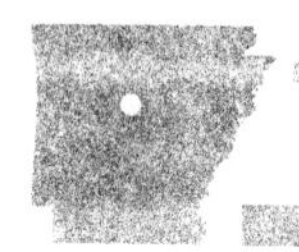

# Petit Jean State Park

Route 3, Box 340 / Morrilton, AR 72110
PARK/CAMPSITE RESERVATIONS: (501) 727-5441
LODGE OR CABIN RESERVATIONS: 1-800-264-2462 (V/TT) or (501) 727-5431

Between the Ouachitas and the Ozarks, Petit Jean Mountain stands 1,100 feet above sea level, offering panoramic views of the Arkansas River Valley. The natural beauty of Petit Jean inspired the creation of Arkansas' state park system in 1923.

*Petit Jean offers dramatic overlooks, wooded campsites, a lodge, and cabins.*

Combining Rustic-style and modern conveniences, facilities of log and stone constructed by the Civilian Conservation Corps are nestled throughout the park. The focal point is Mather Lodge, a grand retreat [24 rooms] that hugs the bluff of an impressive canyon. A meal at the lodge restaurant guarantees a breathtaking view. Nearby are 32 fully-equipped cabins (20 w/kitchens)—many share the same bluff as the lodge. The canyon is the work of Cedar Creek, which cascades as a spectacular 95-foot waterfall. Upstream, a rock dam on the creek forms Lake Bailey, 170 acres for fishing and pedal boating. The boathouse overlooking the lake offers a snack bar, boat rentals and fishing supplies during summer. Trails lead you along forests, canyons, streams, meadows and mountainsides.

**Campsites (127 Class A including Preferred sites)** are near Lake Bailey and in secluded woodlands. The park also offers picnic areas, playgrounds, pavilions, a recreation hall, launch ramp, pool and tennis courts. Interpreters host programs and special events highlighting the resources of this unforgettable state park. Petit Jean Mountain is also home to the Museum of Automobiles, a showcase of antique and classic cars. Petit Jean's airport is open for daytime use only. No flight services available (tie down $4/day -- call lodge for shuttle service rates.)

Take Exit #108 off I-40 at Morrilton and travel nine miles south on Ark. 9, then go 12 miles west on Ark. 154; or from Dardanelle, travel seven miles south on Ark. 7, then go 16 miles east on Ark. 154 to the park.

| | |
|---|---|
| **Cabins with kitchens** - 4 to 6 persons max. depending on cabin size | |
| Rustic-style (fireplace) | $70/two persons/day |
| Rustic-style w/hot tub (fireplace) [2 night min.] | $95/two persons/day (Sun.-Thurs.); $110/two persons/day (Fri.-Sat.) |
| Duplex (fireplace) | $70/two persons/day |
| Each additional person | 5/day |
| Rollaway | $5/day |
| **Cabins without kitchens** - 4 persons maximum | |
| Overnight Duplex Cabin (some w/fireplace) | $45/two persons/day |
| Each additional person (no rollaways available) | $5/day |
| **Mather Lodge Rooms** | |
| Two double beds - 4 persons maximum | $45/two persons/day |
| One double bed - 2 persons maximum | $40/two persons/day |
| Each additional person | $5/day |
| Rollaway | $5/day |
| **Conference Rooms** | |
| Arkansas Room or CCC Room: | |
| Lodge occupancy (10 rooms or more) | No charge |
| Lodge occupancy (Less than 10 rooms) | $30/day |
| Restaurant Conference Room | |
| With 20 meals or more - No charge | With less than 20 meals - $50/day |
| **Camping** | |
| Group Camp (tents only) [Reservable] | $50/day (50 persons maximum) |
| Rally Style & Overflow Area (w/e with limited a/c use) [Reservable by groups] | $8.50/unit/day |
| **Recreation Hall** | $60/use; $100/day |
| **Swimming (Pool)** | $2/person/day |
| **Boat Rentals (summer only)** | |
| Fishing Boat | $5/one-half day; $8/day |
| Pedal Boat | $2.50/one-half hour; $3.75/hour |

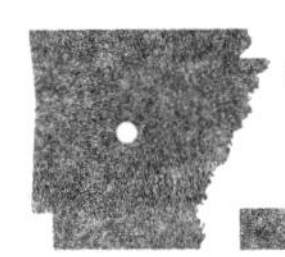

## PINNACLE MOUNTAIN STATE PARK

11901 Pinnacle Valley Road / Roland, AR 72135 (501) 868-5806; Fax (501) 868-5018

Pinnacle Mountain is a day-use park dedicated to environmental education, recreation and preservation. The diversity of habitats, from high upland peaks to bottomlands along the Big and Little Maumelle Rivers, provide many outdoor opportunities. Park interpreters help visitors and students understand man's relationship to the environment, and provide low-impact recreational experiences.

*Pinnacle Mountain's trails lead to beautiful vistas.*

The park features a visitor center with exhibits, A/V programs, a meeting room and gift shop. Special interpretive programs may be scheduled by contacting the park on Mondays. Facilities include picnic sites, a standard pavilion, launch ramps, hiking trails and the

Arkansas Arbortetum which includes one of park's two barrier-free trails.

Camping is available at Maumelle Park, just two miles east on Pinnacle Valley Road.

To reach Pinnacle Mountain State Park, take Exit #9 off I-430 at Little Rock and travel seven miles west on Ark. 10, then go two miles north on Ark. 300.

**Visitor Center Meeting Room**
$30/use
Cleanup deposit
$25/use

**Rent-A-Backpack Equipment**
(Deposit req.)/24-hour period:
Partial Set—$5.25;
Tent—$15.75;
Backpack—$10.50;
Full Set—$21

*Canoeing at Pinnacle Mountain offers many sights including a bald cypress swamp.*

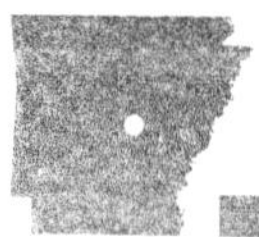

## Plantation Agriculture Museum

P.O. Box 87 / Scott, AR 72142 (501) 961-1409

Exhibits and programs interpret the history of cotton agriculture from 1836 through World War II when agricultural practices quickly became mechanized. See early cultivation tools, the blacksmith shop and rare gins. The museum is in Scott at the junction of U.S. 165 and Ark. 161 [30 minutes from Little Rock/North Little Rock].

**Museum Entrance Fee**
Adult—$2 each; Child (6-12)—$1 each
Group Rates (20 or more with advance notice) $.25 off above fees
Bona Fide School Groups (with advance notice) $.65 per person

**Hours of Operation**
Open—8 a.m.-5 p.m. (Tuesday-Saturday); 1 p.m.-5 p.m. (Sunday)
Closed—Monday (except Monday holidays), New Year's Day, Thanksgiving Day, Christmas Eve and Christmas Day

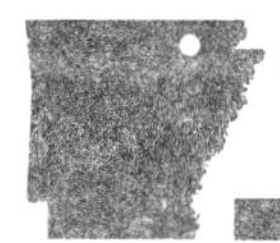

## POWHATAN COURTHOUSE

P.O. Box 93 / Powhatan, AR 72458 (501) 878-6794

From 1869 to 1963, Powhatan served as county seat of western Lawrence County. During the mid-1800s, the town was a busy river port shipping "mother of pearl" button blanks worldwide. In 1888, a stately two-story courthouse with delicate woodwork and a classic cupola was built from red bricks made on-site. Restored in 1970, the courthouse is a regional archive containing some of the oldest records in Arkansas—many predate statehood. Exhibits interpret the rich history of technology, politics and life styles that shaped north Arkansas. Powhatan is on Ark. 25 three mile south of the community of Black Rock.

*The restored courthouse has exhibits and archives.*

**Museum Entrance Fee**

Adult—$2 each; Child (6-12)—$1 each
Group Rates (20 or more with advance notice)
$.25 off above fees
Bona Fide School Groups (with advance notice)
$.65 per person

**Hours of Operation**

Open—8 a.m.-5 p.m. (Wednesday-Saturday); 1 p.m.-5 p.m. (Sunday); 8 a.m.-5 p.m. (Tuesday: Memorial Day thru Labor Day); 1 p.m.-5 p.m. (Tuesday: Rest of year)
Closed—Monday (except Monday holidays), New Year's Day, Thanksgiving Day, Christmas Eve and Christmas Day

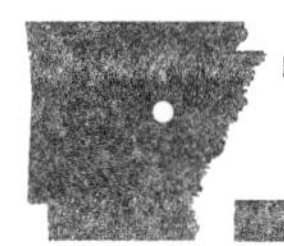

## PRAIRIE COUNTY MUSEUM

Route 2, Box 154 / Des Arc, AR 72040 (501) 256-3711

Learn the story of Arkansas' navigable rivers as a dramatic part of American history. Exhibits interpret early Arkansas settlement, transportation routes and the river based economy including fishing and shelling.

The museum is in Des Arc at the western end of Main Street.

**Museum Entrance Fee**

Adult—$1.50 each; Child (6-12)—$.75 each
[See Page 36, "Plantation Agriculture Museum" for group rates]

**Hours of Operation**

Open—8 a.m.-5 p.m. (Tuesday-Saturday); 1 p.m.-5 p.m. (Sunday)
Closed—Monday (except Monday holidays), New Year's Day, Thanksgiving Day, Christmas Eve and Christmas Day

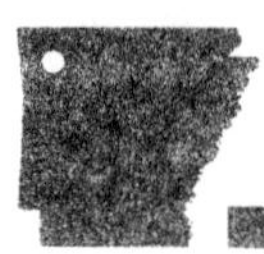

# Prairie Grove Battlefield State Park

P.O. Box 306 / Prairie Grove, AR 72753 (501) 846-2990

The past is the present at this Civil War battlefield park in the Ozarks. See important battle sites along a self-guided driving tour or walking the one-mile Battlefield Trail. Guided tours are offered through structures typical of a 19th century hill community. The life of a Civil War soldier is emphasized at the Battlefield Museum. Interpretive programs and exhibits aid in reliving the Civil War period and its impact on Arkansas. A reenactment of the battle is hosted the first weekend of December on even numbered years. The park is on U.S. 62 in the community of Prairie Grove.

**Museum and Historic Homes Entrance Fee** Adult—$2 each; Child (6-12)—$1 each
[See Page 36, "Plantation Agriculture Museum" for group rates]

| | |
|---|---|
| **Latta Barn** | $25/use plus $8/hour |
| **Group Pavilions** (two)—Small | $20/use; $30/day |
| **Amphitheater/Pavilion** | $30/use; $40/day |
| **Special Events Parking** | $2/car/day |

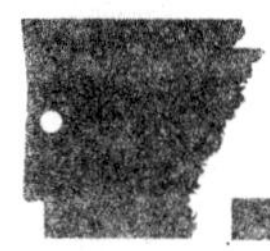

# Queen Wilhelmina State Park

3877 Highway 88 West / Mena, AR 71953
PARK/CAMPSITE RESERVATIONS: (501) 394-2863
LODGE RESERVATIONS: 1-800-264-2477 (V/TT) or (501) 394-2863

Atop Arkansas' second highest peak, this cloud-capped hideaway reigns above the Ouachita Mountains. Located on the Talimena Scenic Drive, the park is as rich in history as in scenery. In the late 1800s, a resort hostelry named Queen Wilhelmina Inn, in honor of the Queen of the Netherlands, was built on Rich Mountain by the Kansas City, Pittsburg and Gulf Railroad. Since then, two inns have replaced the original "Castle in the Sky"—the latest is this state park's focal point. The modern lodge offers 36 guest rooms plus two "Queen's Rooms" with fireplaces, and a restaurant serving fine Southern fare.

*Today's "Castle in the Sky" is known for its comfortable rooms, good food and Arkansas hospitality.*

Park facilities include **40 campsites (35 Class A including Preferred sites; 5 tent),** picnic areas, trails, a miniature scenic railroad, animal park, miniature golf course (open seasonally), laundry and store.

The park is 13 miles west of Mena on Ark. 88. [For an alternate route from Mena, travel six miles north on U.S. 71, then nine miles west on U.S. 270, then two miles south on Ark. 272 to the park.]

**Lodge (38 rooms)**

| | |
|---|---|
| Queen's Room (fireplace) | $85/two persons/day |
| Two double beds | $65/two persons/day |
| One double bed | $55/two persons/day |
| Each additional person | $5/day |
| Rollaway | $5/day |

**Meeting Rooms**

Second Floor Conference Room:
- Lodge occupancy (10 rooms or more) — No charge
- Lodge occupancy (Less than 10 rooms) — $35/use
- Non-lodge guests — $50/use

Heritage Room (on First Floor) — $45/use
- (with $100 food purchase) — No charge

Patio Rose Garden — $40/use
- (with $100 food purchase) — No charge

Heritage Room & Rose Garden (combination) — $60/use

*You'll find spring flowers, fall colors, beautiful trails, scenic drives and dramatic overlooks.*

**Park Facilities (Memorial Day through Labor Day)**

| | |
|---|---|
| Miniature Train | $2/each |
| Animal Park | Adult—$2 each; Child—$1.50 each |
| Miniature Golf | Adult—$2/play; Child—$1.50/play |

## RED RIVER CAMPAIGN

In the spring of 1864, three Civil War battles took place in south central Arkansas. Part of the Union Army's "Red River Campaign," these battles are commemorated as state historic sites.

The first battle occurred near Camden at **POISON SPRING** (April 18) when Confederate troops captured a supply train and scattered Union forces. On April 25 at **MARKS' MILLS,** Confederate troops captured another Union supply train. With the loss of two supply trains and the onslaught of wet spring weather, the Union Army retreated from Camden toward Little Rock. On April 29 and 30, Union troops fought off an attack by the Confederates and crossed the flooded Saline River on a pontoon bridge at **JENKINS' FERRY** and retreated to Little Rock.

*The parks in the Red River Campaign commemorate a disastrous Union foray into south Arkansas.*

Today these parks offer outdoor exhibits and picnic sites. Jenkins' Ferry offers rest rooms, a pavilion (no electricity), swimming and a launch ramp on the Saline River.

Poison Spring is 10 miles west of Camden on Ark. 76; Marks' Mills is at the junction of Highways 97 & 8 just southeast of Fordyce; and Jenkins' Ferry is 13 miles south of Sheridan on Ark. 46.

## TOLTEC MOUNDS ARCHEOLOGICAL STATE PARK

490 Toltec Mounds Road / Scott, AR 72142 (501) 961-9442

Toltec preserves and interprets Arkansas' tallest Native American mounds. These mounds and earthen embankment are the remains of a large ceremonial and governmental complex inhabited from A.D. 600 to 950. Today this interpretive center is managed by Arkansas State Parks and the Arkansas Archeological Survey. Facilities include a visitor center with exhibits, an A/V theater and archeological research laboratory. Site tours are available along the park's 3/4-mile barrier-free trail.

*Visitors to Toltec enjoy guided tours on a barrier-free trail.*

From Little Rock/North Little Rock, take Exit #7 off I-440 and go nine miles southeast on U.S. 165 to the park.

**Archeological Site Walking Tour**
Adult—$2.50 each; Child (6-12)—$1.25 each
**Archeological Site Tour By Tram (when available)**
Adult—$3 each; Child (6-12)—$1.75 each
**Group Rates** (20 or more with advance notice)—$.50 off above fees
**Bona Fide School Groups** (with advance notice)—$.75 per student
**Visitor Center Meeting Room** $25/use; Cleanup deposit—$25/use
(NOTE: Public schools, educational groups and State agencies conducting curriculum-related education or park-related meetings may use the meeting room free-of-charge with advance request.)
**Park Hours of Operation**
Open—8:00 a.m.-5:00 p.m. (Tuesday-Saturday)
Noon-5:00 p.m. (Sunday)
Closed—Monday (except Monday holidays), New Year's Day, Thanksgiving Day, Christmas Eve and Christmas Day

## VILLAGE CREEK STATE PARK

Route 3, Box 49B / Wynne, AR 72396
PARK/CAMPSITE RESERVATIONS: (501) 238-9406
CABIN RESERVATIONS: 1-800-264-2467

Here you can relax and enjoy the lush forest and unique geology of Crowley's Ridge. Five trails lead through the park's unusual vegetation including oak, sugar maple, beech, butternut and tulip poplar.

Fish for bass, bream, catfish and crappie at the park's two lakes. Launch ramps, boat docks, bait, fishing boats, electric motors and pedal boats are available late spring through Labor Day.

Campers will enjoy the **104 Class A campsites including Preferred sites** around Lake Dunn. Nestled on a nearby ridge are 10 fully-equipped cabins with kitchens. At Lake Austell, you'll find picnic sites near a sandy beach and sun deck. Park facilities also include four standard pavilions, playgrounds, baseball and multi-use fields.

The visitor center includes an A/V theater, store and gift shop. A new interpretive center offers a large meeting facility and The Discovery Room with exhibits of prehistoric artifacts and wildlife of Crowley's Ridge. Interpreters offer programs, concerts and special events year-round.

*7,000-acre Village Creek State Park offers lakes, trails, forests, camping and cabins in east Arkansas.*

Take Exit #242 off I-40 at Forrest City and go 13 miles north on Ark. 284 to the park.

| | | |
|---|---|---|
| **Cabins (with kitchens)** | | |
| Three bedrooms (fireplace): | Sun.-Thurs. | $70/two persons/day |
| | Fri.-Sat. | $75/two persons/day |
| Two bedrooms (fireplace): | Sun.-Thurs. | $65/two persons/day |
| | Fri.-Sat. | $70/two persons/day |
| Two bedroom duplex (fireplace): | Sun-Thurs. | $60/two persons/day |
| | Fri.-Sat. | $65/two persons/day |
| One bedroom (fireplace): | Sun.-Thurs. | $60/two persons/day |
| | Fri.-Sat. | $65/two persons/day |
| Each additional person (no rollaways available) | | $5/day |
| **Bicycle Rental** | $1.50/hour; $8/day | |
| **Visitor Center Meeting Room** | $75/use; Cleanup deposit—$25/use | |
| Occupancy rate 5 cabins and over | No charge | |
| Occupancy rate under 5 cabins | $75/use | |

(NOTE: The meeting room may be used free of charge by public schools, education groups and state agencies conducting environmental education or park-related meetings, or groups and individuals with five or more cabin rentals.)

| | |
|---|---|
| **Boat Rentals** | |
| Fishing Boat | $7/day |
| Boat w/Electric Motor | $10/one-half day; $15/day |
| Electric Motor Only | $6/one-half day; $10/day |
| Pedal Boat | $2.50/one-half hour; $3.75/hour |

# White Oak Lake State Park

Route 2, Box 28 / Bluff City, AR 71722 (501) 685-2748 or 685-2132

*White Oak Lake has pine-covered campsites and fishing for everyone.*

This haven for anglers and nature lovers lies on 2,765-acre White Oak Lake, a timber-filled favorite for crappie, bass and bream fishing. Abundant in wildlife, the park has regular sightings of great blue heron, egret, osprey, green heron, and bald eagles are often spotted in winter. Trails wind through the park's woodlands. Facilities include **42 campsites (38 Class A including Preferred sites; 4 tent)**, a store offering supplies, bait and gifts (year-round), boat rentals (year-round), launch ramp, barrier-free fishing pier, standard pavilion, picnic sites, playground, beach and swimming area.

From I-30 at Prescott travel 20 miles east on Ark. 24, then go 100 yards south on Ark. 299, then go two miles southeast on Ark. 387 to the park.

| | |
|---|---|
| **Volleyball and Net** | Deposit—$5/use |
| **Bicycle Rental** | $1.50/hour; $8/day |
| **Marina** | |
| Fishing Boat | $7/one-half day; $10/day |
| Boat w/Motor (fuel extra) | $15/one-half day; $25/day; Deposit—$10/use |
| Rod and Reel Rental | $2.50/one-half day; $5/day |
| Life Jacket Rental | $3/one-half day; $5/day; Deposit—$10/use |
| Transient Slip | $5/day |
| Pedal Boat | $2.50/one-half hour; $3.75/hour |
| Canoe | $3.75/hour; $8/one-half day; $15/day |

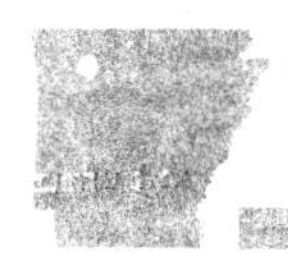

## Withrow Springs State Park

Route 3 / Huntsville, AR 72740 (501) 559-2593

Cradled by the bluffs of the War Eagle River in the heart of the Ozark Mountains, Withrow Springs is a peaceful setting for camping and quiet floats along the river. Canoes and shuttle service are available. Opportunities include swimming, tennis, baseball and softball, crossbow range and river fishing for catfish, bream, perch and bass. Trails lead you along hillsides, ravines, ridges and the river. The **campsites (17 Class B; 8 tent; and 2 group camping sites)** lie near a spring that flows from a small cave. Other facilities include picnic sites, pavilions, a snack bar and gift shop.

The park is five miles north of Huntsville on Ark. 23; or 20 miles south of Eureka Springs on Ark. 23.

**SEE PAGE 2-4 FOR CAMPING FEES, DISCOUNTS AND WINTER RATES.**

*Spring wildflowers and fall colors await you at Withrow Springs State Park.*

| | |
|---|---|
| **Swimming (Pool)** | $2/person/day |
| **Canoe Rental (includes put-in & haul back)** | $20/one-half day; $25/day |

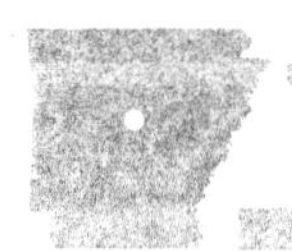

# WOOLLY HOLLOW STATE PARK

82 Woolly Hollow Road / Greenbrier, AR 72058 (501) 679-2098

This park makes a peaceful retreat tucked away in the Ozark foothills of central Arkansas. The waters of 40-acre Lake Bennett offer one of the best swimming and fishing holes in central Arkansas. Canoes, pedal boats, fishing boats and motors are for rent. Boating is limited to electric motors, and a launch ramp is available. [Bring bait and other fishing supplies with you.] A snack bar and bathhouse with hot showers are located near the swimming beach. Facilities include **32 campsites (20 Class A including Preferred sites; 12 Class B)** picnic area, a standard pavilion, gift shop, and a trail encircling the lake. Woolly Cabin, the log home of the area's first settlers, offers a historic perspective to the beautiful hollow.

Take Exit #125 off I-40 at Conway and travel 12 miles north on U.S. 65, then six miles east on Ark. 285 to the park.

| | |
|---|---|
| **Swimming (Beach)** | $1.75/person/day |
| **Boat Rentals** | |
| Fishing Boat | $6/day |
| Boat w/Electric Motor | $10/one-half day; $15/day |
| Electric Motor Only | $4/one-half day; $8/day |
| Pedal Boat | $2.50/one-half hour; $3.75/hour |
| Canoe | $3.75/hour; $5.50/one-half day; $11/day |

---

**Arboretums in the Arkansas State Park System**

Arkansas Arboretum - Located at Pinnacle Mountain State Park near Little Rock, this 71-acre site exhibits examples of native flora representative of Arkansas' six natural divisions: the Ozark Mountains, Ouachita Mountains, Arkansas River Valley, Mississippi Delta, Crowley's Ridge and the Gulf Coastal Plain. Situated below Pinnacle Mountain along the banks of the Little Maumelle River, this arboretum includes a .6-mile barrier-free trail. Open to the public, this phased project is currently under development.

South Arkansas Arboretum - Situated adjacent to the El Dorado High School, this 17-acre site exhibits native plant species indigenous to south Arkansas along with exotic species including flowering azaleas and camellias. Operated by the South Arkansas Community College at El Dorado, the arboretum offers walking trails and ample parking.

Information in this guide is carefully compiled to insure accuracy at time of publication. Conditions, services and rates may change due to unforeseen circumstances. Contact the park for the most current information.

## ROTTWEILERS AND RABBITS

One of the things I've come to love about Arkansas is the remarkable variety of animals that abide in our woods and fields. From my front porch I can watch a daily panoply of acrobatic squirrels, myopic armadillos, an early morning rabbit or two and even an occasional deer.

The one creature in my household that finds all this more fascinating than me is Ra, my Rottweiler. Although a formidable fellow at 140 pounds, he has a gentle nature and the personality of a curious child. The difference between him and the local junk yard dog is that I have raised Ra as a companion, and he has rewarded my efforts tenfold. He loves to chase everything; he has yet to catch anything. It's not for lack of ability, he just figures if he starts catching things, word would get around and no one would want to play anymore. I really believe that's exactly what he thinks. He's that smart.

A while back I decided to teach him to fetch. I got his ball and threw it out on the lawn. Ra looked up at me then out to the ball, but he didn't go get it. I went and picked up the ball, brought it back and showed it to him. He took it out of my hand and with a swing of his massive head, tossed it out into the grass. Then he looked up at me, like what are you waiting for, go get it. So, grumbling about stupid dogs, I went and got the ball and brought it back. He took it out of my hand, threw it again and looked at me, waiting. I'm a pretty smart fellow. It wasn't long before I figured out who was training whom. I went over to his ball and kicked it as far as I could, then I went in the house.

Ra and a local rabbit have become buddies of sorts. I'm sure it's a somewhat tenuous understanding, based on mutual entertainment, but it's an agreement nonetheless. Nearly every morning I'll come out onto the porch and see Ra laying in the grass, and the rabbit munching clover not fifteen feet from him. After a while the rabbit gets bored and begins popping up and down, looking over at the dog. That's the signal for the game to start. The rabbit jumps up, Ra clamors to his feet, and the chase is on. There's a good hundred yards of lawn between the house and the woods. It's just too long a dash for my lazy Rottweiler. Three quarters of the way through the race Ra lumbers to a halt. Just slightly ahead, the rabbit screeches to a stop and looks back, waiting for the dog to catch his breath. It's an impatient rabbit. If Ra doesn't get it together quickly enough, the bunny bounces back a few yards and stares at the dog with anxious disdain. I'm almost certain I've seen him stick out his tongue a couple of times, but I wouldn't swear to it. Soon after the chase continues, until Mr. Cottontail disappears into the underbrush, leaving Ra huffing and puffing and sniffing at the edge of the brambles. It's a wonderful routine, and coffee in hand, my lady and I try to catch the show as often as we can.

This reminds me of a Yorkie named "Dukes" that I once had when I lived in Florida. Lord, that dog loved to swim. You couldn't draw a bath without having to fight to keep him out of the water. I'm convinced his mother must have had more than a passing fancy for Labradors.

Above and beyond his penchant for the water, Dukes had a remarkable sense of humor, a streak of mischievousness about him. When I took him to the beach, he would watch for snorklers bobbing gently in the clear waters along the shoreline. He would spot a close one and swim out to them quietly, using the dog paddle (that was his favorite stroke, although his Australian crawl and his backstroke were fairly proficient). He would virtually sneak up on the unsuspecting tourist paddler, whose attentions would be drawn to the coral sand bottom and whose sense of hearing was muted by the water. Swimming up silently, he would suddenly surge in and nip the hapless tourist on the ear.

Imagine if you will, you're visiting Florida for the first time, from Wisconsin, or Idaho, (or even Arkansas). You're out there floating in all this water, you're having a good time, but you can't seem to get that disconcerting da da da da music of "Jaws" out of your mind, and you keep flashing back on all the Discovery Channel shark shows you've seen recently. Now about that time, when you least expect it, something wet and furry slides up against you and nips your ear. Well, I've seen tourists come straight out of the water like they'd been zapped by a cattle prod, masks filled with water, eyes bulging like a beached sea bass. I've seen them walk across that shallow water a good thirty or forty feet, flippers churning like something out of a Daffy Duck cartoon, before they even look back. Dukes would be out there just treading water and smiling. . . .

I guess the point I'm trying to make is that I've had some wonderfully clever dogs in my life. But the truth is, I made them that way. The more latitude you give an animal to be intelligent, the more intelligent it will be. The more attention and effort you put into your relationship with an animal, the more that creature will become your friend, companion and protector, and the more entertaining that relationship will become.

The world of science, in all it's arrogance, has only just conceded (January issue, *Time Magazine*), what every loving pet owner has known all along; that animals have emotions, react to circumstance intelligently, and yes, they reason. Heck, I could have saved those scientists a lot of trouble by just taking them to the beach with me and Dukes one afternoon.

Well, that's about all I have time for today. I can hear Ra scratching on the door in the living room. He wants out to get the paper. It's Sunday, and he likes me to read him the comics. . . .

## GETTING SKUNKED

5:15 A.M. Friday. It's coal dark and cold outside. I'm tucked in my warm bed, having this wonderful dream I vaguely remember now--something about catching record size bass in a pretty little pond, with the Dallas Cowboy Cheerleaders cheering me on. I'm smiling. . . .

Suddenly this smell comes wafting into my dream, this incredibly noxious odor. The cheerleaders are holding their noses; the scene is beginning to fade. Poof! It's gone . . . I'm awake.

The acrid, eye-watering scent is so strong I can almost taste it. It hurts my teeth; my nosehairs are curling! Bonnie rolls over and sits up next to me. "Skunk," she mumbles in the darkness.

About that time I hear Ra, our Rottweiler, come charging around the house and onto the porch, banging on the door, wanting in.

Fat chance, I think to myself, knowing sure as fire who aggravated that skunk. Ra bangs again. I switch on the night-light and stumble out of bed, grabbing a sweatshirt and a pair of pants. Bonnie starts closing windows. The living room smells like somebody spray painted the air with skunk-whiz. I hit the porch light, open the door a few inches and peer out. I thought the living room reeked, hah. The smell outside that door crams its fingers up my nostrils and jabs the back of my eyeballs, doing permanent damage to my olfactory nerves.

Ra stands banefully at the steps to the porch. He resembles something that might have come out of a Stephen King movie directed by Woody Allen. He has rolled in the ash colored, powdery dirt by the workshop in an attempt to alleviate the smell. The only things that are still black are his eyes. He looks (and smells) like something that's been dead for weeks and dug up.

Foolishly I step out the door. Ra takes this as a signal that everything's fine, that maybe I want to play, and comes bounding across the deck--150 pounds of smiling, slobbering skunk stink. Hands out, and yelling at him not to touch me, I stumble backward, hit the low porch rail and tumble head over heels off the deck.

They say timing is everything. . . . The skunk has chosen this same moment to make its escape from under the house. Hitting the ground with a thump, I see this black and white blur racing out of the shadows at me. I let out a yowl like I've been jabbed with a hot poker. The skunk hisses and jumps, all four feet in the air like a Pepe la Pew cartoon, and tail up, disappears in another cloud of skunk pugh.

6:00 A.M.. The sun has yet to come up. Both Ra and I have banged on the door, trying to get in. Bonnie has opened it just enough to beat us both with the broom, informing us that we're to live in the shed from now on. It is not promising to be a good day. . . .

The upside to this whole affair, if there is one, is that I discovered an excellent formula for neutralizing skunk odor. It was in an article sent to me by a friend. I tried it later that morning and miraculously, it worked!

I'm going to pass it on, in case you or your animals have a run-in with that testy little black and white varmint. No, it's not tomato juice, which works only marginally. This formula, I guarantee, will very nearly eliminate all traces of odor.

Take one quart of 3% Hydrogen Peroxide, 1/4 cup of baking soda and one teaspoon of liquid soap. Blend well and soak all affected area, then rinse. That's it!! Works like a charm! You may need to multiply the formula several times to cover a large dog, or a person, but it virtually extinguishes the odor--not disguising it, but dissolving it chemically.

I must caution you however, that this concoction cannot be bottled or it will explode; something to do with the volatile ingredients.

In closing, I recommend some preventive medicine. Take two cotton balls, spray them with room deodorizer and set them by your nightstand. If your dog gets skunked, and howls and bangs on the door in the middle of the night, stuff one cotton ball up each nostril and go back to sleep.

The Intrepid Arkansas Traveler

## DIAMONDS IN THE ROUGH

For those of you who don't know, Arkansas has the only diamond field in America. Diamonds were discovered on John Huddleson's property, outside of Murfreesboro in 1906, and mined commercially several times over the last 60 years. In 1972 the state bought the mine and the land around it, then turned it into a state park, where now, private individuals can pay to hunt for the shiny stones. We visited the Crater of Diamonds State Park just the other day, in search of sudden wealth, struck with "diamond fever." I felt the experience was worth recounting.

After the affair concerning Ra, me and the skunk, Bonnie was less than happy with all of us. I decided I needed to do something nice for her, to get myself out of the doghouse. (Ra's tough to sleep with; he burps and snores and the fleas were driving me crazy!) They say diamonds are a girl's best friend, so I figured I had the perfect solution.

Now I couldn't afford to buy a diamond outright, but I thought, what if I could find her one. Better yet, if she found the stone, it would save me a lot of work and only cost me the gas to Murfreesboro and the entrance fee at the concession. So, bright and early the following Saturday morning, we headed for the park.

It's actually a very nice park; lots of National Forest campground area, picnic grounds, and the Little Missouri River add to the ambiance. But the main attraction is the diamond field.

We arrived at the information center and took a quick tour, learning about diamonds: how to find them, what they look like before cutting and polishing, etc. Then we rented our equipment and paid our entrance fee. Fueled with the information that three diamonds had already been found that day, we headed out.

The diamond mine is actually a huge field consisting of long, large furrows. It could be the Jolly Green Giant's garden. Everywhere you look there are burrows in the furrows, some with a head protruding above them, pitching out dirt like a Yosemite Sam cartoon. Other burrows have already been abandoned by their luckless architects.

What I discovered is that there are several methods of searching for diamonds. You can dig like a fool for a few minutes then rummage through what you've dug up (not too popular). You can dig and sift with a rented screen (fairly popular). You can crawl along on your hands and knees staring at the ground as if you just lost a contact (surprisingly enough, very popular--there were times when the place looked like a giant farm of nearsighted ants). Or you could shuffle down the furrows, eyes glued to the earth, occasionally doing the "Murfreesboro Squat" (which is a takeoff on the Puka Squat, used by older tourists in Hawaii while picking up seashells). It requires a deep knee bend, slowly lowering your posterior to near ground level while reaching out and snatching something shiny off the ground, then rising up with a groan and continuing to amble forward. I watched an elderly couple perform the Murfreesboro Squat up and down the furrows for about fifteen minutes. Set to good line dance music, it would have been more entertaining than the Saturday Night Movie.

Every once in a while, when things got slow, I would yell "Eureka!", or "Bonanza!", or "Motherlode!", and heads would pop out of the burrows around me like prairie dogs watching a hawk. I quit when the ladies digging closest to me began to get irritated. One of my mottos is never anger a woman with a sharp object in her hand.

When all was said and done, and we'd managed an afternoon of digging, squatting and sifting, we took our equipment, and the handful of stones we thought might be diamonds up to the visitor center for evaluation. I have to admit--diamonds or not--we'd had a great time; the only problem I had with the entire affair was that I wouldn't know an uncut diamond from Jesse Jackson's molars. We had to rely on the fellow at the desk to tell us that almost all of what we had was mica, quartz or barite. There was, however, in the end, one tiny, soapy-smooth stone that turned out to be--yes--a diamond. Eureka! If and when it was cut, it would probably be worth about thirteen bucks (which meant after gas and expenses I was behind about twenty dollars), but it was still a diamond and Bonnie was thrilled. I, too, was thrilled; I was going to get to sleep inside again.

After the whole experience I've come to a conclusion: that diamond mine is really a little gold mine. I mean, they've got people walking in there all day long, paying an average of five bucks apiece for permission to crawl around on their hands and knees in some plowed-up dirt! Now that's a great business!

I'm thinking of buying a pocketful of cheap, industrial diamonds and sprinkling them on my front three acres of pasture, then calling the paper and telling them about the "discovery." I think I'll call it the Menasboro Diamond Mine. We'll make it a family affair. Bonnie can run the gift shop, Ra can guard "the mine" at night, and I'll sit out on the porch in a rocker and take the money.

"Ya'll come back now!"

The Intrepid Arkansas Traveler

# The CAMPGROUNDS and LAKES of ARKANSAS

Show me a bedroll and a warm fire serenaded by the gentle murmur of a mountain stream, and I'll show you a man whose heart does not live in the city.

The Traveler

# NATIONAL PARK SERVICE CAMPGROUNDS

## BUFFALO NATIONAL RIVER

All campgrounds except Lost Valley are directly adjacent to Buffalo River. The 138-mile river is lined with bluffs as high as 440 feet. Riverside stands of willow, sycamore, river birch and cottonwood blend into the predominately oak-hickory upland forest. The Buffalo offers smallmouth bass, goggle-eye and other game fish along with swimming and float trips on this swift-moving river.

Swimming is permitted in Buffalo River but requires special caution. Diving or jumping into river from rocks or bluffs is extremely dangerous due to the likelihood of striking submerged rocks. Limestone and sandstone bluffs are crumbly and slippery when wet and should be completely avoided.

Arkansas state licenses required for fishing, hunting. Canoe rentals nearby.

FOR INFORMATION—Park Superintendent, Buffalo National River, P.O. Box 1173, Harrison, AR 72602-1173. (501) 741-5443

FOR ADDITIONAL LISTINGS, see Wilderness Areas.

BUFFALO POINT CAMPGROUND (B-5) 83 RV with W/E; 20 tent; 5 group tent ........................................................ ♿

14 miles south of Yellville on State 14, then 3 miles east on State 268.

**Attractions:** Rugged mountain scenery and nature trails to hidden springs and caves, overlook. Self-guiding trail brochure at trailhead, 50. Swimming and fishing, naturalist programs in season.

**Facilities:** Housekeeping cabins (Easter through Thanksgiving: 501-449-6206), flush toilets, warm showers, water, picnic sites with nearby grills, 3 pavilions (may be reserved for groups), river access. User's fee charged. (Open year-round; electric and water Apr.-Nov.)

CARVER (B-4) Open Camping

10 miles east of Jasper on State 74, then 2.5 miles north on State 123 to bridge.

**Attractions:** Swimming and fishing.

**Facilities:** Vault toilet, water, fire grates, river access. (Open year-round)

Photo by M. Cates

**ERBIE (B-3) 14 RV sites with no hookups; 16 tent; 10 group tent** ........ ♿
4 miles north of Jasper on State 7, then 6.5 miles west on dirt road past Henry Koen Experimental Forest.
**Attractions:** Swimming and fishing. Historic cabin and farmstead nearby. Hiking trails and bridle paths.
**Facilities:** Vault toilet, water, picnic sites and fire grates, river access. Campsite for equestrians. (Open year-round)

**HASTY (B-4) Open Camping**
5 miles east of Jasper on State 74, then 2 miles to low water bridge.
**Attractions:** Swimming and fishing.
**Facilities:** Vault toilet, river access. (Open year-round)

**HIGHWAY 14 (B-5) Open Camping**
16 miles south of Yellville where State 14 crosses Buffalo River.
**Attractions:** Swimming and fishing.
**Facilities:** Vault toilet, fire grates, river access. (Open year-round)

**KYLES LANDING (B-3) Open Camping**
5 miles west of Jasper on State 74, then 3 miles down rough, steep, winding gravel road.
**Attractions:** Trailhead for wilderness area hiking, including Hemmed-in-Hollow and Indian Creek.
**Facilities:** Drinking water (Apr.-Nov.), vault toilets, fire grates, river access. (Open year-round)
**Note:** Not recommended for large trailers, buses and RVs due to rough, steep and winding road.

**LOST VALLEY (B-3) 15 Tent**
15 miles west of Jasper on State 74, then 1 mile south on State 43.
**Attractions:** 3-mile round-trip hiking trail to Eden Falls and Cob Cave; self-guiding brochure at trailhead, 50.
**Facilities:** Drinking water (Apr.-Nov.), vault toilets, picnic tables and fire grates. (Open year-round)

**MAUMEE SOUTH (B-5) Open Camping**
6 miles east of Marshall on State 27, then 6 miles of paved and dirt road from Morning Star.
**Facilities:** Vault toilet, river access. (Open year-round)

**MOUNT HERSEY (B-4) Open Camping**
17 miles south of Harrison on U.S. 65, then 6 miles of dirt road.
**Facilities:** Vault toilet, river access. (Open year-round)

**OZARK (B-4) Open Camping**
5 miles north of Jasper on State 7, then 2 miles down dirt road.
**Attractions:** Swimming and fishing. Scenic bluff. Trailhead for 2-mile (one way) Ozark-Pruitt trail.
**Facilities:** Drinking water (Apr.-Nov.), fire grates, flush toilets, pavilion (may be reserved for groups), river access. (Open year-round)

**RUSH (B-5) Open Camping**
11 miles south of Yellville on State 14, then 8 miles on paved and gravel road.
**Attractions:** Mining ghost town. Trailhead for wilderness area hiking.
**Facilities:** Vault toilet, fire grates, drinking water (Apr.-Nov.), river access. (Open year-round)

**STEEL CREEK (B-3) Open Camping**
13 miles west of Jasper on State 74, then 2 miles down steep, winding gravel road.
**Attractions:** Scenic bluffs. Trailhead for wilderness area hiking, featuring Hemmed-in-Hollow.
**Facilities:** Drinking water (Apr.-Nov.), vault toilets, fire grates, river access, equestrian campsites and bridle paths. (Open year-round)
**Note:** Not recommended for large trailers, buses and RVs due to steep, winding road.

**TYLER BEND (B-4) 28 RV/Tent with no hookups; 10 tent; 6 group** ........ ♿
35 miles south of Harrison on U.S. 65, then 3 miles off U.S. 65 on paved road.
**Facilities:** Flush toilets, vault toilets, water, warm showers, picnic sites, pavilion, river access, hiking trails and bridle paths. User's fee charged.

**WOOLUM (B-4) Open Camping**
20 miles south of Harrison, then 8.5 miles of dirt road from Pindall; or 26 miles south of Harrison and 7 miles from St. Joe.
**Attractions:** Swimming, fishing. Trail connection with Ozark Highlands Trail (seasonal).
**Facilities:** Vault toilet, river access. (Open year-round)

Early Bathouse Row, Hot Springs

## HOT SPRINGS NATIONAL PARK

**FOR INFORMATION—Park Superintendent, Hot Springs National Park, Fordyce Bathhouse Visitor Center or P.O. Box 1860, Hot Springs, AR 71902. (501) 623-1433**

**GULPHA GORGE CAMPGROUND (F-4) 47 Tent (Self-contained vehicles allowed)** ........ ♿

.5 mile northeast of Hot Springs off U.S. 70B. Exit off U.S. 70 on east side of town.

**Attractions:** The National Park is noted for its thermal springs and bathhouses, hiking trails through forested mountain terrain, and summer interpretive programs. The new Fordyce Bathhouse Visitor Center is located downtown on Bathhouse Row and has interpretive exhibits and an introductory film program on the park and area attractions.

**Facilities:** Central flush toilets, water, and trailer dump station. Camping limit: 14 days per year. No reservations accepted. (Open year-round). User's fee charged for camping.

Photos by M. Cates

# U. S. FOREST SERVICE CAMPGROUNDS

## OUACHITA NATIONAL FOREST

**FOR INFORMATION—Forest Supervisor, Ouachita National Forest, USFS Box 1270, Hot Springs, AR 71902. (501) 321-5202, or contact the Ranger District for each campground. (Ranger Districts are in parenthesis under each recreation area listed and should be contacted for off season availability.)**

**FOR ADDITIONAL LISTINGS—see Wilderness Areas.**

**ALBERT PIKE (F-2) 46 RV/Tent with no hookups**

5 miles southwest of Glenwood on U.S. 70, then west 13 miles on State 84 to Langley, then right on Highway 369 for 6.1 miles. (Caddo Ranger District, Glenwood, AR 71943, (501) 356-4186)

**Attractions:** Natural pool in Little Missouri River, swimming, fishing.

**Facilities:** Central flush toilets, trailer dump station, warm showers, water. (Partially open year-round). User's fee charged.

**BARD SPRINGS (F-2) 17 RV/Tent with no hookups**

19 miles west of Norman on State 8 to Big Fork, then 10 miles south on gravel Forest Road 38. (Caddo Ranger District, Glenwood, AR 71943, (501) 356-4186)

**Attractions:** Small swimming area, hiking trails, fishing.

**Facilities:** Central flush toilets, water, picnic shelter. (Partially open year-round). User's fee charged.

**BIG BRUSHY (E-2) 11 RV/Tent with no hookups**

16 miles west of Mt. Ida on U.S. 270. (Oden Ranger District, Oden, AR 71961, (501) 326-4322)

**Attractions:** Hiking and fishing.

**Facilities:** Vault toilets, water. (Open Apr.-mid Nov.)

**CAMP CLEARFORK (E-3) Group Use Area**

20 miles west of Hot Springs on U.S. 270. (Womble Ranger District, Mount Ida, AR 71957, (501) 867-2101)

**Attractions:** Swimming, fishing, hiking, canoeing and field sports.

**Facilities:** 6 dormitory cabins, 3 staff cabins, dining hall with full kitchen facilities and recreation building. Central bathhouse with flush toilets and warm showers, ball field. (Some facilities are accessible to the physically challenged.) 30 day minimum advance reservations plus deposit.

**CHARLTON (F-3) 69 RV/Tent with no hookups**

20 miles west of Hot Springs on U.S. 270. (Womble Ranger District, Mount Ida, AR 71957, (501) 867-2101)

**Attractions:** Located near Lake Ouachita. Swimming, mountain streams, tree identification interpretive trail. Hiking trail to Lake Ouachita. Outdoor theater programs in season.

**Facilities:** Central flush toilets, cold showers, water, picnic sites/trailer dump station. (Open mid May-mid Nov.) User's fee charged. (Some campsites available by reservation, call 1-800-283-CAMP.)

**CRYSTAL (F-3) 9 RV/Tent with no hookups**

1 mile north of Norman on State 27, then turn east for 3 miles on gravel Forest Road 177. (Caddo Ranger District, Glenwood, AR 71943, (501) 356-4186)

**Attractions:** Swimming, interpretive trail on soil formation, scenic drives.

**Facilities:** Flush toilets, water, picnic sites. (Open year-round) User's fee charged.

**DRAGOVER FLOAT CAMP (E-3) 8 RV/Tent with no hookups**

4 miles east of Sims on State 88, then south on county gravel road, 2 miles. (Oden Ranger District, Oden, AR 71961, (501) 326-4322)

**Attractions:** Float fishing on Ouachita River, swimming, hiking.

**Facilities:** Vault toilets, water, picnic sites, boat ramp. (Open year-round)

**FOURCHE MT. PICNIC AREA (E-3) 5 RV/Tent with no hookups**

5 miles south of Rover on State 27 (Fourche Ranger District, Danville, AR 72833, (501) 495-2844)

**Attraction:** Hiking.

**Facilities:** Vault toilets, water, picnic sites. (Open year-round)

**FULTON BRANCH FLOAT CAMP (E-3) 7 RV/Tent with no hookups**

1 mile northeast of Mount Ida on State 27, then north at sign for 6 miles on gravel road. Watch for signs. (Womble Ranger

District, Mount Ida, AR 71957, (501) 867-2101)

**Attractions:** Float fishing on Ouachita River, swimming, hiking. Womble Trail connects to Ouachita National Recreation Trail.

**Facilities:** Vault toilets, water, picnic sites, boat ramp. (Open year-round)

**HICKORY NUT MT. PICNIC AREA (E-3) 8 RV/Tent with no hookups**

24 miles west of Hot Springs on U.S. 270, then turn north at sign for 6 miles on gravel Forest Road 47. (Womble Ranger District, Mount Ida, AR 71957, (501) 867-2101)

**Attractions:** Provides panoramic view of Lake Ouachita. 1 mile to Lake Ouachita Vista area.

**Facilities:** Vault toilets, picnic sites. (Open year-round)

**IRON SPRINGS (E-4) 13 RV/Tent with no hookups**

26 miles north of Hot Springs on State 7. (Jessieville Ranger District, Jessieville, AR 71949, (501) 984-5313)

**Attractions:** Hiking trails and small wading area. Hunts Trail connects to Ouachita National Recreation Trail.

**Facilities:** Vault toilets, water, picnic sites. (Open year-round)

**JACK CREEK (D-2) 5 RV/Tent with no hookups**

3 miles south of Booneville on State 23, then east for 1 mile on State 116, then south 4 miles on gravel Forest Road. (Cold Springs Ranger District, Booneville, AR 72927, (501) 675-3233)

**Attractions:** Natural pool in creek, swimming, fishing, hiking.

**Facilities:** Vault toilets, water, picnic sites. (Open mid May-mid Sept.)

**KNOPPERS FORD (D-2) 6 RV/Tent with no hookups**

3 miles south of Booneville on State 23, then east 1 mile on State 116, then south at sign for 6 miles on gravel Forest Road. (Cold Springs Ranger District, Booneville, AR 72927, (501) 675-3233)

**Attractions:** Natural pool in creek, swimming, hiking.

**Facilities:** Vault toilets, water (Open year-round)

**LAKE SYLVIA (E-4) 19 RV/Tent with E**

9 miles south of Perryville on State 9, then west at sign for 4 miles on gravel State 324. (Winona Ranger District, Perryville, AR 72126, (501) 889-5176)

**Attractions:** 14-acre lake, swimming beach, boating (no motors), fishing, hiking. Wildlife interpretive trail, and tree identification interpretive trail for handicapped. Outdoor theater programs in season.

**Facilities:** Central flush toilets, water, hot showers, trailer dump station. (Open mid May-early Sept.) User's fee charged.

**LITTLE PINES (E-2) 7 RV/Tent with E; 14 RV/Tent with no hookups**

4 miles west of Waldron on State 248, then west on county gravel road 7 miles. (Poteau Ranger District, Waldron, AR 72958, (501) 637-4174)

**Attractions:** 1000-acre Lake Hinkle, swimming, hiking.

**Facilities:** Central flush toilets, water, hot showers, boat launch. (Open Apr.-Nov.) User's fee charged. (Some campsites available by reservation, call 1-800-283-CAMP.)

**MILL CREEK (E-2) 27 RV/Tent with no hookups**

19 miles northwest of Pencil Bluff on U.S. 270. (Poteau Ranger District, Waldron, AR 72958, (501) 637-4174)

**Attractions:** Natural pool in creek provides swimming and wading area, hiking, fishing. "Briar Patch" loop interpretive trail, equestrian trail under construction.

**Facilities:** Central flush toilets, water. (Open late May-early Sept.) User's fee charged.

**RIVER BLUFF FLOAT CAMP (E-3) 7 RV/Tent with no hookups**

1 mile northeast of Mount Ida on State 27, then north at sign for 5 miles on gravel road. Watch for signs. (Womble Ranger District, Mount Ida, AR 71957, (501) 867-2101)

**Attractions:** Float fishing on Ouachita River, swimming, hiking. Womble Trail connects to Ouachita National Recreation Trail.

**Facilities:** Vault toilets, water, picnic sites, boat ramps. (Open year-round)

**ROCKY SHOALS FLOAT CAMP (E-3) 7 RV/Tent with no hookups**

2 miles southeast of Pencil Bluff on U.S. 270. (Womble Ranger District, Mount Ida, AR 71957, (501) 867-2101)

**Attractions:** Base camp for float fishing on Ouachita River, swimming, hiking. Womble Trail connects to Ouachita National Recreation Trail.

**Facilities:** Vault toilets, water, picnic sites, boat ramp. (Open year-round)

**SHADY LAKE (F-2) 96 RV/Tent with no hookups**

5 miles southwest of Glenwood on U.S. 70; west 23 miles on State 84 to Athens, then north at sign for 5 miles on Forest Road 38. (Mena Ranger District, Mena, AR 71953, (501) 394-2382)

**Attractions:** 25-lake, swimming beach, fishing, and hiking. Outdoor theater programs in season, tree identification interpretive trail.

**Facilities:** Central flush toilets, water, hot showers, trailer dump/station, picnic sites, boat dock (no motors). (Partically open year-round) User's fee charged.

**SOUTH FOURCHE (E-4) 7 RV/Tent with no hookups**

1 mile south of Hollis on State 7. (Jessieville Ranger District, Jessieville, AR 71949, (501) 984-5313)

**Attraction:** Fishing

**Facilities:** Vault toilets, water picnic sites. (Open year-round)

Photo by M. Cates

## OZARK NATIONAL FOREST

**FOR INFORMATION—Forest Supervisor, Ozark National Forest, P.O. Box 1008, Russellville, AR 72801. (501) 968-2354, or contact the Ranger District for each campground. (Ranger Districts are in parenthesis under each recreation area listed and should be contacted for off season availability.)**

**FOR ADDITIONAL LISTINGS, see Wilderness Areas.**

**BARKSHED (B-5) 1 RV/Tent with no hookups**

7 miles north from Mountain View on State 9, then west on State 14, 12 miles, then northeast on gravel Forest Road 1112 for 3 miles. Negotiable by camping trailer rigs. (Sylamore Ranger District, Mountain View, AR 72560, (501) 269-3228)

**Attractions:** Clear mountain stream, hiking trail, fishing.

**Facilities:** 4 picnic sites (or primitive campsites) and pavilion, chemical toilets. (Open year-round)

**BAYOU BLUFF (C-4) 7 RV/Tent with no hookups**

6 miles north of Hector on State 27. (Bayou Ranger District, Hector, AR 72843, (501) 284-3150)

**Attractions:** Illinois Bayou, picturesque bluffs, fishing.

**Facilities:** Chemical toilets, water, picnic shelters, group shelter, reservations taken. (Open May-Nov.) User's fee charged for camp area.

**BLANCHARD SPRINGS RECREATION AREA (B-6) 32 RV/Tent with no hookups**

7 miles north from Mountain View on State 9, then 6 miles west on State 14, then north on Forest Service Road 1110 for 3 miles. Negotiable by camping trailer rigs. (Sylamore Ranger District, Mt. View, AR 72560, (501) 269-3228)

**Attractions:** Crystal clear streams, large flowing spring (12,000 gallons per minute), caves, small lake, scenic trails, picturesque bluffs, swimming, fishing. Daily tours through Blanchard Springs Caverns, outdoor theatre programs in season.

**Facilities:** Central flush toilets, water, trailer dump station, bathhouse with hot showers. 21 picnic sites. (Open year-round) User's fee charged. (Some campsites available by reservation, call 1-800-283-CAMP.)

**Other Information:** Camping in the Blanchard Campground is limited to no longer than three consecutive nights (May 15-Sep. 15). Remainder of year up to 14 days.

**Visitors Information Center:** The Center opens at 9:00 a.m. An audiovisual program in the auditorium presents the geological history of the Caverns. Also available for viewing is an exhibit room where displays depict the intriguing story of life in the underground world. Tours of the Dripstone and the Discovery Trails begin at the Visitors Information Center. The Discovery Trail is open from Memorial Day to Labor Day. The Dripstone Trail is open for an extended period in the off-season that varies each year. Contact the following phone number for availability.

**Note:** A reservation system is available for the tours, DO NOT CALL COLLECT. Phone (501) 757-2213.

Fees for Cave Tours: $7.00 for adults, $3.50 for children 6-15. Special group rates available during off-season. Golden Age and Golden Access Passports entitle bearer to half price of the tour fee. Golden Eagle Passport is not valid. Children under 6 admitted free. No pets or animals other than seeing-eye dogs allowed in Visitors Information Center, exhibit room, audiovisual room, and cave.

**BROCK CREEK (C-4) 6 RV/Tent with no hookups**

5 miles north of Jerusalem on Forest Development Road 1305, then east on Forest Development Road 1309 for .1 mile, then left on Forest Development Road 1331 for 1 mile, then right on Forest Road 1331A for .1 mile.

**Attractions:** 35-acre lake, fishing, hunting nearby in season.

**Facilities:** Pit toilets.

**COVE LAKE (D-3) 28 RV/Tent with no hookups**

1 mile south of Paris on State 109, then 9 miles southeast on State 309. Negotiable by camping trailer rigs. (Magazine Ranger District, Paris, AR 72855, (501) 963-3076)

**Facilities:** Central flush toilets, chemical toilets, water, hot showers, 19 picnic sites, swimming beach, boat ramp (no water skiing on weekends or holidays), fishing, hiking trail. (Open year-round) User's fee charged. (Some campsites available by reservation, call 1-800-283-CAMP.)

**FAIRVIEW (C-4) 11 RV/Tent with no hookups**

28 miles south of Jasper on State 7 (1 mile north of Pelsor). (Buffalo Ranger District, Jasper, AR 72641, (501) 446-5122)

**Attractions:** Located beside scenic State 7, one of the country's 10 most beautiful highways. Access to Ozark Highlands Trail.

**Facilities:** Chemical toilets, water. (Open Oct.-Mar.) User's fee charged.

**GUNNER POOL (B-5) 32 Tent; 16 RV/Tent with no hookups; 10 Tent only**

16 miles northwest from Mountain View on State 9 and 14, then north on gravel Forest Road 1102, 3 miles. Not negotiable by camping trailer rigs. (Sylamore Ranger District, Mt. View, AR 72560, (501) 269-3228)

**Attractions:** Clear mountain stream, small lake, high picturesque bluffs, fishing, hiking.

**Facilities:** Chemical toilets, drinking water. (Open year-round) User's fee charged.

**HAW CREEK FALLS (C-3) 8 RV/Tent with no hookups**

14 miles north from Hagarville on State 123, or 12 miles west from Pelsor on State 123. Negotiable by camping trailer rigs. (Bayou Ranger District, Hector, AR 72843, (501) 284-3150)

**Attractions:** Small mountain stream with picturesque falls, rocks and bluffs; canoeing on Big Piney Creek nearby, fishing. Access to Ozark Highlands Trail.

**Facilities:** Chemical toilets, water. (Open year-round) User's fee charged.

**HORSEHEAD LAKE (C-3) 10 RV/Tent with no hookups**

8 miles northwest of Clarksville on State 103, then west on State 164, 4 miles, then right on gravel Forest Road 1408, 3 miles. Negotiable by camping trailer rigs. (Pleasant Hill Ranger District, Clarksville, AR 72830, (501) 754-2864)

**Attraction:** 98-acre mountain lake, 3 mile hiking loop.

**Facilities:** Central flush toilets, water, boat ramp (10 hp motor limit for boats), 8 picnic sites, beach, bathhouse and showers. (Open Apr.-mid Nov.) User's fee charged.

**LAKE WEDINGTON (B-1) 18 RV/Tent with no hookups**

16 miles west of Fayetteville on State 16. (Boston Mt. Ranger District, Ozark, AR 72949, (501) 667-2191)
**Attractions:** 102-acre lake, hiking, swimming, fishing, canoeing.
**Facilities:** Central flush toilets, bathhouse and showers, trailer dump station, 24 picnic sites, boat ramp (10 hp motor limit). 5 WPA-era rental cabins and lodge. For reservations contact: Wilderness Company, Lake Wedington, Route 4, Fayetteville, AR 72701. Phone: (501) 442-9268. (Open year-round) User's fee charged.

**LONG POOL (C-4) 19 RV/Tent with no hookups**

6 miles north of Dover on State 7, then west on State 164 for 3 miles, then northeast on Forest Road 1801, 3 miles, then northwest on paved Forest Road 1804, 2 miles. (Bayou Ranger District, Hector, AR 72843, (501) 284-3150)
**Attractions:** Large natural pool in Big Piney Creek, high picturesque bluffs, fishing, hiking, swimming, canoeing.
**Facilities:** Chemical toilets, water, 8 picnic sites, pavilion, canoe launch site, change shelter. (Open year-round) User's fee charged.

**MOCCASIN GAP HORSE TRAIL AND CAMP (C-4) 17 RV/Tent with no hookups**

14 miles north of Dover on State 7, turn left follow gravel road .25 mile uphill to the trailhead/horse camp. (Bayou Ranger District, Hector, AR 72843, (501) 284-3150)
**Attractions:** Rugged mountain scenery located on 28 miles of horse trail with four different loops w/varying degrees of difficulty. Scenic views, waterfalls, bluff lines, pine and hardwood forests.
**Facilities:** Chemical toilets, water for horses only, 17 parking spurs for day use and overnight camping. (Open year-round)

**MOUNT MAGAZINE (D-3) 16 RV/Tent with no hookups**

1 mile south of Paris, then southeast on State 309, 17 miles; or 12 miles north of Havana on paved State 309. (Magazine Ranger District, Paris, AR 72855, (501) 963-3076)
**Attractions:** Rugged mountain scenery, cool climate, highest point in Arkansas (2,753 ft.). Access to Cove Lake hiking trail.
**Facilities:** Chemical toilets, water, 30 picnic sites. (Open year-round)

**OZONE (C-3) 8 RV/Tent with no hookups**

18 miles north of Clarksville on State 21. (Pleasant Hill Ranger District, Clarksville, AR 72830, (501) 754-2864)
**Attractions:** Situated in tall pine timber, site of old Ozone CCC Camp. Access to Ozark Highlands Trail.
**Facilities:** Chemical toilets, water. (Open year-round)

**REDDING (C-3) 25 RV/Tent with no hookups**

18 miles north of Ozark on State 23, then east on gravel Forest Road 1003, 3 miles. (Pleasant Hill Ranger District, Clarksville, AR 72830, (501) 754-2864)
**Attractions:** Canoeing on Mulberry River. Trailhead parking for Ozark Highlands Trail, fishing, hiking.
**Facilities:** Flush toilets, water, showers (unavailable during freeze season) (Open year-round) User's fee charged.

**RICHLAND CREEK (B-4) 10 RV/Tent with no hookups**

Ten miles east of Ben Hur near State 16 and Forest Road 1205 (Buffalo Ranger District, Jasper, AR 72641, (501) 446-5122)
**Attractions:** Clear mountain stream, adjacent Richland Creek Wilderness Area, fishing, swimming, hiking.
**Facilities:** Chemical toilets, water. (Open year-round)

**SHORES LAKE (C-2) 23 RV/Tent with no hookups**

15 miles north of Mulberry on State 215, then 1 mile on paved Forest Road 1505. (Boston Mt. Ranger District, Ozark, AR 72949, (501) 667-2191)
**Attractions:** 82-acre lake in mountain setting, access to Ozark Highlands Trail, swimming, fishing, hiking, picnicking.
**Facilities:** Flush toilets, showers, water, 30 picnic sites, group pavilion (reservations taken), dressing rooms, boat ramp (10 hp motor limit). (Open year-round) User's fee charged.

**SPRING LAKE (D-3) 13 RV/Tent with no hookups**

9 miles from Dardanelle on State 27, then west on State 307, 3 miles to gravel Forest Road 1602, 4 miles. Or take State 307 north from Belleville 4 miles to gravel Forest Road 1602, continue on Forest Road 1602, 3 miles. Negotiable by camp trailer rigs. (Magazine Ranger District, Paris, AR 72855, (501) 963-3076)
**Attractions:** 82-acre lake in mountain setting, hiking, swimming, fishing.
**Facilities:** Central flush toilets, water, 19 picnic sites, bathhouse, showers, boat ramp (10 hp motor limit). (Open Memorial

Day through Labor Day.) User's fee charged. (Some campsites available by reservation, call 1-800-283-CAMP)

**WHITE ROCK MOUNTAIN (C-2) 8 RV/Tent with no hookups**

15 miles north of Mulberry on State 215, then 8 miles on Forest Road 1505. (Boston Mt. Ranger District, Ozark, AR 72949, (501) 667-2191)

**Attractions:** Rugged mountain scenery, spectacular bluffs encircling mountain rim trails with panoramic views. Access to Ozark Highlands Trail.

**Facilities:** Chemical toilets, water, 8 picnic sites. (Open year-round) User's fee charged.

**Note:** 3 housekeeping cabins and lodge (capacity 20 persons) are available. Contact: Jack White, Rt. 2, Winslow, AR 72959 (501) 667-1248.

**WOLF PEN (C-3) 6 Tent**

18 miles north of Ozark on State 23, then east on gravel Forest Road 1003, 13 miles; or 22 miles north of Clarksville on State 103, then west on gravel Forest Road 1003, 2 miles. (Pleasant Hill Ranger District, Clarksville, AR 72830, (501) 754-2864)

**Attractions:** Canoeing on Mulberry River, scenic rock bluffs, fishing.

**Facilities:** Chemical toilets, water, 8 picnic sites. (Open year-round)

Photo By M. Cates

## ST. FRANCIS NATIONAL FOREST

**FOR INFORMATION—St. Francis National Forest, St. Francis Ranger District, Marianna, AR 72360. (501) 295-5278**

**BEAR CREEK LAKE (E-9) 41 RV/Tent with no hookups**

7 miles southeast of Marianna on State 44 or 2 miles north of West Helena on State 242, then east on gravel Forest Road 1900, 16 miles.

**Attractions:** 625-acre lake atop Crowley's Ridge, fishing, hiking, swimming, nature trail.

**Facilities:** Chemical toilets, water, bathhouse with showers, 17 picnic sites, boat ramp (10 hp motor limit). (Open year-round) User's fee charged.

**STORM CREEK LAKE (E-9) 12 RV/Tent with no hookups**

2 miles northeast of West Helena on State 242, then east 3 miles on Forest Road 1900, or 7.5 miles southeast of Marianna on State 44, then south on gravel Forest Road 1900, 10 miles.

**Attractions:** 420-acre lake atop Crowley's Ridge, swimming, fishing.

**Facilities:** Chemical toilets, water, boat ramp (10 hp motor limit). (Open April-Labor Day weekend) User's fee charged.

# WILDERNESS AREAS

## BUFFALO NATIONAL RIVER WILDERNESS AREAS

**FOR INFORMATION: Buffalo National River, P.O. Box 1173, Harrison, AR 72602-1173; (501) 741-5443.**

**LOWER BUFFALO WILDERNESS (B-5):** This wilderness area includes almost all Buffalo National River lands downstream from Panther Creek near Buffalo Point. It can be reached via canoe or by driving to Rush which is east off State 14 south of Yellville. 22,500 acres featuring mountain streams and rugged country.

**PONCA WILDERNESS (B-3):** This wilderness area may be reached by canoe from the Ponca bridge or Steel Creek, or by hiking in off State 43 north of Ponca. 11,300 acres featuring waterfalls, bluffs, caves, mountain streams, and rough terrain.

**UPPER BUFFALO WILDERNESS (B-3):** 2 miles south of Boxley on State 21. This 2200 acre wilderness extends south to the park boundary where it adjoins the Upper Buffalo Wilderness Area administered by Ozark National Forest (see below). Features upper stretch of Buffalo River, bluffs, caves, rough terrain.

## OUACHITA NATIONAL FOREST WILDERNESS AREAS

**FOR INFORMATION: Ouachita National Forest, USFS Box 1270, Hot Springs, AR 71902; (501) 321-5202.**

**BLACK FORK MOUNTAIN WILDERNESS (E-1):** 6 miles north of Mena on U.S. 71, then 6 miles west on U.S. 270. 8,400 acres (additional 5,100 acres in Oklahoma) featuring rugged terrain, rock glaciers, and a forest of dwarf oaks.

**CANEY CREEK WILDERNESS (F-2):** 15 miles south of Mena on U.S. 59 and 71, then 17 miles east on State 246, then 9 miles north on Forest Road 38. 14,400 acres featuring secluded forest, flowing streams, and 12 miles of hiking trails.

**DRY CREEK WILDERNESS (D-2):** From the junction of State 10 and 23, go east for 17 miles on State 10, then south 5 miles on county road 309, then south 3.9 miles on Forest Road 18, then west 4 miles on Forest Road 3 to the wilderness boundary. 6,300 acres featuring secluded forest, flowing stream, and sandstone bluffs. There are no developed trails.

**FLATSIDE WILDERNESS (E-4):** From the junction of State 9 and 60, then 13.6 miles south on State 9, then 8.3 miles west on Forest Road 132, then north 3 miles on Forest Road 94 to Flatside Pinnacle. 10,100 acres featuring small creeks, good views, and a section of the Ouachita National Recreation Trail.

**POTEAU MOUNTAIN WILDERNESS (D-1):** From the junction of State 80 and U.S. 71, then north on U.S. 71 for 5.6 miles, then west 2 miles on Forest Road 158 to the southern boundary of the wilderness. 11,300 acres featuring rock outcrops, streams, and secluded forest. There are no developed trails.

## OZARK NATIONAL FOREST WILDERNESS AREAS

**FOR INFORMATION: Ozark National Forest, P.O. Box 1008, Russellville, AR 72801; (501) 968-2354.**

**EAST FORK WILDERNESS (C-4):** From the junction of State 27 and 105 at Hector, follow State 27 north for approximately 13 miles; wilderness will be to the east (and is also accessible via Forest Service Road 1311). 10,700 acres featuring upland swamps, waterfalls, and rugged country.

**HURRICANE CREEK WILDERNESS (B-3):** At the junction of State 7 and 123 (Sand Gap or Pelsor), go west on State 123 for approximately 10.5 miles to the Big Piney Bridge; wilderness is to the north/northeast via the Ozark Highlands Trail (wilderness may also be approached via Forest Road 1209 on its northeast side). 15,100 acres featuring a natural bridge, mountain streams, and black bears.

**LEATHERWOOD WILDERNESS (B-5):** At Big Flat, go east on State 14 approximately 3.8 miles, then turn north on Forest Road 1100 (Push Mountain Road); wilderness lands generally lie west of Forest Road 1100 and between Forest Roads 1118 and 1116. 16,900 acres featuring flowing streams, springs, caves, bluffs, and proximity to the Buffalo National River.

**RICHLAND CREEK WILDERNESS (B-4):** At junction of State 7 and 16 (Sand Gap or Pelsor), turn east on 16 to Ben Hur, then south about 1.5 miles to Forest Road 1205. Keep on Forest Road 1205 for 10-12 miles to Richland Creek Campground, located on the eastern edge of the wilderness. 11,800 acres featuring waterfalls, bluffs, flowing streams, and rugged terrain.

**UPPER BUFFALO WILDERNESS (B-3):** 15 miles south of Jasper on State 7, then west 8 miles on State 16 to Edwards Junction. Or take State 7 north from Pelsor 14 miles, then west on State 16 to Edwards Junction. The wilderness area lies between State 16 (on the south) and State 21 (on the east) to State 16 (on the west) to Cave Mountain Road 1402 (on the north). 11,094 acres featuring caves, bluffs, and the headwaters of the Buffalo National River.

# CORPS OF ENGINEERS LAKES

## River Area Between Arkansas Post and Pine Bluff (G-7, F-7 and F-6)

**FOR INFORMATION: Resident Engineer, U.S. Corps of Engineers, P.O. Box 7835, Pine Bluff, AR 71611, (501) 534-0451.**

**HUFF ISLAND (F-7) 5 RV/Tent with no hookups**
East of Grady on State 11, 7.5 miles.
**Facilities:** Vault toilets, water, 5 picnic sites. (Open Mar.-Nov.; river bank access year-round). No boat ramp.

**MERRISACH (G-7) 51 RV/tent with E; 15 RV/tent with no hookups.**
9 miles south of Tichnor on paved county road.
**Facilities:** Flush toilets, water, hot showers, boat ramp, pavilions, nature trail, dump station, amphitheater, playground. (Open year-round) User's fee charged.

**MOORE BAYOU (G-7) 4 RV/Tent with no hookups**
5 miles south of Gillett on U.S. 165, then 1 mile east on State 16.
**Facilities:** Vault toilets, water, boat ramp, 3 picnic sites. (Open year-round)

**NOTREBES BEND (G-7) 15 RV/Tent with E; 19 RV/Tent with no hookups**
7 miles west on paved road after crossing Arkansas Post Canal Bridge. Adjacent to Wilbur D. Mills Dam.
**Facilities:** Vault toilets, water, boat ramp, dump station. (Open Mar.-Nov.) User's fee charged.

**PENDLETON (G-7) 13 RV/Tent with W/E, 21 RV/tent with no hookups.**
10 miles south of Gillett on U.S. 165 or 13 miles north of Dumas on U.S. 165, then 1 mile east on State 2120.
**Facilities:** Vault toilets, water, boat ramp, 6 picnic sites, pavilion, dump station, playground. (Open year-round)

**RISING STAR (F-7) 19 RV/Tent with E; 6 RV/Tent with no hookups**
5 miles north of Tamo off U.S. 65.
**Facilities:** Flush toilets, water, hot showers, boat ramp, 8 picnic sites, pavilion, playground. (Open Apr.-Sept.) User's fee charged.

**TRULOCK (F-7) 15 RV/Tent with no hookups**
3 miles north of Noble Lake off U.S. 65.
**Facilities:** Flush toilets, water, boat ramp, pavilion, playground, 7 picnic sites. (Open Mar.-Nov.)

## River Area Between Pine Bluff and Little Rock (F-6 and E-6)

**FOR INFORMATION: Resident Engineer, U.S. Corps of Engineers, P.O. Box 7835, Pine Bluff, AR 71611, (501) 534-0451.**

**D.D. TERRY DAM SITE WEST (E-6) 6 Tent with no hookups**
3.2 miles south of Little Rock Port on paved access road.
**Facilities:** Vault toilets, water, boat ramp, 6 picnic sites. (Open year-round)

**TAR CAMP (F-6) 32 RV/Tent with E; 25 RV/Tent with no hookups**
6 miles east of Redfield off U.S. 65.
**Facilities:** Flush toilets, water, hot showers, boat ramp, pavilion, dump station, 4 picnic sites, playground, fishing area for handicapped, nature trails. (Open Mar.-Oct.) User's fee charged.

**WILLOW BEACH (E-6) 21 RV/Tent with E**
2 miles southwest of Baucum off U.S. 165, then .5 mile southwest on paved access road.
**Facilities:** Flush toilets, water, hot showers, boat ramp, pavilions, 29 picnic sites, playground, dump station, fishing area for handicapped. (Open Mar.-Sept.) User's fee charged.

## River Area Between Little Rock and Dardanelle (E-5 and D-5)

**FOR INFORMATION: Lake Manager, Toad Suck Ferry, Route 5, Box 140, Conway, AR 72032, (501) 329-2986.**

**BIGELOW (D-5) 9 RV/Tent with no hookups**
2 miles east of Bigelow on county road.
**Facilities:** Flush toilets, water, boat ramp, pavilion. (Open Mar.-Nov. 15)

**CHEROKEE (D-5) 29 RV/Tent with W/E** ............ ♿
3 miles south of Morrilton off Cherokee Street.
**Facilities:** Flush toilets, water, hot showers, boat ramp, picnic sites, group pavilion, softball field, playground. (Open year-round) User's fee charged.

**CYPRESS CREEK (D-5) 9 RV/Tent with no hookups**
2 miles north of Houston on State 113.
**Facilities:** Vault toilets, water, boat ramp, 9 picnic sites. (Open Mar.-Nov. 15)

**MAUMELLE (E-5) 8 RV/Tent with W/E**
3 miles off State 10 on Pinnacle Valley Road.
**Facilities:** Flush toilets, water, hot showers, boat ramp, 10 picnic sites, pavilion, softball field, nature trail, fishing pier, basketball court, playgrounds. (Open year-round) User's fee charged.

**POINT REMOVE (D-5) 21 RV/Tent with no hookups**
1.4 miles south of Morrilton off Cherokee Street.
**Facilities:** Flush toilets, hot showers, boat ramp, pavilion. (Open Mar.-Nov. 15) User's fee charged.

**SEQUOYA (D-5) 14 RV/Tent with no hookups**
4 miles south of Morrilton on State 9, then right 1.6 miles on Lock and Dam 9 access road.
**Facilities:** Flush toilets, water, showers, dump station, boat ramp, pavilion, 11 picnic sites, playground. (Open year-round)

**SWEEDEN ISLAND (D-4) 27 RV/Tent with E**
8 miles south of Atkins on State 105.
**Facilities:** Vault toilets, water, boat ramp, pavilion. (Open year-round) User's fee charged.

**TOAD SUCK FERRY (D-5) 49 RV/Tent with W/E**
Exit 129 off I-40 at Conway, go 6 miles west on State 286.
**Facilities:** Flush toilets, water, showers, boat ramp, fishing pier, group pavilion, basketball court, softball field, nature trail, playground. (Open year-round) User's fee charged.

### River Area Between Dardanelle and Ozark (D-3 and D-4)

**These sites are listed under Dardanelle Lake, Corps of Engineers Lake section.**

### River Area Between Ozark and Fort Smith (C-1 and C-2)

**These sites are listed under Ozark Lake, Corps of Engineers Lake section.**

## FELSENTHAL NATIONAL WILDLIFE REFUGE

**Felsenthal National Wildlife Refuge was created from the Corps of Engineers Ouachita and Black Rivers Navigation Project. Geographically, the 65,000-acre refuge is located in what is known as the Felsenthal Basin, an extensive natural depression that is laced with a vast, complex of sloughs, bayous and lakes. The region's two major rivers, the Saline and Ouachita, flow through the refuge. These wetland areas in combination with the refuge's diverse forest ecosystem of bottomland hardwoods, pine forests and uplands support a wide variety of wildlife and provide excellent fishing, hunting, boating, wildlife observation opportunities and environmental education opportunities. A visitor center located 5 miles west of Crossett on U.S. 82, contains numerous wildlife exhibits and is open Monday-Friday from 7:00 a.m.-3:30 p.m. and weekends from 1:00 p.m.-5:00 p.m.**

**FOR INFORMATION: Felsenthal National Wildlife Refuge, P.O. Box 1157, Crossett, AR 71635, (501) 364-3167**

**CROSSETT HARBOR (H-5) 119 RV/Tent W/E**
7 miles west of Crossett on U.S. 82. (Crossett Harbor Port Authority, Crossett, AR 71635, (501) 364-6136)
**Facilities:** Flush toilets, water, hot showers, dump station, picnic shelter, 25 picnic sites, boat ramp, paved parking.

**GRAND MARAIS (H-5) 50 RV/Tent W/E**
2 miles north of Huttig off State 129. (Park Office, Huttig, AR 71747, (501) 863-6024 or 943-2930)
**Facilities:** Flush toilets, water, hot showers, dump station, 10 picnic sites, boat ramp.

## BEAVER LAKE AREA

Located in the Ozark highlands of northwest Arkansas on the headwaters of the White River. The surrounding area is known for its tourist attractions ranging from the University of Arkansas at Fayetteville and the Pea Ridge National Military Park near Rogers, to the unique "Stairstep-town" of Eureka Springs. The upper White River tributaries have always been famous for their smallmouth bass fishing. Deer hunting is good throughout the area during season.

FOR INFORMATION: Resident Manager, P.O. Drawer H, Rogers, AR 72757, (501) 636-1210.

**DAM SITE (A-2) 103 RV/Tent with E**

9 miles west of Eureka Springs on U.S. 62, then 2.5 miles south on paved access road State 187 to dam.

**Facilities:** Vault toilets, water, boat ramp, solar heated showers, trailer dump station, overlook, pavilion, swimming, hiking trail. (Open year-round) User's fee charged Mar.-Dec., reduced fees Nov., Dec., Mar.

**HICKORY CREEK (A-2) 67 RV/Tent with E**

4 miles north of Springdale on U.S. 71, then 7 miles east on State 264.

**Facilities:** Flush and vault toilets, water, solar heated showers, boat dock and ramp, trailer and marine dump stations, picnic area, swimming, playground, 2 pavilions. (Open year-round) User's fee charged Mar.-Dec.; reduced fees Nov., Dec., Mar.

**HORSESHOE BEND (A-2) 159 RV/Tent with E**

8 miles east of Rogers on State 94.

**Facilities:** Vault toilets, water, solar heated showers, 2 playgrounds, boat dock and ramp, 3 pavilions, picnic area, trailer dump station, swimming. (Open year-round) User's fee charged Mar.-Dec.; reduced fees Nov., Dec., Mar.

**INDIAN CREEK (A-2) 33 RV/Tent with E**

1.5 miles east of Gateway on U.S. 62, then south 5 miles on paved access road.

**Facilities:** Vault toilets, solar heated showers, water, boat ramp, swimming, hiking trail, picnic area. (Open year-round) User's fee charged Apr.-Oct.

**LOST BRIDGE (A-2) 83 RV/Tent with E**

5 miles southeast of Garfield on State 127.

**Facilities:** Vault toilets, solar heated showers, water, boat dock and ramp, trailer dump station, youth group camp area, playground, 3 hiking trails. (Open year-round) User's fee charged Mar.-Dec.; reduced fees Nov., Dec., Mar.

**PRAIRIE CREEK (A-2) 119 RV/Tent with E**

4 miles east of Rogers on State 12, then 1 mile on access road.

**Facilities:** Flush and vault toilets, water, solar heated showers, boat dock and ramp, trailer and marine dump stations, swimming, picnic area, 2 pavilions, playground, hiking trail. (Open year-round) User's fee charged Apr.-Oct.

**ROCKY BRANCH (A-2) 47 RV/Tent with E**

11 miles east of Rogers on State 12, then 4.5 miles northeast to paved access road on State 303.

**Facilities:** Vault toilets, water, solar heated showers, boat dock and ramp, trailer and marine dump stations, pavilion, playground. (Open year-round) User's fee charged Apr.-Oct.

**STARKEY (A-2) 31 RV/Tent with no hookups**

4 miles west of Eureka Springs on U.S. 62, then 7 miles southwest on paved access road.

**Facilities:** Vault toilets, water, boat dock and ramp, marine dump station, pavilion, playground. (Open year-round)

**WAR EAGLE (A-2) 26 RV/Tent with E**

10 miles east of Springdale on State 412, then 3 miles north on paved access road.

**Facilities:** Vault toilets, water, solar heated showers, boat dock and ramp, trailer dump station, overlook, pavilion, swimming. (Open year-round) User's fee charged Apr.-Oct.

## BLUE MOUNTAIN LAKE AREA

Located on the Petit Jean River in west central Arkansas. The lake is rather small—50 miles of shoreline. Mount Magazine nearby provides opportunities for hiking, and hunting in season.

FOR INFORMATION: Park Manager, Waveland, AR 72867, (501) 947-2372.

**ASHLEY CREEK (D-2) 10 RV/Tent with no hookups**

1.5 miles south of Blue Mountain on paved access road.

**Facilities:** Vault toilets, water, boat ramp, dump station, pavilion. (Open year-round)

**HISE HILL (D-2) 9 RV/Tent with no hookups**
11 miles southeast of Booneville on State 217.
**Facilities:** Vault toilets, water, boat ramp, pavilion. (Open year-round)

**LICK CREEK (D-2) 7 RV/Tent with no hookups; 2 Tent**
5 miles southwest of Waveland on State 309.
**Facilities:** Vault toilets, water, boat ramp, pavilion. (Open year-round)

**OUTLET AREA (D-2) 29 RV/Tent with E.**
3 miles south of Waveland on paved road. Located below the dam on Petit Jean River.
**Facilities:** Vault toilets, water, dump station, overlook. (Open year-round; no electricity Nov. 1-Mar. 15) User's fee charged.

**WAVELAND PARK (D-2) 51 RV/Tent with E**
2 miles southwest of Waveland on paved road.
**Facilities:** Vault toilets, water-borne toilet, showers, water, boat ramp, dump station, group pavilion. (Open year-round; no electricity Nov. 1-Mar. 15) User's fee charged.

## BULL SHOALS LAKE AREA

**Located in the Ozarks in north central Arkansas and southeastern Missouri, Bull Shoals Lake has received national recognition from fishermen and outdoor writers as the home of "lunker bass." The hardwood and pine-clad hills around the lake provide scenic beauty and a ready haven for the hiker and nature lover, while the over 1,000 miles of shoreline provide hidden coves and inlets popular with the fisherman and water sportsman.**

**FOR INFORMATION: Resident Engineer, P.O. Box 369, Mountain Home, AR 72653, (501) 425-2700.**

**BUCK CREEK (A-4) 34 RV/Tent with E; 3 RV/Tent with no hookups** ........ ♿
5.5 miles south of Protem, MO, on Arkansas State 125.
**Facilities:** Flush, vault and chemical toilets, water, hot showers, swimming beach, change shelter, group pavilion, playground, boat dock and ramp, trailer and marine dump station. (Open year-round) User's fee charged.

**BULL SHOALS (A-5) 12 RV/Tent with E**
West of the town of Bull Shoals on State 178.
**Facilities:** Vault toilets, water, boat dock and ramp, marine dump station. (Open year-round) User's fee charged.

**DAM SITE (A-5) 14 RV/Tent with E; 21 RV/Tent with no hookups** ........ ♿
1 mile southwest of town of Bull Shoals.
**Facilities:** Flush toilets, water, hot showers, boat ramp, trailer dump station, playground, basketball court, swimming beach. (Open Apr.-Oct.) User's fee charged.

**HIGHWAY 125 (A-4) 38 RV/Tent with E** ........ ♿
14 miles northwest of Yellville on State 14, then north on State 125 for 13 miles.
**Facilities:** Vault and chemical toilets, water, hot showers, boat dock and ramp, trailer and marine dump stations, swimming beach, playground, group pavilion. (Open year-round) User's fee charged.

**LAKEVIEW (A-5) 90 RV/Tent with E; 7 RV/Tent with no hookups** ........ ♿
North of Lakeview on State 178.
**Facilities:** Flush, vault and chemical toilets, water, hot showers, dump station, swimming beach, playground, group pavilion, 1 mile nature trail. (Open year-round) User's fee charged.

**LEAD HILL (A-4) 73 RV/Tent with E** ........ ♿
4 miles north of Lead Hill on State 7.
**Facilities:** Vault and chemical toilets, water, hot showers, trailer and marine dump stations, boat dock and ramp, swimming beach, change shelter, group pavilion, playround. (Open year-round) User's fee charged.

**OAKLAND (A-5) 32 RV/Tent with E; 1 RV/Tent with no hookups** ........ ♿
8 miles north of Midway on State 5, then 10 miles west on State 202.
**Facilities:** Flush and vault toilets, water, hot showers, boat dock and ramp, trailer dump station, swimming beach, change shelter, group pavilion, playground. (Open year-round) User's fee charged.

**OZARK ISLE (A-5) 14 RV/Tent with E; 92 RV/Tent with no hookups** ........ ♿
5 miles southwest of Oakland.
**Facilities:** Flush and vault toilets, water, hot showers, boat ramps, swimming beach, change shelter, group pavilion, playground. (Open Apr.-Oct.) User's fee charged.

**POINT RETURN (A-5) 22 RV/Tent with no hookups**
Northeast of town of Bull Shoals on access road.
**Facilities:** Vault and chemical toilets, water, boat ramp, dump station, swimming beach, change shelter, 8 picnic sites, pavilion. (Open Apr.-Nov.) User's fee charged.

**TUCKER HOLLOW (A-4) 29 RV/Tent with E** ........ ♿
7 miles northwest of Lead Hill on State 14, then 3 miles north on State 281.
**Facilities:** Flush toilets, vault toilets, water, showers, boat dock and ramp, trailer dump station, pavilion, swimming beach, change shelter, playground. (Open year-round) User's fee charged.

## DARDANELLE LAKE AREA

**Located on the Arkansas River in the west-central part of the state, this lake is a major unit of the Arkansas River Navigation Project. The lake stretches 50 miles up the Arkansas River Valley from Dardanelle Lock and Dam to Ozark-Jeta Taylor Lock and Dam. About 315 miles of shoreline give the visitor ample fishing and camping opportunities.**

**A visitors center, located 1.5 miles west of State 7 at the Old Post Road Park, explains the development of the Arkansas River Valley from the days of the Indians to the present through interpretive exhibits entitled "Renaissance of a River."**

**FOR INFORMATION: Resident Engineer, P.O. Box 1087, Russellville, AR 72801, (501) 968-5008.**

**CABIN CREEK (D-3) 9 RV/Tent with no hookups**
1.5 miles west of Knoxville on paved access road.
**Facilities:** Vault toilets, water, boat ramp, pavilion. (Open year-round)

**CANE CREEK (D-3) 16 RV/Tent with no hookups**
3.5 miles northeast of Scranton on State 197, then north 2 miles on paved road.
**Facilities:** Vault toilets, water, boat ramp, pavilion. (Open year-round) User's fee charged May-Labor Day.

**DELAWARE (D-4) 13 RV/Tent with no hookups**
.25 mile east of Delaware on State 22, then north 2 miles on State 393.
**Facilities:** Vault toilets, water, boat ramp, overlook, pavilion. (Open year-round) User's fee charged May-Labor Day.

**DUBLIN (D-3) 16 RV/Tent with no hookups** ........ ♿
7.3 miles east of Scranton on State 197.
**Facilities:** Vault toilets, water, boat ramp, swim beach, group shelter. (Open year-round) User's fee charged May-Labor Day.

**FLAT ROCK (D-4) 15 RV/Tent with no hookups**
.66 mile east of Piney on U.S. 64, then north on State 359 for mile, then west mile on access road.
**Facilities:** Vault toilets, water, boat ramp, pavilion. (Open year-round) User's fee charged May-Labor Day.

**HORSEHEAD (D-3) 7 RV/Tent with no hookups**
1 mile east of Hartman on U.S. 64, then 2 miles east on State 194, then 1.75 miles south on access road.
**Facilities:** Vault toilets, water, boat ramp. (Open year-round)

**OLD POST ROAD PARK (D-4) 12 RV/Tent with no hookups** ........ ♿
1.3 miles west of State 7 on paved road to Lock and Dam.
**Facilities:** Flush toilets, water, boat ramp, dump station, tennis courts, basketball court, playground, baseball field, soccer-football field, pavilions. Arkansas River Visitor Center open weekends during summer and fall. (Open year-round) User's fee charged May-Labor Day.

**PINEY BAY (D-3) 88 RV/Tent with E;** ........ ♿
3 mile west of London on U.S. 64, then 3.5 miles north on State 359.
**Facilities:** Boat ramps, water, rest rooms, swim beach, dump station, 8 picnic sites, amphitheater, pavilion. (Open year-round) User's fee charged.

**RIVERVIEW (D-4) 18 RV/Tent with no hookups** ........ ♿
.75 mile north of Dardanelle on paved road to Dam.
**Facilities:** Vault toilets, water, 5 picnic sites, pavilion. (Open year-round) User's fee charged May-Labor Day.

**SHOAL BAY (D-3) 82 RV/Tent with E** ........ ♿
2 miles north of New Blaine on State 197.
**Facilities:** Flush toilets, water, showers, boat dock and ramp, marina, trailer dump station, group pavilion, swim beach, playground, Bridge Rock Nature Trail, amphitheater. (Open year-round) User's fee charged.

**SPADRA (D-3) 30 RV/Tent with E** ............................................ ♿
2 miles south of Clarksville on State 103 to Jamestown, then 1 mile on access road.
**Facilities:** Flush toilets, water, showers, boat dock and ramp, pavilion, 5 picnic sites, marina and restaurant. (Open year-round) User's fee charged.

## DeGRAY LAKE AREA

**On 31,800 land and water acres with 13,500 water acres and 207 miles of shoreline located on the Caddo River in the Ouachita Mountains of southwest Arkansas, eight miles north of Arkadelphia (Exit 78 off I-30 at Caddo Valley/ Arkadelphia). The Arkansas Game and Fish Commission has stocked the lake with a variety of game fish.**

**FOR INFORMATION: Corps of Engineers Resource Manager, No. 30 I.P. Circle, Arkadelphia, AR 71923, (501) 246-5501.**

**ALPINE RIDGE (F-4) 49 RV/Tent with E** ............................................ ♿
10 miles east of Alpine Community off State 8.
**Facilities:** Flush toilets, water, heated showers, boat ramp, trailer dump station, registration booth, day use area, 4 picnic sites, swim beach, playground. (Open year-round) User's fee charged.

**ARLIE MOORE (F-4) 72 RV/Tent with E; 15 Tent with E** ............................................ ♿
Halfway between DeGray Dam and Bismarck on State 7, turn left at Gibson's Country Store, then 2 miles.
**Facilities:** Flush toilets, water, 2 boat ramps, dump station, heated showers, playground, pavilion, swim beaches, day use area, registration booth, nature trail, amphitheater, 20 picnic sites. (Open year-round) User's fee charged.

**CADDO DRIVE (F-4) 45 RV/Tent with E; 27 Tent with E** ............................................ ♿
15 miles north of Arkadelphia, turn off State 7 at Tri-County Marina, then 3 miles.
**Facilities:** Flush toilets, water, heated showers, boat ramp, dump station, playground, swimming beach, registration booth, day use pavilion, 30 picnic sites. (Open May 15-Aug. 15) User's fee charged.

**EDGEWOOD (F-4) 51 RV/Tent with E** ............................................ ♿
15 miles north of Arkadelphia, turn off State 7 at Tri-County Marina, then 4 miles.
**Facilities:** Flush toilets, water, heated showers, registration booth, playground, swim beach, dump station (Open Mar. 1-Nov. 15) User's fee charged.

**IRON MOUNTAIN (F-4) 69 RV/Tent with E** ............................................ ♿
Off State 7, 2.5 miles west of DeGray Dam.
**Facilities:** Flush toilets, water, heated showers, boat ramp, dump station, playground, registration booth, day use area, 25 picnic sites. (Open year-round) User's fee charged.

**LENOX MARCUS (F-4) Open Camping** ............................................ ♿
3 miles south of Lambert off State 84.
**Facilities:** 200 acres of remote camping. Flush toilets, water, boat ramp, 30 picnic sites. (Open year-round)

Photo by M. Cates

**OAK BOWER (F-4) Group Use Only** ♿
2 miles south of Lambert off State 84.
**Facilities:** 8 cabins, kitchen/dining hall combination, showers, flush toilets, playground, electricity. By reservation only. (246-5501)

**OZAN POINT (F-4) 50 Tent** ♿
12 miles east off State 8 near Alpine Community.
**Facilities:** Flush toilets, water, boat ramp, 4 picnic sites. (Open year-round)

**POINT CEDAR (F-4) 58 RV/Tent with no hookups; 4 Tent** ♿
10.5 miles west of Bismark on State 84, turn left at Point Cedar community, then 2 miles.
**Facilities:** Flush toilets, registration booth, water, boat ramp, 9 picnic sites. (Open Mar. 1-Dec. 1) User's fee charged.

**SHOUSE FORD (F-4) 100 RV/Tent with E** ♿
10.5 miles from Bismarck on State 84, turn left at Point Cedar, then 2 miles.
**Facilities:** Flush toilets, water, heated showers, boat ramp, dump station, playground, day use area, 25 picnic sites, swim beaches, amphitheater. (Open year-round) User's fee charged.

## DeQUEEN LAKE AREA

**DeQueen Lake is located on the Rolling Fork River in the foothills of the Ouachita Mountains. The lake covers 1,680 surface acres and has 35 miles of shoreline. The lake is a fine fishing resource with deep open water and flooded standing timber. Major fish species include black bass, crappie, bream and catfish. Other recreational activities include camping, boating, water skiing, swimming, picnicking, and hunting. Over 1,000 of the project's 5,000 land acres are intensively managed for both game and non-game species of wildlife by the Corps of Engineers. Major game species include deer, rabbit, turkey, quail and ducks.**

**FOR INFORMATION: Park Ranger, Tri Lakes, Rt. 1, Box 358C, DeQueen, AR 71832, (501) 584-4161.**

**BELLAH MINE (G-1) 20 RV/Tent with E**
7 miles north of DeQueen on U.S. 71, then 5 miles west on Bellah Mine Road.
**Facilities:** Vault toilets, water (Mar.-Oct.), boat ramp, trailer dump station. (Open year-round) User's fee charged.

**OAK GROVE (G-1) 36 RV/Tent with E**
3 miles north of DeQueen on U.S. 71 and 5 miles west on project access road, then .25 mile north on county road.
**Facilities:** Flush and vault toilets, water, hot showers, boat ramp, playground, dump station, swimming beach, amphitheater, picnic shelter, 8 picnic sites. (Open year-round; no electricity Oct.-Mar.) User's fee charged Mar.-Oct.

**PINE RIDGE (G-1) 10 RV/Tent with E; 37 RV/Tent with no hookups**
3 miles north of DeQueen on U.S. 71 and 5 miles west on project access road, then 2 miles north on county road.
**Facilities:** Vault toilets, water (Mar.-Oct.) boat ramp, showers. (Open year-round) User's fee charged Mar.-Oct.

## DIERKS LAKE AREA

**Surrounded by beautiful hardwood and pine forests, Dierks Lake offers recreational opportunities to boaters and non-boaters alike. For the fisherman there are many coves, inlets, and flooded timber to fish for largemouth bass, smallmouth bass, crappie, catfish and several species of sunfish. The main area of the 1,360 acre lake offers ample room for water skiers and recreational boaters. Below the lake at Horseshoe Bend, canoeists and kayakers enjoy exciting sport when sufficient water is being released. The natural beauty of the steep ridges, dense forests, and abundant wildlife make this area a favorite for the hunter. Located on the Saline River about 5 miles northwest of the town of Dierks, Dierks Lake has easy access off of Highway 70.**

**FOR INFORMATION: Park Ranger, Dierks Lake, P.O. Box 8, Dierks, AR 71833, (501) 286-2346.**

**BLUE RIDGE (F-2) 22 RV/Tent with no hookups**
3 miles north of Dierks on U.S. 70, then 4 miles northwest on State 4, and 3 miles west on paved county road.
**Facilities:** Vault toilets, boat ramp, swimming beach, group camp area. (Open year-round)

**HORSESHOE BEND (F-2) 11 RV/Tent with no hookups**
2 miles west of Dierks on U.S. 70, then 4 miles northwest on paved county and project access road.
**Facilities:** Vault toilets, water, swimming beach, change shelter, pavilion. (Open year-round)

**JEFFERSON RIDGE (F-2) 84 RV/Tent with W/E**
2 miles west of Dierks on U.S. 70, then 7 miles northwest on county and project access road.
**Facilities:** Water, boat ramps, showers, pavilion, swimming beach. (Open year-round) User's fee charged.

## GILLHAM LAKE AREA

"The Bright Spot on the Cossatot," Gillham Lake, is located on the Cossatot River, one of the most challenging white water streams in Arkansas. The lake lies in Howard and Polk Counties about 16 miles north of the town of DeQueen and 6 miles northeast of Gillham. At normal pool Gillham

Lake covers 1,370 acres with a shoreline of 37 miles. The deep, clear blue lake in the foothills of the Ouachita Mountains is surrounded by a beautiful hardwood/pine forest and offers boating, fishing, skiing and swimming. The wide expanse of white, sandy beach provides hours of pleasure for picnicking and building "sand castles." The canoe launch area downstream of the dam provides an easy access to the river for kayakers and canoeists and for float trips when sufficient water is being released. In addition, the forest around the lake offers hunting, hiking and nature study. Gillham Lake offers something for everyone.

FOR INFORMATION: Park Manager, Gillham Lake, Rt. 3, Box 184, Gillham, AR 71841, (501) 386-2141.

COON CREEK (F-2) 26 RV/Tent with E; 5 RV/Tent with no hookups

6 miles northeast of Gillham via county road.

**Facilities:** Vault toilets, water, boat ramp, swimming beach, amphitheater, playground. (Open year-round) User's fee charged.

COSSATOT REEFS (F-2) 22 RV/Tent with E; 8 RV/Tent with no hookups

6 miles northeast of Gillham via county road, close to the dam.

**Facilities:** Flush and vault toilets, water, showers, boat ramp, swimming area, covered picnic shelter, playground. (Open year-round) User's fee charged.

LITTLE COON CREEK (F-2) 10 RV/Tent with no hookups

6 miles northeast of Gillham via county road and approximately 3 miles north via public use and county road.

**Facilities:** Vault toilet, boat ramp. (Open year-round)

## GREERS FERRY LAKE AREA

Greers Ferry Dam, completed in December 1962, spans the Little Red River three miles north of Heber Springs. The dam and lake are nestled in the foothills of the scenic north central Arkansas Ozark Mountains. This clean, clear lake has been stocked with almost every known game fish native to the tate by the Arkansas Game and Fish Commission. Hybrid bass, the most recently added species, are now reaching excellent size. The U.S. Fish and Wildlife Service operates a trout hatchery below the dam and stocks the lake and river with rainbow trout.

Sugar Loaf Mountain Island National Nature Trail provides an exciting two-hour island hike with panoramic views of the surrounding lake and countryside from the summit, 540 feet above the water. Mossy Bluff National Nature Trail, downstream of the dam, meanders along a buff overlooking the Little Red River and fish hatchery, and provides an excellent view of the dam and lake from the overlook shelter. Buckeye National Trail is located adjacent to Mossy Bluff Trail and features a paved trail surface for persons unable to negotiate the rougher areas.

A visitors center, located 2.5 miles north of Heber Springs on State 25, explains the role of the U.S. Army Corps of Engineers in the exploration and development of the Little Red River area through interpretive exhibits and a multi-image, audiovisual presentation entitled "The Saga of the Little Red, a Tale of Two Centuries." Advance reservations are required for picnic shelters and group camping areas. Fee dates are approximate. Contact resident engineer.

FOR INFORMATION: Resident Engineer, P.O. Box 1088, Heber Springs, AR 72543, (501) 362-2416.

CHEROKEE (C-6) 16 RV/Tent with E; 33 RV/Tent with no hookups ........ ♿

7.5 miles west of Drasco on State 92, then 4.5 miles south on paved access road.

**Facilities:** Vault toilets, water, dump station, boat ramps, swimming beach. (Open year-round) User's fee charged Apr.-Oct.

CHOCTAW (C-5) 78 RV/Tent with E; 68 RV/Tent with no hookups ........ ♿

5 miles south of Clinton on U.S. 65, then 3.5 miles east on State 330.

**Facilities:** Flush and vault toilets, water, hot showers, boat dock and ramps, dump station, marine dump station, swimming beaches, amphitheater, group picnic shelter, playground, 5 picnic sites. (Open year-round) User's fee charged all year.

COVE CREEK (C-6) 31 RV/Tent with E; 34 RV/Tent with no hookups ........ ♿

8 miles southwest of Heber Springs on State 25, then 3 miles northwest on State 16, then 1.25 miles northeast on access road.

**Facilities:** Flush and vault toilets, water, hot showers, dump station, boat ramp, 4 picnic sites, group picnic shelter, swimming beaches. (Open year-round) User's fee charged Apr.-Oct.

**DAM SITE (C-6) 156 RV/Tent with E; 113 RV/Tent with no hookups** ........ ♿
3 miles north of Heber Springs on State 25.
**Facilities:** Flush and vault toilets, water, hot showers, trailer and marine dump stations, boat dock and ramp, 14 picnic sites, swimming beaches, amphitheater, playground, group picnic shelter (200 capacity pavilion by advance reservation only). (Open year-round) User's fee charged Apr.-Oct.

**DEVILS FORK (C-6) 40 RV/Tent with E; 15 RV/Tent with no hookups** ........ ♿
.25 mile north of Greers Ferry on State 16.
**Facilities:** Flush and vault toilets, hot showers, water, boat ramp, dump station, swimming beach, playground, group picnic shelter. (Open year-round) User's fee charged all year.

**HEBER SPRINGS (C-6) 52 RV/Tent with E; 90 RV/Tent with no hookups** ........ ♿
2 miles west of Heber Springs on State 110, then .5 mile north on paved access road.
**Facilities:** Flush and vault toilets, water, boat dock and ramp, trailer and marine dump stations, cold showers, swimming beaches, playground, 11 picnic sites, group picnic shelter. (Open year-round) User's fee charged all year.

**HILL CREEK (C-6) 25 RV/Tent with E; 16 RV/Tent with no hookups** ........ ♿
12 miles west of Drasco on State 92, then 3 miles northwest on State 225, then 2 miles south on paved access road.
**Facilities:** Vault toilets, water, boat dock and ramp, swimming beach, group picnic shelter. (Open year-round) User's fee charged Apr.-Oct.

**JOHN F. KENNEDY (C-6) 74 RV/Tent with E** ........ ♿
4 miles north of Heber Springs on State 25, then 1 mile east on paved access road. Located on the left bank of the Little Red River.
**Facilities:** Flush toilets, water hookups at 13 sites, playground, group picnic shelter, hot showers, dump station, boat ramp, 6 picnic sites. (Open year-round) User's fee charged all year.

**MILL CREEK (C-6) 39 RV/Tent with no hookups** ........ ♿
14 miles northeast of Bee Branch on State 92, then 3 miles north on paved access road.
**Facilities:** Vault toilets, water, boat ramp, swimming beach, group picnic shelter. (Open year-round) no fee.

**NARROWS (C-6) 60 RV/Tent with E** ........ ♿
2.5 miles southwest of Greers Ferry on State 16.
**Facilities:** Flush and vault toilets, water, hot showers, boat dock and ramp, dump station, 2 group pcinic shelters, 9 picnic sites. (Open year-round) User's fee charged Apr.-Oct.

**OLD HIGHWAY 25 (C-6) 64 RV/Tent with E; 36 RV/Tent with no hookups** ........ ♿
6.25 miles north of Heber Springs on State 25, then 3 miles west on old State 25.
**Facilities:** Flush and vault toilets, water, hot showers, boat ramps, dump station, swimming beach, group picnic shelter, group camp area, 3 picnic sites. (Open year-round) User's fee charged Apr.-Oct.

**SHILOH (C-6) 60 RV/Tent with E; 56 RV/Tent with no hookups** ........ ♿
3.5 miles southeast of Greers Ferry on State 110.
**Facilities:** Flush and vault toilets, water, hot showers, boat dock and ramp, trailer and marine dump stations, group picnic shelter, group camp area, 4 picnic sites, playground. (Open year-round) User's fee charged Apr.-Oct.

**SOUTH FORK (C-5) 13 RV/Tent with no hookups** ........ ♿
2 miles east of Clinton on State 16, then 7 miles southeast on gravel access road.
**Facilities:** Vault toilets, water, boat ramp. (Open year-round) no fee.

**SUGAR LOAF (C-5) 56 RV/Tent with E; 39 RV/Tent with no hookups** ........ ♿
12 miles northeast of Bee Branch on State 92, then 1.5 miles west on State 337.
**Facilities:** Vault toilets, water, boat dock and ramp, dump station, swimming beach, group picnic shelter, playground, 3 picnic sites. (Open year-round) User's fee charged Apr.-Oct.
**Note:** National Nature Trail on nearby Sugar Loaf Mountain Island.

**VAN BUREN (C-5) 18 RV/Tent with E; 47 with no hookups** ........ ♿
2 miles south of Shirley on State 16, then 5 miles on State 330.
**Facilities:** Flush and vault toilets, water, hot showers, boat dock and ramps, trailer and marine dump stations, swimming beach, 2 group picnic shelters. (Open year-round) User's fee charged Apr.-Oct.

## LAKE GREESON AREA

**Located on the Little Missouri River in the foothills of the Ouachita Mountains of southwest Arkansas, this crystal clear lake is popular with scuba divers. Many coves and inlets around the lake provide excellent fishing and protected areas for water skiing. Bare rock outcroppings contrast with the tall pines along the shores to provide interesting areas for hikers and nature lovers.**

**FOR INFORMATION: Resource Manager, Lake Greeson, Murfreesboro, AR 71958-9720, (501) 285-2151.**

**ARROWHEAD POINT (F-3) 23 RV/Tent with no hookups**
5 miles east of Newhope on U.S. 70, then .25 mile south on access road.
**Facilities:** Flush toilets (mid Mar.-Nov.), water, boat ramp, swimming area. (Open year-round) User's fee charged mid Mar.-Sept.

**BEAR CREEK (F-3) 19 RV/Tent with no hookups**
.5 mile south of Kirby on State 27, then 1.75 miles west on access road.
**Facilities:** Vault toilets, water, cycle trails. (Open year-round)

**BUCKHORN (F-3) 9 RV/Tent with no hookups**
6 miles north of Murfreesboro on State 19, 3 miles northwest of dam, then 2 miles east on gravel access road.
**Facilities:** Vault toilets. (Open Mar.-mid Nov.)

**COWHIDE COVE (F-3) 40 RV/Tent with E; 10 RV/Tent with no hookups** ........ ♿
6 miles south of Kirby on State 27, then 2 miles west on access road.
**Facilities:** Flush toilets, water, hot and cold showers, boat ramp, dump station, nature trail, amphitheater, 5 picnic sites. (Open year-round; water-borne facilities available mid Mar.-mid Nov.) User's fee charged.

**KIRBY LANDING (F-3) 87 RV/Tent with E** ........ ♿
2.5 miles west of Kirby on U.S. 70, then 1.25 miles south on access road.
**Facilities:** Flush toilets (mid Mar.-mid Nov.), water, hot and cold showers, dump station, boat dock and ramp, marina, nature trail, amphitheater, cycle trails, swimming beach, bathhouse. (Open year-round; water-borne acilities available mid Mar.-mid Nov.) User's fee charged.

**LAUREL CREEK (F-3) 24 RV/Tent with no hookups**
5.25 miles south of Kirby on State 27, then 4 miles west on gravel access road.
**Facilities:** Vault toilets, water, boat ramp, nature trails, cycle trails. (Open Mar.-mid Nov.)

**NARROWS DAM SITE (F-3) 18 RV/Tent with E; 6 RV/Tent with no hookups** ........ ♿
6 miles north of Murfreesboro on State 19.
**Facilities:** Flush toilets (year-round), water, hot and cold showers (year-round), dump station, marina and ramp, nature trails, boat rental, 34 picnic sites, pavilion, 2 overlooks, swimming area. (Open year-round; water-borne facilities available year-round) User's fee charged.

**PARKER CREEK (F-3) 24 RV/Tent with E; 36 RV/Tent with no hookups** ........ ♿
6 miles north of Murfreesboro on State 19, then 3 miles northwest of dam on gravel access road.
**Facilities:** Flush toilets (mid Mar.-mid Nov.), water, hot and cold showers (mid Mar.-mid Nov.), boat ramp, nature trail. (Open mid Mar.-Nov.) User's fee charge.

**PIKEVILLE (F-3) 12 RV/Tent with no hookups**
6 miles north of Murfreesboro on State 19, 2 miles northwest of dam, then 2 miles east on gravel access road.
**Facilities:** Vault toilets, water, nature trail, 4 picnic sites. (Open Mar.-mid Nov.)

**SELF CREEK (F-3) 41 RV/Tent with E; 41 RV/Tent with no hookups** ........ ♿
1 mile west of Daisy on U.S. 70.
**Facilities:** Flush toilets, water, showers, dump station, marina and ramp, 14 picnic sites, swimming beach, pavilion, boat rental. (Partially open year-round) User's fee charged.

**STAR OF THE WEST (F-3) 21 RV/Tent with no hookups**
2.75 miles east of Newhope on U.S. 70.
**Facilities:** Vault toilets, water. (Open year-round)

## LAKE OUACHITA AREA

**Located on the Ouachita River in the Ouachita Mountains of west central Arkansas, the lake is surrounded by the Ouachita National Forest and private timberlands. Unsurpassed scenic beauty, excellent fishing, water sports of all kinds**

**and a prolific area for rockhounds are just a few of the natural attractions of this area. Most camping areas are just a few miles from all the tourist attractions of Hot Springs National Park.**

**FOR INFORMATION: Resource Manager, P.O. Box 4, Mountain Pine, AR 71956, (501) 767-2108.**

**BIG FIR (E-3) 17 RV/Tent with no hookups**

6 miles northeast of Mt. Ida on State 27, 6 miles east on State 188, then 4 miles east on gravel road.

**Facilities:** Vault toilets, water, boat ramp. (Open year-round)

**BRADY MOUNTAIN (E-4) 57 RV/Tent with E; 17 Tent** .................................................... ♿

10 miles west of Hot Springs on U.S. 270, then 7 miles north on access road.

**Facilities:** Flush toilets, water, hot showers, boat ramp, dump station, nature trail, restaurant, marina, store, playground, scenic overlook, scuba shop, pavilion, lodge. (Open year-round) User's fee charged.

**BUCKVILLE (E-3) 6 RV/Tent with no hookups**

10 miles northeast of Hot Springs on State 7, then west for 18 miles on State 298, then 7 miles south on Buckville Rd.

**Facilities:** Vault toilets, water, boat ramp, beach. (Open year-round)

**CRYSTAL SPRINGS (E-3) 53 RV/Tent with W/E; 21 Tent** .................................................... ♿

15 miles west of Hot Springs on U.S. 270, then 2 miles north on access road.

**Facilities:** Flush toilets, water, hot showers, boat ramp, dump station, picnic sites, 2 pavilions, day use swimming beach with change house and playground, restaurant, marina, store, cottages. (Open year-round) User's fee charged.

**DENBY POINT (E-3) 58 RV/Tent with E; 9 Tent**

8 miles east of Mt. Ida on U.S. 270, then 1 mile north on access road.

**Facilities:** Flush and chemical toilets, water, hot showers, dump station, 4 picnic sites, amphitheater, nature trails, restaurant, marina, 2 group camping areas (6-site and 7-site reservations accepted), swimming beach, lodge. (Open year-round) User's fee charged.

**HIGHWAY 27 (E-3) 19 RV/Tent with E.**

9 miles northeast of Mt. Ida on State 27.

**Facilities:** Flush toilets, water, boat ramp, trailer dump station, beach, restaurant, marina, ballfield, horseshoe pits. (Open year-round) User's fee charged.

**IRONS FORK (E-3) 5 RV/Tent with no hookups**

8 miles east of Story on State 289, then 1.5 miles on access road.

**Facilities:** Vault toilets, water, boat ramp. (Open year-round)

**JOPLIN (MOUNTAIN HARBOR) (E-3) 65 RV/Tent with no hookups**

11 miles east of Mt. Ida on U.S. 270, then 2 miles north on access road.

**Facilities:** Flush toilets, water, showers, boat ramp, dump station, picnic sites, beach, restaurant, marina, lodge. (Open year-round) User's fee charged Apr.-Sept.

Photo by M. Cates

**LENA LANDING (E-4) 10 RV/Tent with no hookups**
12 miles west of Blue Springs on State 298, 1 mile south on Navy Landing Road.
**Facilities:** Flush toilets, water, boat ramp, trailer dump station, restaurant, marina, convenience store, scuba shop. (Partially open year-round) User's fee charged Apr.-Sept.

**LITTLE FIR (E-3) 25 RV/Tent with no hookups**
6 miles northeast of Mt. Ida on State 27, then 9 miles east on State 188.
**Facilities:** Flush toilets, water, boat ramp, trailer dump station, marina. (Open year-round) User's fee charged Apr.-Sept.

**STEPHENS PARK (E-4) 9 RV/Tent with E**
At Blakely Mountain Dam, 1 mile west of Mt. Pine on State 227.
**Facilities:** Flush toilets, water, boat ramp, pavilion, 8 picnic sites, playground. (Open year-round) User's fee charged.

**TOMPKINS BEND (SHANGRI LA) (E-3) 47 RV/Tent with E; 16 RV/Tent with no hookups; 14 Tent**
10 miles east of Mt. Ida on U.S. 270, then 3 miles north on access road.
**Facilities:** Flush toilets, water, hot showers, boat ramp, dump station, amphitheater, restaurant, marina, cabins. (Open year-round) User's fee charged.

**TWIN CREEK (E-3) 15 RV/Tent with no hookups**
8 miles east of Mt. Ida on U.S. 270, then 1 mile north on access road.
**Facilities:** Flush toilets, water, boat ramp, trailer dump station, swimming beach. (Open year-round)

## MILLWOOD LAKE AREA

**Millwood Lake is located on State 32, 9 miles east of Ashdown, in the lowlands of southwestern Arkansas. Of the 29,500 acres inundated by the lake, approximately 6,000 acres are cleared. On the remaining 23,500 acres, the dense growth of timber and brush was left standing, providing an excellent habitat for the wide variety of fish native to this area. Cleared boat lanes, old roads and creek and river channels provide access to the favorite fishing places on the lake.**

**FOR INFORMATION: Resident Manager, Route 1, Box 37A, Ashdown, AR 71822, (501) 898-3343.**

**BEARD'S BLUFF (G-2) 33 RV/Tent with E; 1 RV/Tent with no hookups** ............ ♿
13 miles east of Ashdown. Recreation area is upstream of the east embankment of the dam.
**Facilities:** Flush toilets, water (Feb. 28-Nov. 1), showers, dump station, boat ramp, beach, amphitheater, playground, overlook, pavilion. (Open year-round; no electricity Nov. 1-Feb. 27) User's fee charged Mar. 1-Oct. 31. Gate attendants.

**BEARD'S LAKE (G-2) 5 RV/Tent with W/E** ............ ♿
13 miles east of Ashdown. Recreation area is downstream of the east embankment of the dam.
**Facilities:** Vault toilets, water, boat ramp courtesy dock, 4 picnic sites, playground. (Open year-round no electricity Nov. 1-Feb. 27). User's fee charged Mar. 1-Oct 31.

**COTTONSHED LANDING (G-2) 50 RV/Tent with E**
8 miles southwest of Mineral Springs and Tollette.
**Facilities:** Vault toilets, water, showers, fish cleaning station, boat ramp, dump station, playground. (Open year-round; no electricity Nov. 1-Feb. 27) User's fee charged Mar. 1-Oct. 31. Gate attendants.

**PARALOMA LANDING (G-2) 34 RV/Tent with E**
1.5 miles south of Paraloma on access road.
**Facilities:** Vault toilets, water, boat ramp, dump station. (Open year-round; no electricity Nov. 1-Feb. 27) User's fee charged Mar. 1-Oct. 31.

**RIVER RUN EAST (G-2) 7 RV/Tent with no hookups**
Below Millwood Dam on State 32, 12 miles east of Ashdown.
**Facilities:** Vault toilets, boat ramp. (Open year-round)

**RIVER RUN WEST (G-2) 4 RV/Tent with no hookups**
Below Millwood Dam on State 32, 10 miles east of Ashdown.
**Facilities:** Vault toilets, boat ramp. (Open year-round)

**SARATOGA LANDING (G-2) 38 RV/Tent with no hookups**
1 mile south, then 1 mile west of Saratoga.
**Facilities:** Vault toilets, water, boat ramp, pavilion, fish cleaning station, playground. (Open year-round)

**WHITE CLIFFS (G-2) 18 RV/Tent with no hookups**
6 miles south of State 27 on gravel road.

**Facilities:** Vault toilets, boat ramp, archaeological site. (Open year-round)

## NIMROD LAKE AREA

**Located on the Forche LaFave River in the Ouachita highlands of west central Arkansas, this small lake has long been known for its crappie fishing. Hiking and hunting are excellent in season.**

**FOR INFORMATION: Resident Manager, Plainview, AR 72857, (501) 272-4324.**

**CARDEN POINT (E-4) 9 RV/Tent with no hookups**
6 miles east of Plainview on State 60.
**Facilities:** Vault toilet, water, boat ramp. (Open year-round)

**CARTER COVE (E-4) 16 RV/Tent with E**
3 miles east of Plainview on State 60, then 1 mile south on access road.
**Facilities:** Vault toilet, water, boat ramp, dump station, beach, pavilion, playground, fish cleaning station. (Open year-round) User's fee charged.

**COUNTY LINE (E-4) 20 RV/Tent with E**
6 miles east of Plainview on State 60, then .25 mile south on access road.
**Facilities:** Flush toilets, water, hot showers, boat ramp, dump station, beach, fish cleaning station, playground. (Open year-round) User's fee charged.

**PROJECT POINT (E-4) 6 RV/Tent with E**
8 miles southeast of Ola on Highway 7, then .25 mile west on Highway 60 to access road.
**Facilities:** Vault toilets, water. (Open Apr.-Nov.) Entire campground may be reserved. User's fee charged.

**QUARRY COVE (E-4) 31 RV/Tent with E**
8 miles southeast of Ola on State 7, then .5 mile west on State 60 to access road.
**Facilities:** Flush toilets, hot showers, playground, water, boat ramp, dump station, beach, pavilion, amphitheater, fish cleaning station. (Open year-round) User's fee charged.

**RIVER ROAD (E-4) 15 RV/Tent with E**
8.25 miles southeast of Ola on State 7, then .33 mile on River Road below dam.
**Facilities:** Flush toilets, water, boat ramp, dump station, pavilion, playground. (Open year-round) User's fee charged.

**SUNLIGHT BAY (E-4) 28 RV/Tent with E**
1.5 miles east of Plainview on State 60, then 2.33 miles southwest on gravel access road.
**Facilities:** Vault toilets, water, boat ramp, dump station, pavilion, playground. (Open year-round) User's fee charged.

## NORFORK LAKE AREA

**Located on the North Fork River in the Ozark highlands of north central Arkansas and southern Missouri, this crystal clear lake is a favorite of scuba divers. The wooded hills surrounding the lake abound in deer and turkey and other small game. Hiking, all types of water sports, and hunting in season are featured attractions.**

**FOR INFORMATION: Resident Engineer, P.O. Box 369, Mt. Home, AR 72653, (501) 425-2700.**

**BIDWELL POINT (A-5) 48 RV/Tent with E**
9 miles northeast of Mt. Home on U.S. 62 then 2 miles north on State 101, cross lake on bridge and take first access road to the right.
**Facilities:** Vault toilets, water, hot showers, dump station, beach, pavilion, playground. (Open Apr.-Oct.) User's fee charged.

**BUZZARD ROOST (A-5) Camping By Permit Only**
1 mile northeast of Mt. Home on U.S. 62, then 4 miles on Highway 178. (Camping by permit only which may be obtained by calling, writing, or visiting the Resident Engineer's Office, (501) 425-2700.)
**Facilities:** Boat ramp, rest rooms, marina, marine dump station.

**CRANFIELD (A-5) 74 RV/Tent with E** ............ ♿
5.5 miles northeast of Mt. Home on U.S. 62, then 2 miles north on Baxter County Road 34.
**Facilities:** Vault toilets, water, hot showers, dump station, beach, change shelter, marina, pavilion, playground. (Open Apr.-Oct.) User's fee charged.

**GAMALIEL (A-5) 64 RV/Tent with E**
9 miles northeast of Mt. Home on U.S. 62, then 4.5 miles north on State 101, then 3 miles southeast on Baxter County

Road 42.
**Facilities:** Vault and flush toilets, water, hot showers, boat ramp, beach, group pavilion, playground, marina. (Open Mar.-Nov.) User's fee charged. Reservations accepted.

**GEORGE'S COVE (A-5) 12 RV/Tent with no hookups**
6.5 miles southeast of Mt. Home on State 5, then 3 miles east on State 342.
**Facilities:** Vault toilets, water, boat ramp, dump station, beach. (Open year-round)

**HENDERSON (A-5) 38 RV/Tent with E**
10 miles east of Mt. Home on U.S. 62, cross lake on bridge and turn left.
**Facilities:** Vault toilets, water, boat ramp, dump station, beach, pavilion, marina, marine and trailer dump stations. (Open Apr.-Oct.) User's fee charged.

**HOWARD COVE (A-5) 12 RV/Tent with E**
9 miles northeast of Mt. Home on U.S. 62, then north 3 miles on State 101, then east on access road.
**Facilities:** Vault toilets, water, marina and marine dump station. (Open year-round) User's fee charged. Park operated by concessionaire. Reservations accepted.

**JORDAN (A-5) 33 RV/Tent with E; 7 Tent**
3 miles east of Norfork Dam on State 177, then 3 miles north on Baxter County Road 64.
**Facilities:** Vault toilets, water, beach, pavilion, marina. (Open Apr.-Oct.) User's fee charged.

**PANTHER BAY (A-5) 15 RV/Tent with E; 13 RV/Tent with no hookups**
9 miles east of Mt. Home on U.S. 62, then 1 mile north on State 101.
**Facilities:** Vault toilets, water, boat ramp, marina, trailer and marine dump stations, beach. (Open Apr.-Oct.) User's fee charged.

**QUARRY COVE (A-5) 52 RV/Tent with E; 28 RV/Tent with no hookups** ............ ♿
3 miles northeast of Norfork on State 5, then 2 miles east on State 177.
**Facilities:** Flush toilets, water, hot showers, trailer dump stations, marina, playground, beach, pavilion. (Open Mar.-Nov.) User's fee charged. Reservations accepted.

**RED BANK (A-5) 12 RV/Tent with no hookups**
9 miles northeast of Mt. Home on U.S. 62, then north 5 miles on State 101, then 3 miles west on access road.
**Facilities:** Vault toilets, water, boat ramp. (Open Apr.-Oct.) User's fee charged.

**ROBINSON POINT (A-5) 102 RV/Tent with E**
9 miles east of Mt. Home on U.S. 62, then 2.5 miles south on Baxter County Road 279.
**Facilities:** Vault toilets, water, hot showers, dump station, beach, change shelter, pavilion, hiking trail, playground. (Open Apr.-Oct.) User's fee charged.

**TRACY (A-5) 7 RV/Tent with no hookups**
6.5 miles southeast of Mt. Home on State 5, then 3 miles on State 341.
**Facilities:** Vault toilets, water, marina, marine dump station. (Open year-round)

**WOODS POINT (A-5) 11 RV/Tent with no hookups**
16 miles east of Mt. Home on U.S. 62, then 9 miles south on access road.
**Facilities:** Vault toilets, water, boat ramp, dump station. (Open Apr.-Oct.) User's fee charged.

## OZARK LAKE AREA

**As the Arkansas River flows through the state, it reaches its northernmost point in a sweeping bend. Now a part of Ozark Lake, this big bend was called "Aux Arc" by the French and it is from the French that the lake and the nearby city of Ozark received their names. Fishing, camping, and other recreational opportunities may be found within and around the lake's 173 miles of shoreline.**

**FOR INFORMATION: Lake Manager, Rt. 1, Box 267X, Ozark, AR 72949, (501) 667-2129 or 1-800-844-2129.**

**AUX ARC (pronounced Ozark) (C-2) 60 RV/Tent with E; 4 RV/Tent with no hookups**
1.3 miles south of Ozark on State 23, then left 1 mile on State 309, and then left on access road.
**Facilities:** Flush toilets, water, boat ramp, dump station, warm showers, pavilions, playground. (Open year-round) User's fee charged.

**CITADEL BLUFF (C-2) 36 RV/Tent with no hookups**
1.2 miles north of Cecil on State 41.

**Facilities:** Vault toilets, water, boat ramp, pavilion. (Open year-round) User's fee charged Apr.-Oct.

**CLEAR CREEK (C-2) 31 RV/Tent with E; 16 RV/Tent with no hookups**
5.2 miles south of Alma on State 162, then left on paved highway 3.6 miles.
**Facilities:** Flush toilets, water, warm showers, boat ramp, dump station, pavilion. (Open year-round) User's fee charged.

**LEE CREEK (C-1) 10 RV/Tent with no hookups**
From U.S. 64-71 in Van Buren, travel Main Street west, then south to floodwall, turn right to park.
**Facilities:** Flush toilets, water, warm showers (Apr.-Sep.), dump station, boat ramp, pavilion, 4 picnic sites. (Open Apr.-Oct.) User's fee charged.

**RIVER RIDGE (C-2) 24 RV/Tent with no hookups**
12 miles west of Cecil on State 96, then right 1.5 miles on county road.
**Facilities:** Vault toilets, water, boat ramp, historical marker (Open year-round)

**SPRINGHILL (C-2) 38 RV/Tent with E; 10 RV/Tent with no hookups**
Park entrance located immediately south of the State 59 Arkansas River bridge 8 miles south of Van Buren.
**Facilities:** Flush toilets, water, warm showers, boat ramp, playground, pavilions. (Open year-round) User's fee charged.

**VACHE GRASSE (C-2) 29 RV/Tent with no hookups**
2.4 miles west of Lavaca on State 255, then right 1.2 miles on paved county road.
**Facilities:** Flush toilets, water, boat ramp, pavilion. (Open year-round)

**VINE PRAIRIE (C-2) 13 RV/Tent with E; 7 RV/Tent with no hookups**
1.7 miles south of Mulberry on State 215.
**Facilities:** Flush and vault toilets, water, boat ramp, dump station, pavilion. (Open year-round) User's fee charged Apr.-Oct.

**WHITE OAK (C-2) 7 RV/Tent with no hookups**
5.4 miles east of Mulberry on U.S. 64, then right on paved county road 1.7 miles.
**Facilities:** Vault toilets, boat ramp. (Open year-round)

Photo by M. Cates

## TABLE ROCK LAKE AREA

**Although the main body of Table Rock lies in the Ozarks of southwest Missouri, a segment dips into northwest Arkansas where Boone and Carroll Counties meet. Like Beaver and Bull Shoals, Table Rock is another White River Reservoir serving water enthusiasts and fishermen from throughout mid-America.**

**FOR INFORMATION: Resident Engineer, Branson, MO 65616, (417) 334-4101.**

**CRICKET CREEK (A-3) 21 RV/Tent with E; 16 RV/Tent with no hookups** ........................................................................ ♿
6 miles southwest of Ridgedale, MO, on State 14.
**Facilities:** Flush and vault toilets, water, hot showers, boat ramp, trailer and marine dump stations, swim beach, boat and motor rental. (Open Apr.-Oct.) User's fee charged.

# PRIVATE & MUNICIPAL CAMPGROUNDS

**ALMA**

**KOA-Fort Smith/Alma (120 sites)** -- 3 miles north of Alma on U. S. 71, Rt. 3, Box 422, Alma, AR 72921 -- Phone: (501) 632-2704

**ARKADELPHIA**

**KOA-Arkadelphia (62 sites)** -- Exit 78, Jct. I-30 & Highway 7, 221 Frost Road, Arkadelphia, AR 71923 -- Phone: (501) 246-4922

**BALD KNOB**

**Barnes RV Park (30 sites)** -- Exit 55 S. On U. S. 67-167, 1.5 miles on Highway 365 South, 1601 Hwy. 367 N, Bald Knob, AR 72010 -- Phone (501) 724-5026

**BEAVER**

**Beaver Town RV Park (39 sites)** -- 6 miles north of Eureka Springs on State 187 at Beaver on Table Rock Lake, Box 0025, Beaver, AR 72613 -- Phone: (501) 253-5700

**BENTON**

**Benton RV Park (105 sites)** -- 19 miles west of Little Rock on I-30, 19719 I-30, Benton, AR 72015 -- Phone: (501) 778-1244

**Salem Pines RV Park (113 sites)** -- I-30 Exit 121, 15 miles west of Little Rock, Rt. 1, Box 772, Benton, AR 72015 -- Phone: (501) 794-2950

**BLUE MOUNTAIN**

**Little Bear Cabin & Campgrounds (18 sites)** -- 1 mile south and .5 mile east of Blue Mountain on Highway 10, Box 64, Blue Mountain, AR 72826 -- Phone: (501) 947-2363 or (501) 947-2265

**CALICO ROCK**

**Cedar Ridge RV Park (20 sites)** -- Junction Highways 56 and 5, Box 236, Calico Rock, AR 72519 -- Phone: (501) 297-4282

**CLINTON**

**Whispering Pines Camping Park (65 sites)** -- 7 miles north on U. S. 65, HC-63, Box 157, Clinton, AR 72031 -- Phone: (501) 745-4291

**COTTER**

**White River campground (110 sites)** -- U. S. 62B west of cotter, Box 99, Cotter, AR 72626 -- Phone: (501) 453-2299

**DOGPATCH**

**Mill Creek Campground (35 sites)** -- Highway 7 south, 2.5 miles south of Dogpatch, HC 73, Box 46, Dogpatch, AR 72648 -- Phone: (501) 446-5507

**DOVER**

**Mack's Pines & Cabins (18 sites)** -- 20 miles north of I-40 on Highway 7, HCR 30, Box 29, Dover, AR 72837 -- Phone: (501) 331-3261

**EL DORADO**

**Country Living Park (23 sites)** -- 2 miles south of Highway 82 Bypass on U.S. 167, 100 Country Living Park, El Dorado, AR 71730 -- Phone: (501) 863-6565

**EMMET**

**Lazy W Overnight Campground (20 sites)** -- I-30 at Emmet Exit 36, Box 206, Emmet, AR 71835 -- Phone: (501) 777-2980

**EUREKA SPRINGS**

**Myers' Beaver Dam RV Park (15 sites)** -- 8 miles west of Eureka Springs on U.S. 62 and one mile south on Highway 187, Rt. 2, Box 406, Eureka Springs, AR 72632 -- Phone: (501) 253-6196

**Dinosaur World (28 sites)** -- 8 miles west of Eureka Springs, Rt. 2 Box 408, Eureka Springs, AR 72632 -- Phone: (501) 253-8113

**Fox Fire Camping Resort & Cabins (120 sites)** -- Junction Highways 12 and 45, Rt. 1, Box 198, Hindsville, AR 72738 -- Phone: (501) 789-2122

**Green Tree Lodge & RV Park (24 sites)** -- On U. S. 62 W., 4 miles west of The Great Passion Play, Rt. 2, Box 130, Eureka Springs, AR 72632 -- Phone: (501) 253-8807

**Kettle Kampground (50 sites)** -- On U.S. 62 East - .25 mile east of Passion Play entrance, Rt. 4, Box 615, Eureka Springs, AR 72632, Phone: (501) 253-9100

**KOA-Eureka Springs (100 sites)** -- 5 miles west of Eureka Springs on U. S. 62, then .75 mile south on Highway 187, Rt. 2 Box 331, Eureka Springs, AR 72632 -- Phone: (501) 253-8036

**Lake Leatherwood (30 sites)** -- 3 miles west of Eureka Springs on U. S. 62, P.O. Box 230, Eureka Springs, AR 72632 -- Phone: (501) 253-8624

**Pine Haven Campground (82 sites)** -- On U. S. 52 East in Eureka Springs, Rt. 1, Box 447, Eureka Springs, AR 72632 -- Phone: (501) 253-9052

**Wanderlust RV Park (81 sites)** -- U. S. 62 East, on Passion Play Road, Rt. 1, Box 946, Eureka Springs, AR 72632 -- Phone: (501) 253-7385 or (800) 253-7385

**FAYETTEVILLE**

**Fayetteville RV Park (12 sites)** -- 2306 S. School Street, Fayetteville, AR 72701 -- Phone: (501) 443-5864

**FORDYCE**

**Lavelock RV Park/MHP (15 sites)** -- Highway 8 East, 1008 Morton, Fordyce, AR 71742 -- Phone: (501) 352-5067

**FORT SMITH**

**Terry Campground RV Park (30 sites)** -- 4520 Plum, Ft. Smith, AR 72904 -- Phone: (501) 782-2401

**GILBERT**

**Buffalo Camping and Canoeing/Gilbert General Store (16 sites)** -- 30 miles south of Harrison on U. S. 65, then 3 miles on 333 to Gilbert, P.O. Box 504, Gilbert, AR 72636 -- Phone: (501) 439-2888

**GOULD**

**Jones RV Park & Landing (60 sites)** -- 7 miles east of Gould on Highway 114 on Douglas Lake, Rt. 2, Box 652, Gould, AR 71643 -- Phone: (501) 263-4074

**HACKETT**

**Sugarloaf Lake Resort (24 sites)** -- 25 miles south of Ft. Smith off Hwy. 45,

8314 Northshore Dr., Hackett, AR 72937 -- Phone: (501) 639-2537

**HARDY**

**HardyCamper Park (99 sites)** -- Downtown - on Spring River, Rt. 2, Box 50, Hardy, AR 72542 -- Phone: (501) 856-2356

**Kamp Kierl Camping & Canoeing Outfitters (150 sites)** -- On Highway 63, 1 mile from Hardy on Spring River, P.O. Box 365, Hardy, AR 72542 -- Phone: (501) 856-3747

**HARRISON**

**Harrison Village Campground (80 sites)** -- 3.5 miles south of Harrison on Highway 65, Rt. 4 Box 15, Harrison, AR 72601 -- Phone: (501) 743-3388

**High Country Pines Campgrounds & RV Park (20 sites)** -- 5 miles south of Harrison on Highway 7; 3 miles from Dogpatch, Rt. 8, Box 319B, Harrison, AR 72601 -- Phone: (501) 743-4325

**Ozark Safari Camp (75 sites)** -- 7 miles south of Harrison on Highway 7, then 1 mile east on Highway 206, Rt. 1 , Box 249A, Harrison, AR 72601 -- Phone: (501) 743-2343

**Parkway RV Travel Park (26 sites)** -- 6 miles south of Harrison on Hwy. 7 South; 3 miles north of Dogpatch, Rt. 1, Box 231, Harrison, AR 72601 -- Phone: (501) 743-2198

**HEBER SPRINGS**

**Lindsey's Rainbow Resort (40 sites)** -- On Rainbow Rd. Off Highway 25 North, 350 Rainbow Rd., Heber Springs, AR 72543 -- Phone: (501) 362-3139 or (501) 362-8857

**Lobo Landing resort (50 sites)** -- Highway 337 South, 3525 Libby Rd., Heber Springs, AR 72543 -- Phone: (501) 362-5801 or (800) 659-8330

**Red River Trout Dock and Campground (20 sites)** -- Highways 110 and 210 east, 285 Furreson Rd., Heber Springs, AR 72543 -- Phone: (501) 362-2197

**Swinging Bridge Trout Dock & Campground (12 sites)** -- Highway 110 east, 100 Swinging Bridge Rd., Heber Springs, Ar 72543 -- Phone: (501) 362-3327

**HENDERSON**

**Wilderness Point Camping Resort (400 sites)** -- 12 miles east of Mt. Home on U. S. 62, P.O. Box 09, Henderson, AR 72544-0009 -- Phone: (501) 488-5340

**HETH**

**KOA-West Memphis/Shell Lake (74 sites)** -- I-40 at Highway 149, Rt. 1, Heth, AR 72346 -- Phone: (501) 657-2422

**HOPE**

**Fair Park RV Park (400 sites)** -- Exit 30 off I-30, south on Hwy. 4 to U. S. 67, west two blocks, then south on Hwy. 174 five blocks, then west on Park Drive. Follow signs. Hope, AR 71801 -- Phone: (501) 777-7500

**HOT SPRINGS**

**All Season Mobile & RV Park (10 sites)** -- Highway 7 South, 4.5 miles south of Hot Springs Mall, 6507 Central Ave., Hot Springs, AR 71913 -- Phone: (501) 525-1248

**Camp Lake Hamilton (40 sites)** -- Highway 7 South, 6191 Central Ave. South, Hot Springs, AR 71913 -- Phone: (501) 525-8204

**Hot Springs Nat'l Park KOA (112 sites)** -- U. S. 70 East, 838 McClendon Rd., Hot Springs, AR 71901 -- Phone: (501) 624-5912

**Lakeside Trailer Park & Cottages (20 sites)** -- Highway 7 South, one mile from Hot Springs Mall, 451 Lakeland Dr., Hot Springs, AR 71913 -- Phone: (501) 525-8878

**Mill Pond Village (20 sites)** -- 5 miles from Hot Springs Mall on Highway 7 South, 1 Preakness Dr., Hot Springs, AR 71913 -- Phone: (501) 525-3959

**Phil's Trailer City (30 sites)** -- Highway 7 to Majextic Hotel, then 9 blocks west on Whittington Ave., 938 Whittington, Hot Springs, AR 71901 -- Phone: (501) 623-3062

**Rovin' Ramblers Mobile & RV Park (15 sites)** -- 15 miles southwest of Hot Springs, U. S. 70, Rt. 1, Box 180, Bonnerdale, AR 71933 -- Phone: (501) 356-4412

**Shoreline Campground (23 sites)** -- Highway 7 South on Lake Hamilton, 5321 Central Ave., Hot Springs, AR 71913 -- Phone: (501) 525-1902

**Wagon Wheel Campground (62 sites)** -- U. S. 270 West on Lake Hamilton - Ouachita River Bridge, 205 Treasure Isle Rd., Hot Springs, AR 71913 -- Phone: (501) 767-6852

**Wester Village (78 sites)** -- 2345 E. Grand, Hot Springs, AR 71901 -- Phone: (501) 623-5559

**JASPER**

**Heritage Woodstock Farm (10 sites)** -- 5 miles east on Highway 74, HCR 72, Box 24, Jasper, AR 72641 -- Phone: (501) 446-2281

**JONESBORO**

**Craighead Forest Park Campground (26 sites)** -- Approximately 3.5 miles south of Jonesboro on Highway 141, 1212 S. Church, Jonesboro, AR 72401 -- Phone: (501) 933-4604

**Perkins RV Park (13 sites)** -- U. S. 63 bypass exit S. on Caraway Road, west on service road .5 mile, 1821 E. Parker, Jonesboro, AR 72401 -- Phone: (501) 935-4152

**LAKEVIEW**

**Gunga-La Trout Dock (7 sites)** -- White River Road, Rt. 1, Box 147, Lakeview, AR 72642 -- Phone: (501) 431-5606

**Riverside Mobile & RV Park (40 sites)** -- .3 mile from Bull Shoals State Park on White River Road, P.O. Box 167, Lakeview, AR 72642 -- Phone: (501) 431-8260

**LAKE VILLAGE**

**Chicot County Park (98 sites)** -- Across Lake Chicot from Lake Village, Rt. 884, Box 250, Lake Village, AR 71653 -- Phone: (501) 265-3500

**Pecan Grove RV Park (42 sites)** -- 3 miles south of U. S. 82 and U. S. 65 Jct., P.O. Box 9, Lake Village, AR 71653 -- Phone: (501) 265-3005

**LITTLE ROCK**

**Sands RV Park (21 sites)** -- Chicot Road S. & I-30, 8123 Chicot Rd., Little Rock, AR 72209 -- Phone: (501) 565-7491

**MAMMOTH SPRING**

**Many Islands Camp & Canoe Rental (150 sites)** -- Rt. 2, Mammoth Spring, AR 72553 -- Phone: (501) 856-3451

**MARION**

**Best Holiday Trav-L Park (100 sites)** -- 7 miles north of West Memphis on I-55, Rt. 2 Box 1, Holiday Lane, Marion, AR 72364 -- Phone: (501) 739-4801

**MENA**

**KOA-Mena (70 sites)** -- 5 miles south of Mena on U. S. 71 & Hwy. 59, Rt. 4 Box 612AA, Mena, AR 71953 -- Phone: (501) 394-3021

**MORRILTON**

**KOA-Morrilton/Conway (86 sites)** -- at Exit 107 off I-40, Rt. 1, Box 270-30, Morrilton, AR 72110 -- Phone: (501) 354-8262

**MOUNTAIN HOME**

**White Buffalo Resort (32 sites)** -- 14 miles southwest of Mountain Home on Highway 126 S. At Buffalo City, Rt. 2 Box 438, Mountain Home, AR 72653 -- Phone: (501) 425-8555

**MOUNTAIN PINE**

**Cozy Acres Resort (28 sites)** -- Below Blakely Dam on Lake Hamilton, 1100 Cozy Acres Road, Mountain Pine, AR 71956 -- Phone: (501) 767-5023

**MOUNTAIN VIEW**

**Blue Sky RV Park (116 sites)** -- 3 miles north of Mountain View at Junction of Highways 5, 9, & 14, HC 72, Box 135, Mountain View, AR 72560 -- Phone: (501) 269-8132

**Green Acres RV Park (72 sites)** -- .5 mile north on Highways 5, (, & 14, Rt. 72, Box 43, Mountain View, AR 72560 -- Phone: (501) 269-3497

**Holiday Mountain Resort (113 sites)** -- 5 miles north of Mt. View on Highway 14, HC 72 Box 10, Mt. View, AR 72560 -- Phone: (501) 585-2231

**Ozark RV Park and Primitive Camping (36 sites)** -- Adjacent to Ozark Folk Center, HC 72, Box 540 Mountain View, AR 72560 -- Phone: (501) 269-2542

**Shady Grove RV Park (30 sites)** -- .25 mile north of Mountain View at Junction of Highways 5, 9, & 14, HC 72, Box 29, Mountain View, AR 72560 -- Phone: (501) 269-4588

**Whitewater Travel Park (62 sites)** -- .5 mile south of the Ozark Folk Center next to City Park, or 2 blocks north of downtown court square, P.O. Box 446, Mountain View, AR 72560 -- Phone: (501) 269-8047

**MT. IDA**

**Mt. Ida Trailer Park (5 sites)** -- Highway 270, HC, Box 67-R, Mt. Ida, AR 71957 -- Phone: (501) 867-2682

**MURFREESBORO**

**Miner's Camping (33 sites)** -- 2 miles south of Murfreesboro on Hwy. 301, Rt. Box 365, Murfreesboro, AR 71958 -- Phone: (501) 285-2722

**NORTH LITTLE ROCK**

**Burns Park Campground (37 sites)** -- Off I-40 at Burns Park Exit 150, S. Of I-40, Burns Park, North Little Rock, AR 72118 -- Phone: (501) 753-0086

**KOA-North Little Rock (100 sites)** -- From I-40 Exit 148-Crystal Hill Road, then southwest 1 mile. From I-30 take I-430 to Exit 12-Crystal Hill Road, then .5 mile east, 7820 Crystal Hill Road, North Little Rock, AR 72118 -- Phone: (501) 758-4598 or 1-800-289-4598 in-state.

**OMAHA**

**Ozark Vue RV Park & Campground (32 sites)** -- 12 miles north of Harrison on Highway 65, Rt. 1, Box 126-D, Omaha, AR 72662 -- Phone: (501) 426-5166

**OLD JOE**

**Red's Landing Campground (20 sites)** -- 3 miles south of Norfork on Hwy. 5 S, HC 62, Box 362, County Rd. 68, Old Joe, AR 72658 -- Phone: (501) 499-7574

**PALESTINE**

**P&L Campground (20 sites)** -- Nest to I-40 south side Exit 233, P. O. Box 10, Palestine, AR 72372 -- Phone: (501) 581-2744

**PELSOR**

**The Red Barn (22 sites)** -- 40 miles south of Harrison and 40 miles north of Russellville on Hwy. 7, HCR 30, Box 96C, Pelsor, AR 72856 -- Phone: (501) 294-5284

**PERRYVILLE**

**Coffee Creek Landing (50 sites)** -- On Highway 300 at Harris Break Dam, Rt. 2, Box 27E, Perrybille, AR 72126 -- Phone: (501) 889-2745

**Vurl's Landing & Campgrounds (80 sites)** -- 2.5 miles south of Perrybille off Highways 9 & 10 at Harris Brake Lake, Rt. 2, Box 184, Perryville, AR 72126 -- Phone: (501) 889-2829

**PINE BLUFF**

**Hestand Stadium Fairgrounds (105 sites)** -- 1 block north of U. S. 65 - 410 N. Blake, 711 W. 6th, Pine Bluff, AR 71601 -- Phone: (501) 534-4424 or 535-2900

**Pine Bluff Convention Center (150 sites)** -- One Convention Center Plaza, Pine Bluff, AR 71601 -- Phone: (501) 536-7600

**PONCA**

**Lost Valley Canoe & Lodge & General Store (25 sites)** -- 22 miles west of Harrison on State Hwy. 43, Ponca, AR 72670 -- Phone: (501) 861-5522

**ROGERS**

**Beaver Lake Safari Campground (100 sites)** -- Highway 303 - Rocky Branch Area, Rt. 6, Box 228, Rogers, AR 72756 -- Phone (501) 925-1333

**KOA-Rogers/Pea Ridge (45 sites)** -- U. S. 62 east of Rogers, P.O. Box 456, Rogers, Ar 72756 -- Phone (501) 451-8566

**Monte Ne Beaver Lake Resort (90 sites)** -- 5.5 miles fromrogers on Hwy. 94 East, Rt. 1, Box 756, Rogers, AR 72756 -- Phone: (501) 925-1265

**RUSSELLVILLE**

**Lakeside Resort & Motel (35 sites)** -- Highway 7 north, Rt. 7 N., Box 35, Russellville, AR 72801 -- Phone: (501) 968-9715

**Mission RV Park (45 sites)** -- 4 miles west on U. S. 64 at west end of bridge, Rt. 3, Highway 64 West, Box 24, Russellville, AR 72801 -- Phone: (501) 967-3576

**SHERIDAN**

**Southland Village (14 sites)** -- .5 mile from downtown Sheridan on Highway 167 S., Rt. 4, Box 11D-4, Sheridan, AR 72150 -- Phone: (501) 942-3907

**SHIRLEY**

**Golden Pond RV Park (40 sites)** -- Highways 16 and 330, P.O.a Box 226, Shirley, AR 72153 -- Phone: (501) 723-8212

**SILOAM SPRINGS**

**Smith's Landing (50 sites)** -- From Highway 412 take 43 N. To Mt. Olive road, follow signs, Rt. 2, Box 675, Siloam Springs, AR 72761 -- Phone: (501) 524-3072

**SPRINGDALE**

**Motor Inn Trailer Park (24 sites)** -- Highway 71B North, Rt. 7, Box 102, Springdale, AR 72764 -- Phone: (501) 751-1562

**Whisler Park (64 sites)** -- Approximately .5 mile north of Highway 412E on Highway 265, State 265, Springdale, AR 72764 -- Phone: (501) 751-9081

**TEXARKANA**

**KOA-Texarkana (100 sites)** -- I-30 Mandeville Exit 7, Rt. 8, Box 254, Texarkana, AR 75502 -- Phone: (501) 772-0751

**VAN BUREN**

**Oaks Campground (12 sites)** -- 2 miles west of Alma on U. S. 64-71, 6918 Alma Highway, Van Buren, AR 72956 -- Phone: (501) 632-2524

**Circle G Campground (28 sites)** -- North 1 block off I-40 on Highway 59, Rt. 2 Box 4, Rena Road, Van Buren, AR 72956 -- Phone: (501) 471-1272

**WEST HELENA/HELENA**

**Town & Country Mobile & RV Park (12 sites)** -- 1.5 miles north of West Helena on Hwy. 242, P.O. Box 2595, West Helena, AR 72390 -- Phone: (501) 572-5341

**WEST MEMPHIS**

**Tom Sawyer's Mississippi River RV Park (38 sites)** -- 7th St. exit off I-40 and I-55, follow signs, 1719 E. Broadway, West Memphis, AR 72301 -- Phone: (501) 735-9770

**WINSLOW**

**Silver Leaf Campark (24 sites)** -- 20 miles south of Fayetteville on U. S. 71, Rt. 1 Box 436, Winslow, AR 72959 -- Phone: (501) 634-5861

**"Y" CITY**

**"Y" City Mountain Inn (50 sites)** -- 60 miles south of Ft. Smith on U. S. 71, Rt. 69, Box 199,Boles, AR 72926 -- Phone: (501) 577-2489

**YELLVILLE**

**Sherwood Forest Campground (45 sites)** -- 5 miles south of Yellville on Highway 14E, HCR 66, Box 260, Yellville, AR 72687 -- Phone: (501) 449-4260

Introductory photograph courtesy of Eureka
Photos in Camping and Lakes sections courtesy of Looking Glass Graphics
(501) 285-2244

# The Civil War in Arkansas

You can trace the heritage of the Civil War at historic sites throughout Arkansas. There are preserved battlefields, restored structures that played prominent roles in the conflict, and exhibits that tell the story of the struggle that pitted brother against brother in the 1860s.

Places like Pea Ridge National Military Park, Prairie Grove Battlefield State Park, Jenkins' Ferry Battlefield State Park, Headquarters House in Fayetteville and the McCollum-Chidester House at Camden bring the Civil War to life for today's travelers. Old Washington Historic State Park, Helena, St. Charles, and Marks' Mills Battlefield State Park are other locations with sites related to the Civil War.

You'll find Civil War reenactments and other special observances listed in this calendar at Hot Springs National Park, Petit Jean State Park, Poison Spring State Park, and Prairie Grove Battlefield State Park (see the Index for dates).

An excellent source for finding out more about the Civil War in Arkansas is Rugged and Sublime: The Civil War in Arkansas by Mark Christ, published by the University of Arkansas Press. It sells for $22 (hard cover) or $18 (paperback) at bookstores throughout the state.

Nationally, the Civil War Discovery Trail links more than 300 sites in 16 state to inspire and to teach the story of the Civil War and its haunting impact on America. The Trail, an initiative of The Civil War Trust, allows visitors to explore battlefields, historic homes, railroad stations, cemeteries, parks and other destinations that bring history to life. For more information on the Trail and the Trust, or to order a copy of Civil War Discovery Trail Official Guidebook for $4.95, call 1-800-CWTRUST.

## GUNS, PLANES, AND GOVERNMENT CLAIMS

Just for fun, let's lambaste the government today. There's such a wealth of material here I hardly know where to begin, but what say we start with the truth in government's statements.

Most of us have come to realize that when someone from the government shows up at your front door and says, "Trust me, I'm here to help you," you're probably in the deep muckety-muck.

Let's examine for a moment these words, "trust me." They carry a whole bundle of negative connotations, from seedy salesmen and shady deals, to supposedly mailed checks and unilaterally pleasing sexual encounters. Still, it's a very popular bureaucratic phrase.

"We're here to help you." Hmmmm. . . . That's another dandy. If you're not a foreign national, or on welfare, (or both), when was the last time the government "helped" you?

So it is generally with some trepidation that we face encounters with the government. This brings me to the little tale I have for you today: the story of an innocent's blunder into bureaucratic barbed wire. True story, cross my heart. . . .

A few months ago I had to attend a five-day seminar in Little Rock. Now I lived in South Florida for quite a while before moving here. Even so, one never quite gets used to the idea of people wanting to shoot you for your wallet. As a precautionary measure, reminiscent of other times and places, I packed my 9mm pistol in my carry bag.

I did my seminar, fortunately without incident, and returned home Friday. Sunday morning I grabbed my carryall, never considering the gun therein, and left for Little Rock Airport. I was flying out to meet with my publisher in Salt Lake City, to discuss my new book.

I arrived ahead of time Sunday morning; the flight was on schedule. So far so good. I checked in at the counter and walked to the correct gate. Shoving my bag into the X-ray machine, I strolled through the metal detection frame. It was about that point when things began to take a decidedly downhill turn. The two girls watching the monitor went bug-eyed as constipated Pekingese, both suddenly staring at the screen like they'd just found a finger in their Hostess twinkie. They glanced at me, looked at each other, then their eyes ricocheted back to the monitor. I was still standing there without a clue.

One girl nervously sidled over to the counter and began frantically pressing something underneath the desktop. Hmmmm. . . . At first I thought she was storing her chewing gum for later. What did I care? But boy, it sure seemed like she was really into getting that gum attached to the desk! The other girl was already backing up so she could get a running start in case I yelled "Viva Castro!" and pulled a grenade out of my armpit.

About this time several things began to happen. My bag came through the machine, and with a sudden incandescence I finally realized what was going on. But before I could slap myself in the head and say stupid, stupid, the cavalry arrived from several different directions.

As they surrounded me, one officer stepped forward and asked the inevitable question. "Whatcha got in the bag, fella?"

"Well, a gun," I said, launching into a high-pitched, hasty explanation that they were only partly interested in as they carried me and my bag, quite separably, to "the little room."

The long and the short of it is, they asked me a bunch of questions, then they ran me and my pistol through the computer. Finally satisfied I wasn't a guest star of Unsolved Mysteries or America's Most Wanted, they let me go--without, of course, the pistol. I thought that was the end of it. Hmmmm. . . .

****

About a month later I get a letter from the Federal Aviation Administration. In essence, it says you're in deep muckety-muck. But not to worry, 'cause we're here to help you. You have committed a violation that carries a $10,000.00 fine. Send us a detailed explanation of the whole incident, along with a complete record of any and all crimes you have committed in your entire life. Be sure to include every one, even those you got away with, and maybe we can get this straightened out. Hmmmm.

Okay, so I send them this clever little letter with a complete explanation and an amusing Reader's Digest version of my life, explaining that the only time I had ever been arrested was for sneaking into a drive-in movie, locked in the trunk of a car, when I was 19. My friends were nervous--they broke the key off in the lock trying to get me out. It was a sweltering August night. Three hours later, when the police finally got me out of the trunk, I was glad to be arrested.

Well, two weeks later I get another letter. Hmmmm. It says: We read your explanation, and we don't think you're as cute as you do. We've decided that you're not dangerous enough to be jailed, but you certainly screwed up enough to be fined. Please send a civil penalty in the amount of $500.00

Now I'm reading this, feeling my ankles sinking into the muckety-muck, when down at the bottom of the page the last paragraph reads: You can contest the matter, but if you do, we're going to go after you for the whole ball of wax--10K, and who knows, maybe a federally funded vacation. Or you can take advantage of our special thirty-day offer: plead no contest and pay only half the above fee immediately--that's right, only half the retail fine--$250.00, and we'll forget the whole thing.

Now I don't know about you, but the whole thing seems like a cross between a shakedown and a late night TV advertisement to me. I'm waiting for them to throw in a free set of Ginsu knives if I get my money in the mail today.

So I wrote them back, saying, just $250.00, huh? Does this deal come with any kind of guarantee?

Two weeks later I get another letter. It says basically: We guarantee this is your last chance sucka. . . .

****

I sent them the $250.00. I'm looking forward to having this whole thing over, and getting my Ginsu knives. . . .

The Intrepid Arkansas Traveler

## ILLEGAL GARDENS AND SLEIGH RIDES

Ah, fall is in the air; cool winds ruffle the trees, sheets of leaves cascade to the ground in gentle billows. The sweet autumn fragrance of plants in final bloom fills the air; moonflowers, jasmine, and gee, is that marijuana I smell?

Yes folks, it's that time again when those daring cultivators of Midwest wacky weed discreetly begin their harvest, gambling that they'll stay one step ahead of the jailer.

As perilous an enterprise as it may be, there are still a handful of audacious souls out there who just can't resist the smell of green--in whatever form. And let's face it, they probably come by their penchant for the illegitimate quite honestly. Seems to me it wasn't long ago that moonshining was pretty popular in these parts.

Now I don't know much about pot, and I certainly never inhaled it, I can assure you of that! But I do know a good tale when I hear one, and the other day I was in just the right place at the right time to be privy to a yarn. . . .

I was sitting in a quiet little place just over the state line, washing down that county road dust with a cold one, when I overheard the fellow at the table next to me telling a story. . . .

Seems a couple friends of his, two brothers, had grown a patch of pot up on a mountainside in a remote area of Oklahoma. Two or three hundred yards below the garden ran a wide swathe of the Mountain Fork River, which supplied their water.

Lem and Larry, we'll call them, had carefully nurtured their crop through summer and into fall, but only days before harvest an early Northerner had rolled through and deposited three inches of snow on everything. Now they had to get their crop off the mountain, pronto. Lem, the smarter of the two, suggested they use an old three-man sled, and tow it down the mountain. Without thinking about it much, Larry agreed, but then thinking wasn't one of Larry's strong points. Truth was, when it came to intellect, about the only difference between Larry and a Tyson chicken was the feathers.

Well, bright and early the next day the two guerilla gardeners bounced their way down the old logging road in their battered pickup, stopping at the edge of the river. There they unloaded the sled, pruning shears and garbage bags, then began climbing the hill. By midmorning they had the pot cut, bagged and tied to the sled.

They had been so busy working they failed to notice the two county sheriffs' cars that pulled up behind their truck, and the handful of deputies that spread out and began climbing the hill. You see, the day before, the boys in the surveillance helicopter had spotted the neat little patch of pot laying stark green against the white snow of the mountain.

As the deputies silently climbed the hill, the unsuspecting duo prepared to depart. Larry suggested to Lem that they try sitting on top of the bundles of pot and riding the sleigh slowly down the mountain. Lord knows why, but Lem agreed (which doesn't do much for Lem's credibility as the smart one). About then things took a decidedly downhill turn for the bunco brothers.

Larry sat on the front of the sled, holding the steering rope like a bull rider just before the gate opens. Lem gave them a push and swung himself up, straddling the bundles in the back, holding onto one of the ropes that bound the garbage bags of pot to the sled.

At first, Larry was laughing and yelling, "Mush! Mush!" to imaginary dogs while Lem sat behind him smiling, pleased as peaches that his little plan was going so well. Sad to say, neither of them remembered how steep that old hill got just past the ridge.

In a few moments they'd gone from coasting leisurely, to zipping along at an alarming speed. Trees were suddenly blurring by. Larry, eyes bulging like goose eggs, was edging rapidly toward panic and starting to make little whining noises in the back of his throat. Lem tried to dig his heels into the snow to slow them down, but his feet barely reached the ground. The sled was careening down the hill like a demented version of the Batmobile now, bouncing and jagging at breakneck speed. Larry's whine had burbled into a full-fledged shriek. Just when it looked like things couldn't get any worse, they saw the police. . . .

They shot through the line of startled deputies, yipping and yelling like a Jamaican bobsled team. Heck, at that point either of the plummeting pair would gladly have traded a jail cell for the sleighride from hell. But they were not to be so lucky. They were three-quarters of the way down the mountain and miraculously still on the sled. That was the good news. The bad news was the raging, rain-swollen river and the cliff that lay in wait not fifty yards ahead.

Lem decided he'd had all the fun he could handle and stood up to jump, but at that moment they shot under a tree and a low branch took him off the sled like he'd been swatted by the hand of God. That left crazy Larry, the sleigh, the pot, and the river, in that order. Screaming like a banshee and frozen to the reins, Larry shot across the road, over the last of the snow-covered precipice and sailed off the cliff looking like Slim Pickins riding the bomb in "Dr. Strangelove." Behind him, the deputies watched in slack-jawed amazement as he flew a good fifty feet out over the river and landed with a splash in the rolling torrent of brown water.

Nobody ever found the sled or the pot. Well, at least nobody reported it. Lem was taken into custody right there. Larry was found about nightfall, five miles down river, soaked to the bone, mud-spattered and shivering like a wet puppy. I guess it just goes to show, crime doesn't pay.

In the end though, the police had to let them go; there was no evidence. What could they charge them with, failure to yield on a runaway sleigh? It didn't matter, the bunco brothers had had enough, they were going straight. It was said they changed their names to Gonzales, took the government test and became U.S. Postal employees.

Don't ya just love this place? America!

The Intrepid Arkansas Traveler

# TRAVELIN' BY TRAIL
## in
# ARKANSAS

Have you ever on a misty morn, set foot on mountain trail, and had the new sun breach that gold-green canopy above you, casting trellises of light and warmth, painting hazy shafts of brilliance on the still, dewed landscape of bough, and flower, and leaf about you?

Could you doubt then, at that moment, that there is a God?

The Traveler

# HIKING THE OUACHITA NATIONAL FOREST

1. ***Boardstand Trail and Old Military Road Trail***
   This historical Military Road Trail starts along Holson Valley Road and connects with the Ouachita National Recreation Trail on the south side of Winding Stair Mountain. These two trails, along with the Boardstand Trail can be combined to form a looped hike of about 23 miles. Since the trail has so many options, it may be used for day hiking or overnight backpacking. (Choctaw Ranger District)

2. ***Cedar Lake Trail and Old Pine Trail***
   Hikers may access the Cedar Lake Trail from any of the established camping areas. The trail hugs the shoreline and completely encircles Cedar Lake. This trail offers an array of opportunities to day hikers who want to view waterfowl and wading birds which frequent the lake. (Choctaw Ranger District)

3. ***Horsethief Spring Trail***
   The Horsethief Spring Trail is one of the most beautiful trails in the area. The trail begins at Cedar Lake and loops through many different tree types. The hiker will cross several small streams before connecting with the Ouachita National Recreation Trail. The trail then loops back down the northern face of Winding Stair Mountain to Cedar Lake. Using the Ouachita National Recreation Trail to form the loop results in about an 11 mile hike. (Choctaw Ranger District)

4. ***Kerr Arboretum Trails***
   Located at the Kerr Nature Center on the Talimena Scenic Byway, these three Interpretive trails feature a variety of plants which are identified by trail signs. The trails are an easy walk for the day hiker and provide an opportunity to experience the variety of ecological areas that exists on a single mountain. (Choctaw Ranger District)

5. ***Billy Creek Trail***
   The Billy Creek Trail winds down from the Talimena Scenic Byway atop Winding Stair Mountain. It offers year-round day hiking as well as horseback riding. Bicycles and motorized vehicles are prohibited. The trail curves down the southern face of the mountain to Billy Creek Campground. (Choctaw Ranger District)

6. ***Big Brushy Trail Complex***
   ***(Brushy Mountain, Mountain Top, Rockhouse and Brushy Creek Trails)***

The Trails in the Brushy Mountain Trails Complex, combined with the Ouachita National Recreation Trail, allow many opportunities for loop-trail hiking, ranging from 3 to 12 miles in length. Hikers will see flowing streams, waterfalls, geologic formations, and quiet woodlands along the trail. The trails are all located near parking and camping areas at the Big Brushy Campground. (Oden Ranger District)

### 7. *Little Missouri Trail*

This trail provides many glimpses of the spectacular Little Missouri River, which is known for its scenic beauty. Cascading waterfalls, stately hardwoods, old-growth pine stands, wildlife, and seasonal leaf colors are just a few of the natural delights awaiting hikers. The area where Raven Branch flows into the Little Missouri, known as *Winding Stairs,* features breathtaking views of the forest, river and large novaculite rock outcrops.

The trail is fairly level and crosses the Little Missouri river six times and Crooked, Brier, Long, and Blaylock creeks once. There are no foot bridges across these areas, so hikers should be very careful during periods of high water. The Little Missouri Trail is an ideal place for day hiking. (Caddo Ranger District)

### 8. *Serendipity Interpretive Trail*

The trail is highlighted by interpretive signs which identify forest vegetation, food plots, and wildlife ponds. They also tell how these attributes attract and enhance wildlife. Moreover, the signs will help you become more familiar with plants which are found along the trail. (Oden Ranger District)

### 9. *Ouachita National Recreation Trail*

The trail spans 192 miles of the Ouachita National Forest, between Talimena State Park on U.S. Hwy. 271 near Talihina, Okla., and Arkansas Hwy. 9 south of Perryville, Ark. Another 32 miles of trail, located on private and other public lands, extend to Pinnacle Mountain State Park, 15 miles west of Little Rock. Elevations range from 600 to 2,600 feet as the trail passes through forested mountains, across sweeping valleys and near clear-running streams. Spur trails connect to various recreation areas and point of interest. Numerous road crossings and access points provide opportunities for point to point hikes of various distances. (The Supervisor's Office)

### 10. *Charlton Trail*

The Charlton trail begins at Charlton Campground and ends at beautiful Crystal Springs Recreation Area on popular Lake Ouachita. Both areas provide camping, picnicking, and swimming opportunities. The trail is a popular day-use hiking area. It is also open to mountain biking. (Womble Ranger District)

### *11. Hole in the Ground Mountain Trail*

The trail follows the ridge line of the Hole in the Ground Mountain. It offers views of the Petit Jean River Valley to the north and the Jack Creek Drainage to the south. Surrounding pine and hardwood forests provide opportunities for viewing deer, squirrel and black bear (highest density in Arkansas). Rugged, steep terrain is the norm; geologic formations are abundant. Jack Creek Campground (trailhead) offers free developed camping, picnicking, and swimming. Jack Creek and Sugar Creek offer fishing and seasonal Class IV whitewater. A short day hike on the Hole in the Ground Trail allows visitors to explore exciting outdoor opportunities. (Cold Springs Ranger District)

### *12. Little Blakely Trail*

On this trail, hikers see spectacular views of beautiful Lake Ouachita, stately old-growth pines and hardwoods. The hardwoods become especially scenic during the autumn and spring when trees display an array of brilliant colors or white blossoms. (Jessieville Ranger District)

### *13. Hunts Loop Trail*

Along this trail, hikers can enjoy panoramic views from Short Mountain vista while observing interesting geologic features on the steep rocky slope above Iron Springs. They can also hike through open woods on ridge tops. This trail is an ideal day hike. (Jessieville Ranger District)

## HIKING/MOUNTAIN BIKING

---

### *1. Earthquake Ridge Trail*

The trail parallels the Talimena Scenic byway on the north and south sides of Rich Mountain. The day hiker will view several interesting rock formations as well as a variety of plane and animal life. Mountain bikers find this trail an exciting challenge. (Mena Ranger District)

### *2. Womble Trail*

The Womble Trail stretches 37 miles between Northfork Lake and the Ouachita National Recreation Trail. The Womble Trail meanders along the scenic shores of Lake Ouachita for about a mile offering the hiker or mountain biker breathtaking views of one of Arkansas' most beautiful lakes. Visitors can use the short spur trails to access three float camps. The free camping areas offer fire rings, picnic tables, and vault toilets. Hikers may also combine the roundtop Trail with the Womble and Ouachita Trail to form an eight-mile loop. (Womble Ranger District)

### 3. *Shady Lake Trail*

The Civilian Conservation Corps developed the Shady Lake Recreation Area in 1937. The Shady Lake trail traverses Saline Creek and passes the historic Shady Lake Dam. It continues along the opposite side of the lake up West Saline Creek. The trail is ideal for day hiking. Mountain bikers may also use the trail. (Mena Ranger District)

## MOUNTAIN BIKE

### 1. *Buffalo Gap Mountain Bike Trail*

Along this trail, bike riders will see numerous panoramic views of the Ouachita National Forest and Buffalo Gap. Fall colors area at their best in October, while early April offers a scenic display of spring's shades of greenery. (Jessieville Ranger District)

### 2. *Possum Kingdom Bike Trail*

This bike trail offers a variety of roads, varying from the very primitive to the paved county road. Vegetation types vary from pure pine forests to mixed pine and hardwood stands, with varying ages. The trail has a primitive portion that can be used by all-terrain vehicles. (Jessieville Ranger District)

## EQUESTRIAN

### 1. *Cedar Lake Equestrian Trail*

The Cedar Lake Equestrian Trail is a network of looping horse trails that winds over various types of terrain and through a variety of tree types. Rides range from moderately easy to more difficult. Connecting loops offer riders an opportunity to create their own type of experience. Trails extend from the Cedar Lake Camp to Blue Mountain (north), Holson Valley (west), and Winding Stair Mountain (south). (Choctaw Ranger District)

### 2. *Mill Creek Equestrian Trail*

The Mill Creek Equestrian Trail offers breathtaking views of Fourche Mountain and Buck Knob. Abandoned silver mines, beautiful streams, and several spectacular views of the Ouachita Mountains area among the trail sites. While this trail's network provides horseback riding opportunities, it also offers day hiking and mountain biking. (Poteau Ranger District)

### *3. Eight West Equestrian Trail*

The western portion of the trail follows along Self Mountain and offers an outstanding view to the South. The lowlands of this trail system offer a picturesque setting through beautiful bottomland hardwoods with clear running streams. While enjoying the trail, the visitor will pass several old home sites. These sites are evidenced by old rock fences. (Mena Ranger District)

## AREA OFFICES:

**Caddo Ranger District**
P.O. Box 369, Glenwood, AR 71943
(501) 356-4186

**Jessieville Ranger District**
P.O. Box 189, Jessieville, AR 71949
(501) 984-5313

**Mena Ranger District**
Hwy 71 N, Mena, AR 71953
(501) 394-2382

**The Supervisor's Office**
P.O. Box 1270, 100 Reserve St, Hot Springs, AR 72958 -- (501) 321-5202

**Choctaw Ranger District**
HC 64 Box 3467, Heavener, OK 74937
(918) 653-2991

**Oden Ranger District**
Rt. 9 Box 16, Oden, AR 71961
(501) 326-4322

**Poteau Ranger District**
P.O. Box 2244, Waldron, AR 72958
(501) 637-4174

**Womble Ranger District**
P.O. Box 255, Mt. Ida, AR 71957
(501) 867-2101

A fellow from Neosho took his fourteen children to the county fair, and there was a big bull in the tent which some folks said the critter was worth ten thousand dollars. The fellow wanted to see the bull, but you had to pay fifty cents to get in. "Is these kids all your'n?" says that man that was selling the tickets. The fellow from Neosho says yes. "Well, you can all go in the tent free," says the ticket-seller, "I want that bull to take a look at *you!*"

# TRAVELIN' BY TRAIL in the OZARK - ST. FRANCIS NATIONAL FORESTS

## HIKING

1. ***Alum Cove Trail*** is located in the Alum Cove Natural Bridge area near Deer, AR. This 1.1-mile trail takes hikers near rock outcrops and a 120-foot natural bridge. This trail is located 15 miles south of Jasper, off Ark. Hwy. 7. (Buffalo Ranger District)

2. ***Bear Creek Lake Nature Trail*** is located 5 miles southeast of Marianna, AR. This .8 mile trail takes hikers across wooden bridges and through the beautiful and unique Mississippi Flood plain hardwood forests of the St. Francis National Forest. (St. Francis Ranger District)

3. ***Horsehead Lake Trail*** is a 3-mile loop trail located at the Horsehead Lake Recreation area 12 miles northwest of Clarksville, on Hwy 103 to Ark. Hwy. 164. (Pleasant Hill Ranger District)

4. ***Mt. Magazine to Cove Lake Trail*** is a 10.8-mile trail which connects the Cameron Bluff Campground atop Mt. Magazine (the highest point in Arkansas) with the Cove Lake Campground in the valley below. Magazine mountain is located in Logan County 18 miles south of Paris on Ark. Hwy. 309. (Magazine Ranger District)

5. ***North Sylamore Creek Hiking Trail*** is a 13-mile trail which follows North Sylamore Creek from Allison to Barkshed Recreation Area. It is located 8 miles northwest of Mtn. View, AR. (Sylamore Ranger District)

6. ***Ozark Highlands Trail*** begins at Lake Fort Smith on Hwy. 71 and goes east for 160 miles, ending at Wooten on the Buffalo National River. This trail passes some of the most scenic areas in the state. The trail can be accessed at several places. (Supervisor's Office)

7. ***Pedestal Rock Trail*** is a 1-mile trail which begins at Pedestal Rock parking area. This trail takes hikers to the unusual pedestal rock formations and rock bluffs. This trail is located 38 miles north of Russellville, off Ark. Hwy. 7. (Bayou Ranger District)

8. ***Redding Loop - Spy Rock Spur*** is an 8.5-mile loop trail located 18 miles north of Ozark, off Ark. Hwy. 23. The trail takes the hiker to Spy Rock for a spectacular view of the Mulberry River Valley or to a junction with the Ozark Highlands Trail. (Pleasant Hill Ranger District)

9. ***Shores Lake - White Rock Loop Trail*** is a 15-mile loop trail off the Ozark Highlands Trail that links Shores Lake to White Rock Mountain. It is located 12 miles north of Mulberry off Interstate 40. (Boston Mtn. Ranger District)

## BIKING/HIKING/HORSEBACK

***Huckleberry Mountain Horse Trail*** offers 40 miles of deep winding valleys, rugged mountain bluffs and cool creeks starting just off Hwy. 308 near Mt. Magazine. Campsites along the trail provide a choice for equestrians who like to stay in a different place each trip. Group camping and daytime parking area available at the Mt. Magazine Camp, just off of Scenic Byway 309 on Forest Road 1638. (Magazine Ranger District)

## BIKING/HORSEBACK

***Sylamore Horse Trail*** is a 58-mile trail located just north of Mountain View, AR. Four loops of the trail travel through old roads and up and down Ozark hollows taking riders along streams, ridges and the beautiful White River. (Sylamore Ranger District)

## AREA OFFICES:

**Bayou Ranger District**
Rt. 1 Box 36; Hector, AR 72843
(501) 284-3150

**Boston Mountain Ranger District**
P.O. Box 76; Ozark, AR 72949
(501) 667-2191

**Buffalo Ranger District**
P.O. Box 427; Jasper, AR 72641
(501) 446-5122

**Cass Job Corp Center**
HC 63, Box 210; Ozark, AR 72949
(501) 667-3686

**Magazine Ranger District**
P.O. Box 511; Paris, AR 72853
(501) 963-3076

**Pleasant Hill Ranger District**
P.O. Box 190; Clarksville, AR 72830
(501) 754-2864

**St. Francis Ranger District**
Rt. 4 Box 14-A; Marianna, AR 72360
(501) 295-5278

**Sylamore Ranger District**
P.O. Box 1279; Mtn. View, AR 72560
(501) 269-3228

## THE TRAIL OF TEARS

The other night I watched a documentary hosted by none other than Kevin Costner, of "Dances With Wolves" fame. It was about early America's manifest destiny, the westward migration of those tenacious souls across the new frontier. It presented an enlightening look at the lands, the people they conquered, and the nations they dispossessed in the process.

I am proud of my American heritage, as are most Arkansans, but watching that film I found myself strangely sad and slightly ashamed.

I am certain that the noble savage was in some instances, not quite as noble as we are led to believe, for they were human and perfection is not a characteristic of this creature, man. Yet watching that movie and listening to their words, there seemed to be a quality of integrity, a guilelessness and a love of the earth, and yes, a nobility, that far transcended what virtues could be found in those who had subdued them.

In an age where we are so critical of atrocities of any sort, so haughty and so quick to condemn, we should occasionally be reminded of our own transgressions, so that we do not repeat them. To that end I would share a poem with you. It is called "Somewhere on the Trail of Tears . . . "

### SOMEWHERE ON THE TRAIL OF TEARS . . .

Hey na hey Great Spirit, sing our song of passing and open wide your arms, for I am coming home. . . .

They took our lands and sent us away with promises. They placed our feet upon a bitter path and pointed towards the setting sun, and we went. Even though the small voices inside us cried, "No, this is wrong...." But we trusted. We did not understand, or we refused to see, the width and the depth of the white man's guile and greed. . .

For of the things the white man did, he promised best of all. . . .

Hey na hey Great Spirit, set my feet upon the path. Take me past the sorrow, to the village of my father . . .

So it was that we began the journey of a nation. Four thousand souls who traded their freedom and their future for a handful of empty pledges . . . And when the white man's words changed like the seasons and his summer promises turned to winter lies, we looked at each other and cried, "What have we done?" But our feet were on the trail and there was no turning back. You cannot change the color of the moon nor the course of the sun for the wanting of it . . .

So on we pressed, to camp that cold night, somewhere on the Trail of Tears . . .

Hey na hey Great Spirit, light a sweetwood fire to warm the lodge, for I am coming home . . .

When there was no more food in our bellies, we dreamt of the full fields we had left and we starved.

When the winter wind ate at our skin and we stumbled in cold despair across the flat hard plains, we dreamt of the warm hills of home and our tears froze on our cheeks.

And when there was no more room in our bodies for pain and no more hope in our hearts to sustain our spirits, we died. Somewhere on the Trail of Tears. . . .

Hey na hey Great Spirit, lay back my buffalo robes for the long sleep, for I am coming home . . .

One bitterly cold night, as I slept beneath a wagon with my child in my arms, I dreamt. I saw my husband and I riding through warm summer meadows of dandelion and marigold, past peaceful stands of birch and cedar, painted in the colors of the season.

I could feel my child move, contented, in my belly. I felt the caress of the sun on my hair and shoulders, as it gilded the leaves of the trees around us. My husband smiled and held his hand out, and I reached for it. . . . But I awoke then, holding only my child's death cold body in my arms, for her spirit had passed in the night.

Hey na hey Great Spirit, light the trail for our loved ones to the happy hunting ground, for they are coming home . . .

New moon followed old as we plodded on in silent desperation, adversity chasing us like winter wolves, bringing down the frail and the weak.

And when hope had turned to ashes and faith had faded like the waning sun, when there was no more blood in the body of this nation, the great Cherokee heart stopped and the spirit fled . . .

Somewhere on the Trail of Tears . . .

Hey na hey Great Spirit, make them remember. Let our passing not have been in vain. To the everlasting shame of those who sent us and the everlasting sorrow of those remained.

For now, I too, am coming home. . . .



The Intrepid Arkansas Traveler

## NEW RULES . . .

Quote from the Rev. Willy Johanahan:

"BEHOLD, YE OF LITTLE FAITH IN GOD AND NATURE, BROOD OF A MORALLY WOUNDED SOCIETY. BEAR WITNESS TO THE COMING CLEANSING.

"YE HAVE AEROSOLED, INSECTACIDED AND WASTED WITHOUT CONSCIENCE. YE HAVE SQUANDERED THE GIFTS OF GOD'S GREEN EARTH SINCE THE DAYS OF YOUR FATHER'S FATHERS. NOW, AS SURE AS ARROGANT PRIDE GOETH BEFORE A FALL, AND WICKEDNESS BEGETS CALAMITY, IT'S TIME TO PAY THE PIPER FOR ALL YOUR DIRTY DANCIN' WITH MOTHER NATURE'S DAUGHTERS . . . ."

The other day I ran into ol' "Reverend" Willy Johanahan. He's sort of a self-ordained environmental evangelist. I don't think he's spent much time behind a pulpit; in fact, I think he got his ministry by mail order, but he can thump a bible and shout His praises with the best of them--and louder than most.

Now old Willy was about as excited as a person gets without spittled lips. Seems he'd just received a message from God. Better than that, he claimed to have been issued a handful of brand new commandments, directly from the burning bush. (Well, in this case it was a burning tree.) I'll explain.

It appears Willy was out hunting in the Ouachitas one recent afternoon when he became lost. I suspect the inability to determine his position may have stemmed from his trusty bottle of Ole Turkey, which is never far from his side during most outdoor excursions.

Night fell, a storm rolled in, and flashing daggers of lightning seared a dark sky. Dazed but determined, Willy was stumbling through the murky, rainswept woods when a jagged bolt of lightning sliced through the foliage and struck a tree not twenty feet from him. Over the crash of the lightning there came a voice, as powerful as thunder but sweet and strange (this is Willy's story), a voice that came from everywhere, a voice that called his name.

Willy claims he passed out then, in heavenly rapture. I think the rapture was much more earthly and caused mostly from bourbon. Nonetheless, he said when he woke up, there, burned in the trunk of the tree before him were ten new commandments . . . of sorts.

Now I don't know where Willy got these--he can't seem to find the tree they were supposedly seared into. Heck, he can't even remember what mountain he was on. But the "commandments" are pretty good, so I thought I'd share them with you.

## The Latest Ten

1. Thou shalt not lay waste to forest's bough and branch--to supply the Japanese with housing. . . . Leave them dern trees where they are. Better the Japanese should learn to live in Toyotas.

2. A few thousand years ago I said go forth and multiply. Let me clarify that; I meant with reason. I didn't mean breed yourselves into poverty. Don't take what you can't pay for, and don't make what you can't feed.

3. Remember when I said, "An eye for an eye and a tooth for a tooth?" Well, that's exactly what I meant--not a few years in prison with time off for good behavior.

4. Thou shalt not cause the animals of this earth to perish for the sake of vanity and ego; tiger skin rugs, alligator shoes and rhino horn aphrodisiacs. (Let me tell you up front, rhino horn ain't gonna help.)

5. There ain't no such thing as sexual preference. If the birds don't do it, and the bees don't do it. . . .

6. All rapists, murderers, and their attorneys, will go directly to hell--no exceptions.

7. It will henceforth be a sin to show more than five commercials during a single TV station break.

8. Thou shalt not use God-given talents to seduce the flesh or the intellect of your admirers. Let me clarify; Madonna and Mike Tyson are coming back as one-legged frogs in a stork pond.

9. All liberal bureaucrats go to hell--no exceptions.

10. The first Ten I gave you were commandments, not suggestions.

AMEN

As Arkansas is blessed with thousands of acres of rolling ranch land, and boots and hats are still standard apparel for most of our rural areas, I felt it only fitting to include a few pages on the cowboy and his lady. . . .

## WOMEN!

by Baxter Black

She cried over the cat. After all that had happened she cried over the dang cat.

Christmas had been hectic. Feeding and watching out for 12 relatives for 5 days. Then in January when the blizzard hit I was at the state capital for a committee meeting. The power was out at the ranch and the water was off for 48 hours. She and the hired man managed to feed the cows, but we lost four of them anyway. When I finally got through to her on the phone, she said they were managing but hurry home if I could.

We held our little bull sale. She did the programs, mailed the flyers, planned the lunch and smiled at prospective buyers for a day and a half. It went smoothly, but she didn't get much rest that week.

It rained in March. The new calves got the scours. I was calvin' so she sorta took over treating the calves. She divided her time between haulin' the kids back and forth to town and nursin' sick calves.

Right before the regional track meet our oldest broke his leg. He was bitterly disappointed and was bedridden for two weeks. She waited on him hand and foot.

At our brandin' she fed 34 people outta the back of the pickup in the far pasture.

The first day it got over 85° she went to town for parts. One the way home her car broke down and she walked the last four miles. Her crock pot shorted out and the beans froze to the bottom. That was the night the school superintendent dropped by.

Well, she finally went to the doctor about the pain in her hands. Arthritis. Sorta what she'd suspected all along. Gettin' older.

In the last six months we've had two car wrecks, the well pump went out, my mother came to live with us, we found a leak in the roof above the kitchen sink, gophers got in her garden, the meat freezer gave up the ghost, I sold her favorite cow, our insurance went up, I started takin' high blood pressure pills and they canceled her favorite TV show.

It's been kind of a tough go at our place these last few months. But she never complained. Just bowed her back and kept goin'.

We had company last night. After they left, this morning we found the cat dead in the driveway. A black tom cat. One of the barn cats. I didn't even know she cared about him. He hardly ever came in the house.

I found her in the bedroom cryin' her eyes out. "The cat?" I asked. She nodded. I held her.

Women cry over the strangest things.

## EVOLUTION OF THE RANCH WIFE
by Baxter Black

**October** **(NEWLYWEDS)**

"Honey, the boys and I will be workin' cows all day. It's dangerous and dirty, especially for a pretty little thing like you. We'll be up to the house at noon. I'd sure appreciate it if you could fix us some lunch. There'll only be five of us but if you need help don't hesitate to call my mother."

**April** **(MARRIED 3 YRS)**

"Emily Jean, you stand behind that barrel. Sometimes these heifers get feisty after they calve. Once I get her tied down you hand me those chains and the calf puller. Be careful, Darlin', it's heavy."

**July** **(MARRIED 6 YRS)**

"Emily, sugar, the hayin' crew will be in at lunch time. I think there's 12 of 'em. I don't wanna stop this mornin' so when you bring out the coffee and sweet rolls at 9:30 would you mind just catchin' up to each baler and give it to the driver on the run. By the way, the tax man will be here at one o'clock. Take care of him, will ya?"

**November** **(MARRIED 10 YRS)**

"Emily, you sure you got that chain hooked good enough? Let the clutch out easy. When you feel the tractor starting to lug, drop to a lower gear and go slow. I don't want to lose any bales off the back of the pickup. Just follow the tracks. When we get out to the cows, I'll trade you. You can toss the bales and I'll drive. You wanna borrow my slicker?"

**September** **(MARRIED 13 YRS)**

"Em, crawl under here and hold this nut. I'll get up under the hood and turn the bolt from above. Watch out for that grease spot."

**May** **(MARRIED 17 YRS)**

"Mother, you spray the fly dope and keep the blackleg gun full. I'll rope 'em. Junior and Jenny can help you flank the big calves."

**October** **(MARRIED A LONG TIME)**

"Ma, we're running outta cows! Push 'em up!"

**March** **(NOT LONG AGO)**

"Dang it, I checked the heifers at midnight. It's your turn."

# RIVERS, FLOAT-TRIPS and OUTFITTERS of ARKANSAS

Floating softly on crystal waters, carefree as an autumn leaf.
Wrapped in the rapture of still beauty, captured by the colors of the season.
Eagles cry greeting on soaring wing above while jagged thrusts of granite tower about you in quiet reverence, like sentinels at the gates of mystic journey.

Slice the water deftly traveler, with sure stroke.
For around yon bend, swirl and eddy meld with rushing torrent, and you shall soon find yourself somewhere 'tween the terror and the thrill.

The Traveler

# THE ARKANSAS FLOATER'S KIT

## 1995-96 OUTFITTERS' DIRECTORY

—NOTE: Addresses and telephone numbers are listed at the end of this chart.

| THE ARKANSAS FLOATER'S KIT | CANOE RENTAL | JOHNBOAT RENTAL | RAFT RENTAL | SHUTTLE SERVICES | GUIDE SERVICES | LODGING | CAMPGROUND | SUPPLIES | RESTAURANT |
|---|---|---|---|---|---|---|---|---|---|
| **Big Piney Creek** | | | | | | | | | |
| Fish & Game Guaranteed | | | | | • | | | | |
| Kyles Landing Cabin & Canoe Rental | • | | | | • | • | • | • | |
| Moore Outdoors | • | | • | • | | | • | • | |
| Paulette Helton | | | | • | | | | | |
| Razorback Wilderness Center | • | | • | • | • | | • | | |
| **Upper Buffalo River** | | | | | | | | | |
| Buffalo Adventures Canoe Rental | • | | • | • | • | | • | • | |
| Buffalo Outdoor Center, Ponca | • | | • | • | | • | | • | |
| Gordon Motel & Canoe Rental | • | | • | • | • | • | | • | |
| Keller's Kanoes | • | | • | • | | | | • | |
| Kyles Landing Cabin & Canoe Rental | • | | | | • | • | • | • | |
| Lost Valley Canoe & Lodging | • | | • | • | | • | • | • | |
| Razorback Wilderness Center | • | | • | • | • | • | | • | |
| Riverview Motel Canoe Rental | • | | • | • | | • | | | |
| **Middle Buffalo River** | | | | | | | | | |
| Buffalo Camping & Canoeing | • | | • | • | • | • | • | • | |
| Buffalo Outdoor Center, Silver Hill | • | • | • | • | • | • | | • | |
| Silver Hill Canoe Rental | • | | • | • | | • | | • | |
| Tomahawk Canoe Rental & RV Park | • | | • | • | | | • | • | |
| **Lower Buffalo River** | | | | | | | | | |
| Bennett's Canoe Rental | • | | | • | | • | | • | |
| Buffalo Point Canoe Rental, Inc. | • | | • | • | | | | • | |
| Cotter Trout Dock | | | | | • | | | • | |
| Crockett's Country Store & Canoe Rental | • | | | • | | | | • | |
| Dirst Canoe Rental & Log Cabins | • | | • | • | • | • | | • | |
| Dodd's Canoe & Johnboat Rental | • | • | | • | • | | | • | • |
| Newland's Float Trips & Lodge | | | | | • | • | | • | |
| Rose's Trout Dock | | • | | • | • | | | • | |
| Sportsman's Resort | | • | | | • | • | • | • | • |
| White Buffalo Resort | • | • | | • | • | • | • | • | |
| Wild Bill's Outfitters | • | • | • | • | • | • | • | • | • |
| Woodsman's Sport Shop & Fishing Service | • | | | • | • | • | • | • | |
| **Caddo River** | | | | | | | | | |
| Arrowhead Cabin & Canoe Rentals | • | | | • | • | • | • | | |
| Two Rivers Canoe Rental, Inc. | • | | | • | • | | | | |
| Wright Way Canoe Rental | • | | | • | • | • | | | |
| **North Cadron Creek** | | | | | | | | | |
| Ozark Funtime Canoe | • | | • | • | | | | | |
| **Cossatot River** | | | | | | | | | |
| Arkansas River Runner | • | • | • | • | • | | | | |
| Arrowhead Cabin & Canoe Rentals | • | | | • | • | • | • | | |
| **Crooked Creek** | | | | | | | | | |
| Bull Shoals Famous Floats, Inc. | | | | | • | | | | |
| **Crooked Creek** —CONTINUED | | | | | | | | | |
| Kyles Landing Cabin & Canoe Rental | • | | | | • | • | • | • | |
| Razorback Wilderness Center | • | • | | • | • | | | | |
| **Current River** | | | | | | | | | |
| Current River Beach Campground | • | | | • | | • | • | • | |
| **Eleven Point River** | | | | | | | | | |
| Woody's Canoe Rental & Campground | • | • | | • | | • | • | • | |
| **Illinois Bayou** | | | | | | | | | |
| Fish & Game Guaranteed | | | | | • | | | | |
| **Kings River** | | | | | | | | | |
| Fletcher's Devil's Dive Resort | | • | | • | • | • | | | |
| Trigger Gap Float Service | • | | | • | | | • | | |
| **Little Missouri River** | | | | | | | | | |
| Arrowhead Cabin & Canoe Rentals | • | | | • | • | • | • | | |
| Clear Fork Canoeing | • | | | • | | | | | |
| **Little Red River (Below Greers Ferry)** | | | | | | | | | |
| Dripping Springs Trout Dock | | • | | | • | | • | • | |
| Lindsey's Rainbow Resort | | • | | | • | • | • | • | • |
| Little Red River Trout Dock | | • | | | • | • | • | • | |
| Lobo Landing Resort | | • | | | • | • | • | • | • |
| River Ranch Resort | • | • | | • | • | • | • | • | • |
| Swinging Bridge Resort | • | • | | • | • | • | • | • | |
| **Mulberry River** | | | | | | | | | |
| Byrd's Mulberry River Canoe Rental | • | | • | • | • | | • | • | |
| Kyles Landing Cabin & Canoe Rental | • | | | | • | • | • | • | |
| Turner Bend Canoe Rental | • | | • | • | | | • | • | |
| Wayfarer of the Ozarks | • | | | • | | | • | • | |
| **Ouachita River** | | | | | | | | | |
| M & M Canoe Rentals | • | | | • | | • | • | • | |
| Ouachita Joe's Canoe Rental | • | | | • | • | | | • | |
| Ouachita & Rocky Shoals Canoe Rentals | • | • | | • | • | • | • | • | |
| Rockport Rapids Canoe Rental & RV Park | • | | • | • | • | | • | • | |
| Two Rivers Canoe Rental, Inc. | • | | | • | • | | | | |
| **Saline River** | | | | | | | | | |
| Ozark Funtime Canoe | • | | • | • | | | | | |
| **Spring River** | | | | | | | | | |
| Beach Club BBQ & Canoe Rental | • | | | • | • | • | • | | • |
| Kamp Kierl | • | | | • | | | • | | |
| Mammoth Spring Canoe Rental | • | | | • | | | • | • | |
| Many Islands Camp & Canoe Rental | • | • | | • | | • | • | • | |
| Riverside Campground & Canoe Rental | • | | | • | | • | • | • | |
| Saddler Falls Canoe Rental | • | | | • | | | • | • | |
| Southfork Canoe Rental & Resort | • | • | | • | • | • | • | • | |
| Spring River Oaks Camp & Canoe Rental | • | | | • | | | • | • | |

# THE ARKANSAS FLOATER'S KIT

## 1995-96 Outfitters' Directory —Continued

THE ARKANSAS FLOATER'S KIT

| | CANOE RENTAL | JOHNBOAT RENTAL | RAFT RENTAL | SHUTTLE SERVICES | GUIDE SERVICES | LODGING | CAMPGROUND | SUPPLIES | RESTAURANT |
|---|---|---|---|---|---|---|---|---|---|
| **War Eagle Creek** | | | | | | | | | |
| Withrow Springs State Park | • | | | • | | | • | | |
| **White River & North Fork** | | | | | | | | | |
| Bull Shoals Famous Floats, Inc. | | | | | • | | | | |
| Bull Shoals State Park Trout Dock | • | • | | • | | | • | • | |
| Bull Shoals White River Landing | | | | • | • | • | • | • | |
| Chamberlain's Trout Dock | • | • | | • | • | • | • | • | |
| Cotter Trout Dock | | | | | • | | | • | |
| Gaston's White River Resort | | • | | • | • | • | | • | • |
| Gene's Trout Fishing Resort | • | • | | • | • | • | • | • | |
| Gunga-La Lodge & River Outfitters | • | • | • | • | • | • | • | • | |
| Hurst Fishing Service | | • | | • | • | | | • | |
| Jack's Fishing Resort | • | • | • | • | • | • | • | • | • |
| Jenkins Fishing Service & Motel | | • | | | • | • | | • | |
| McClellan Trout Dock | | • | | | | • | • | • | |
| Miller's Fishing Service | • | • | | • | • | | | • | |
| Newland's Float Trips & Lodge | | • | | • | • | • | | • | |
| Norfork Trout Dock | • | • | | • | • | | | • | |
| P.J.'s Lodge | | | | | • | • | | • | • |
| Rainbow Drive Resort | | • | | | • | • | | • | |
| Rainbow Trout Resort | | • | | | • | • | • | • | |
| Red Bud Dock | | • | | | • | • | | • | |
| Rivercliff Trout Dock | | • | | | • | | | • | |
| Rose's Trout Dock | | • | | • | • | | • | • | |
| Sportsman's Resort | | • | | | • | • | • | • | • |
| Stetson's Resort | | • | | | • | • | | • | • |
| White Buffalo Resort | • | • | | • | • | • | • | • | |
| White Hole Resort | | • | | | • | • | • | • | • |
| Wildcat Shoals Resort | | • | | | • | • | | • | |
| Woodsman's Sport Shop & Fishing Resort | • | | | • | • | • | • | • | |
| **Upper White River** | | | | | | | | | |
| Charlie's Canoe Rental | • | | | • | | • | | | |
| Riverview Resort | • | • | | • | • | • | | • | |

| | CANOE RENTAL | JOHNBOAT RENTAL | RAFT RENTAL | SHUTTLE SERVICES | GUIDE SERVICES | LODGING | CAMPGROUND | SUPPLIES | RESTAURANT |
|---|---|---|---|---|---|---|---|---|---|
| **Statewide** | | | | | | | | | |
| Unlimited Outdoors, Inc. | • | | | • | • | | | • | |

### *Big Piney Creek*

**Fish & Game Guaranteed**
Route 2, Box 247
Dover, Arkansas 72837
(501) 331-2712 or 858-4061

**Kyles Landing Cabin & Canoe Rental**
HCR 70, Box 145
Kyles Landing Road
(6 Miles West of Jasper)
Jasper, Arkansas 72641
(501) 446-2060

**Moore Outdoors**
Route 2, Box 303M
Dover, Arkansas 72837
(501) 331-3606

**Paulette Helton**
16525 SR 7 North
Dover, Arkansas 72837
(501) 331-3305
(Shuttle Only)

**Razorback Wilderness Center**
Route 1, Box 185
Dogpatch, Arkansas 72648
(501) 446-2255

### *Upper Buffalo River*

**Buffalo Adventures Canoe Rental**
P.O. Box 414
Highway 74 West
Jasper, Arkansas 72641
(501) 446-5406

**Buffalo Outdoor Center, Ponca**
P.O. Box 1
Ponca, Arkansas 72670
(501) 861-5514 or
1-800-221-5514

**Gordon Motel & Canoe Rental**
P.O. Box 60
Jasper, Arkansas 72641
(501) 446-5252 or 446-2399 or
1-800-477-8509

**Keller's Kanoes**
Dogpatch, Arkansas 72648
(501) 446-2644 or
1-800-352-6637

**Kyles Landing Cabin & Canoe Rental**
HCR 70, Box 145
Kyles Landing Road
(6 Miles West of Jasper)
Jasper, Arkansas 72641
(501) 446-2060

**Lost Valley Canoe & Lodging**
Highway 43
Ponca, Arkansas 72670
(501) 861-5522

**Razorback Wilderness Center**
Route 1, Box 185
Dogpatch, Arkansas 72648
(501) 446-2255

**Riverview Motel Canoe Rental**
P.O. Box 352
Jasper, Arkansas 72641
(501) 446-2616 or 446-5581

### *Middle Buffalo River*

**Buffalo Camping & Canoeing**
P.O. Box 504
Gilbert, Arkansas 72636
(501) 439-2888 or 439-2386

**Buffalo Outdoor Center, Silver Hill**
Route 1, Box 56
Highway 65 South
St. Joe, Arkansas 72675
(501) 439-2244 or
1-800-582-2244

**Silver Hill Canoe Rental**
Route 1, Box 47
St. Joe, Arkansas 72675
(501) 439-2372

**Tomahawk Canoe Rental & RV Park**
Route 1, Box 11A
St. Joe, Arkansas 72675
(501) 439-2617

### *Lower Buffalo River*

**Bennett's Canoe Rental**
HCR 66, Box 331
Yellville, Arkansas 72687
(501) 449-6431

**Buffalo Point Canoe Rental, Inc.**
HCR 66, Box 383
Yellville, Arkansas 72687
(501) 449-4521 or
1-800-85-CANOE

**Cotter Trout Dock**
P.O. Box 96
Cotter Springs Access
(Off Hwy. 62B)
Cotter, Arkansas 72626
(501) 435-6525

# THE ARKANSAS FLOATER'S KIT

**Crockett's Country Store & Canoe Rental**
Highways 27 & 14
Harriet, Arkansas 72639
(501) 448-3892 or
1-800-355-6111

**Dirst Canoe Rental & Log Cabins**
HCR 66, Box 385
Yellville, Arkansas 72687
1-800-537-2850

**Dodd's Canoe & Johnboat Rental**
HCR 66, Box 365
Yellville, Arkansas 72687
(501) 449-6619 or 449-6297 or
1-800-423-8731

**Newland's Float Trips & Lodge**
Route 1, River Road
Lakeview, Arkansas 72642
(501) 431-5678 or 431-5604 or
1-800-334-5604

**Rose's Trout Dock**
P.O. Box 82
Norfork, Arkansas 72658
(501) 499-5311

**Sportsman's Resort**
HCR 62, Box 96
Flippin, Arkansas 72634
(501) 453-2424 or 453-2422

**White Buffalo Resort**
Route 2, Box 438
(Located in Buffalo City)
Mountain Home, Arkansas 72653
(501) 425-8555

**Wild Bill's Outfitter**
HCR 66, Box 380
Yellville, Arkansas 72687
(501) 449-6235 or
1-800-554-8657

**Woodsman's Sport Shop & Fishing Service**
HCR 61, Box 461
Norfork, Arkansas 72658
(501) 499-7454

## *Caddo River*

**Arrowhead Cabin & Canoe Rentals**
191 Peppermint Terrace
Hot Springs, Arkansas 71913
(501) 356-2944 or 767-5823

**Two Rivers Canoe Rental, Inc.**
Caddo River Bridge
Highway 7
Caddo Valley, Arkansas 71923
(501) 246-2773 or 366-4251

**Wright Way Canoe Rental**
P.O. Box 180
Glenwood, Arkansas 71943
(501) 356-2055

## *North Cadron Creek*

**Ozark Funtime Canoe**
16605 I-30
Benton, Arkansas 72015
(501) 776-3626

## *Cossatot River*

**Arkansas River Runner**
Route 3, Box 301
Highway 71 East
DeQueen, Arkansas 71832
(501) 642-4919

**Arrowhead Cabin & Canoe Rentals**
191 Peppermint Terrace
Hot Springs Arkansas 71913
(501) 356-2944 or 767-5823

## *Crooked Creek*

**Bull Shoals Famous Floats, Inc.**
P.O. Box 44
1515 Central Blvd.
Bull Shoals, Arkansas 72619
(501) 445-7160

**Kyles Landing Cabin & Canoe Rental**
HCR 70, Box 145
Kyles Landing Road
(6 Miles West of Jasper)
Jasper, Arkansas 72641
(501) 446-2060

**Razorback Wilderness Center**
Route 1, Box 185
Dogpatch, Arkansas 72648
(501) 446-2255

## *Current River*

**Current River Beach Campground**
P.O. Box 184
(Highway 67 North)
Biggers, Arkansas 72413
(501) 892-5455

## *Eleven Point River*

**Woody's Canoe Rental & Campground**
9931 Highway 93
Pocahontas, Arkansas 72455
(501) 892-9732 or
1-800-892-9732

## *Illinois Bayou*

**Fish & Game Guaranteed**
Route 2, Box 247
Dover, Arkansas 72837
(501) 331-2712 or 858-4061

## *Kings River*

**Fletcher's Devil's Dive Resort**
HCR 1, Box 1050
Eagle Rock, Missouri 65641
(417) 271-3396

**Trigger Gap Float Service**
Route 1, Box 654
Eureka Springs, Arkansas 72632
(501) 253-9247

## *Little Missouri River*

**Arrowhead Cabin & Canoe Rentals**
191 Peppermint Terrace
Hot Springs, Arkansas 71913
(501) 356-2944 or 767-5823

**Clear Fork Canoeing**
Route 4, Box 159 A
Highway 27
Murfreesboro, Arkansas 71958
(501) 285-2729

## *Little Red River (Below Greers Ferry)*

**Dripping Springs Trout Dock**
263 Dripping Springs Road
Pangburn, Arkansas 72121
(501) 728-4711

**Lindsey's Rainbow Resort**
350 Rainbow Road
Heber Springs, Arkansas 72543
(501) 362-3139

**Little Red River Trout Dock**
285 Ferguson Road
Heber Springs, Arkansas 72543
(501) 362-2197

**Lobo Landing Resort**
3525 Libby Road
Heber Springs, Arkansas 72543
(501) 362-5802

**River Ranch Resort**
630 River Ranch Road
Heber Springs, Arkansas 72543
(501) 362-9003 or
1-800-366-9003

**Swinging Bridge Resort**
100 Swinging Bridge Drive
Heber Springs, Arkansas 72543
(501) 362-3327

## *Mulberry River*

**Byrd's Mulberry River Canoe Rental**
HCR 61, Box 131
Ozark, Arkansas 72949
(501) 667-4066

**Kyles Landing Cabin & Canoe Rental**
HCR 70, Box 145
Kyles Landing Road
(6 Miles West of Jasper)
Jasper, Arkansas 72641
(501) 446-2060

**Turner Bend Canoe Rental**
HCR 63, Box 216
Highway 23 North
Ozark, Arkansas 72949
(501) 667-3641

**Wayfarer of the Ozarks**
HCR 61, Box 131
Ozark, Arkansas 72949
(501) 667-4998

## *Ouachita River*

**M & M Canoe Rentals**
Highway 88
(Between Pencil Bluff & Sims)
HC 64, Box 72
Pencil Bluff, Arkansas 71965
(501) 326-4617 or
1-800-99-FLOAT

**Ouachita Joe's Canoe Rental**
P.O. Box 65
Pencil Bluff, Arkansas 71965
(501) 326-5517

**Ouachita & Rocky Shoals Canoe Rentals**
Star Route 2, Box 200
Mount Ida, Arkansas 71957
(501) 867-2382

**Rockport Rapids Canoe Rental & RV Park**
I-30 (1 Mile From Malvern Exit 97)
P.O. Box 22696
Little Rock, Arkansas 72221
(501) 844-1900

**Two Rivers Canoe Rental, Inc.**
Caddo River Bridge
Highway 7
Caddo Valley, Arkansas 71923
(501) 246-2773 or 366-4251

## *Saline River*

**Ozark Funtime Canoe**
16605 I-30
Benton, Arkansas 72015
(501) 776-3626

# THE ARKANSAS FLOATER'S KIT

## *Spring River*

**Beach Club BBQ & Canoe Rental**
P.O. Box 239
Hardy, Arkansas 72542
(501) 856-3292

**Kamp Kierl**
Highway 63
(1 Mile North of Hardy)
P.O. Box 365
Hardy, Arkansas 72542
(501) 856-2824

**Mammoth Spring Canoe Rental**
P.O. Box 244
Highway 63
(15 Miles North of Hardy)
Mammoth Spring, Arkansas 72554
(501) 625-3645 or
(417) 264-7592

**Many Islands Camp & Canoe Rental**
Route 2
Mammoth Spring, Arkansas 72554
(501) 856-3451

**Riverside Campground & Canoe Rental**
Highway 63 South
(4-1/2 Miles South of Mammoth Spring)
Mammoth Spring, Arkansas 72554
(501) 625-7501

**Saddler Falls Canoe Rental**
Highway 63
(1 Mile North of Hardy)
P.O. Box 365
Hardy, Arkansas 72542
(501) 856-2824

**Southfork Canoe Rental & Resort**
Route 3, Box 124A
Highway 289
Mammoth Spring, Arkansas 72554
(501) 895-2803

**Spring River Oaks Camp & Canoe Rental**
Route 2, Box 66 (Off Highway 63)
Mammoth Spring, Arkansas 72554
(501) 856-3885

## *War Eagle Creek*

**Withrow Springs State Park**
Route 3
Highway 23
Huntsville, Arkansas 72740
(501) 559-2593

## *White River & North Fork*

**Bull Shoals Famous Floats, Inc.**
P.O. Box 44
1515 Central Blvd.
Bull Shoals, Arkansas 72619
(501) 445-7160

**Bull Shoals State Park Trout Dock**
P.O. Box 205
Bull Shoals, Arkansas 72619
(501) 431-5557 or 431-5521

**Bull Shoals White River Landing**
P.O. Box 748
Highway 178
Bull Shoals, Arkansas 72619
(501) 445-4166

**Chamberlain's Trout Dock**
Route 1, Box 620
Denton Ferry Road
Cotter, Arkansas 72626
(501) 435-6535

**Cotter Trout Dock**
P.O. Box 96
Cotter Springs Access
Cotter, Arkansas 72626
(501) 435-6525

**Gaston's White River Resort**
#1 River Road
Lakeview, Arkansas 72642
(501) 431-5202 or 431-5204

**Gene's Trout Fishing Resort**
Route 3, Box 348
(1/2 Mile Below Norfork Dam)
Mountain Home, Arkansas 72653
(501) 499-5381 or
1-800-526-3625

**Gunga-La Lodge & River Outfitters**
Route 1, Box 147
(1 Mile Below Bull Shoals Dam)
Lakeview, Arkansas 72642
(501) 431-5606 or
1-800-844-5606

**Hurst Fishing Service**
P.O. Box 129
Cotter, Arkansas 72626
(501) 435-6414

**Jack's Fishing Resort**
HCR 72, Box 185
Mountain View, Arkansas 72560
(501) 585-2211

**Jenkins Fishing Service & Motel**
P.O. Box 303
605 Highway 56 East
Calico Rock, Arkansas 72519
(501) 297-8181

**McClellan Trout Dock**
HCR 61, Box 24
County Road 63
Norfork, Arkansas 72658
(501) 499-5589

**Miller's Fishing Service**
Box 277
Cotter, Arkansas 72626
(501) 435-6313

**Newland's Float Trips & Lodge**
Route 1, River Road
Lakeview, Arkansas 72642
(501) 431-5678 or 431-5604 or
1-800-334-5604

**Norfork Trout Dock**
P.O. Box 129
Norfork, Arkansas 72658
(501) 499-5500

**P.J.'s Lodge**
P.O. Box 61
County Road 68
Norfork, Arkansas 72658
(501) 499-7500

**Rainbow Drive Resort**
Route 1, Box 1185
Cotter, Arkansas 72626
(501) 430-5217

**Rainbow Trout Resort**
Route 3, Box 340
Mountain Home, Arkansas 72653
(501) 499-7214

**Red Bud Dock**
Route 2, Box 541
Gassville, Arkansas 72635
(501) 435-6303

**Rivercliff Trout Dock**
#1 River Road
P.O. Box 469
Bull Shoals, Arkansas 72619
(501) 445-4420

**Rose's Trout Dock**
P.O. Box 82
Norfork, Arkansas 72658
(501) 499-5311

**Sportsman's Resort**
HCR 62, Box 96
Flippin, Arkansas 72634
(501) 453-2424 or 453-2422

**Stetson's Resort**
HCR 62, Box 102
Flippin, Arkansas 72634
(501) 453-8066

**White Buffalo Resort**
Route 2, Box 438
(Located in Buffalo City)
Mountain Home, Arkansas 72653
(501) 425-8555

**White Hole Resort**
HCR 62, Box 100
Flippin, Arkansas 72634
(501) 453-2913

**Wildcat Shoals Resort**
HCR 62, Box 166
Flippin, Arkansas 72634
(501) 453-2321

**Woodsman's Sport Shop & Fishing Service**
HCR 61, Box 461
Norfork, Arkansas 72658
(501) 499-7454

## *Upper White River*

**Charlie's Canoe Rental**
Route 2, Box 451
Eureka Springs, Arkansas 72632
(501) 253-9125

**Riverview Resort**
Route 6, Box 475
Eureka Springs, Arkansas 72632
(501) 253-8367

## *Statewide Outfitters*

**Unlimited Outdoors, Inc.**
P.O. Box 1187
North Little Rock, Arkansas 72115
(501) 753-9873

***Information shown on this list of outfitters was provided by the various businesses and does not represent an endorsement by the State of Arkansas. Outfitters wishing to be included in future editions should contact:***

***Arkansas Department of Parks & Tourism,***
***Tourism Director's Office,***
***One Capitol Mall,***
***Little Rock, Arkansas 72201***

***Phone: 501-682-1088***
***FAX: 501-682-1364***

# THE ARKANSAS FLOATER'S KIT

Produced by the Arkansas Department of Parks and Tourism, the Arkansas Game and Fish Commission, and the Arkansas Natural and Scenic Rivers Commission

## INTRODUCTION

Arkansas has over 9,000 miles of streams, and a good deal of this mileage is perfect for floating — be it by canoe, johnboat, or raft. The variety of enjoyable experiences provided by this assortment of rivers is remarkably wide-ranging: from matchless trout fishing trips, to rugged whitewater runs, to peaceful passages ideal for first-timers. The streams of Arkansas are, in a word, inviting.

Introductions to 17 of the state's favorite waterways are found in this "floater's kit." Seasons, access points, fishing tips, and basic characteristics of the rivers are included along with locator maps. What the reader won't find are mile-by-mile descriptions of the streams; these details are for you to discover!

First, though, ten important reminders:

- Wear those life jackets.
- Take along a spare paddle.
- Pay attention to local weather forecasts.
- Dress appropriately for the season.
- Don't travel alone.
- Avoid camping in areas subject to sudden rises.
- Know your ability and don't exceed it.
- Refrain from drinking creek or river water no matter how clean it appears.
- Carry out whatever you carry in.
- Should you capsize, try to stay with your boat and swim it to shore, making certain that you're on the upstream side of the craft to avoid getting pinned between it and rocks or willows.

### ENCLOSURES

Big Piney Creek
Buffalo River
Caddo River
Cadron Creek
Cossatot River
Crooked Creek
Eleven Point River
Illinois Bayou
Kings River
Little Missouri River
Little Red River
Mulberry River
Ouachita River
Saline River
Spring River
Strawberry River
White River
Outfitters' Directory

## BACKGROUND INFORMATION

### Maps

Several of the stream write-ups in the "floater's kit" recommend the purchase of "general highway maps" for particular counties. These can be obtained, at a cost of $1.10 per county (postpaid), from: Map Sales, Room 203; Arkansas State Highway and Transportation Department; P.O. Box 2261; Little Rock, Arkansas 72203.

For a more detailed look at the land, refer to topographic maps published by the U.S. Geological Survey. These are available at a cost of $2.50 each (plus postage and handling charges), but first write for a free "Index to Topographic Maps for Arkansas" from: Arkansas Geological Commission; Map and Publication Sales; 3815 West Roosevelt Road; Little Rock, Arkansas 72204.

### Degree of Difficulty: Classes I-VI

The narratives also occasionally refer to class ratings for the streams, based on an international scale of six levels of difficulty:

**Class I:** EASY. Moving water with few riffles and small waves. Few or no obstructions. Correct course is easy to determine.

**Class II:** MEDIUM. Fairly frequent, but unobstructed rapids. Course generally easy to recognize. Some maneuvering is required.

**Class III:** DIFFICULT. Numerous rapids with high and irregular waves. Narrow passages that often require complex maneuvering. Course not always easily recognizable.

**Class IV:** VERY DIFFICULT. Long rapids characterized by high and irregular waves with boulders directly in swift current. Course often difficult to recognize requiring some scouting from bank.

**Class V:** EXCEEDINGLY DIFFICULT. Continuous rocky rapids with high and irregular broken water which cannot be avoided. Extremely fast flow, abrupt bends, and strong cross currents. Difficult rescue conditions. Frequent inspections from bank necessary.

**Class VI:** LIMIT OF NAVIGABILITY. Class V difficulties increased to the upper limits of skill and equipment. Extremely dangerous. Only for teams of experts.

### Additional Information

Many of the streams mentioned in this collection flow through or near Arkansas's two national forests — the Ouachita National Forest and the Ozark-St. Francis National Forest. Both offer superb hiking, camping, and hunting opportunities in addition to their river recreation possibilities. For more information, write:

- Forest Supervisor
  Ouachita National Forest
  P.O. Box 1270
  Hot Springs, Arkansas 71902
- Forest Supervisor
  Ozark-St. Francis National Forests
  P.O. Box 1008
  Russellville, Arkansas 72801

The Arkansas Game and Fish Commission is the agency charged with managing the state's wildlife resources. It has established a fine network of hatcheries, public fishing lakes, and wildlife management areas. More information, including order forms for hunting and fishing licenses, may be obtained by writing:

- Information and Education Division
  Arkansas Game and Fish Commission
  2 Natural Resources Drive
  Little Rock, Arkansas 72205

The Arkansas Department of Parks and Tourism manages the state park system, produces the Arkansas Vacation Kit, and houses the Arkansas Trails Council. For details on these or similar topics, write:

- Director
  Arkansas Department of Parks
  and Tourism
  1 Capitol Mall
  Little Rock, Arkansas 72201

In 1979 the legislature established the Arkansas Natural and Scenic Rivers Commission, a body charged with developing a system to protect "natural beauty along certain rivers of the state." For more information on the Commission and its activities, write:

- Director
  Arkansas Natural and Scenic Rivers
  Commission
  c/o Department of Arkansas Heritage
  Heritage Center East, Suite 200
  225 East Markham
  Little Rock, Arkansas 72201

# BIG PINEY CREEK

# THE ARKANSAS FLOATER'S KIT

## #1 IN A SERIES

At 67 miles, Big Piney Creek is not particularly long by Arkansas standards. But mile for mile, there's no doubt it ranks among the best float streams in the state.

For one thing, the Piney is situated in some very interesting country — the heart of the Ozarks. Its headwaters region is rugged and remote, and the few communities to be found have appropriate names like Fallsville, Limestone, and Deer.

The Piney itself is a clear mountain stream wasting little time on its journey toward the Arkansas River. It hurries pell-mell over ledges and numerous rapids in a twisting course through Newton, Johnson, and Pope counties. It flows past bluffs, alongside gravel bars, and under overhanging hardwoods. Some consider the Piney to be "the classic Ozark stream."

If nothing else, the Piney offers a classic mix of recreational opportunities. The creek and adjacent public lands provide an ideal setting for floating, fishing, camping, hiking, hunting, and swimming — not to mention other rituals like rock-skipping and plain old relaxing. In short, the Piney has something for everyone.

### SECTION DESCRIBED

Source to Lake Dardanelle (Arkansas River), a distance of approximately 67 miles.

### CHARACTERISTICS

Depending on one's point-of-view, Big Piney Creek is either a series of short pools interrupted by rapids, or a series of rapids interrupted by stretches of relative calmness. Fishermen probably prefer the first description, while canoeists will generally opt for the latter. In any event, the creek offers good water for both users.

The Limestone to Arkansas Highway 123 run is not a common float (the water's usually too low), but when conditions are right, the 10-mile section is worth considering. In this stretch the Piney has numerous rapids (some up to a class III rating), along with a good supply of those traditional canoe-catchers — willow thickets.

The next section is the Arkansas 123 to Treat run, a float covering about eight miles. As with the upper stretch, the water's clear and the scenery's good. Here, though, the valley is not so tight, and the stream's pace slackens a bit. The rapids are a little more subdued (all of the class I and II varieties), but willows — while not so plentiful as upstream — can still cause problems.

The third section of Big Piney Creek — the Treat to Long Pool float — is where the stream has earned its reputation among whitewater enthusiasts. The hills start crowding the creek for space along this 10-mile run, and one result is rapids — rapids with names like "Roller Coaster," "Surfing Hole," and even "Cascades of Extinction." Gravel bars are conveniently located just below most of these rapids and provide ideal spots for a breather, a picnic, or, in some cases, a salvage operation.

The Piney's next section — Long Pool to Arkansas 164 (or Twin Bridges) — slows down considerably in its five-mile journey. As the creek leaves the Ozarks, its pools become longer, and the rapids are generally in the class I category. Willow strainers, if anything, are more common here than in the upper reaches.

The stream's final stretch — Arkansas 164 to Lake Dardanelle (or points in-between) — isn't for those who require their water to be white. In these last few miles, the Piney slowly meanders toward Piney Bay, an arm of Lake Dardanelle.

### SEASONS

Big Piney Creek offers year-round recreation. The canoe season usually begins in late fall and can last through mid-June, depending on local rainfall. Fishing is a year-long possibility for those willing to wade-fish or drag their boats over the shoals during the drier months. And after the first frost has discouraged ticks and chiggers, hiking and backpacking are highly recommended, particularly in the 15,000-acre Hurricane Creek Wilderness just northeast of the 123 bridge.

### ACCESS POINTS

Considering the ruggedness of the country, access to Big Piney Creek is surprisingly good. At Limestone, the stream can be reached by Forest Road 1004. Forest Road 1002 also provides access a few miles south of the 1004 crossing. The next put-in or take-out points are at Arkansas 123 and Forest Road 1802. Perhaps the most popular beginning point for float trips is the Helton Farm access at Treat (Forest Road 1805), where local landowners allow canoeists to put-in for a small fee. Ten miles downstream is Long Pool, a Forest Service campground complete with restrooms, changing rooms, loading/unloading areas, and a parking lot. (The Long Pool site is a fee area except for the winter season.) The last major access point is another five miles downstream at Arkansas 164.

### SCENERY

While the Piney doesn't have the towering bluffs of the Buffalo River, it has no shortage of good scenery. The steep hillsides are covered with a mixed hardwood and pine forest and occasionally offer glimpses of deer, turkeys, or even black bears. Along the way floaters will pass an astonishing assortment of rocks — some house-sized — that over the eons have toppled into the stream. In addition, quiet travellers may discover great blue herons, wood ducks, or beavers along their route.

### FISHING

A vast majority of those floating the Big Piney don't carry fishing equipment. No doubt some fear they'll lose their rods and reels at the first rapid, but most probably don't realize that the stream is a good place to fish. A veteran fisherman, though, will note the cool, clear water with its rocky cover and come to one conclusion — smallmouth bass. That fish can be caught in the pools of the Piney and so can spotted and largemouth bass, longear and green sunfish and rock bass.

Fishing the Big Piney can be a twelve-month pastime, but most authorities will recommend the late spring/early summer period. In the hotter months, diehards may have some luck in the creek's deep pools, but getting there may require dragging boats over shallows or even bushwacking through cane thickets. Anglers seldom visit the Piney during late fall and winter months, but it's during this period the largest bass are often taken.

### SERVICES AVAILABLE

Supplies can be obtained in Dover or Russellville, and the latter city also offers numerous motels. Camping is permitted just about anywhere in the Ozark National Forest, but two "developed" campgrounds — Long Pool and Haw Creek Falls — are available. Canoes can be rented in the vicinity, and several local families are willing to provide car shuttles for a fee.

### OTHER INFORMATION

**The best time to float the Piney is when its water level is in the 3.0-5.0 range (call the Corps of Engineers' recording—501-324-5150—for a daily report), although the uppermost reaches may require a higher minimum reading for best conditions. At five feet and beyond, the stream is considered dangerous.**

**Lastly, a good deal of private property borders the stream. Visitors should take care to avoid trespassing problems.**

# BUFFALO RIVER

# THE ARKANSAS FLOATER'S KIT

## #2 IN A SERIES

North Arkansas's Buffalo River was the country's first national river, is roughly 150 miles long, and includes nearly 95,000 acres of public land along its corridor. It has been the topic of a full-length book, the subject of a *National Geographic* feature article, and the cornerstone for the state's environmental movement. Describing the Buffalo in 1,000-1,200 words won't be easy, but here goes:

Like the Mulberry River and Big Piney Creek, the Buffalo originates in the rugged Boston Mountains division of the Ozarks near Fallsville in southwestern Newton County. Unlike the other two streams which eventually head south to meet the Arkansas River, the Buffalo goes east where, ultimately, it joins the White River. Along the way it descends nearly 2,000 feet through layers of sandstone, limestone, and chert. One immediately obvious result is bluffs and more bluffs — the highest in all the Ozarks. Hidden away, ready for discovery, are other geologic marvels — springs, caves, waterfalls, natural bridges, and box-like canyons.

But the Buffalo is much more than an ongoing display of natural curiosities. It is, in the words of the National Park Service, "an island of time and space." It is a valley where turn-of-the-century lifestyles and landscapes still exist. It is a place that refreshes the spirit.

### SECTION DESCRIBED

Entire length — 150 miles.

### CHARACTERISTICS

The Buffalo River gets its start in national forest country, nearly within rock-throwing distance of the highest point in the Ozarks. Some floating takes place in the headwaters area (the "Hailstone" trip from Dixon Road to Arkansas 21 is almost legendary among serious paddlers), but, for most, this is a good place to put on the hiking boots. A real treat is the Upper Buffalo Wilderness, a 14,200-acre tract managed by the Ozark National Forest and the Buffalo National River. Visitors to the area can expect to see caves, bluffs, waterfalls, old cabin sites, and maybe even a local black bear.

The Buffalo's next section — from the Highway 21 bridge south of Boxley to the Ponca low-water bridge at the Highway 74 crossing — is another that doesn't get a great deal of use; the water's usually too low. But when conditions are right, this six-mile stretch offers a fast-moving series of class II rapids, many of which are laced with willows.

Perhaps the most famous of all Buffalo River floats are those that take place between Ponca and the Arkansas Highway 7 crossing (known until recent years as the community of Pruitt). Something for everyone can be found in this 25-mile section: class I and II rapids (complete with hazards like "Gray Rock"); the highest waterfall in mid-America (at Hemmed-in-Hollow); the 11,300-acre Ponca Wilderness; towering cliffs including the 500-foot tall Big Bluff; and an excellent assortment of swimming holes. In addition, there are several conveniently located access points/campgrounds — Steel Creek, Kyles Landing, Erbie, and Ozark — between Ponca and Highway 7.

The Buffalo's next stretch — from Arkansas 7 to Highway 123 (or Carver) — is about 10 miles in length. While it doesn't offer the spectacular scenery available just upstream, this is a fine float, especially for families. It features class I rapids, gravel bars, and numerous bluffs. Campsites and access are available at Carver or two and a half miles upstream at Hasty.

Another major section of the river begins at Carver and concludes about 32 miles downstream at the U.S. 65 bridge (in-between access and camping areas are available at Mount Hershey and Woolum). Many Buffalo veterans consider this to be among the stream's finest stretches. While other sections feature higher bluffs and more challenging rapids, this portion of the river is one of its quietest and most peaceful trips. The scenery is good, too, including such things as "The Narrows" — a tall but narrow rock outcrop separating the Buffalo and Richland Creek.

The 27 mile trip from U.S. 65 to Buffalo Point (still referred to by many as "the old state park") is a long, lazy float ideally suited for those interested in casual canoeing. The scenery's good, and the rapids are interesting but easy. Other access points within this part of the river include Gilbert, Maumee North, Maumee South, and the Highway 14 crossing.

The Buffalo's final stretch — from Buffalo Point to Buffalo City (on the White River) — is 30 miles in length, with only a single take-out point (Rush) in between. The 7.5-mile float from Buffalo Point to Rush is short, safe, and scenic — perfect for families. The remaining 23 mile trip passes through some of Arkansas's wildest country, including better than 39,000 acres of wilderness (the Lower Buffalo Wilderness and the adjacent Leatherwood Wilderness). This is the one for those wanting to get away from it all.

### SEASONS

The Buffalo is a river for all seasons. Canoeing is a year-round possibility except in the upper reaches where it's limited to the winter and spring months. Camping, too, is a year-long pursuit, though visitors should remember the state's lowest winter temperatures traditionally occur along this stream. The Buffalo's corridor is also a great locale for hiking and backpacking, but expeditions should be scheduled outside the tick/chigger season.

### ACCESS POINTS

Visitors can get to the Buffalo River via U.S. Highway 65 and a whole host of Arkansas highways — 21, 74, 7, 123, 333, 14, and 268. In addition, a good many county roads provide access to points between the highway crossings.

### SCENERY

Spectacular is the best word to describe scenery along the river. For 150 miles, the Buffalo offers an unmatched mixture of clear water, lofty cliffs, overhanging hardwoods, and inviting gravel bars. There's excellent scenery off the river, too. One place that shouldn't be missed is Lost Valley, a unique bluff-lined canyon between Boxley and Ponca. The Richland Creek Valley is also a sight-seer's paradise, especially in its upper reaches where an 11,800-acre wilderness area awaits the adventurous.

### FISHING

To many anglers, the hordes of visitors attracted to the Buffalo destroy the peaceful, aesthetic values that are the reason for going fishing in the first place. But this spirited colt of a stream has a remarkable capacity for swallowing up people in a maze of bluffs and canyons. And the Buffalo is a gem among Arkansas' float fishing streams.

Considered a model smallmouth bass stream, the Buffalo has fast, clear, oxygen-rich water with the kind of gravel bottom and boulder beds smallmouths love. Floating in a johnboat or canoe is the accepted method of fishing, but during spring, try beaching your craft at the head of a deep, swift chute and drifting a lure near a boulder in the fast water. Many fishermen make the mistake of working the holes where the bass aren't and floating through the swift water where they are. The knowing locals often work surface lures at night for the big ones, and they catch them regularly.

The Buffalo's cool, clean waters also provide perfect habitat for channel catfish, green and longear sunfish and spotted bass. Veterans frequently rely on natural baits — crayfish, minnows and worms — in their efforts to entice a keeper.

### SERVICES AVAILABLE

About two dozen concessionnaires rent canoes along the Buffalo and offer other related services. In addition, several rent johnboats and can provide complete fishing packages.

Lodging choices will depend upon individual preferences but can range from genuine log cabins to bed and breakfast facilities to modern motel rooms. And, of course, designated campgrounds are located at frequent intervals on the river. Most all supplies can be obtained at Harrison, Marshall, Jasper, Yellville or other nearby communities.

### OTHER INFORMATION

The National Park Service maintains Information Stations at the Highway 7 crossing (Pruitt), near the U.S. 65 crossing (Silver Hill), and at Buffalo Point. Maps and river guides are available for purchase at these sites, from the Park Headquarters in Harrison, or from local outfitters. Additional information may be obtained by writing: Superintendent, Buffalo National River; P.O. Box 1173; Harrison, Arkansas 72602.

Kenneth L. Smith's *Buffalo River Country* provides a fascinating introduction to the river and its surrounding landscape. The book may be ordered through the Ozark Society; P.O. Box 3503; Little Rock, Arkansas 72203.

# CADDO RIVER

# THE ARKANSAS FLOATER'S KIT

#3 IN A SERIES

Flowing out of the Ouachita Mountains in west central Arkansas is one of the state's most unappreciated streams — the Caddo River. Those that know it, however, describe the Caddo as among the best "family outing" type streams in the state.

It begins in southwestern Montgomery County, and flows near or through the communities of Black Springs, Norman, Caddo Gap, Glenwood, and Amity before entering the backwaters of DeGray Lake. In fact, throughout this 40-mile journey, the Caddo is never very far from civilization. Railroad tracks parallel the stream for several miles, a few houses can be spotted from the river, and cattle frequently gaze down at passing floaters. This surrounding landscape may not be original wilderness, but it sure is peaceful.

The Caddo itself is also peaceful — at least in most places. But to prevent paddlers from becoming too complacent, a handful of faster rapids (class I/class II) have been strategically placed in the stream. The river also features some top-notch gravel bars — ideal places to stop, lean back, and contemplate the mysteries of moving water.

### SECTION DESCRIBED

Source to DeGray Lake, a stretch about 40 miles in length.

### CHARACTERISTICS

While the Caddo River is "floatable" above Norman (the water has to be high, and it's a very fast float), most trips on the stream's upper reaches begin at the southwest edge of this small town. The eight-mile float down to Caddo Gap is scenic, but is possible only after extended periods of rainfall.

Probably the most popular Caddo River float is the six-mile journey from Caddo Gap to Glenwood. One highlight is a swinging footbridge over the river at the put-in (the low-water bridge west of the Caddo Gap community) which, for safety's sake, should be appreciated from below. Rock gardens are common along this stretch and can cause consternation when the water's low. The actual "gap" for the Caddo occurs about a mile and a half into the trip (just above the Arkansas 240 bridge). At this point the river passes through a narrow opening between the ridges, and so do Arkansas 8 and the railroad — all three bunched closely together. The gap is also the site of a geological oddity: some hot springs bubble up into the streambed here (for those wishing to experience these thermal waters, here are some rough directions: go upstream 200-300 yards from the old low-water bridge; springs will be on the west bank, and are usually at or below the river's surface; barefoot waders will have no trouble recognizing the spot!). Two and a half miles later, the Caddo's South Fork enters from the west. Small rapids, long gravel bars, and an occasional willow thicket characterize the stream as it approaches Glenwood.

The float from Glenwood to Amity is a slower version of the upper sections. Pools are longer, and the rapids lose some of their intensity. Yet it's a fine float, perfectly suited for those wishing to gain encouraging experience in a canoe.

### SEASONS

Like most of Arkansas's canoeing streams, the Caddo usually gets too low in the summer and early fall for good floating. The best months for a successful trip are March through June.

### ACCESS POINTS

The Caddo River is an easy stream to get to. Access points are numerous, and the shuttle routes are almost always along paved roads. Traditional put-in and take-out points include: the bridge immediately west of Norman; the low-water bridge west of Caddo Gap; the old low-water bridge on Arkansas 182 north of Amity; and the Arkansas 84 bridge northeast of Amity.

### SCENERY

The Caddo may lack dramatic views, but it has plenty of good scenery. The floater often travels next to forested hillsides and past rocky outcrops. In several places the stream flows under a green canopy of overhanging hardwoods.

### FISHING

The Caddo is one of the most underrated and overlooked cold-water fishing streams in Arkansas. That's unfortunate, for this small river offers excellent fishing in a peaceful setting that's ideal for a weekend family "getaway."

Smallmouth and spotted bass are the most notable sportfishes inhabiting the Caddo. The n ost productive bass angling begins near Caddo Gap and ends below Amity. During low water periods, portions from Caddo Gap to Glenwood can be floated. Longear and green sunfish are often caught in this stretch as well.

This is one of the few cold-water streams where white bass are an important species. These scrappy fighters migrate upstream from DeGray Lake during their spring spawning runs and are taken by boaters and bankfishermen alike using live minnows, jigs, spinners and minnow-replica crank-baits. Hybrid bass and walleyes are also occasionally taken during their spring spawning runs.

### SERVICES AVAILABLE

Most of the communities along the Caddo River include gas stations and grocery stores. Glenwood, by far the largest town along the route, also features several restaurants and at least three motels, one of them within sight of the river.

### OTHER INFORMATION

Because nearly every acre along the Caddo is privately owned, floaters need to be particularly careful not to aggravate local landowners. Camping sites are available at the Crystal Recreation Area north of Norman off Forest Road 177.

# CADRON CREEK

# THE ARKANSAS FLOATER'S KIT

#4 IN A SERIES

Each spring dozens and dozens of canoeists load up their gear and head for north Arkansas's famed Buffalo River. Many coming from central and southern parts of the state drive up U.S. 65 north of Conway and never realize that they pass right over another great canoeing stream — Cadron Creek.

The Cadron begins way up in Cleburne County, nearly within the city limits of Heber Springs. It flows in a westerly direction, is joined by its North Fork near Quitman, then continues on a southwesterly course toward its eventual destination — the Arkansas River. Along the way the stream passes by things most might expect — fields and occasional farm houses — and, for many, some startling surprises — rapids, bluffs, and canyon-like surroundings.

## SECTION DESCRIBED

Source to Arkansas River, a distance of about 59 miles.

## CHARACTERISTICS

The Cadron doesn't receive much canoeing use above the Arkansas 124 bridge west of Quitman, although the North Fork can be floated downstream from Gravesville. The first major run begins at the Highway 124 crossing and goes down to a county bridge — sometimes called the "Iron Bridge" — northeast of Guy. The float is about 4.5 miles long with class I rapids. Incidentally, history buffs might enjoy knowing that the bridge marks the site of the Hartrick Mill which operated on the creek from 1868 until the great flood of 1927. Rocks from the old mill dam still can be seen in the creekbed.

The second section of the Cadron starts at the county bridge northeast of Guy (local storeowners can provide directions) and is roughly 10 miles in length. The take-out point is in an area known as Pinnacle Springs that was once the site of a flourishing resort community in the 1880's. A dozen bath houses were found in the town, along with two hotels, a college, a saloon, a skating rink, and even a cotton gin. To get to this historic take-out, go west from Guy for three miles or so on Arkansas 310. The road will end at the creek. The float is a good one, particularly during its last few miles where the current picks up. Class II rapids — some with willow thickets — can be expected.

The Cadron's third section — Pinnacle Springs to U.S. 65 — is the shortest of the four, but may be the best of the lot. In its three and a half mile run, the paddler will find rocky shoals (up to class II), quiet pools, and rugged bluffs. Willow strainers will also be present.

The last float on the Cadron is the 10-11 mile trip from the U.S. 65 bridge down to the Arkansas 285 crossing 10 miles north of Wooster. It, too, offers a good experience, complete with class I/class II rapids, the highest bluffs on the creek, and occasional wildlife.

## SEASONS

Cadron Creek is a pretty reliable stream. One published account claims it can be floated "90% of the time between December and June." For a more accurate day-to-day reading, check the gauge under the U.S. 65 bridge; levels of 2.00 feet and above are desirable (6.00 and up is not recommended).

## ACCESS POINTS

Points of access include: the Arkansas 124 crossing; the county bridge northeast of Guy; Arkansas 310 going west from Guy; the U.S. 65 bridge; and the Arkansas 285 crossing.

## SCENERY

First-time visitors to the Cadron are invariably surprised at the scenery. Most have no idea that a whitewater stream exists in central Arkansas — much less that it features bluffs, pinnacles, and caves. But all of these attractions are found on Cadron Creek. Not only that, the scenery changes from season to season. Many of the bluffs will be ice-encrusted during the winter months; later on they'll be the locations for waterfalls.

## FISHING

By all appearances, Cadron Creek should be a great little smallmouth stream. But surprisingly, smallmouth bass are virtually absent from these waters. Because the water is warmer than on most Arkansas float streams, the Cadron hosts a variety of species more commonly found in the sluggish streams of the lowlands.

Here anglers pursue tailwalking largemouth bass, feisty crappie and the good-things-come-in-small-packages bluegill. Flathead catfish, which may tip the scales at 50 pounds or more, are also present in good numbers, giving the visiting angler an outstanding opportunity to land a real leviathan.

## SERVICES AVAILABLE

Most all supplies can be obtained in Greenbrier or other nearby communities. Conway, about 15 miles south of the Cadron on U.S. 65, is a major commercial center with overnight accommodations available. Campgrounds are located at Woolly Hollow State Park a few miles northeast of Greenbrier, and also at the more distant Corps of Engineers' parks on Greers Ferry Lake.

## OTHER INFORMATION

Cadron Creek is also "floatable" downstream from the Arkansas 285 bridge. While it doesn't offer the whitewater recreation of the upstream reaches, this lower section can be enjoyable.

In addition, the Cadron has a sister stream — East Cadron Creek — that can provide several good float trips. One — the eight-mile section between Arkansas 36 and 107 — goes past Mansfield Bluff, Rainbow Falls, Buzzard's Roost, and an interesting array of tupelo gum trees. A 10-mile float from the 107 crossing down to a county bridge is also possible.

Finally, Cadron Creek and its East Fork flow almost entirely through private property. Canoeists, therefore, need to respect the rights of riparian landowners.

# COSSATOT RIVER

# THE ARKANSAS FLOATER'S KIT

#5 IN A SERIES

The National Park Service describes it as "probably the most challenging" whitewater float in the state. The U.S. Army Corps of Engineers is a little more emphatic, saying it "is the most difficult whitewater stream in the state of Arkansas." Early Indians simply called it Cossatot — their word for "skull crusher." Today the Cossatot River is still crushing things, but they're mostly canoes, ice chests, and the egos of over-confident paddlers.

The stream heads up in rugged Ouachita mountain country just southeast of Mena. It flows in a southerly direction for about 26 miles before its current ceases at Gillham Lake. Along the way the Cossatot travels through the Ouachita National Forest, alongside a wilderness area, and over and around upended layers of jagged bedrock. This last characteristic is what gives the stream its class IV/class V rating among river-runners.

The Cossatot, however, is not just for floaters. In fact, much of its whitewater is not recommended for casual canoeists. Yet, as the following paragraphs will show, the stream offers something for nearly everyone interested in Arkansas's outdoors.

## CHARACTERISTICS

The Cossatot's first section is the headwaters run from its source to the Arkansas Highway 246 bridge northwest of Athens. Not much floating activity takes place on this stretch (the water's usually too low), although the three-mile trip from the lower Forest Road 31 crossing to the 246 bridge can be an exciting class II/class III journey. What this area offers is an interesting landscape — whether it be seen from a car, by foot, or in a canoe. Forest Road 31 parallels the stream for several miles, providing the pleasure driver with views of a small mountain stream and attractive rural countryside. In these upper reaches the Cossatot also flows next to and through the Caney Creek Wilderness, a 14,400-acre area perfect for hikers, photographers, bird-watchers, and backpackers. And immediately upstream from the 246 bridge is a traditional swimming hole — complete with a huge gravel bar perfect for sunning and picnicking.

Just above the Highway 246 crossing, the Cossatot leaves the Ouachita National Forest. For most of the rest of its journey to Gillham Lake, the stream flows through property owned by the Weyerhaeuser Company, and access to the Cossatot is via Weyerhaeuser roads and bridges.

The Cossatot's second stretch begins at the 246 bridge and ends about three miles downstream at a low-water crossing known as Ed Banks Bridge. Good scenery, rock gardens, and class II/class III rapids are typical of this fast-moving section.

The third stretch of river is the float from Ed Banks Bridge to the low-water bridge just above Cossatot Falls. It's short — about two miles — but steep, dropping around 60 feet in the process. The trip gets down to business very quickly with a solid class III rapid — Zig Zag — during the first few hundred yards. Coming up next, and soon, is a hazard to navigation known as the "Esses." It's a 200-yards long rapid that resembles a rock-filled flume — narrow, noisy, and nonstop. Several more class III drops take the floater to another low-water bridge (at Weyerhaeuser Road 52600) upstream from the falls.

The Cossatot's final stretch — from the 52600 bridge to Arkansas 4 — is its most difficult. In this five-mile section, the river has ripped through several ridges creating some mighty interesting rapids. The first of these — located a quarter of a mile or so below the low-water bridge put-in — is Cossatot Falls itself. It's not a single drop, but a series of cascades over which the river descends 35 to 40 feet (Note: other published reports claim that the elevation change is on the order of 80 feet!). In any event, it's a very exciting place with strong currents, big waves, six to eight foot drops, and tricky channels. All of this adds up to a class IV/class V rating.

For those having second thoughts (and this is to be recommended for all but the most experienced paddlers), Cossatot Falls can be portaged to the left (east bank), although the portage has been described "as easy as carrying your boat six flights down a fire escape." Survivors of the float (or portage) can look forward to several more class III rapids in the next two miles, followed by another two miles of quiet water before reaching the Highway 4 bridge. Incidentally, this bridge is the state's highest (the roadway is 87 feet above the water) and offers an appealing view of the narrow river valley.

## SEASONS

Floating is a wet weather phenomenon on the Cossatot, requiring a stream flow between 500 cubic feet per second and 2,000 cfs (for daily readings, call the Corps of Engineers at 378-5150). The best months for these preferred levels are December through June.

The Cossatot, however, should not be viewed as solely a float stream. Sight-seers, campers, fishermen, hunters, rock hounds, and photographers are among the many other groups that will find a season for this stream.

## ACCESS POINTS

The river may be reached via two state highways (4 and 246), Weyerhaeuser roads (particularly #52000 which leads to Ed Banks Bridge and #52600 which goes to the bridge above Cossatot Falls), and Forest Service Road 31.

## SCENERY

The Cossatot River is one of the state's most scenic streams, although this fact is not always appreciated by paddlers who spend most of their time trying to stay afloat. For those visitors who can slow down and enjoy the sights, it's quickly apparent that the Legislature was correct in designating the Cossatot as one of four components in Arkansas's Natural and Scenic Rivers System.

## FISHING

Smallmouth and spotted bass are the noteworthy inhabitants of the Cossatot River. Getting to them is the biggest problem facing most fishermen; the stream just doesn't lend itself to a casual fishing/floating trip. The quiet streamside hiker, however, may find good bass fishing around boulders and downed trees that break the current in deep pools and chutes, especially when using live crayfish or jig-and-pig artificials. Green and longear sunfish are also abundant in the Cossatot, and anglers may occasionally hook channel catfish, largemouth bass, rock bass, bluegill, grass pickerel or white bass.

## SERVICES AVAILABLE

Basic supplies can be obtained in the nearby communities of Athens, Langley, and Wickes. Campsites are available in the Ouachita National Forest (Shady Lake and Bard Springs) and at Gillham Lake.

## OTHER INFORMATION

The Cossatot River country is rugged, largely uninhabited, and criss-crossed by logging roads. It's easy to get lost in. To help visitors keep their bearings, the Weyerhaeuser Company has published a handy guide — "Southwest Arkansas Recreation Map" — that is available — on a single copy basis — by writing: Weyerhaeuser Company; Public Affairs; P.O. Box 1060; Hot Springs, Arkansas 71902.

Also, canoeists should be advised that another 15.5 miles of the Cossatot can be floated between Gillham Dam and U.S. Highway 70/71 east of DeQueen. Excellent scenery — complete with bluffs, islands, and rapids (class I/classII) — characterizes the first five miles; the last ten feature slower water and a pastoral landscape. Several bridges and fords provide access along this stretch. A brochure describing this float may be obtained by writing: U.S. Army Corps of Engineers; Millwood/Tri-Lakes Resident Office; Route 1, Box 37A; Ashdown, Arkansas 71822 (a similar brochure for upper river is also available).

# CROOKED CREEK

# THE ARKANSAS FLOATER'S KIT

#6 IN A SERIES

Arkansas's stream inventory includes ten Crooked Creeks (not to mention a healthy collection of Crooked Bayous, Branches, and Sloughs), but only one has been described as "the blue-ribbon smallmouth stream of the state." That particular Crooked Creek is found way up in the north central part of Arkansas. It originates near Dogpatch in Newton County, flows north and then east through Boone County, and continues east across Marion County where it empties into the White River. Along the way it passes through the communities of Harrison, Pyatt, and Yellville, but most of its journey is through rural countryside.

## SECTION DESCRIBED

Source to mouth, a distance of about 80 miles.

## CHARACTERISTICS

As it meanders across northern Arkansas on the way to the White River, Crooked Creek passes through typical Ozark landscapes featuring rolling hills, cedar glades, bluffs, bottomland thickets, and lush pasturelands. The stream itself is characterized by deep pools, fast chutes, and clear water.

In addition to its nationally known smallmouth fishery, Crooked Creek also provides habitat for many other species including channel catfish and several varieties of sunfish. Living along the stream corridor are numerous mammals — beaver, mink, and deer to name a few — and an abundant assortment of water-oriented birds including kingfishers, ospreys, and great blue herons.

While the stream's upper reaches offer opportunities for wade-fishing and occasional float trips, most recreational use along Crooked Creek occurs in the lower 50 miles below Pyatt. A particular favorite of many smallmouth anglers is the Pyatt to Yellville section which can be broken down into at least three separate trips:

a) Pyatt to Turkey — This half-day float features riffles, gravel bars, and overhanging limbs. To reach the take-out by car, go east of Snow for about two miles, then turn south off U.S. 62 onto a country road which provides access to the stream.

b) Turkey to Kelly's Slab — The longest of the three floats in the section, this one-day trip also offers good scenery, fast chutes, and occasional hazards (willow thickets, flood debris, and fallen timber). The take-out point is one mile due west of Yellville at a low-water bridge known locally as "Kelly's Slab."

c) Kelly's Slab to Yellville — This half-day float is similar to the upper trips, but shorter. The trip concludes on the east side of Arkansas 14 where the City of Yellville is constructing a public park.

Float trips are also possible past Yellville, but, as one account noted, this lower portion "is recommended only for the serious, dedicated fisherman." The very ruggedness of the float — rocky shoals, tight chutes, and willow thickets — discourages most visits. Also, in late spring, a very peculiar thing happens to Crooked Creek below Yellville. It disappears, literally sinking into the ground. (Recent tests with colored dye revealed that the stream flows underground several miles and emerges at Cotter Spring on the White River near Cotter. The spring has been designated as a trout sanctuary by the Arkansas Game and Fish Commission and is now closed to fishing).

## SEASONS

The best time for floating Crooked Creek is during spring, and that season's early months are recommended for fishing. Good fishing is also reported in mid-fall.

## ACCESS POINTS

In addition to using the access points previously listed (Pyatt, Turkey, Kelly's Slab, and Yellville), Crooked Creek visitors can reach the stream at several other places between Yellville and the White River. A Marion County General Highway Map can be a great aid in locating points of access.

## SCENERY

Clear water, colorful gravel bars, tree-lined banks, and a pastoral countryside make any Crooked Creek float a scenic experience.

## FISHING

Crooked Creek has received national acclaim as one of the top smallmouth bass streams anywhere, and its reputation is well deserved. Ideal habitat and an abundance of crayfish, hellgrammites and other smallmouth foods combine to produce large numbers of quality fish. Two to three pounders are fairly common, and four to six pound smallmouths are not unusual.

Below Yellville, the going is rough, but this is the stretch that produces six and seven-pound "brownies." May is perhaps the best month to fish Crooked Creek. During this season, live minnows and jigging frogs (one-eighth-ounce brown jig and a brown pork frog) do exceptionally well. Fall fishing is also fantastic, especially when using crank-baits, spinner-baits and live hellgrammites or crayfish. Popping bugs and streamers on a fly rod offer great sport for smallmouths, as well as for rock bass and longear sunfish that are also common in Crooked Creek.

## SERVICES AVAILABLE

Supplies may be obtained at Yellville, Cotter, Harrison, Flippin, and other communities in the area. Canoes and johnboats are available for rent in the vicinity, and guide services are also available. While there are no public campsites on Crooked Creek itself, campgrounds can be found nearby at Bull Shoals Lake, Bull Shoals State Park, or Buffalo Point (on the Buffalo National River).

## OTHER INFORMATION

Visitors to Crooked Creek should remain mindful that nearly every acre along the creek is in private ownership. Floaters should take special care to avoid potential trespassing problems.

Like most Ozark streams, Crooked Creek can rise rapidly following heavy rains. In flood stage, it's dangerous and should not be floated.

# ELEVEN POINT RIVER

# THE ARKANSAS FLOATER'S KIT

#7 IN A SERIES

A year-round float stream, the Eleven Point is fed by numerous springs making it an ideal destination for floaters any month. About 70 percent of its flow is supplied by these springs. Even when the river is low after a period of drought, all shoal areas can be navigated.

Rising in the Ozarks of Missouri, the Eleven Point flows southward through the Mark Twain National Forest, passing rocky, dramatic country. But once it enters Arkansas, the terrain becomes more alluvial. Its pace slows, and the scenery becomes pastoral and bucolic. From the river, a fringe of forest hides the pastures and farmhouses just beyond.

A clear, unpolluted stream, the Eleven Point is a favorite of canoeists because of its frequent rapids. Sand and gravel bars on the lower river, some of considerable height, are subject to cave-ins due to the natural action of the water. This can be a problem to floaters, since the resulting debris can obstruct the stream's flow.

Islands are characteristic of the Eleven Point, probably formed in times past by these cave-ins. Passage around some of these islands may be blocked, requiring an occasional portage. In addition to the islands, there are five old stone dams providing their own form of hazard if the stream is high. Below the community of Dalton, inexperienced canoeists should avoid the river due to the tricky nature of these dams. However, above Dalton, the stream is reasonably safe for all when the water is low to medium in height.

## SECTION DESCRIBED

From Missouri State Highway 142 to the stream's confluence with the Spring River, a distance of 44 miles.

## CHARACTERISTICS

A traditional put-in point is at the east end of the Missouri 142 bridge near the Calm community. Five miles downstream, the Missouri-Arkansas line is crossed, marked by an "Entering Arkansas" sign. Another mile or two and floaters come to the first of the old stone dams. The best way to navigate this one is to walk the canoe through a small chute on the left.

The second old stone dam is at the 15-mile mark. While it can be negotiated to the left of the center island with a sharp right turn, it's perhaps simpler and safer to drag your canoe over gravel on the right.

Just beyond is the Arkansas 93 bridge at Dalton. Campsites are available on private land here; inquire at the grocery store for details, and for directions to the nearby put-in point. The swift current along the shore is difficult to maneuver in, and it might be best to walk a canoe through, keeping it out of the current before getting underway.

A third stone dam lies just about eight miles downstream, shortly after an island and its accompanying brush-filled channels. There is a break in the dam to the right that can be run, but because of willows just beyond, it might be best to walk the craft through. Less than a mile beyond is the Arkansas 90 bridge, supported by high banks. There is deep water on the left, and a landing beyond the bridge, but the property is private and posted.

Next comes the Black Ferry Bridge, on a county road. Steep banks and deep water makes this a difficult launching site. (The Corps of Engineers has proposed in times past the damming of the Eleven Point at a site just beyond, to be called Water Valley Dam. The resulting impoundment would have extended to the state line.)

Just above the U.S. Highway 62 bridge is the fourth dam, which can be run at low water. On the upstream side of the bridge you'll find a put-in on the east bank. Seven-tenths of a mile below the 62 crossing is an emergency exit on the left at the site of the old bridge for the highway.

The fifth stone dam comes into view next, complete with several breaches for lining a canoe through. Within a few miles the Eleven Point enters the Spring River, and four and a half miles later the Spring joins up with the Black River. The Game and Fish Commission maintains a public landing ramp on the right bank of the Black River just below the junction. Access is provided by a county road from Black Rock, a little over a mile away.

## SEASONS

Because of its numerous springs, the Eleven Point is a year-round stream. However, when the river is up and charging southward, all but the most experienced canoeists should stay on the bank.

## ACCESS POINTS

Principal access points are: Missouri 142; Dalton (Arkansas 93); Arkansas 90; the county road at Black Ferry Bridge; and U.S. 62.

## SCENERY

Although farmland borders the Eleven Point throughout most of its Arkansas length, the heavy growth along the banks tends to conceal the signs of civilization and to give the floater the sense of being miles from anywhere. Black gum, sycamore, bois d'arc, oak, sweet gum, willow, walnut and river birch are found in this lush growth. Wildflower displays are frequent and a special treat of the Eleven Point. Herons often stand sentinel in quiet reaches of the stream. And, on hot summer days, the Eleven Point makes a delightful swimming hole because of its spring-fed coolness.

## FISHING

The Eleven Point's gravelled path is an ideal spawning ground for smallmouth bass. While an occasional three or four-pounder is taken, most will weigh from one to two pounds. Even so, the number of smallmouths in the river is phenomenal, and it's not unheard of to haul in a pair of smallmouths on a single crank-bait. When the water is clear, minnow-replica crank-baits on fairly light line are recommended. On those rare occasions when rains give the water some turbidity, large spinner-baits and crank-baits are also good producers.

One of the most overlooked fish species in Arkansas's cold-water streams is the channel catfish. While most people associate channels with muddy, slow-moving waters, they actually prefer clear, gravel-bottomed streams. Channel cats are abundant in the Eleven Point and will accept a variety of offerings including chicken liver and stinkbaits. The flathead catfish, another common Eleven Point sportfish, prefers live baits such as minnows and small sunfish. Anglers will also find good action for spotted bass and longear sunfish.

The Eleven Point offers fish a smorgasbord of aquatic foods such as crayfish, hellgrammites, leeches, salamanders, mayfly and stonefly nymphs, a variety of chubs, darters and small fish, worms, mussels and an occasional terrestrial insect washed in during a cloudburst. It goes without saying that fish use these foods on a day-to-day basis in this and other float streams, and a fresh, well-fished live bait offering is often more enticing than an artificial lure.

## SERVICES AVAILABLE

The nearby city of Pocahontas is a major trade center for the area around the Eleven Point. Public campsites are available at Old Davidsonville State Park southwest of Pocahontas.

## OTHER INFORMATION

Since along most of its Arkansas length, the Eleven Point flows past privately-owned farmland, visitors need to be mindful to avoid trespassing problems.

# ILLINOIS BAYOU

## THE ARKANSAS FLOATER'S KIT

#8 IN A SERIES

For most of us, the term "bayou" means one thing: a sluggish body of water. But anybody getting on the Illinois Bayou with that thought in mind is in for a big and wet surprise.

The Bayou, as many of its floaters know it, has its origins high up on the south slopes of the Ozarks. As the stream works its way toward Russellville and the Arkansas River, there's nothing slow and lazy about it. It may be the only bayou in the country featuring class II/III whitewater.

### SECTION DESCRIBED

Entire length from backwaters of Lake Dardanelle to headwaters in the Ozarks.

### CHARACTERISTICS

The Illinois Bayou really is not one stream but four: 1) the North Fork; 2) the Middle Fork; 3) the East Fork; and 4) the main stem (downstream from Bayou Bluff). Because of these divisions in what is a relatively small watershed, it takes a good amount of rainfall to get them up to floating levels. But once there, they offer some of the state's best whitewater. In fact, the Bayou is recommended for experienced paddlers. It is not a good "first time" float.

The North Fork offers a trip through truly remote country. During the 10-mile float from the Dry Creek put-in (on Forest Road 1310) to the Forest Road 1001 take-out, visitors will be well removed from civilization, passing no roads, bridges, houses, or fields. Prospective floaters are warned that the shuttle is an ordeal involving considerable driving. The float itself is a delight — class II and III rapids (19 feet/mile gradient), short pools, narrow channels, great scenery, and a wonderful sense of solitude. In times of high water, floaters may put in at Forest Road 1000, but again, the stream is strictly for the experienced paddler.

The Bayou's Middle Fork offers a two-mile float that is one of Arkansas's best for continuous whitewater. It begins at the Snow Creek put-in (two miles up Forest Road 1312, off Arkansas Highway 27) and concludes at Bayou Bluff Campground, just below the junction of the Middle and East Forks. Along the way, the stream drops 20 feet per mile, creating all kinds of excitement including some class II/III rapids. Unlike the North Fork's float, this Middle Fork section is seldom far from roads, yet it also offers a sense of remoteness.

A good float can also be had on the East Fork — when conditions are right. A 12-mile trip from Forest Road 1301 to Bayou Bluff is steep, dropping 25 feet per mile, and wild, passing through the middle of the 10,800 acre East Fork Wilderness Area. Like its companion floats, this one is not for the novice.

The main stem of the Illinois Bayou begins where the Middle and East Forks run together near Bayou Bluff and continues, for floating purposes, to the Arkansas 164 bridge north of Scottsville. This stretch includes the most commonly floated section of the Bayou — the four-mile trip from Bayou Bluff to the Arkansas 27 bridge north of Hector. Throughout this trip the paddler can expect many class II rapids, including one just upstream from the take-out that features large standing waves. The second float — from the 27 bridge to the 164 crossing — is about seven miles long and considerably calmer than the others. The North Fork joins up with the main stem about halfway along this float. Rapids are present, but most are of the class I variety.

### ACCESS POINTS

Primary points of access for the Bayou and its forks are the Arkansas 164 and 27 bridges, and several Forest Road crossings (chiefly 1000, 1001, 1301, and 1312). The Highway 27 access is less than 20 miles north of Interstate 40.

### SEASONS

The Illinois Bayou is a seasonal stream, floatable only after periods of extended rainfall. A good indicator of "floatability" is the Scottsville reading on the Corps of Engineers' recording (378-5150). Levels between 6.0 and 7.0 are best (6.5 minimum for the North Fork), and much beyond 7.5 is considered risky.

### SCENERY

The scenery is superb for all floats on the Bayou. The three forks — North, Middle, and East — provide exposure to rugged and remote country. Rocky outcrops, steep hillsides of dense forest, and periodic glimpses of wildlife can be expected. The main stem offers overhanging trees, interesting vistas, and occasional scenes of pastoral landscapes.

### FISHING

Bass are king on Illinois Bayou, and anglers will find healthy populations of three species — the largemouth, smallmouth and spotted basses. Bass fishing is generally best in spring and early summer, although some anglers prefer to fish the pot holes that form during drier months.

Anglers who want to land a real lunker may want to bait up with small sunfish or large minnows and try for one of the flathead catfish lurking in these waters. Coldwater flatheads may reach weights up to 50 pounds or more, making them the largest fish available to float stream fishermen. The best flathead fishing is at night, and the best areas to try include washouts around downed timber and deep holes in the outside bends of the stream.

Multi-colored green and longear sunfish are also abundant in Illinois Bayou. These fish readily accept worms, crickets, mini-jigs and tiny crank-baits, and while they rarely reach even a pound in weight, they can provide hours of fishing fun for kids and adults alike.

### SERVICES AVAILABLE

Most any necessity (other than rental canoes) can be obtained in the nearby towns of Hector and Atkins. The nearest outfitter is located on Big Piney Creek to the west.

Camping is possible at the Bayou Bluff Campground at the confluence of the Middle and East Forks. In addition, the Forest Service has other developed campgrounds — like Brock Creek and Long Pool — that are within easy driving distance.

### OTHER INFORMATION

One of Arkansas's more interesting geological marvels can be observed at Pedestal Rocks, a site within the watershed of the Illinois Bayou's North Fork. In addition to seeing the large, weathered limestone columns, visitors to the area can poke around in caves and bluff shelters. Photographers will also enjoy the panoramic views of the North Fork's valley. To get there, turn east off Arkansas 7 onto Arkansas 16, and then go for about five miles toward Ben Hur. The parking area will be visible on the south side of the highway.

Another interesting area is the East Fork Wilderness. While it is accessible by canoe at times, the best way to see the wilderness is by foot. Features include upland swamps, waterfalls, and generally rugged country. The best times for visits are during fall, winter, and spring months.

Finally, floaters should bear in mind that private property does exist within the Ozark National Forest. "Posted" land should not be entered.

# KINGS RIVER

# THE ARKANSAS FLOATER'S KIT

## #9 IN A SERIES

High in the Boston Mountains of Madison County lie the beginnings of the Kings River. From this steep country the stream twists its way northward to the White River and finally flows into southern Missouri's Table Rock Lake. In its upper reaches, the Kings cuts a narrow gorge through sandstone, shale, and limestone. On downstream the surrounding countryside is not quite so precipitous, but the water is the same — clear and cool.

The Kings' most attractive features are found along the rocky banks and bluffs where floaters will notice wild azaleas, ferns, umbrella magnolias, and other fascinating plants. In addition, observant visitors can view a great many signs of wildlife — beaver cuttings and deer and raccoon tracks, for instance — and may even spot some of the local creatures.

### SECTION DESCRIBED

Headwaters to the Arkansas-Missouri border, a distance of approximately 90 miles.

### CHARACTERISTICS

The headwaters area is, of course, no place to float, but it does offer some hiking opportunities. One good place in particular is the Kings River Falls Natural Area, a preserve of the Arkansas Natural Heritage Commission. In addition to observing the falls themselves (which drop about 6 feet over a water-sculpted ledge), visitors can inspect a great many interesting plants in the area, and history buffs might try to envision the grist mill which was once located at the site. To get there, travel to the community of Boston, located on Arkansas 16. At Boston, go north on the county road for about 2 miles until the road forks. Keep to the right and continue north for another 2½ miles or so, at which point the road again forks. Take the left fork, ford the creek, and then park your car to the right. A trail — about three-quarters of a mile along and paralleling the river — will lead downstream to the falls.

While some floating takes place in the Kingston area, Marble is a traditional starting-off place for many Kings River visitors (note: the put-in is northwest of Marble at a county road crossing). After eleven miles of deep pools, overhanging trees, occasional rapids, and several large bluffs, floaters will arrive at Marshall Ford, an access point northeast of Alabam.

The second Kings River stretch is the Marshall Ford to Rockhouse run, a 15-mile trip through quiet and attractive country. Access to the river at Rockhouse is a little out-of-the-ordinary; floaters must navigate a feeder stream (Warm Fork Creek) for a few hundred yards before entering or exiting the Kings.

A seven-mile stretch from Rockhouse to Trigger Gap is the third in the series, and offers a peaceful float. The take-out point is a low-water bridge on Arkansas Highway 221 about 9 miles southwest of Berryville.

The next section — Trigger Gap to the U.S. Highway 62 crossing — is a favorite of Kings River veterans. The 12-mile trip combines good scenery with good fishing. Osage Creek, the Kings River's largest tributary and a float stream in its own right early in the year, enters on the right about a quarter of a mile above the U.S. 62 bridge.

A 12-mile float from the 62 crossing to Summers Ford (off Arkansas 143) is another memorable run, and a popular choice for fishermen. Some fine gravel bars are found in this stretch of the river.

The last Kings River trip begins at Summers Ford and concludes eight miles later in Missouri at the Highway 86 bridge. Halfway into the trip floaters will encounter backwaters of Table Rock Lake.

### SEASONS

Upstream from U.S. 62, the April-June period is considered best for a float, although fall rains, if sufficient, can make for good canoeing. Below 62, floating extends into early summer.

### ACCESS POINTS

General Highway Maps for Carroll and Madison counties will help floaters locate the entry points listed in earlier paragraphs. (note: Visitors are advised that access is not recommended at the U.S. Highway 68 bridge east of Marble).

### SCENERY

Overhanging hardwood forests, fine gravel bars, and rugged bluffs give the Kings River good marks in the scenery department. Also attesting to the stream's beauty is the fact that in 1971 the General Assembly passed legislation to protect that portion of the river in Madison County, noting that it "possesses unique scenic, recreational, and other characteristics in a natural, unpolluted and wild state." Thus the Kings River was actually the state's first stream to receive governmental recognition and protection, predating the Buffalo National River legislation by a year.

A float on Kings River is a return to fishing in its purest form — no motors, no loaded bass boat, only your partner quietly paddling as you both absorb the untainted outdoor grandeur. The Kings has countless rock bass and hefty channel cats, but when fishing this stream, first and foremost on the minds of most anglers are the big smallmouth bass.

If you want to catch the real Kings River lunker smallies, take along heavy tackle. Some people expect bass from this smallish stream to be small, too, and that can cost trophy fish which commonly reach four to six pounds. A baitcasting reel, a medium-action rod, and 10- to 12-pound line are appropriate.

Two sportfishes often overlooked by Kings River anglers are the walleye and white bass. Both species are common in the portion of the river near Table Rock Lake during the spring spawning runs in March, April and early May. White bass will hit a variety of shad-imitation lures and minnows, while walleyes are usually taken on live baits such as minnows, crayfish and worms or artificial lures, particularly deep-running crank-baits and jigs.

### SERVICES AVAILABLE

Berryville and Eureka Springs are both located near the Kings River and can meet the needs of most visitors. In addition, several outfitters have operations in the area for those wishing to experience the stream.

### OTHER INFORMATION

Folks who enjoy floating the Kings River will be equally delighted by its sister stream, War Eagle Creek. War Eagle, which flows west of the Kings and parallel to it, is chiefly a springtime float offering good scenery and fine fishing. Canoes may be rented at Withrow Springs State Park which borders the stream north of Huntsville.

# LITTLE MISSOURI RIVER

# THE ARKANSAS FLOATER'S KIT

#10 IN A SERIES

From its headwaters south of the Big Fork community to the backwaters of Lake Greeson, the Little Missouri River descends some 1,035 feet. For the 29-mile journey, that's an average drop of 35 feet per mile, and that means one thing — whitewater.

But the stream offers more than excitement, although it has plenty of that. It also provides a solid introduction to the Ouachita Mountain country of southwest Arkansas. Pine-covered ridges tower hundreds of feet above the rocky channel. In several places, the Little Missouri has cut through the twisted rock layers that are the very essence of the Ouachitas. It is, in short, an interesting stream.

### SECTION DESCRIBED

Headwaters area to Lake Greeson, a total of 29 miles.

### CHARACTERISTICS

The stream's first section — from its source to the Albert Pike Campground — is not one for floating. This upper stretch has its merits, however. A chief attraction is the Little Missouri Falls area which has been developed for day-use activities (i.e., no camping) by the Ouachita National Forest. While there are no developed facilities between the falls and Albert Pike, the river corridor offers possibilities for all kinds of outdoor pursuits — swimming in deep pools, hiking along the streambank, and wildlife photography, just to name a few.

The Albert Pike Campground to Arkansas 84 run is one of the best in the state. It begins on national forest property near the junction of Forest Roads 73 and 106, and continues for about 8.5 rough-and-tumble miles. This stretch of the river heads downhill at a good clip — 25 feet per mile. The rapids are exciting (up to class IV in high water), with many featuring standing waves at their bases. Along the way floaters will pass the mouth of Greasy Creek, near which Albert Pike — the famed pioneer lawyer, general, and poet — once lived in a well-appointed cabin. More noticeable will be Winding Stair Rapid, a series of drops that may well put water into one's boat. The rapid — which is approximately three miles below the put-in — can, and should, be scouted from the left (east) bank; heavy flows can put it in the class IV level. The remainder of the float features numerous rapids in the class I-class III categories, including a diagonally-running ledge about a quarter mile below Winding Stair that can be tricky.

While the Arkansas 84 to Lake Greeson section doesn't require the technical paddling skills of the upper section, it, too offers gunnel-grabbing excitement. Its claim to fame is standing waves — some of the biggest in the state when the water is up. The floating distance is 10-11 miles.

### SEASONS

The Little Missouri River is among the most seasonal of Arkansas streams, primarily because of its small watershed. It's "floatable" only after periods of considerable rainfall, and even then the stream may not stay navigable for long. The wet months of spring offer the best chances for catching it at a good level. An old low-water bridge just below the Arkansas 84 bridge offers a primitive but acceptable gauging system: one to two feet of water over the slab means that conditions are desirable.

### ACCESS POINTS

The stream's major access points are: the Albert Pike Campground area at Forest Road 106 north of Langley; the Arkansas 84 bridge west of Langley; and the U.S. 70 bridge at the Star of the West area on Lake Greeson. All roads are paved with the exception of those in the Ouachita National Forest.

### SCENERY

It doesn't take a geologist to note some differences between the Ouachita mountains and the Ozarks. Floaters can pick up on them, too. Bluffs, which are common on many Ozark rivers, are unusual in the Ouachitas. Unlike the flat-topped mountains found in the northern parts of the state, steep ridges — many of them the hogback variety — are the rule in the Ouachitas. And where streams have worked their way through these ridgelines, they've exposed upturned rock strata whose rough, jagged edges are unlike anything in the Ozarks. Floaters beware! In short, the Ouachitas are no less scenic than their sister mountains to the north; they're just built differently.

Finally, the Arkansas General Assembly has even recognized the beauty of the Little Missouri River. In 1985 the legislature passed an act placing this 29-mile stretch into the Arkansas Natural and Scenic Rivers System — one of only four such designations.

### FISHING

Like many of Arkansas's other mountain streams, the Little Missouri harbors smallmouth bass, spotted bass, green sunfish and longears which may be taken year-round. White bass are also present in the headwaters of Lake Greeson during the spring spawning run.

The Little Missouri seldom comes to mind when the state's great trout streams are mentioned. However, thousands of rainbow trout are stocked in the stream both above and below Lake Greeson, providing exciting sport for trout enthusiasts.

The lower Little Missouri (below Narrows Dam) differs from other Arkansas trout streams in that it is primarily a cold-weather fishery. When there is no demand for electricity, the flow from Narrows Dam is cut to a mere 15 cubic feet per second, which isn't sufficient to sustain lower water temperatures required by trout. As a result, the trout season here runs from early December (when the Game and Fish Commission begins its annual stocking program on the river) to Memorial Day or thereabouts. Stocking is finished by early April each year, and by late May, fishing pressure and rising water temperatures have just about wiped out the trout. Few fish manage to survive through the summer, but the lower Little Missouri offers excellent fishing for about five months each year for trout in the one-half to three-quarter pound range, and that's nothing to sneeze at. Rainbow trout can be caught in the river above Lake Greeson, especially near the Albert Pike area, year-round.

### SERVICES AVAILABLE

In addition to the public campsites (Albert Pike), there's a privately operated campground just across the river (east side). This operation also features rental cabins, a grocery store/snack bar, and gasoline. Other services are available at the nearby towns of Langley, Kirby, and Daisy. Several public campgrounds can be found on Lake Greeson, including one — Star of the West — at the take-out point for the lower float.

### OTHER INFORMATION

Few people realize that much of the Little Missouri River and the surrounding landscape nearly became a national park back in the late 1920s/early 1930s. Only a last-minute veto by then-President Calvin Coolidge prevented establishment of the 165,000-acre Ouachita National Park.

The Little Missouri River can also be floated below Lake Greeson, and is popular with trout fishermen for the first half-dozen miles below the dam.

# LITTLE RED RIVER

# THE ARKANSAS FLOATER'S KIT

#11 IN A SERIES

One of the most popular fishing and floating streams in Arkansas, the lower Little Red River flows from the base of Greers Ferry Dam near the town of Heber Springs to eventually merge with the White River at the Hurricane Lake Wildlife Management Area just east of Searcy. The chief reason for its popularity is trout — thousands and thousands of which are stocked in the stream on a regular basis. Good scenery and convenient access also work in the river's favor.

### SECTION DESCRIBED

From Greers Ferry Dam to Ramsey Public Access, a distance of approximately 29 miles.

### CHARACTERISTICS

The Little Red River is generally a good year-round float. The condition of the river is dependent upon generation periods of the powerhouse at the dam. It becomes very swift and dangerous in spots when water is released, but after generation ceases, the Little Red reverts to a peaceful Ozark mountain stream with long, gentle pools and numerous shoals. During periods of high flow, the river should be floated only by experienced boaters.

The first few miles of river below Greers Ferry Lake are strewn with boulders, making a challenging float for canoers, but a difficult one for crafts larger than a johnboat. Beyond this stretch, there is a long pool of deep water. Farther downstream, an island hinders river travel. The usual approach is to veer left at the island, which will take floaters into one of the river's largest fishing holes. Approximately one and one-half miles downstream, a series of shoals impedes travel of large boats when water levels are low. Beyond this shoal area, canoes are the best choice for shallow areas and a series of bends. Next is a three-mile-long deep hole, followed by a narrowing of the river into another long shoal. These shoals give way to deep pools above Pangburn, then the river's pace picks up with a series of rapids upstream of the low water bridge north of town. Beyond the rapids, the river widens as it flows through another series of shoals. The last access point, Ramsey Access, is a few miles downstream. Total distance from the dam to the last access is 29 miles. Trout waters end a few miles beyond the Ramsey area at Arkansas 305.

### ACCESS

A Corps of Engineers public ramp on the north bank, located next to the Federal Fish Hatchery, is the easiest access to the upper portion of the river. Other public access points on the middle and lower stretches of the river, maintained by the Arkansas Game and Fish Commission, include Barnett (Winkley Bridge), Lobo (adjacent to Lobo Landing Trout Dock), Dripping Springs, and Ramsey. Four commercial boat docks also offer launch ramps.

Most of the land bordering the river is privately-owned and is posted. Always check with landowners before attempting access to the river via private property.

### SEASONS

Water conditions on the Little Red don't vary so much by season as they do by day of the week. On weekdays, when power demand is usually at its greatest, water is frequently released around mid-morning. Demand for electricity drops over the weekends, and so do water levels. When the river reading is low, expect to wade and drag boats over the shoals.

### SCENERY

The scenery is outstanding, easily good enough to offset one of those rare occasions when the fish aren't biting. As it cuts through beautiful Ozark foothills, the Little Red provides excellent year-round viewing.

### FISHING

The Little Red is among the real blue-ribbon trout streams of America and takes her place alongside the White as one of the best in the South. Hundreds of thousands of rainbow trout are stocked here annually, and periodic releases of brown trout have produced an excellent fishery for that species as well.

The secret to fishing the Little Red is light tackle and small lures. Ultralight spinning rigs and two- to four-pound line are popular. Most trout are taken on bait, rather than artificials, simply because more anglers use it. Whole kernel corn, redworms, nightcrawlers, waxworms, salmon eggs, and Velveeta cheese all take their share.

Favorite artificials for Little Red trout include marabou jigs, small spinners and spoons, and crayfish- and minnow-imitation crank-baits. But one of the most productive techniques involves a curious marriage between bait and artificials. This rig consists of a small, clear bobber rigged about four or five feet above a brown feather jig, on the barb of which is impaled a small white waxworm. The rig is cumbersome to cast, but that's acceptable since the proper fishing technique is to work the lure in as slowly as possible.

During highwater, driftfishing with the current is favored. Bait is cast upstream and allowed to bump the bottom as it drags behind the boat. On low water, stillfishing deep holes, weedbeds, and timber from an anchored boat is preferred. The Little Red is also one of Arkansas's most popular flyfishing streams, and the many shoals exposed during low water periods offer ideal locations to hook a hefty trout on a variety of fly patterns. Arkansas's trout season never closes, but many of the larger fish are taken from October through February.

Although trout get most of the publicity on the Little Red, anglers shouldn't overlook opportunities for taking other species as well. The river has healthy populations of chain pickerel, spotted and smallmouth bass, green and longear sunfish, rock bass and bluegills.

### SERVICES AVAILABLE

A network of resorts, private campgrounds, restaurants, bait shops, and guide services has been established to serve the recreating public. In addition, the nearby city of Heber Springs serves as a trade center for the surrounding area. Public camping spots are located on Greers Ferry Lake.

### OTHER INFORMATION

In the spring, the forks of the Little Red are floatable above Greers Ferry Lake, and the best of the lot is probably the Middle Fork. Flowing between the towns of Leslie and Shirley, the Middle Fork cuts a 30-mile path through some of the state's most rugged terrain. The river boasts a sharp fall creating a series of rapids that can be treacherous during periods of heavy rainfall. Only experienced canoeists should attempt this float when water levels are high. Another of the tributaries, the South Fork, flows for 13 miles between Scotland and Clinton, and is not a bad fishing stream.

Canoeists interested in getting on new water might also check out Big Creek, one of the Little Red's major tributaries. Several put-in points are located on county roads east of Wilburn (see a Cleburne County map for details), while the traditional take-out is an old iron bridge near the stream's confluence with the Little Red. To get to the iron bridge, go north on Arkansas 110 from Pangburn, then turn east on a county road about three-quarters of a mile beyond the Little Red River bridge. Highlights of the float include deep pools, class I/II rapids, towering bluffs, and — believe it or not — cypress trees and knees.

Floaters will also find several interesting attractions in the area. One is the Greers Ferry Visitors Information Center, an impressive structure housing a museum, a Corps of Engineers display, and an exciting audiovisual presentation of the region's history. Two nearby trails, Mossy Bluff and Buckeye (handicapped accessible), provide lofty views and interpretive stops along the way. In addition, visitors can tour Greers Ferry Dam and the National Fish Hatchery, located just downstream from the dam.

# MULBERRY RIVER

# THE ARKANSAS FLOATER'S KIT

#12 IN A SERIES

It wouldn't be completely accurate to describe the Mulberry River as 50 miles of whitewater, but it would not be far from the truth for several months of the year. According to one publication, the stream "is definitely the state's wildest river during spring." From its beginnings deep in the Ozarks to its confluence with the Arkansas River, the Mulberry pours over ledges, shoots through willow thickets, and whips around sharp turns. These "wild" characteristics are what give the stream its class II/III rating, and high marks from the floating public.

In drier times, the river takes on a completely different personality. It's a good place to swim, wade, skip rocks, and stalk the wary smallmouth. The best floating during the summer months is on an air mattress at one of the local swimming holes.

In short, the Mulberry River is a seasonal stream, but the good news is that it offers a season for just about anybody. The General Assembly recognized this fact in 1985 when it officially declared the Mulberry to be "a scenic river of the State of Arkansas."

### SECTION DESCRIBED

Source to Arkansas River, a distance of 50-55 miles.

### CHARACTERISTICS

The Mulberry flows in a west-southwesterly course in its rush to leave the Ozarks. Access points are fairly common, particularly where the stream is within the Ozark National Forest.

The first major put-in point is at the Arkansas 103 crossing about two miles southwest of the Oark community. Take-out for this float is frequently the Forest Road 1504 crossing (11.5 miles downstream), although the Wolf Pen Recreation Area, a U.S. Forest Service development situated 2.5 miles below the 103 bridge, can also serve as a put-in/take-out location. This section of the river is fast moving with a good mixture of class II rapids, standing waves, and willow strainers. The Little Mulberry joins up with the main stem about two miles below Wolf Pen; paddlers will note its entry on the right side (north shore) of the Mulberry.

The second float begins at the 1504 access and concludes six to seven miles later at the Arkansas 23 crossing, known for years now as Turner's Bend. There is plenty of class II excitement along this route, including some rather large boulders that tend to influence the streamflow. Redding Campground, a Forest Service development, is located midway through this trip, while a private camping area is found at Turner's Bend.

The third major float originates at the Highway 23 bridge and continues for some 8.5 miles to a place known as Milton's Ford (located on Forest Road 1501 west of Arkansas 23). Like the Mulberry's earlier floats, this one features solid class II whitewater, plus several notorious willow thickets that should be negotiated with caution.

The Mulberry's last section — from Milton's Ford to Arkansas 215 north of the city of Mulberry — is the favorite of some floaters. During this 18-20 mile trip, canoeists pass through remote, virtually inaccessible country. The pools are longer, requiring a bit more paddling, but many feel this is more than offset by the solitude offered during this stretch. Class II rapids and the ever-present willow thickets can be expected.

### SEASONS

Traditional floating months are late fall to June, but conditions can vary according to local rainfall. The best bet for canoeists is to call the Corps of Engineers' river level recording (378-5150); readings between 2.0 and 4.0 are ideal, while 4.5 and beyond are considered dangerous.

### ACCESS POINTS

Primary points of access include Arkansas Highways 23, 103, and 215 (all paved), and Forest Roads 1003, 1501, and 1504. And while the Mulberry is located in some of the state's wildest country, the stream is amazingly convenient; the Highway 23 crossing is less than a dozen miles north of Interstate 40.

### SCENERY

Visitors to the Mulberry can expect basic Ozark Mountain scenery — narrow canyons, tree-lined bluffs, and dense woods. A good assortment of wildlife is found in the immediate area, including one of the state's largest concentrations of black bears. The stream itself is clear, cool, and challenging.

### FISHING

The Mulberry River is a fine fishing stream provided you're on it at the right time. In early spring, it's frequently too high and fast for a "laid back" fishing trip. In late spring and early summer, though, when things have calmed down somewhat, the river is an excellent choice when angling for smallmouth, largemouth and spotted bass and green and longear sunfish. The potholes can be fished during drier months but getting to them may require some hiking up or down a slippery streambed.

### SERVICES AVAILABLE

Supplies and overnight accommodations are available in Ozark, a city located about 15 miles south of the Highway 23 crossing. In addition, several outfitters are located on or near the river.

The Forest Service operates two campgrounds — Redding and Wolf Pen — on the river, and three others — Shores Lake, Ozone, and White Rock Mountain — within easy driving distance. Campsites are also available in conjunction with a couple of the outfitting operations.

### OTHER INFORMATION

While much of the Mulberry River is within the boundaries of the Ozark National Forest, the stream frequently flows through private property, a good bit of which is posted. Visitors, therefore, are urged to take câre not to abuse the rights of riparian property owners.

Canoeists should also make a point of checking into local weather forecasts. A heavy rain can quickly transform the Mulberry into a rampaging torrent. Because of the chance for these sudden rises, visitors are advised that camping on islands and gravel bars is generally not recommended.

Finally, anyone desiring more information on the stream should read Margaret and Harold Hedges' "The Mighty Mulberry," a 16-page guide to the entire river. It is available through the Ozark Society Foundation; P.O. Box 3503; Little Rock, Arkansas 72203.

# OUACHITA RIVER

# THE ARKANSAS FLOATER'S KIT

#13 IN A SERIES

For many first-time visitors, the most difficult thing about the Ouachita River is learning to say it correctly. For some reason, the pronunciation — Wash-i-taw — bears little resemblance to the spelling. Regardless of how it's said, though, the Ouachita is a fine stream, ideally suited for family outings.

From its beginnings where two small creeks converge at the base of Rich Mountain in Polk County, the river winds its way through the scenic Ouachita Mountains and beyond. It is in these higher elevations that the stream offers a good range of recreation opportunities for floating and fishing enthusiasts alike.

A major draw is its location within the Ouachita National Forest. The Forest Service provides campgrounds, picnic areas, and access points along the river and several of its tributaries. In addition, the Arkansas Game and Fish Commission maintains several access areas along the stream. These developments attract not only experienced river travellers, but many people venturing out for their first trip in a canoe.

## SECTION DESCRIBED

Headwaters to Lake Ouachita, a distance of about 70 miles.

## CHARACTERISTICS

In its upper reaches, the Ouachita is a narrow, fast-moving stream with class I (and occasionally class II) rapids. Further downstream, the river still has some interesting shoals, but the pools are a little longer and deeper.

The uppermost float on the Ouachita begins at the McGuire Access, a Game and Fish Commission development. It's located on the south side of Arkansas Highway 88 about halfway between the communities of Ink and Cherry Hill. The seven-mile trip down to the Cherry Hill Access — another Game and Fish project — should be scheduled after periods of extended rainfall to avoid a good deal of dragging. The float features narrow channels, tight turns, and quiet pools. Paddlers should be on the lookout for logjams and overhanging limbs.

The second Ouachita River float is the 13-mile journey from Cherry Hill to Pine Ridge. The take-out point is a county bridge about one mile east of Pine Ridge, just to the southeast of Highway 88. Like the earlier float, this one requires plenty of rain and cautious canoeists.

A 10-mile trip from Pine Ridge to Oden is next in the series of Ouachita excursions. Noisy shoals, quick turns, and a tunnel of overhanging trees characterize this section. The Arkansas Highway 379 bridge south of Oden is the take-out point.

One of the most popular trips on the river is the journey from Oden to the Rocky Shoals Campground at the U.S. 270 crossing. This 10-mile trip features some of the best scenery on the Ouachita, including a towering bluff a few miles above the take-out..Deep pools, stimulating rapids, and shady banks are also found along this stretch. In the springtime, quiet canoeists may hear the calls of wild turkeys up on the steep hillsides.

Canoeists putting in at Rocky Shoals have several options. They can take out at the Sims Campground, located four miles downstream, or at the Fulton Branch Campground which is another three miles down the river. Each of these camping/launching areas also is a good starting point for trips down to the last two public take-outs — Dragover and River Bluff. Both offer toilets, boat ramps, and campsites. The Fulton Branch to Dragover trip covers about two miles, while the float on to River Bluff covers another three miles. Several other take-outs are possible on the backwaters of Lake Ouachita around the Arkansas Highway 27 crossing.

## SEASONS

The Ouachita can be floated much of the year, particularly if its visitors don't mind getting their feet wet and pulling their boats through the shallows during drier months. The best period for good canoeing in the upper reaches is late fall to late spring — generally November through June. The lower stretches (below the 270 bridge) come closest to offering year-round floating conditions.

## ACCESS POINTS

Major access points include the U.S. 270 crossing, the Arkansas 379 bridge, several county road crossings off Arkansas 88, and a handful of Forest Service Campgrounds.

## SCENERY

The Ouachita River's scenic beauty is due in part to the noticeable bluffs along the route. Though they are common sights in north Arkansas's Ozarks, these occurrences are few and far between in the Ouachita Mountain range.

Other features of the Ouachita River are its clear water, intriguing rock formations, and a canopy of overhanging trees. In its upper reaches, the dogwoods and redbuds which bloom in the spring make for an unmatched setting of beauty. With only sparse population along its banks, the river also offers a sense of solitude. The Ouachita's long, lazy pools and sparkling shoals make the river especially inviting for families wishing to pause for a swim and/or picnic along the way.

Wildlife viewing is another distinct possibility on this river. Floaters report seeing beaver, deer, wild turkeys, and an assortment of wading birds.

## FISHING

The Ouachita has been a favorite fishing spot among sportsmen for decades. Heavy stringers of smallmouth and spotted bass come from the stream year-round, although the best angling for big bass (four-pounders are not uncommon) is usually during the cooler months from October through March. In the lower reaches just above Lake Ouachita, the spawning runs of white bass always attract large numbers of spring fishermen, and, as might be expected, this cool stream supports large numbers of green and longear sunfish. Anglers will also land an occasional walleye, largemouth bass, rock bass, catfish or bluegill.

## SERVICES AVAILABLE

Supplies can be obtained in Pencil Bluff, Mount Ida, or more distant towns like Mena and Hot Springs. In addition to the Forest Service campgrounds along the river, the Corps of Engineers has developed numerous camping sites on Lake Ouachita. Rental canoes are available in Pencil Bluff.

## OTHER INFORMATION

The Ouachita is the longest and largest river in the Ouachita Mountain region. The river is also "floatable" (and "fishable") below Lake Hamilton to Arkadelphia and well beyond. Supplies, including rental canoes, are available in Malvern for this stretch.

The newest recreation developments on the stream are found in extreme southern Arkansas where the U.S. Fish and Wildlife Service and the Corps of Engineers are constructing facilities within the Felsenthal National Wildlife Refuge. Hunters and fishermen are already giving the area rave reviews.

# SALINE RIVER

# THE ARKANSAS FLOATER'S KIT

#14 IN A SERIES

The Saline River maintains the intangible quality of timelessness. Born of the rivulets that flow out of the eastern foothills of the rugged Ouachita Mountains, its three major divisions — Middle, Alum and North forks — merge above Benton. Below this point the river flattens out to begin its long journey through Grant, Cleveland, Bradley and Ashley counties to its confluence with the Ouachita River in the heart of Felsenthal National Wildlife Refuge.

The Saline River is the last major undammed stream in the entire Ouachita Mountain drainage, and its watershed contains some of the finest deer, turkey and squirrel hunting in Arkansas. That, combined with the excellent fishing, scenery and backcountry floating the river produces, makes it no wonder that Arkansans who know it regard the river with almost fanatical devotion.

## SECTION DESCRIBED

Source to Ouachita River, a distance of 204 river miles.

## CHARACTERISTICS

The upper portion of the Saline, above Benton, is characterized as a clear, cold-water section with a series of fast-running shoals interspersed with short, quiet pools. The middle section of the river (Benton to Warren) contains long pools and few riffles with clear to murky water. The river's lower section below Warren has sluggish current with slightly murky water. The Saline is one of only a few rivers that has a gravel bottom throughout its entire length.

## SEASONS

The Saline is a good year-round float stream except in the uppermost portions.

## ACCESS POINTS

Access to the Saline is generally at state highway crossings, county road crossings and numerous little-known fords and ferry sites. The Game and Fish Commission has developed several access points along the river, including (working downstream): a boat ramp off Highway 229 on a forest road between Traskwood and Poyen; Lee's Ferry Access from Highway 35; Pool access at Highway 79; Mt. Elba off Highway 35; Highway 4 out of Warren; at Longview off Highway 189 between Fountain Hill and Johnsville; and Stillion at the mouth of the canal right below Lake Georgia Pacific. There is also access in Grant County at Jenkins' Ferry Historical Monument between Sheridan and Leola. Local inquiry will generally uncover others on or near forest roads.

## SCENERY

The Saline remains relatively unspoiled by man and creates an illusion of wilderness along much of its length. Dense forests line the river banks. Visitors may be treated to the sight of deer, mink, otters, beaver, muskrats and a variety of bird species.

## FISHING

The Saline is one of the most underrated fishing rivers in Arkansas. Smallmouth bass abound in the upper reaches; largemouth bass occupy the lower reaches; and the intermediate water between has a healthy population of spotted bass that overlaps into both areas. The warmouth, longear, and green sunfish top the panfish offering, with some bluegills and crappie. The river also has a good walleye fishery, and channel catfish are common. Rock bass are found in association with smallmouth bass on the upper third of the river.

Fishing during much of the year is a "wade a little, fish a little" proposition, and for this reason, canoes are much preferred over the traditional flatbottom johnboat. A motor is normally more trouble than it's worth on headwater float trips, though a light electric trolling motor can be a real boon at times.

## SERVICES AVAILABLE

Gas, groceries, restaurants and overnight accommodations are available in nearby communities. Picnicking and swimming are available at Jenkins' Ferry Historical Monument south of Sheridan.

## OTHER INFORMATION

The best time to float the Saline is when it's low and clear. When the current is swift, logjams, brushpiles and uprooted trees can make even travel difficult in some areas.

# SPRING RIVER

# THE ARKANSAS FLOATER'S KIT

#15 IN A SERIES

Although the Spring River begins somewhere up in Missouri, it doesn't get serious until it reaches the state line and enters Arkansas. That's where Mammoth Spring flows into it, adding about nine million gallons of water every hour to the streamflow. Instantly the river is transformed into a racing stream, just right for fishing and floating.

### SECTION DESCRIBED

Mammoth Spring State Park to the Black River, a distance of about 57 miles.

### CHARACTERISTICS

There's no getting around the fact that Spring River is chilly. After all, nine million gallons — every hour — of 58° water is hard to ignore. But it is this volume of cool water that: 1) makes the Spring River a year-round float stream; and 2) allows the river to be regularly stocked with rainbow trout.

Most Spring River canoe trips take place in the 17 mile stretch between Mammoth Spring State Park and Hardy, an historic town in northern Sharp County. This section is recommended for beginning to intermediate canoeists, and is very popular for family outings.

The first half of this section begins at the base of Dam #3, a former hydropower structure located south of Mammoth Spring. To get to the launching area, take Arkansas 342 (west off U.S. 63) for slightly less than a mile. Floaters of this nine-mile portion can look forward to numerous rapids, and even a couple of small waterfalls (both of which should be portaged in high water). The take-out point is Many Islands Camp, a private development located between Hardy and Mammoth Spring, and about two and one-half miles west of U.S. 63 (directional signs are present).

The second half of the Spring River's upper portion begins at Many Islands and concludes about eight miles downstream at Hardy Beach, a public park below the U.S. 62-167 bridge on the stream's southwest (right) bank. Like the previous section, this one also features rapids and waterfalls although they're not as frequent. One especially noteworthy spot is High Falls, a six foot waterfall which looks considerably taller than that from a canoe going over its brink.

Another Spring River float is the ten-mile stretch from Hardy to Williford. The water slows down in this run, although interesting rapids can be expected. The take-out point for this leisurely trip is a public launch area behind the United States Post Office at Williford, a small town two miles south of U.S. 63 on Arkansas 58.

The Spring River remains "floatable" for another thirty or so miles below Williford. While this section is seldom visited by canoeists because of the long, slow pools, folks strictly interested in a quiet fishing trip might find it ideal.

### SEASONS

The constant flow from Mammoth Spring makes the Spring River a dependable year-round stream for floating, even in the summer months when most other creeks are too low.

### ACCESS POINTS

The Spring River is one of Arkansas's more accessible streams, with U.S. Highway 63 paralleling much of its length. Major public access points include: Cold Springs and Dam #3 (both reached off U.S. 63 between Hardy and Mammoth Spring), Bayou Access (off Arkansas 289 on the river's west side), Hardy Beach, the Williford Launch Area (off Arkansas 58), two entry/take-out points at Ravenden (one south of town on a county road; the other to the east at U.S. 63), and a final launch site at Imboden (at U.S. 62 crossing). In addition, access can also be obtained at several private developments along the river.

### SCENERY

Clear water, overhanging trees, and occasional wildlife make the Spring a scenic float. The very construction of the river itself (a stairstep series of ledges and pools) makes it one of the most interesting and appealing in the state.

### FISHING

The cool waters of the Spring River provide ideal conditions for stocking trout. Rainbow trout are by far the most abundant and popular species, but recent stockings of brown trout have also proven successful. The likelihood of catching a lunker trout on the Spring is minimal, but what the fish lack in poundage by comparison with trout fishing on the White or Little Red is compensated by the fierce fight that the fish can wage in the relatively calm water.

The stretch of river from Mammoth Spring to Dam No. 3 is best waded and fished afoot except for the deep portion of the river near the dam. The first mile or two is an ideal flyfishing stretch. The heart of the Spring's trout waters lies in the three-mile stretch below the dam. This portion of the river, which is difficult to fish from the bank, holds some of the larger trout. One to three-pounders are fairly common in the shoals and pools down to Many Islands, but the flow of water from Myatt Creek a few miles further on increases the water temperature to such a degree that very few trout are found in the river below.

The best fishing spots for trout are immediately below the falls where the falling water hits, creating a frothing white mass. Back under the ledges is where the rainbows lie, waiting to nip out and grab food coming over the falls. The most deadly method is to stand on the lip of the falls and let lure or bait drift over the lip with the current. Strikes are lightning fast and hard to feel in the churning water.

In addition to trout, the Spring offers high-quality smallmouth bass fishing and seasonal walleye fishing. These two species are scattered in the river from Myatt Creek to well below Hardy. Spring River anglers will also find good action for jumbo channel and flathead catfish, tailwalking spotted bass, and small but sassy rock bass, warmouths and longear sunfish.

### SERVICES AVAILABLE

The nearby towns of Mammoth Spring and Hardy can supply the needs of most any visitor. Private resorts, campsites, motels and canoe outposts are readily available in the area.

### OTHER INFORMATION

One attraction that should not be missed is Mammoth Spring State Park. In addition to viewing one of the largest springs in the country, visitors can hike, picnic, or even examine an exhibit of train memorabilia.

Next door to the park is the Mammoth Spring National Fish Hatchery, the nation's leading producer of smallmouth bass (and also a source for largemouth and striped bass, walleye, channel catfish, and redband trout). Visitors can take a self-guided tour of the hatchery, and also view one of the nicest public aquariums in the region.

Another place worth a closer inspection is Hardy, one of those towns which has managed to retain a good deal of its original character. Attractive old buildings are still in place, with many of them housing shops featuring antiques or local arts and crafts.

And one last bit of news for floaters: the Spring River's South Fork is "canoeable" during many months of the year. The first float — a twelve-miler — is from Saddle (on Arkansas 289) to the bridge at the Cherokee Village Campground. A six-mile trip from this bridge down to Hardy Beach is also possible. While the South Fork's gravel bars are great for picnicking, potential campers should note that these same gravel bars can be quickly inundated following local or upstream rainfall.

# STRAWBERRY RIVER

# THE ARKANSAS FLOATER'S KIT

#16 IN A SERIES

Flowing out of the Ozark foothills in north central Arkansas is the Strawberry River, a friendly stream good for family excursions. It begins just a few miles west of Salem in Fulton County, and meanders in a southeasterly direction for slightly over 100 miles before merging with the Black River. While it does not offer the whitewater of the Mulberry or the bluffs of the Buffalo, the Strawberry has a lot going for it: convenient access, interesting scenery, and a smallmouth bass fishery. In fact, because of its fine qualities the stream's upper section has been placed in Arkansas's Natural and Scenic Rivers System.

### SECTION DESCRIBED

Entire length, a distance of approximately 109 miles.

### CHARACTERISTICS

The upper one-third of the Strawberry River is generally too low for good floating, although wade fishing is a possibility for the die-hard. The best bet for a good outing is in the river's middle third — the section between the U.S. 167 crossing north of Evening Shade and the Arkansas 115 bridge northeast of Jesup.

The first float, a nine to 10 mile journey, begins at Highway 167 and concludes at a low-water bridge which is about two miles north off Arkansas 56 and roughly halfway between Evening Shade and Poughkeepsie. A second float — also nine to 10 miles in length — begins at this same crossing and ends at the next low-water bridge about two miles north of Poughkeepsie, just west of Arkansas 58. The third float is from this second low-water bridge to the Arkansas 58 crossing, a distance of about two and a half miles.

These three floats offer certain similarities. They all possess fine gravel bars, and something else not too common to Arkansas streams — sandy beaches. In addition, these sections all include some very fishable waters, with bass (smallmouth, largemouth, rock, and spotted) and sunfish receiving the most attention.

The Strawberry can also be floated from the Arkansas 58 crossing on down to the 115 bridge near Jesup, but it's a lengthy trip (around 20 miles). Rather than floating the entire distance, some fishermen prefer to paddle (or motor) upstream from either of these access points, and then leisurely fish their way back down to the vehicles.

### SEASONS

For floating, the time to visit the Strawberry is in the spring of the year. The river is also a prime candidate for wade fishing when water levels are too low for a successful boat trip.

### ACCESS POINTS

Primary points of access include U.S. 167 near Evening Shade; a low-water bridge north of Arkansas 56 and about halfway between Evening Shade and Poughkeepsie; the Arkansas 58 crossing; and the Arkansas 115 crossing near Jesup. The Sharp County General Highway Map helps in locating these and other put-in/take-out points.

### SCENERY

The scenery, in a word, is attractive. The river itself has easy rapids, deep pools, and good-looking water. In many places canoeists are sheltered by over-hanging trees. And the surrounding country, while not wild, is very quiet and peaceful.

### FISHING

The gravel-bottomed Strawberry offers ideal habitat for channel catfish, one of the primary sportfishes found here. These sleek underwater bulldogs usually lurk near rocks and downed timber out of strong current. Crayfish are their primary forage and consequently the best bait, but channel cats will take a variety of other offerings, including worms, minnows, catalpa worms, liver and stinkbaits. Huge flathead catfish also haunt the Strawberry, offering heart-pounding thrills to catfishermen in-the-know.

While catfish abound in the Strawberry, they are often overlooked by anglers who usually come here to try their luck for spotted and smallmouth bass. Wade fishing for bass is popular in the upper reaches where a fly rod and popping bug can produce non-stop fishing entertainment. However, most bass are taken in the lower two-thirds of the river using ultralight rods and reels equipped with small spinner-baits, jigs, plastic worms or salamanders or crayfish-lookalike crank-baits. Other less important, but often caught, fishes include crappie, bluegills, saugers and warmouths.

### SERVICES AVAILABLE

Supplies can be obtained in the nearby communities of Ash Flat, Evening Shade, or Cave City, but bring your own boat since rentals are not available locally. The nearest camping facilities are at Lake Charles State Park, located about 15 miles east of Jesup.

### OTHER INFORMATION

The Strawberry is another one of those streams receiving a good deal of public recreational use, despite the fact that there is little if any public land along the river. Traditional access points may, in fact, be on private property. Therefore visitors are encouraged to check with local residents concerning recommended put-in and take-out locations.

# WHITE RIVER

# THE ARKANSAS FLOATER'S KIT

#17 IN A SERIES

To a casual reader of maps, the White River appears mostly, well, indecisive. It flows west in its headwaters region before turning north in the Fayetteville-Springdale area. On toward Eureka Springs, the river bends back to the east, then wanders up through southern Missouri before reentering Arkansas and angling to the southeast past Cotter, Calico Rock, and Batesville. At Newport, the stream makes an abrupt turn to the south and flows some 257 miles in that direction before joining up with the Mississippi River.

In this 720-mile journey, the White undergoes several transformations. It begins as a small, mountain stream (complete with rapids), and ends up as a broad, meandering waterway serving the barge and towboat industry. In between, the river's flow is interrupted by at least eight dams, six in Arkansas and two more in Missouri. The largest of these — Bull Shoals — is responsible for converting what had been a warm-water fishery into one of the nation's premier stretches of trout habitat. Today this cold-water section of the White River is among the state's major tourist destinations.

But the White River is more than an attraction for outdoor recreation-types. As it passes through or alongside nearly a fourth (18) of Arkansas's 75 counties, it exerts a steady though sometimes subtle influence on a vast portion of the state.

### SECTION DESCRIBED

Entire length of 720 miles, with emphasis on headwaters region and trout fishing section.

### CHARACTERISTICS

The first 31 miles of the White River are similar to the beginning stretches of other Ozark streams — fast and furious in the wet months, and comparatively calm the rest of the year. In this upper stretch above the first impoundment — Lake Sequoyah — the stream offers a series of pools and shoals with overhanging trees, tight turns, and gravel bottoms. While Arkansas 16 is seldom more than a quarter of a mile away, it goes virtually unnoticed by floaters. The bluffs, forests, and quiet pastures hold visitors' interest.

The next "floatable" section of the White begins many miles downstream, right at the base of Bull Shoals Dam. Here the river is considerably larger and, because of the hydro-power discharges from deep within the lake, very cold — just right, in fact, for rainbow, brown, and cutthroat trout. Each year thousands of people try their luck with these fish, and numerous guide services, outfitters, trout docks, and resorts have been established to help out. Also contributing to their success is the Arkansas Game and Fish Commission which annually stocks great quantities of trout into the stream. Many of these are caught fairly soon after their release, but others manage to hide out year after year, getting bigger all the time. Some get exceptionally large, like the 19 pound, 1 ounce rainbow or the 33 pound, 8 ounce brown trout which are discussed in the "fishing" section.

But trout are only one part of the White River picture. There's the scenery itself, featuring some of the best bluffs in all of the Ozarks. Others remember the river by the thin layer of fog suspended delicately above the stream each morning around sunrise. And not to be overlooked are the famous "shore lunches" on handy gravel bars, cooked up on the spot by experienced outfitters.

The trout section of the river stretches all the way to Guion, or a distance of about 90 miles. Flowing into the White along the route are two superb smallmouth streams — Crooked Creek and the Buffalo River — and another fine trout stream — the North Fork River. The latter offers a scenic six-mile float between Norfork Dam and the town of Norfork.

There are numerous ways to get to know the White. One extreme — and the choice of thousands of vacationers every year — is to hire a guide and a johnboat, relax in a deck chair, and head for a fishing hole. Another extreme is to emulate the annual Boy Scout pilgrimage by putting a canoe in at Bull Shoals State Park and paddling like crazy all the way to Batesville — a distance of 120 miles.

No matter how they get on the river, visitors need to remember that the stream is subject to sudden fluctuations because of power generation at the dam. When all the turbines are in operation, the White River can become bank-full and very swift. At normal operating levels, however, the stream's shoals and pools provide an ideal combination for a memorable fishing trip.

### SEASONS

The White's upper reaches are strictly seasonal, with the late October through April/May period traditionally the best time for float trips. Below Bull Shoals Dam, the White River is a year-round float stream, with some of the best fishing reported during the winter months.

### ACCESS POINTS

Launch sites for the White are too numerous to list. The Game and Fish Commission has constructed many access points downstream from Bull Shoals, and the Arkansas State Parks Division has a handy launch ramp at Bull Shoals State Park. In addition, many of the resorts along the river have developed launching areas for their guests. →

# WHITE RIVER

# THE ARKANSAS FLOATER'S KIT

CONTINUED

## SCENERY

People have been commenting on the beauty of the White River since at least 1819 when explorer Henry Rowe Schoolcraft said of the stream: "It unites a current which possesses the purity of crystal, with a smooth and gentle flow, and the most imposing, diversified, and delightful scenery . . . Our canoe often seemed as if suspended in the air, such is the remarkable transparency of the water."

Today's visitors will not be in quite the wilderness that Schoolcraft experienced, but there's still plenty of good scenery — towering bluffs, wildflowers, thickly forested hillsides, and lots of wildlife.

## FISHING

The upper White River with its assortment of bass (smallmouth, largemouth, rock, and Kentucky), catfish (channel, blue, and flathead), and sunfish should satisfy nearly any angler. Spinnerbaits, crawfish imitators, and skirted jigs (with pork tails) are recommended, along with minnows, crawfish, and other natural baits.

Below Bull Shoals Dam, the White River takes on an entirely different character. Here it is one of the most famous float fishing streams in the world. And with good reason. Probably more rainbow trout are caught here each year than in any other trout stream in America. The Game and Fish Commission stocks hundreds of thousands of rainbows in the White annually, and more than 90 percent of them are caught each year by anglers who come here from all corners of the globe.

Brown trout? Well, let the figures speak for themselves. In 1972, Gordon Lackey landed a monster brown weighing 31 lbs. 8 ozs. This stood as the North American record until fellow guide Leon Waggoner landed a 33½ lb. giant in 1977, now just mere ounces under the world record brown. Missouri angler Tony Salamon landed a 30 lb. 8 oz. leviathan in 1986 that set a new world line-class record for 6-pound-test line. Very few browns grow that large, of course. But frankly, 5-10 pounders are common, and anglers have a good chance of landing an 11-20 pound trophy. And, yes, a few 20 pound plus monsters are usually corralled each year.

Although White River rainbows don't approach North American record size, the river still boasts the 19 lb. 1 oz. Arkansas state record. Ten pound fish are considered large, but there are plenty of real thoroughbreds in the 2-6 pound class.

As an added bonus, White River anglers can also find cutthroat and brook trout in these fine waters. Cutthroats were first stocked in 1983, but the river has already produced 9-pound-plus fish. Brook trout are a rare catch, but they have reached up to four pounds in the North Fork of the White.

Bull Shoals to Cotter is the stretch best known for trophy browns. Many are taken on live crayfish or sculpins, but a variety of other live baits and artificials can also be employed successfully, especially at night since brown trout are nocturnal feeders. Fly-fishing is extremely popular on the White during low water periods, but most anglers opt for the standard White River rig — a 16- to 20-foot johnboat equipped with a 10-20 hp motor.

The North Fork of the White from Norfork Dam to the White has produced two record rainbows and the state record brook trout. The Crooked Creek and Buffalo River junctions are also good lunker trout holes. Smallmouth bass fishing is good at the mouths of feeder streams, including the mouths of Sylamore Creek, Buffalo River, Rocky Bayou and Piney Creek. Fishing is good for channel catfish and rock bass, and in lake headwaters, white bass, hybrid stripers and walleyes are important sportfishes.

## SERVICES AVAILABLE

For the upper reaches, the cities of Fayetteville and West Fork can supply most needs of floaters and fishermen. The nearest campground is at Devil's Den State Park located west of Winslow on Arkansas 74.

Visitors to the trout-fishing section of the White River can choose from numerous resorts and guide services. Many are located around Cotter, a city which modestly bills itself "Trout Capital of the World." Public campgrounds are found along the river at Bull Shoals State Park and at Corps of Engineers facilities on Bull Shoals Lake.

## OTHER INFORMATION

The Norfork National Fish Hatchery, located near the base of Norfork Dam, is an interesting stop for area visitors. So is the Wolf House, an historic cabin located in Norfork at the confluence of the White River and its North Fork.

Many, many miles downstream is another point of interest — the White River National Wildlife Refuge. This 113,000-acre tract is the home for waterfowl, songbirds, deer, and one of Arkansas's largest black bear concentrations.

Finally, the reader should be advised that the lower White River is well known for its catfish. Restaurants in DeValls Bluff, Des Arc, and other river towns have taken full advantage of this resource and can serve some of the best food to be had anywhere.

# The Traveler's Outfitters ...

## Canoe Rentals, Fishing Guides, Float Trips

*Red Bud Dock*

• Lodging •
• Guide Service •
• Boat & Motor Rentals •

Route 2, Box 541
Gassville, AR 72635-9510
Phone (501) 435-6303

**Jeff Evans**

*** COME AND ENJOY A LEISURELY FLOAT***
*** FISH FOR SMALLMOUTH IN THE WILD ***
*** WITHOUT ANOTHER SOUL IN SIGHT ***

**TRIGGER GAP**
**FLOAT SERVICE**
***On the King's River***

**The King's River is relatively untouched. As the only outfitter on the King's, we service the length of the river, from Arkansas to Missouri. Canoe rental and shuttle service available. Group rates.**

THE JEPPSEN FAMILY 501-253-2225
RT.1, BOX 643, EUREKA SPRINGS, ARKANSAS

**RESORT**

*"Home Of The World Record Brown Trout"*

**RAINBOW TROUT FISHING AT ITS BEST**

| CABINS | CAMPSITES |
|---|---|
| BOATS | GUIDES |
| MOTORS | TACKLE |

3 Miles East Of
Heber Springs, AR
Paved State Highway 110

100 Swinging Bridge Drive
Heber Springs, AR 72543
(501) 362-3327

*George and Joan Heine, Owners*

**Boats-Motors**
**Guide Services**
**Baits - Licenses - Canoes !!!**

Float fish by yourself or with a guide who knows the water...plus when and how to catch fish! You will enjoy the excellent fishing and the magnificent scenery of the world-famous White and Norfork Rivers
*"Leave the world behind and relax with us."*

**( 501 ) 499-5500**

Mike & Tammy Harrison
Box 129 • Norfork, Arkansas 72658

At the junction of the White and Norfork Rivers

CADDO RIVER — FLOAT TRIPS

**CABIN & CANOE RENTALS, INC.**

*The Only Complete Recreational Facility on the Beautiful Caddo River*

***FEATURING:***

- Bunkhouse Accommodation for 60 *(Separate Quarters for Boys & Girls)*
- Screened Pavilion with Kitchen
- Canoe Floating, Swimming & Fishing
- Volleyball Court, Horse Shoes & Tether Ball
- New for 1996 – *Authentic Indian Tipi*

*For Reservations Call Toll Free:*
**1-800-538-6578**
or call
(501) 356-2944 – Caddo Gap, Arkansas

Route 1, Box 1185
Cotter, AR 72626
(501) 430-5217

**On The White River**
**In The Arkansas Ozarks**

***Relaxed and Refreshed***

Here at the resort, we offer fully-equipped cabins with dishes, cooking utensils, towels, dish towels, etc. All units have air conditioning, TV and a deck, all within 100 feet of the river. Our units will accommodate from 2 to 20 persons. We also have a swimming pool, tackle shop, gift shop, and meals on request. Boats, motors and guides, are available.

**Your Hosts:**
**PHIL AND ANN BYRAM**
**HCR 62, Box 100 • Flippin, AR 72634**
**(501) 453-2913 • FAX: (501) 453-2376**

**Canoes**
**1 - 800 - 99 FLOAT**

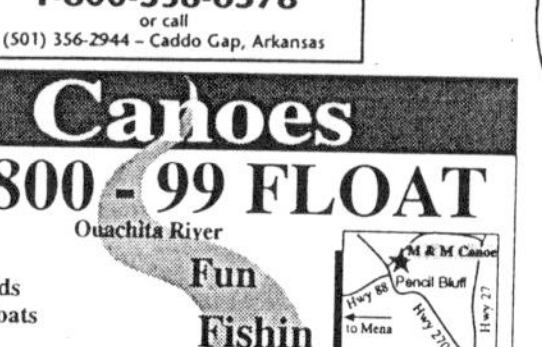


Canoes
Cabins
Campgrounds
Camping Floats
FloatTrips
Taxi Service
Shuttles

Fun
Fishin
Floatin

*"Open year round"*

Pencil Bluff, Arkansas

M & M
**Canoe Rentals**

**MOORE OUTDOORS**

Canoe & Raft Sales & Rentals

Camping
BackPacking & Hiking
Whitewater Instruction

**( A trip down Big Piney Creek is a trip you'll never forget. )**

The most picturesque, as well as one of the most challenging streams in the state.
Enjoy the towering granite bluffs & scenic beauty through the calm waters; then feel the thrill of the ride as you navigate the many rapids on your journey.

**501-331-3606**
**3827 SR 164W**
**Dover, Arkansas 62837**

**SOUTHFORK CANOE RESORT**

**Highway 289**
**Saddle, Arkansas**
**(501) 895-2803**

**Guided Fishing Trips**
**Fly Fishing**
**Bank Fishing**
**Hiking**
**Exploring**
**Birdwatching**
**Deluxe, Fully furnished Cabins**
**Camper Cabins**
**RV & Tent Sites**
**Boat & Canoe Rentals**

501-425-8555

## FEDERAL PRIORITIES, OR DO CONGRESSMEN REALLY HAVE PLOOP FOR BRAINS?

The other day I came across and article in a local magazine that really got my hackles up. If you're an Arkansan and a fisherman, today's column is required reading.

The Federal Government, notorious for mismanagement of funds, has declared for lack of monies it is closing eleven fish hatcheries in the Southeastern U.S. this coming year. Fifteen more are scheduled for closing in 1997, but they have yet to be selected.

Although none of the initial eleven are in Arkansas, there is great concern by the Arkansas Fish and Game Commission, as well a local citizenry, that one or more of the hatcheries in our state are earmarked for extinction. I don't know about you, but this just plain #$%@#s me off. In very simple terms, the loss of warmwater river habitat due to Federal Flood Control and hydropower projects in the White River basin absolutely requires the continual restocking of trout and other specimens such as small mouth, walleye and perch. Without this restocking we can eventually expect to see most of these species diminish and very possibly disappear from Arkansas' large rivers and streams.

Fishing in Arkansas provides more than 200 million dollars in revenue each year, creates thousands of jobs and generates more than 20 million dollars in federal and state taxes. But aside from that, and even more important, it is an essential part of our children's heritage. Fishing is as integral to Arkansas as its mountains and its pines, and as much a part of our outdoor traditions as hunting the deer and the turkey of our heartland. Yet if our government, with its screwed up sense of priorities has its way, this may begin to change within a few short years.

The whole thing made me so mad I was compelled to do a little research. I've told you what the government doesn't have the money to support. (This is the same government you pay all those taxes to each year.) Now let me tell you what they are funding with your dollars.

First, let's talk big money, then we'll get into a couple smaller absurdities.

#1. This year alone we spent 226 million dollars on the Federal Bilingual Education Act, so we could teach immigrant children attending U.S. schools in their own languages, rather than have them learn English. That sure makes good sense.

#2. How about this: Last year 67,000 drug addicts and alcoholics collected more than 350 million dollars in "Supplemental Security Income." What's that? Well, it's a nifty little piece of legislation that says drug and alcohol addiction qualifies as a disability that keeps people from working. (I'll bet it does!) So they are entitled to monthly social security benefits. Okay, let me make sure I've got this right. All I have to do is get hooked on drugs, and the government will pay me a minimum of $5,000.00 a year. That makes good sense. . . . I guess you could call it the "Getting

High with a Little Help From My Friends" program.

I promised you a couple of lesser priced federal spending absurdities, and I won't let you down. These are real zingers.

The Environmental Protection Agency gave the state of Utah almost a million dollars this year, to fit cows with special plastic devices gauging bovine flatulence and its effect on global warming. Now I gotta ask you, have our congressmen gone mad, or do they just have cowpies for brains? I mean, they just spent the equivalent of the combined yearly federal tax payment of an average Arkansas township so that someone could bungee strap baggies on the butts of a bunch of cows and measure how much methane is expelled when a heifer passes gas.

I know you're thinking that last one is going to be hard to top, but my final example deals with the Federal Grants Program, which I'm certain is staffed exclusively by lobotomy patients.

I had a friend who owned a construction company. Two of his employees, young college graduates, had studied the Federal Grant procedure extensively. They were determined not only to take advantage of it, but to demonstrate the inanity of the system.

Following federal guidelines, they applied for a grant. They filled out all the forms in triplicate, sent in the required letters of recommendation and qualifications, then waited patiently. One day several months later they showed up for work all chuckles and smiles, and gave their notice. Their $300,000.00 grant had been approved--they were off to Alaska to do a comprehensive study on the internal temperature of hibernating Brown Bears. (I know you think I'm making this up, but I'm not!) Yes, $300,000.00 (a good portion of which I'm sure was spent on Alaskan girls and Yukon Jack whiskey) for taking the temperature of sleeping bruins.

Now you've got to figure they ain't gonna get that thermometer under the bear's tongue, so that leaves only one other port of entry, and as challenging an enterprise as that might be, I can't see the results being worth a third of a million of our tax dollars. Yet some pointy-headed bureaucrat with more responsibility than brains decided it was a worthy endeavor. These, my friends, are some fine examples of what they're doing with our tax money.

They are closing National Parks and federally funded state fisheries, diminishing our most precious heritage, the outdoors, while they fund projects ranging from the sublime to the ridiculous--projects that rend the fabric of this society rather than mend it. It isn't right. It isn't even American, and it won't change--in fact it'll get worse--unless we do something about it. Write the Governor, call your congressmen, tar and feather a liberal bureaucrat.

The Intrepid Arkansas Traveler

## LOOK OUT, THE PHONE'S RINGING

I guess it doesn't matter whether you live in the hills of Arkansas or in a beach bungalow in L.A. If you've got a phone, you automatically fall prey to the dreaded telephone solicitor; that friendly fellow with the artificial attitude who won't take no for an answer, who's certain he has a service or an item that you just can't live without. . . .

It's two o'clock on Sunday afternoon. I've raked the leaves in the front yard and cut a cord of wood for the cold front they say is coming in. Bonnie's done the breakfast dishes and straightened up inside while I showered. It's an unseasonably pleasant day; a cool breeze is coming through the open windows. Seems like a great time for a nap, or whatever. We sidle into the bedroom, kick off our slippers and snuggle up, but we no sooner get the covers pulled over our heads when the phone rings.

I struggle out of bed with a groan and grab the receiver. "Hello."

"Hello, is this Michael, Michael Reisig?" says a disgustingly congenial voice that could only belong to a salesman of some sort.

A part of me wants to say, "No, no this is not Michael; unfortunately he died yesterday; got run over by the tractor and the hogs ate him." But I don't.

"Yes?"

"Michael, I'm Gerald from *Time/Life Books*. Michael, how are you doing today, Sir?" (There's that generous use of my first name, followed with a question about the weather or my health. It's a salesman for sure.)

Now I feel the urge to contradict the initial acknowledgment of my name. (Excuse me, did I say I was Michael? No, no, I'm sorry. I'm Fred, his cousin. Michael moved to Argentina yesterday; doing research on the Mabuto tree frog -- endangered species, you know. He probably won't be back for a year or two.) But I don't.

"Fine, I'm fine. What can I do for you?"

At that point Gerald launches into a spiel on the deal he has for me today: all these magazines he can get for me at only one-third the cover price. I've been picked out special, 'cause I've got great credit and I'm a wonderful person and this deal wouldn't even be possible if it wasn't for a survey they were conducting on what people read. You know -- intelligent people like me . . . I'm beginning to feel like I'm knee deep in muckety-muck, wishing I was back in bed with the covers pulled over my head. I decide to get out of this, tastefully, artfully.

"Excuse me. Gerald, wasn't it?"

"Yes, Michael?"

"Gerald, did I mention to you that I'm blind? Yep, blind as a bat. I'm so blind my seeing eye dog needs a seeing eye dog. I couldn't even tell you where the magazine rack is, let alone read something from it!" I smile; I'm sure I've got him.

But Gerald is hard core. . . .

There's a pause. "Does your wife read, Michael? This would make a great gift for her. In fact, I'm certain you would want her to have such a wonderful opportunity. . . . " I have to think fast.

"Yes, I would get it for her, if she was still around."

"Still around?" Gerald says cautiously, sensing a trap.

"Yeah, sad to say, she's gone -- abducted by aliens about a week ago."

"You mean like spaceships and blinking lights?" I can hear the smile in Gerald's voice.

"No, she was kidnaped by two Latinos in a '65 Chevy, and hasn't been heard from since."

Gerald senses that he's losing, but he's tough. He's a closer if I've ever heard one. No more ploys now, no more Mr. Nice Guy, Gerald goes in for the kill, one more shot.

"You got a dog or a cat?"

"Yeah, both. Why?"

"Let me tell you, Mr. Reisig, (not Michael, I noticed) I don't think there's much in these magazines worth reading anyway, but the paper has really great absorption qualities. I mean, if you've got a puppy, or a cat with the squirts, you can pull out the pages and spread them on the floor. Works really great; it'll save your rug. . . . Have you got a fireplace? This stuff burns better than dry tinder . . . !" At this point I resort to my final tactic.

I reach for the cordless electric shaver that I leave by the phone for occasions such as this. I turn the shaver on and run it across the mouthpiece of the receiver while shouting in the background, "Hello? Hello? Are you still there? Hello? Damned line's gong out again!" After about 15 seconds, I notice the line's gone dead. Gerald realized he had met his match.

Now I know I could have just told Gerald to kiss my posterior and hung up, but he gets that all the time. This way, being beaten at his own game, will eat at him for weeks; might even cause him to quit his job. Then there'll be one less solicitor to bother me on Sunday afternoon.

The Intrepid Arkansas Traveler

## FACING DEATH HEAD-ON

I was driving home from work the other day when there, on the side of the road, I noticed a raccoon. He was dead as dirt, upside-down, legs sticking up and stiff as a board. He'd obviously been looking right when he should have been looking left. As sad as it was for me to see one of God's creatures having met his fate, I couldn't keep a small smile from the corners of my mouth, for it reminded me of my very first trip through Arkansas, just over ten years ago. Most of all, the sight of the raccoon was a particular and poignant reminder of the fellow I had been traveling with, Loony Tony Lamar. I can hardly see a legs-up animal on the side of the road, or smell peach brandy and not think of that guy. Now, I know you must think that's a pretty strange combination, but I can explain.

Loony Tony, who came by his name honestly, and I were returning from Wichita, Kansas, where I'd just bought another giant portable BBQ machine for my catering business in South Florida. Tony worked for me, on and off (mostly off), for about two years. If the fish weren't biting and the dogs weren't racing, or if the weather got too cold for the beach, he'd probably show up; otherwise it was a roll of the dice. But when he did show, he was a hard worker and good company. Tony was also an excellent cross country driver, which was why he was with me that afternoon, as we came down Hwy. 40 headed for Little Rock.

We were driving straight through to Miami in five-hour shifts, stopping just long enough to fuel, feed ourselves and use the restroom. It was my turn to drive, so at our last stop Tony picked himself up a pint of his favorite, Morton's Peach Brandy.

We got to laughing and telling stories, and Tony began nipping seriously at that bottle. Pretty soon it was empty, and he was high as a kite, crazy as a road lizard. I was thinking maybe we should find some coffee when all of a sudden he yelled, "Stop! Stop the car!" his hands waving as he pointed at something ahead, to the side of the road, a psychedelic gleam in his eye. It was a Monday afternoon; there was little or no traffic. I slammed on the brakes and swerved off the road, screeching to a halt.

There in front of us was the biggest raccoon I'd ever seen. I mean, this son-of-a-gun must have weighed in at seventy pounds. He was also dead as last week's news, on his back, legs straight out and rigid as a fur-covered card table. Before the truck even stopped moving, Tony's out the door yelling something about dignity and death, headed for the animal.

Sitting in the truck, I couldn't believe what I was seeing. Loony Tony had grabbed the giant raccoon, turned him over and stood him up, facing the oncoming traffic. Tony stepped back, admiring his work, and I found myself smiling, then laughing. Suddenly we were both laughing our fool heads off, and finally I understood. What was a painful last grimace had been turned into a defiant snarl as the raccoon proudly faced his nemesis', man and the automobile. He had been given a modicum of dignity in death, stubbornly standing there as if to say, "Come on sucka, give me your best shot!" (And I'm quite sure someone did not long after we left. Nonetheless, it was still rewarding to see Rocky Raccoon staring onward as we drove away.)

We were feeling so good, I let Tony buy another pint of Morton's best, and we stood up animals for the next 200 miles. Why, we managed a little dignity for three armadillos, two 'possums, four raccoons, a Labrador, a Chihuahua and a four-point buck before we cleared Louisiana.

I guess the point I'm trying to make here was best put by Tony the next day when he had sobered up. He said most everyone he knew, including himself for the longest time, was afraid of dying. We seem to perceive it as some dark, confusing affair. Somewhere along the line he realized that if your take something less seriously, it can't frighten you; that dying should be viewed with less fear and trepidation and more a simple acceptance of what it is: the final, essential part of life.

Now I'm not saying we should take this final communion with the Great One lightly, and I'm not saying that when Grandma kicks the bucket you should stand her up on the highway (that would freak out the tourists, wouldn't it?). But I have often wondered, at somber funerals marked with dark clothes and hushed tones, whether the one who had just passed into that bright realm would really have wanted everyone acting that way.

For me, I think I'd like to go out with a little dignity and a little levity, like a nice coffin and a Groucho Marx mask.

You all watch out for those raccoons, hear?

The Intrepid Arkansas Traveler

# HUNTING REGULATIONS

The act of hunting satisfies an ancient, primal part in the heart of modern man, but we must be reminded that this communion with nature is a ritual of survival and a celebration of life, not a veneration of death. The true sportsman finds more sadness than elation in the final moment, having drawn his pleasure from the journey, not the arrival.

The Traveler

# Licenses

**What kinds of licenses or permits do I need to hunt in Arkansas?**
If you are 16 years or older, a hunting license is required to hunt wildlife in Arkansas unless you are on a licensed commercial shooting resort that supplies pen-raised birds for you to shoot. The license must be carried with you. You may not possess a license that belongs to someone else or one that has been altered, backdated or counterfeited. If you are a nonresident you may not possess a resident license. If you guide, aid or assist someone else for a fee, you must have a guide license. Nonresidents (under 16 years of age) are not ordinarily required to purchase a license until they actually bag a deer, turkey or bear; however, anyone using the new $10 "bonus" antlerless deer tag must purchase it before hunting.

**How do I get the licenses I need?**
You can buy many licenses at sporting goods stores, hunting and fishing supplies stores, some discount chains, the Arkansas Game and Fish Commission's Little Rock or regional offices or you can call 1-800-364-GAME (1-800-364-4263), at any time. If you intend to order by phone, please have your credit card and driver's license number ready. Your hunting or fishing privileges will become effective immediately and your license will arrive in the mail in a few days. Lifetime licenses are not available by phone order.

**Do I qualify for a resident license?**
A resident is someone who has established an actual residence at least 60 days prior to applying for a license and who intends to become a citizen of Arkansas. Also included are nonresidents enrolled as full-time students at colleges and universities in Arkansas who carry proof of full-time enrollment while hunting or fishing. Possession of Arkansas real estate by a person living outside the state does not qualify the owner as a resident. Servicemen and women stationed (permanently assigned) in Arkansas are granted resident privileges for hunting and fishing. Servicemen and women who were Arkansas residents at the time of entering service are also granted resident privileges for hunting and fishing, regardless of where they are currently stationed.

**Who needs a Hunter Education Card?**
Hunters born after 1968 must carry a valid Hunter Education card. Youngsters (under 16 years) under the direct supervision of an adult (over 21 years old) do not need to have a card. Call 1-800-482-5795 to find out about Hunter Education classes. Arkansas honors the home state Hunter Education cards of nonresidents.

**How do I replace a lost license or Hunter Education card?**
Call 223-6349 if you have lost your license and 223-6377 to replace your Hunter Education card.

**What other wildlife-related activities require licenses?**
Call 223-6386 during office hours about these licenses or permits: fur dealer, commercial game breeder, commercial special quail, commercial shooting resort, falconry, commercial nongame breeder or alligator farming.

# Hunting License

## RESIDENT

$37.50 **Resident Combination Sportsman's License (CS)** entitles the holder to hunt all game species using modern gun, muzzleloader or archery/crossbow, to hunt or trap furbearers; and to fish the waters of the state with non-commercial tackle. State and federal waterfowl stamps must be purchased to hunt waterfowl and a resident trout permit must be purchased to fish in certain waters

*****

$26.00 **Resident Sportsman's License (RS)** entitles the holder to hunt all game species using modern gun, muzzleloader or archery, and to hunt or trap furbearers. State and federal waterfowl stamps must also be purchased to hunt waterfowl.

*****

$11.50 **Resident Wildlife Conservation License (HNT)** entitles holder to hunt small game (except furbearers), and to take one deer using modern gun. State and federal waterfowl stamps must be purchased to hunt waterfowl.

*****

$7.00 **Resident Arkansas Waterfowl Stamp (DS)** is required to hunt waterfowl in addition to a resident hunting license and federal Duck Stamp. Not required of youth under 16 or holders of a non-expiring $1,000 Lifetime Resident Sportsman Permit. Must be signed across the face in ink. Expires June 30th.

*****

$10.00 **Resident Antlerless "Bonus" Deer (ABD).** See top of next page.

*****

## NONRESIDENT

$185.00 **Nonresident Annual All Game Hunting License (NBG)** entitles holder to hunt all game species except furbearers for the 5-day period specified. A NWP and federal waterfowl stamp must also be purchased to hunt waterfowl.

*****

$125.00 **Nonresident 5-Day All Game Hunting License (AG5)** entitles holder to hunt all game species except furbearers for the 5-day periods specified. A NWP and federal waterfowl stamp must also be purchased to hunt waterfowl.

*****

$95.00 **Nonresident 3-Day All Game Hunting License (AG3)** entitles holder to hunt all game species except furbearers for the 3-day period specified. A NWP and federal waterfowl stamp must be purchased to hunt waterfowl.

*****

$65.00 **Nonresident Annual Small Game Hunting License (NRH)** entitles holder to hunt small game (except furbearers). A NWP and federal waterfowl stamp must also be purchased to hunt waterfowl.

*****

$40.00 **Nonresident 5-Day Small Game Hunting License (SG5)** entitles holder to hunt small game (except furbearers) for 5-day period specified. A NWP and federal waterfowl stamp must also be purchased to hunt waterfowl.

*****

$100.00 **Nonresident Fur Taker's Permit (NFT):** In addition to a nonresident hunting license, entitles holder to hunt and trap furbearers.

*****

$12.00 **Nonresident Waterfowl Hunting Permit (NWP)** is required for waterfowl hunting in addition to a nonresident hunting license and federal Duck Stamp. Expires June 30th.

*****

$10.00 **Nonresident Antlerless "Bonus" Deer (NAB).** See top of next page.

*****

# The New $10 "Bonus" Anterless Deer Tag

With this tag, resident or nonresident hunting license holders may hunt antlerless deer in zones 12, 15, 16, 17, 19 and 20 when regular deer seasons are open. This deer is not part of the regular seasonal bag limit. Only 1 tag is allowed per hunter.

**MISCELLANEOUS LICENSES AND TAGS**

$2.50 **Hunting Dog Tag (DOG)** (resident and nonresidents) is required of each dog used for hunting, chasing or retrieving game species. Metal tag must be affixed to dogs collar. See page 23 for exempt dogs. Expires June 30th of each year.

*****

$20.00 **Casey Jones Leased Lands Permit (LCJ)**: In addition to hunting license, required to hunt, trap or camp on Casey Jones Leased Lands.**

*****

$20.00 **Cherokee Leased Lands Permit (LCH)**: In addition to hunting license, required to hunt, trap or camp on Cherokee leased Lands.**

*****

$20.00 **Big Timber Leased Lands Permit (LBT)**: In addition to hunting license, required to hunt, trap or camp on Big Timber Leased Lands.**

*****

$25.00 **Guide License-Hunting (GLH)** is required of any person who guides or assists another person, for pay or other consideration, in hunting game species on land which is not owned or leased by AGFC.

*****

$150.00 **Guide License-Special (GLS)** entitles holder to same privileges as the GLH plus the privilege to guide or assist another person for pay or other consideration in hunting on land owned or leased by AGFC .

*****

**map available from area license dealers

# INFORMATION HOT LINES

## (501) 688-8000

When asked, press the desired 4-digit code.
For help or additional information, press 4

| | | | |
|---|---|---|---|
| 4250 | Big Game Seasons | 4255 | Licenses |
| 4251 | Small Game Seasons | 4256 | Water Levels |
| 4252 | Fishing | 4257 | Firing Range |
| 4253 | Waterfowl | 4258 | Boat Registration |
| 4254 | Hunter/Boater Education | 4259 | Current Events |

# General Regulations

## You may not hunt wildlife:

- except during open seasons.
- from or across a city, county, state or federally maintained road or its right-of-way.
- within 50 yards from the center of a city, county, state, or federally maintained road during a modern gun deer season.
- from or across the main levee of the Mississippi River and Arkansas River from the Louisiana border to the intersection of state highway 11 (north of Grady in Lincoln County).
- from a boat at night.
- using deadfalls, drugs, chemicals, poisons or explosives.
- from an aircraft.
- using electronic tracking or telemetry equipment to locate wildlife.
- for scientific studies without a scientific collection permit from the Commission; phone 223-6430 for more information.
- that is fleeing from floods or fires.
- that is damaging crops or personal property during closed seasons without a depredation permit from the Commission (and complying with the permit's terms).
  Phone 223-6381 for more information.

*** The possession of tackle or hunting device in fields, forests, along streams or in a location known to be game cover, may be considered along with other evidence as prima facie evidence that the possessor is hunting or fishing.***

## Either a Winner or a Loser

Years ago there was a regular Sunday Afternoon dice game near Big Flat. One of the stories coming from this meeting is the one about one of the members who was stumbling home from the game drunk as a skunk late one Sunday afternoon, carrying a bridle on his shoulder.

A passing motorist stopped to give him a ride. Knowing where his rider had been, the driver asked how his luck had been that day.

The gambler picked up the bridle and told the driver he wasn't sure. Said that he'd been walking along trying to remember whether he'd won a bridle or lost a horse.

## MAKING BUCKS FROM BUCKS

The other day I went to the doctor for my annual physical, a debasing ritual of nakedness, poking, prodding and coughing that I could gladly do without. It does, however, lend perspective to one's overall health; so each year about this time I grit my teeth and do it.

Slumped in a plastic chair in the reception room I picked up a copy of an Arkansas outdoor magazine, and while paging through it I came across an advertisement in the "New Products" section that set me to giggling maniacally and scribbling notes.

The product was called Supreme Buck Urine. Yep, that's right, Supreme Buck Urine. Not regular stuff, this, but high test twaddle for the wholesale attraction of deer of all kinds, or perhaps for the hunter who wants a really rugged cologne. I've heard of a lot of strange sales businesses, from marketing bottled tap water to Florida swampland, but I think this might top them all. I mean, for goodness sake, these people are making a living selling . . . urine!

The ad went on to mention that Supreme Buck Urine is collected at the company's state-of-the-art collection facilities. (I'm not making this up, I swear!) Now that got my curiosity piqued. How exactly is state-of-the-art buck urine collection done? Is there a very quiet guy in a camouflage suit and a measuring cup hiding in the woods, discreetly following deer around until that special moment. He'd have to get awfully close, and have a very steady hand.

Well, I took the number at the bottom of the page and called the company that afternoon. I had a couple of what I thought were legitimate questions. A girl answered on the third ring. I told her I wanted some info on her urine. She said, "Excuse me?"

"You know, Supreme Buck Urine?"

"Oh yeah, that."

I said I wanted to know the inside scoop on buck urine collection. And what about rutting versus non-rutting buck urine as mentioned in the ad. I mean, was a rutting buck more, or less cooperative? I struggled to make the conversation a straight transaction, but try as I might I couldn't keep the smile out of my voice. Pretty soon we were both giggling. Finally we were laughing so much she said I'd have to call back, maybe talk to the boss about the technical side of buck urine collection. I said, "Okay, who do I ask for?"

She said, "Buck."

I said, "You gotta be kidding!"

Seems Buck was out doing some collecting and field testing, whatever that means. I suppose you can use your imagination. . . .

The Intrepid Arkansas Traveler

## THE GREAT TURKEY HUNT

It's hunting season again. Guns are being pulled from rack and cabinet and cleaned with care, ammunition purchased with eager anticipation, and Supreme Buck Urine is being snatched off the shelves by the gallon. (Keep up the good work, Buck!)

Ah, the aroma of damp earth on a misty autumn morn, the crisp crackle of leaves underfoot, that heavy, satisfying feel of a cold weapon in your hands, and the startling first sight of your prey: these are the reasons we hunt. These and of course the reassuring knowledge that we're shooting something that can't shoot back. But then, even with those odds, every once in a while something goes awry....

I have a hunting buddy who lives in Mt. Ida. We'll call him Rodge. Now, they tell me Rodge was wrapped a little loose even before he went to Nam. The field trips to Cambodia didn't help. Though he loves the outdoors (he's one of the few people I know who wishes the deer could shoot back), Rodge's approaches to the primitive instinct sports are a little unconventional, and the tangents he goes off on occasionally land him in trouble.

His idea of fishing is a baitcasting rod, twenty pound test line and a grenade. He likes guns with sufficient stopping power to disable a bulldozer, and he owns an armory that would make the National Guard jealous.

A while back Rodge called me and asked if I'd like to go turkey hunting with him. "With guns?" I asked.

"Yeah, sure, with guns," he replied. "Grenades mess 'em up too much...."

Now, knowing Rodge's history with this sort of enterprise I should have said no, but I really wanted a turkey for the larder, and the season was nearing an end. My primal instincts got the better of me, and I reluctantly agreed, though my concern escalated when Rodge assured me we would get a turkey 'cause he had a plan....

The following morning, as the first rays of the sun began to edge the darkness, we were already in position deep in the National Forest. Rodge had brought a large duffle bag with him, but when I asked him what was in it, he wouldn't tell me. He just smiled and said it was part of "the plan".

He was maybe thirty yards from me and I could hear him rustling around in the darkness, but I couldn't see him. In the distance I heard an old Tom call. A few moments later I heard my partner use his diaphragm caller, the kind that fits in the roof of your mouth. I looked over, and suddenly, out of the gloom came Rodge. My jaw just dropped. I didn't know whether to laugh out loud or shoot him and put him out of his misery. Crazy ol' Rodge was dressed in a giant turkey suit, complete with a beak protruding over his forehead, full feathered wings that his arms fit into, beige colored leggin's and clawed tennis shoes. One arm tucked his gun to his side. The surprising part was how damned much he looked like a turkey! "Wetti ool, uh?" he said.

"Take the diaphragm out of your mouth."

"Pretty cool, huh?" he repeated. "I'll just be another big ol' turkey; get those suckers to walk right up to me!"

Closer, the old Tom gobbled again. "Get down!" I whispered tensely. "Behind that log!"

As Rodge settled in behind a giant fallen oak, he put his diaphragm back into his mouth and called again. The turkey answered, insistent. Everything was going perfectly; it looked like a piece of cake. I should have known better.

Seems there were a couple of factors that we were unaware of. First, two other hunters were moving in to the west of us, stalking what they thought were a pair of turkeys calling to each other. Second was the nest of fire ants that Rodge had sat in; ants that were at that moment crawling into his feathers and his leggin's.

Fire ants are crafty little creatures. It's almost like they wait until they're all in position, then bite on cue....

All of a sudden Rodge grunted, and his eyes bulged. He stood straight up and stumbled over the log, his arms flapping, doing some kind of demented turkey jig. The turkey caller caught in his throat, and he started clacking and gobbling, performing some of the finest turkey calling I'd ever heard, but I was sure that dance thing was gonna scare the bird.

Before I could yell at him to get back down, I heard someone call from the other side of the clearing, "Look, Jeb! There's the biggest goll derned turkey I ever seen! Get 'em! Shoot that son of a #$%#@!"

The roar of a shotgun shattered the stillness of the morning, and a patch of feathers on Rodge's haunches exploded. He did a standing broad jump of about fifteen feet (probably a record of some sort), coughing up the diaphragm as he shrieked and spitting it about twenty-five feet (probably another record). Rodge dashed for the woods, zig-zagging, screaming and flapping while shotgun blasts chewed the bark off trees around him. I kept my head down until the shooting stopped.

When the smoke cleared, Rodge was gone. The other hunters had disappeared as well, probably still in search of the Loch Ness Turkey. Two hours later I found Rodge back at the car, nursing a load of birdshot--the turkey suit gone, left in the woods.

I looked at him. "Don't say a word," he said. "Just take me home. I want a beer and a TV dinner, in that order."

"Turkey and dressing?" I asked.

The Intrepid Arkansas Traveler

## THE UNWELCOME GUEST

The other day I ran into Rodge, my crazy hunting buddy from Mt. Ida. You might remember him from the disastrous turkey hunt I wrote about a few weeks ago. Not surprisingly, he had experienced another "adventure" and had to relate it to me. Typically of Rodge, it's quite a story, and I thought I'd pass it on. . . .

Rodge lives in a 60' by 12' mobile home just off Hwy. 27. It's not a bad place, except that it's decorated in early bachelor. Cast-off clothes, unwashed dishes and an assortment of beer cans are usually an accepted part of the ambience; nothing a good woman and a good cleaning couldn't fix. Rodge occasionally experiences both, though neither seem to last long enough to change that old hippie.

Rodge's latest problem dealt with an unwanted guest -- a rat. It seems this giant rat (Rodge's version) had decided to homestead in the walls of my friend's trailer. Now, I don't know if you've ever experienced this, but a rodent in the walls of your home can be a really disconcerting thing. It oftentimes doesn't matter how fastidious you are, they just seem to choose you, and they can be hell to get rid of.

Late at night Rodge would be having a bite to eat while watching TV, and he would hear that soft patter of padded feet across ceiling beams, a whisper of scratching, the rasping of tiny claws on wood, wallboard and insulation, as the creature gathered up the ingredients essential for a comfortable little nest. He tried traps; he caught the neighbor's cat. He tried poison; he killed two raccoons, a squirrel and a gecko lizard, but no rat. The little fellow was clever.

The rat would scratch inside the wall and Rodge would bang on the outside and yell at him. Terrible things -- he called that rat, could have burned the ears off a sailor, but the furry little guy seemed unaffected and went right on building his nest.

Now Rodge is not known for his patience nor his decorum. Remember, this is the guy who fishes with grenades. Gradually it began to gnaw at him, the derned rodent was outsmarting him. It was eating his house, for God's sake, like it was a gingerbread cottage in some demented fairy tale!

It all came to a head one night: a sordid story of whiskey, vengeance and a twelve-gauge shotgun. . . .

Rodge had been hunting earlier that day. Having capped off the event with a sixpack, he was sitting on the couch, working on his third Jack and water (very little water), cleaning his shotgun, when the scratching began. Staring at the wall, he folded up his bore rod and put away the cleaning rags. "Dirty little $#@#$#," he muttered as he threw down the last of his drink and poured another, straight. As the scratching grew in intensity, he was sure that he could hear a squeaky little voice laughing at him from behind the paneling. He took a drink. The voice and the scratching continued, louder now. He began loading the gun, four rounds of number-eight shot, one in the chamber. He focused his bloodshot eyes as best he could on the area where the rasping, taunting sounds seemed to emanate from, and the barrel of the gun came around.

The cannon-like report of the weapon inside the room took even Rodge by surprise. Unfortunately Rodge's approximation of the location of the rodent was a few inches off, for suddenly out of the smoking, jagged hole in the wall came a terrified Harry the Rat. It flew out the hole and landed on the coffee table in front of my besotted friend. Disoriented and frightened, it bounded straight ahead onto Rodge's chest. Rodge let out a shriek and struggled to rise, knocking over the couch as he and the rat went head over heels behind it. In the interim, the shotgun discharged again, vaporizing the small chandelier on the ceiling and instantly installing a ten-inch skylight. Harry the Rat bounced off Rodge's forehead and headed down the hallway toward the bedrooms. Rodge was quick to recover, even as toasted as he was. He was a Veteran; he'd been in combat before. He scrambled for his weapon and got off two rounds as the rat squealed and jagged down the corridor. The whiskey, however, didn't improve his aim. His first shot mortally wounded the air handler for the central air system. The second round went through the bathroom wall and disintegrated the top half of the commode. Harry the Rat made it to the bedroom.

The next day, in the process of cleanup (and $500.00 worth of repairs), Rodge found specks of blood in the hallway, but no sign of Harry anywhere. The scratching had ceased, and my friend began to savor his hard-won victory. He figured it was over, and it was, almost. . . .

A few days later Rodge began to sense a slightly unpleasant odor in his bedroom. A week later the room smelled like a men's room in a Guatemalan prison. It was fairly evident that Harry was getting revenge. Rodge looked everywhere; he even pulled the paneling off a couple of walls. No Harry. He had almost given up, having taken to wearing deodorized cottonballs in his nose while he slept, when one cold morning he took his heavy army fatigue jacket out of the closet. Putting it on and walking outside, he noticed there seemed to be a particular aura of dead rat about him. The neighbor's coon dogs had taken to following and yipping at him. The cold wind whipped across his face. He shivered and stuck his hands in his pockets . . .

The little fellow must have had a great sense of humor, for in his last moments he had crawled into his nemesis' favorite coat. It must have been a sight seeing Rodge trying to rip that jacket off, then having to fight the coon dogs for it. I'd have to say the last laugh went to Harry.

The Intrepid Arkansas Traveler

# FISHING REGULATIONS

Of all the primal instinct sports, fishing is the most amazing. It is remarkable that the quest for a simple, scaled creature should be cause for such an amalgamation of hardware and paraphernalia; that something as intrinsic as the insistent tap tap and the tautening of a line should draw such riveting attention and quickening of pulse in the most sophisticated of souls.

The Traveler

# Fishing License

**What must I have to fish legally in Arkansas?**
If you are 16 years or older, a fishing license is required to take or attempt to take fish, frogs, minnows or mussels in Arkansas, unless you are fishing in a licensed "put and take pay lake." The license must be carried with you. You may not possess a license that belongs to someone else or one that has been altered, backdated or counterfeited. If you are a nonresident, you may not possess a resident license. If you guide, aid or assist someone else in fishing for hire, you must have a guide license.

**How do I get the licenses I need?**
You can buy licenses at many sporting goods stores, hunting and fishing supplies stores, some discount chains, many boat docks, directly form the Arkansas Game and Fish Commission's Little Rock office or you can call 1-800-364-GAME (1-800-364-4263), at any time. If you intend to order by phone, please have your VISA or MASTERCARD and drivers license number ready. Your hunting or fishing privileges will become effective immediately and your license will arrive in the mail in a few days.

**Do I qualify for a resident license?**
A resident is someone who has established an actual residence at least 60 days prior to applying for a license and who declares his or her intentions of becoming a citizen of Arkansas. Also considered as residents are nonresidents enrolled as full-time students at colleges and universities in Arkansas and carrying proof of full-time enrollment while hunting or fishing. Possession of Arkansas real estate by a person living outside the state does not qualify the owner as a resident. Servicemen and women stationed (permanently assigned) in Arkansas are granted resident privileges for hunting and fishing . Servicemen and women who were Arkansas residents at the time of entering service are also granted resident privileges for hunting and fishing, regardless of where they are currently stationed.

**Do I need a license to fish on my own land?**
Yes.

**How long is my fishing license good for?**
Unless it is a 3, 7 or 14 day license, one year from the date of purchase.

**How do I replace a lost license?**
You may be able to get a replacement for a lost license at a reduced cost. Call 501-223-6349 for details.

**FREE FISHING INFORMATION FOR ARKANSAS AND OTHER STATES**
**CALL 1-800-ASK-FISH**
**Provided by the Sport Fishing Promotion Council**

CS $35.50* **Resident Combination Sportsman's License** entitles the holder to the privileges of a Resident Sportsman's License (hunting) and a Resident Fisheries Conservation License (fishing). A resident trout permit must also be purchased to fish in certain waters.

*****

FSH $10.50* **Resident Fisheries Conservation License** entitles the holder to fish the waters of the state with non-commercial tackle. A resident trout permit must also be purchased to fish in certain waters.

*****

RT3 $ 6.50* **Resident 3-Day Trip Fishing License** entitles the holder to fish the waters of the state with non-commercial tackle for the 3 day period specified. A resident trout permit must also be purchased to fish in certain waters.

*****

TPR $ 5.00 **Resident Trout Permit** is required to fish in certain waters (see page 10) in addition to a Resident Fisheries Conservation License, a Resident Trip License, a Resident Combination Sportsman's License or a Lifetime Fishing License. Not required for holders of the non-expiring $1000 Lifetime Resident Hunting and Fishing Sportsman's Permit. No trout stamp will be issued.

*****

TPN $ 7.50 **Nonresident Trout Permit** is required of a nonresident to in certain waters (see page 10) in addition to a Nonresident Annual Fishing License, a nonresident 3-day Trip Fishing License or a Nonresident 14-Day Trip Fishing License. No trout stamp will be issued.

*****

NRF $30.00 **Nonresident Annual Fishing License** entitles a nonresident to fish the waters of the state with non-commercial tackle. A nonresident trout permit must also be purchased to fish in certain waters.

*****

NT3 $10.00 **Nonresident 3-Day Trip Fishing License** entitles a nonresident to fish the waters of the state with non-commercial tackle for the 3 day period specified. A nonresident trout permit must also be purchased to fish in certain waters.

*****

NT7 $15.00 **Nonresident 7-Day Trip Fishing License** entitles a nonresident to fish the waters of the state with non-commercial tackle for the 7 day period specified. A nonresident trout permit must also be purchased to fish in certain waters.

*****

N14 $20.00 **Nonresident 14-Day Trip Fishing License** entitles a nonresident to fish the waters of the state with non-commercial tackle for the 14 day period specified. A nonresident trout permit must also be purchased to fish in certain waters.

*****

GLF $25.00 **Guide License, Fishing** is required of any person who guides, aids or assists another person, for pay or other consideration, in taking any species of fish.

*****

***Subject to increase by the Arkansas Legislature in 1995**

## STATEWIDE

### GAME FISH LIMITS

| | Daily Limit | Minimum Length Limit |
|---|---|---|
| **Alligator gar** | 2 | |
| **Black basses** (largemouth, spotted, smallmouth combined) | 10 | |
| **Smallmouth bass** | 6 | 10 inch |
| **Rock bass** | 10 | |
| **Bream** (bluegill, redear, longear, warmouth and other sunfishes combined) | 50 | |
| NOTE: no limit on bream four inches or smaller | | |
| **Catfish** (other than bullhead | 10 | |
| NOTE: no limit on bullhead | | |
| **Crappie** (black, white combined | 20/30/50 | |
| **Tiger muskie** | 6 | |
| **Northern pike** | 6 | |
| **Paddlefish** | 5 | |
| **Pickerel** | 6 | |
| **Sauger** | 6 | |
| **Saugeye** | 6 | |
| **Striped bass (including hybrid stripers)** | 6 | |
| **Trout** (rainbow, brown, cutthroat, brook combined) | 6 | |
| **Brown trout** | 2 | 16 inch |
| **Cutthroat trout** | 2 | 16 inch |
| **Walleye** | 6 | |
| **White bass** | 25 | |
| NOTE: no limit on yellow bass | | |
| Aggregate limit (total number of fish allowed to be taken in a 24-hour period 12 o'clock midnight to 12 o'clock midnight) | 75 | |
| Possession limit | Double the daily limit | |
| Spearfishing limit | Half the daily limit | |

DAILY LIMIT - The number of fish of one species allowed to be taken in 24 hours (from 12 o'clock midnight to 12 o'clock midnight).

## STATEWIDE

## THE ONE THAT DIDN'T GET AWAY

Like most Arkansans, I like to fish. I take the sport fairly seriously, using the proper rods, reels and tackle, but beyond that I generally just put the boat in the water and go.

I have a friend however, I'll call him Jim, that has relegated the sport of fishing to something very near a religion. He has tackle boxes that would rival Hillary Clinton's luggage. Lures? Let me tell you about lures. If it resembles anything that might fit in a bass's mouth, he's got one. If someone tied a hook on a doorknob and advertised it on late night TV as the latest Crappie Killer, Jim would have one the next day.

Like any number of religions, he has costumes and rituals that go with it. He's got trout fly hats, BASS jackets, and belt buckles the size of dinner plates with life-like reliefs of fish that look like they're jumping out of his bellybutton.

He spits on his bait before casting. He sprays all sorts of noxious scents on lure and bait, odors only a fish or a starving raccoon could appreciate.

He even kisses his lures, but generally not after spraying them. His wife broke him of that habit. She told him, "You can kiss your lures, you can kiss me, but if you spray them lures with that #@%@ and kiss 'em, your only chance of gettin' lucky relates strickly to fishin'."

Jim looks at this fishing thing as a contest of intelligence between him and the fish. He's one of my closest friends, but he's not one of my brightest friends and for all the accessories, ceremony and effort, the fish sometimes win. This can throw him into a depression that makes Barbara Streisand's bad moods look like tea time with Shirley Temple.

As for myself, if I have a particularly bad day of fishing and need to boost my spirits, I have one little ritual. I take the stringer of big bass I caught two years ago out of the freezer. I let them thaw out enough to get the frost off, and I shoot an instant picture of me holding them up and smiling. Then I send it to one of my old fishing buddies with a note saying, "Boy, we killed them today! You should have been here!" Works every time.

This brings to mind a particular fishing trip that my friend Jim and I took to Bull Shoals Lake, just above the community of Mountain Home. Actually it was our last fishing trip together. Come to think of it, I haven't heard much from him since then. I'll explain....

It's a great lake, Bull Shoals. It has thousands of acres of clean water, lots of dead trees around the shore for crappie and bass cover, big catfish and stripers in the middle and good trout fishing.

We eased the boat into the water a half-hour after dawn. Pale white shrouds of mist still blanketed the lake. The soft swirls of early morning feeders could be seen on the surface around us. A big bass whorled the water next to the boat, sucking down a luckless insect. It was the kind of scene that both warms your heart and gives you a mild case of the hangover shakes as you try to thread the eye of your lure.

Jim was bait casting; I was fly fishing that day. I'm not a great fly fisherman, and I think that's where the trouble began.

About midway into the morning, I drew back my rod for a cast, the line and the fly floating effortlessly over us. The line straightened perfectly behind me, but just as I came forward with the rod, my attention was caught by a beaver surfacing next to the boat. The line and the fly tracked slightly sideways. About that time two things happened: Jim set his rod down and stood up to stretch, and my fly whizzed by, solidly snagging him in the earlobe. He let out a yelp like a salt-rocked coon dog, flailed with both hands and took a step to turn. I think that was his first mistake. Stepping on his tackle box, he lost his balance, and in less time than it takes a lizard to snatch a gnat, Jim was headed for the water.

He went in headfirst and came up gasping and splashing, eyes the size of saucers, water spiting out his mouth like one of those fountains in Hot Springs. My first thought was, *There goes the fishing in this area*. My second, as I watched him begin to flounder, was that Jim doesn't swim real well.

In his panic he had turned away from the boat a bit. I figured I better redirect his attention, so tightening my line I gave the top of the rod a little pop. Jim screamed like a pubescent schoolgirl, grabbed for his ear and my firmly attached fly, and grasped the line.

He was a big one, I knew I was going to have to play him. I loosened my drag and let him run a little, giving him some line as he splashed with one hand in an awkward circle. But if he started to sink or get too far from the boat, I gave him a short tug and immediately got his attention again. Finally, after one of the best fights I could remember in recent fishing history, I got him close enough to the boat to consider landing him. Problem was, he was too big for my net and I didn't bring the gaff. Besides, though grateful to be boat-side, Jim had a look in his eyes that said he was less than pleased with me. So, in the end I elected to tow him the short distance to shore with the electric motor.

As he crawled out of the water like early man and blew his cookies on the grass, making sounds like a cat hacking up a rat, I was pretty sure fishing was over for the day. I was right. After removing the fly from his ear, Jim didn't speak to me all the way home. Like I said, I haven't heard much from the ungrateful cuss since.

In closing, just remember, if you head out to Bull Shoals and catch a bunch of big ones, take 'em home and freeze 'em, stringer and all, 'cause you never can tell when you're going to have a bad day fishing.

The Intrepid Arkansas Traveler

# CALENDAR of EVENTS
# FALL and WINTER

DATES ARE SUBJECT TO CHANGE. CONTACT LOCAL CHAMBER OF COMMERCE FOR VERIFICATION.

## A

**Alread**
Sep 9: 5th Annual ACRDC Benefit Concert

**Altus**
Sep 23-24: 32nd Annual Wiederkehr Village Weinfest
Nov 23: Thanksgiving Dinner at St. Mary's

**Arkansas Oil & Brine Museum**
Thru Sep 9: Laurie Delezen Exhibit
Sep 2-Dec 31: Portraits of Pride Exhibit
Sep 10-Oct 21: Artists of the Future Exhibit
Oct 22-Dec 2: Arkansas Perspectives Exhibit
Dec 2-Jan 13: Upon Reflection Exhibit
Dec 3: Remember When...?
Jan 14-Feb 24: Youthful Impressions

**Ash Flat**
Dec 2: 6th Annual Christmas Parade

**Ashdown**
Nov 22-Jan 1: Land O' Lights
Dec 8-10: Celebration of Lights

## B

**Banks**
Nov 10-12: 9th Annual Buck Fever Festival

**Batesville**
Sep 23: 8th Annual Air Festival
Dec 2: 10th Annual Country Christmas Craft Fair

**Bauxite**
Dec 2: 10th Annual Arkansas Bluegrass Assn. Christmas Party

**Beebe**
Nov 25: 4th Annual Christmasfest Craft Show
Dec 1: 4th Annual Christmas Parade

**Bella Vista**
Oct 19-21: 27th Annual Arts & Crafts Festival

**Benton**
Oct 28: 3rd Annual Festival of the Scots

**Bentonville**
Sep 2-4: 4th Annual The Ole Applegate Place Labor Day Weekend Arts & Crafts Festival
Sep 17: Pops in the Park Concert
Oct 19-22: 9th Annual The Ole Applegate Place Autumn Arts & Crafts Festival
Oct 19-22: 11th Annual Sugar Creek Arts & Crafts Fair
Nov 24-25: 2nd Annual Christmas at The Ole Applegate Place Arts & Crafts Festival
Dec 1-2: 2nd Annual Christmas at The Ole Applegate Place Arts & Crafts Festival
Dec 8-9: 2nd Annual Christmas at The Ole Applegate Place Arts & Crafts Festival
Dec 15-16: 2nd Annual Christmas at The Ole Applegate Place Arts & Crafts Festival

**Berryville**
Sep 21-24: 40th Annual Saunders Memorial Muzzleloading Matches

**Bismarck (See DeGray Lake Resort State Park)**

**Blytheville**
Oct 7: 16th Annual Chili Cook-Off & Fall Festival

**Booneville**
Sep 12-15: South Logan County Fair & Livestock Show
Sep 23-24: Arkansas Association for Morgan Horses Trail Rides & Drive
Nov 20-Dec 3: American Brittany Club National Championship
Dec 4: 14th Annual Christmas Parade
Dec 9: 2nd Annual Tour of Decorated Homes

**Brinkley**
Sep 30: 12th Annual Fall Round-Up

**Bryant**
Sep 30: 8th Annual Fallfest

## C

**Cabot**
Oct 14: 17th Annual Cabotfest

**Camden**
Sep 12-16: 42nd Annual Ouachita County Livestock Show & Fair
Sep 23: South Arkansas Symphony Gala Season Opening
Sep 30: 27th Annual BPW Barn Sale
Oct 7-8: 5th Annual Indian Summer Pow Wow
Oct 28: 4th Annual Harvest Festival
Dec 9: 8th Annual Christmas Parade

**Cane Hill**
Sep 16-17: 4th Annual Harvest Festival

**Cherokee Village**
Sep 16: 9th Annual Indian Summer Day
Dec 4: Christmas Festival of Lights
Dec 9-17: Lake Thunderbird Christmas Lights Tour

**Clarksville**
Sep 29-Oct 1: River Valley Antique Machinery Show & Auction
Oct 12-13: "Talley's Folly"
Feb 1-3: "Pinocchio"
Feb 1-3: "3 X 3"

**Clinton**
Sep 1-3: 10th Annual National Championship Chuckwagon Races
Oct 19-21: 10th Annual Arkansas Heritage Quilt Festival

**Conway**
Sep 27: 45th Annual Faulkner County Fair Parade
Oct 28: 5th Annual Hunt of the Scavengers
Oct 28: 4th Annual Chips-N-Chili
Nov 12: 27th Annual Christmas Open House
Dec 2: 25th Annual Christmas Parade

**Corning**
Oct 28: 9th Annual Harvest Festival

**Crossett**
Oct 7: 17th Annual Wiggins Cabin Festival
Dec 4: Christmas Parade

## D

**Dardanelle**
Sep 22-23: 4th Annual Shade Tree Pickin'
Nov 4: 9th Annual Rotary Club Arts & Crafts Show
Dec 1: Christmas Parade

**DeGray Lake Resort State Park**
Sep 7-8: 8th Annual Moonlight Cruises
Sep 9: 8th Annual Great Arkansas Clean-Up
Oct 7-8: 23rd Annual Street Rod Car Show
Oct 7-8: 8th Annual Moonlight Cruises
Oct 13-15: 9th Annual Autumn Avian Affair
Oct 14-15: Ladies Halloween Scramble
Oct 20-29: 9th Annual Fall Foliage Frenzy
Nov 12: 37th Annual South Arkansas Quartet Convention
Nov 23-26: 9th Annual Thanksgiving Get-Away
Jan 26-28: 17th Annual Eagles Et Cetera Weekend

**DeQueen**
Oct 7-8: 7th Annual Hoo-Rah Days
Feb 11: 7th Annual Tea for Poets & Lovers

**Deer**
Oct 13-15: 3rd Annual Yard Sale

**Delight**
Dec 2: 5th Annual Holiday Open House

**Des Arc**
Sep 16: 3rd Annual Indian Games, Myths & Legends
Oct 20-21: Exhibition of Indian Artifacts
Nov 4: Flintknapping Demonstration
Dec 2: 2nd Annual Christmas Open House
Jan 20: Storytelling Time
Feb 9-23: 3rd Annual Doll Exhibit

**Devil's Den State Park**
Sep 16-17: 7th Annual Arkansas Mountain Bike Championships
Oct 14-15: 6th Annual Fall Backpacking Trip
Oct 21-22: 4th Annual Ozark Heritage Weekend

**Dover**
Oct 20-22: Mugwump Yuletide Craft Fair

**Dumas**
Nov 11-12: 21st Annual Delta Arts & Crafts Fair

## E

**El Dorado**
Oct 13-14: 9th Annual Musicfest
Oct 28: Orchestral Fireworks with Guitarist Benjamin Verdery
Nov 19-Dec 31: 8th Annual Christmas Open House & Festival of Lights
Dec 7: Annual Christmas Parade
Dec 10: Holiday Celebration with Guest Artist, Louis Nabors
Feb 17: All Tchaikovsky Concert with Guest Artist Andreas Klein

**England**
Oct 21-22: 2nd Annual Fluff 'N Feather Fest

**Eureka Springs**
Sep 9: 8th Annual Toy, Doll & Train Show & Sale
Sep 9-10: 25th Annual Antique Car Show
Sep 14-17: 11th Annual Jazz Festival
Sep 15-17: 4th Annual Woodcarver's Jamboree
Sep 16: 17th Annual Original Doll Show & Sale
Sep 23-24: 8th Annual Fall Village Crafters Show
Sep 28-Oct 1: 48th Annual Original Ozark Folk Festival
Oct 6-8: 5th Annual Corvette Weekend
Oct 6-8: 4th Annual Festival of Quilts
Oct 12-14: 22nd Annual Ozark Creative Writers Conference
Oct 14: Flamenco Guitarist Ronald Radford in Concert
Oct 20-22: 30th Annual Arkansas Craft Guild Fall Show & Sale
Oct 28: Chili Cook-Off
Nov 3-5: 2nd Annual Food & Wine Weekend
Nov 10: 10th Annual Christmas Lighting Extravaganza
Nov 10-11: 2nd Annual Early Bird Shopping Days
Nov 11: Jingle Bell Stroll
Nov 18-19: 7th Annual Antique Show & Sale
Nov 19: 2nd Annual Christmas Parade
Nov 24: Santa in the Park
Nov 24-25: "The Nutcracker"
Nov 24-25: 2nd Annual Victorian Christmas in Music
Dec 2: 23rd Annual Christmas Tour of Victorian Homes
Dec 2: Arkansas Symphony Quapaw Quartet in Concert
Dec 9: Gallery Walk
Dec 16: Eureka on Sale Day
Dec 26-Jan 1: Shopping Week

## F

**Fairfield Bay**
Oct 12-14: 14th Annual Oktoberfest
Nov 4: 5th Annual Winterfest
Nov 24-25: 10th Annual Christmas Arts & Crafts

**Fayetteville**
Sep 1-Oct 14: William McNamara Exhibit
Sep 1-Oct 31: 21st Annual Farmer's Market
Thru Sep 2: Washington County Fair
Sep 8: Pops in the Park Concert
Sep 9: Mark Twain Starring Hal Holbrook
Sep 15-17: Home Show
Sep 16: Elaine Elias in Concert
Sep 21-24: Antique Show
Sep 24: Christopher Taylor in Concert
Oct 7-8: "The Velveteen Rabbit"
Oct 8: American Chamber Players Concert
Oct 10: ODC Dance Repertory Show
Oct 13-14: 14th Annual Autumnfest
Oct 14: Opening Gala Concert

| | |
|---|---|
| Oct 14: | "Wiley & The Hairy Man" |
| Oct 15: | "Jesus Christ, Superstar" |
| Oct 20-21: | "Five Guys Named Moe" |
| Oct 20-22: | 23rd Annual Antique Show & Sale |
| Oct 20-Nov 19: | Baker Prairie Project Exhibition |
| Oct 22: | Mozart Piano & Violin Forte |
| Oct 28: | Oomph! |
| Nov 4-5: | "The Faure Requiem" |
| Nov 10: | Keith Terry & Crosspulse |
| Nov 17: | River North Dance Company in Concert |
| Nov 19: | Miami String Quartet with Pianist Alan Chow |
| Jan 20: | "Chicago City Limits" |
| Nov 22-Jan 6: | 3rd Annual Lights of the Ozarks Festival |
| Nov 24-Dec 26: | Recent Works by Pat Musick Exhibit |
| Dec 1: | 3rd Annual Jingle Bell Jog |
| Dec 2-3: | "The Nutcracker" |
| Dec 9: | Puppets & Storytelling Featuring The Lizard's Song |
| Dec 16: | Cirque Zoppe Europa |
| Jan 2-28: | Memories of Childhood Exhibit |
| Jan 18: | Dave Brubeck in Concert |
| Feb 2-3: | "Crazy for You" |
| Feb 3-29: | Hung Liu: Chinese American Artist |
| Feb 10: | Hometown/Concerto-Aria |
| Feb 14: | Anonymous Four in Concert |
| Feb 22: | Ballet Hispanico Presents Latin Beat |
| Feb 23-24: | "Always...Patsy Cline" |

**Fordyce**

| | |
|---|---|
| Oct 27-28: | The Fall Hunting Special |
| Dec 1: | 8th Annual Christmas Parade |

**Foreman**

| | |
|---|---|
| Dec 2: | Christmas Parade |

**Fort Smith**

| | |
|---|---|
| Sep 2-24: | Native American Invitational Exhibit |
| Sep 16: | 5th Annual Riverfront Blues Festival |
| Sep 16-17: | 8th Annual Classic Truckers |
| Sep 17: | Open Horse Show |
| Sep 21-30: | "I Hate Hamlet" |
| Sep 22-30: | 57th Annual Arkansas-Oklahoma State Fair |
| Sep 23: | Native American Festival |
| Sep 29-Oct 1: | 2nd Annual ZONTA Club Antique Show & Sale |
| Oct 1-29: | Lee Smith: Paintings Exhibit |
| Oct 1-29: | Catlin Prints—A Plains Portfolio |
| Oct 7: | Flights of Fantasy |
| Oct 13-14: | 10th Annual Oktoberfest |
| Oct 21: | Superior Federal Kinderkonzert Concert |
| Oct 31: | 22nd Annual Halloween Magic Show |
| Nov 2-4: | 2nd Annual Holiday Market |
| Nov 9-18: | "Who's Afraid of Virigina Woolf?" |
| Nov 5-26: | 19th Annual Photography Competition |
| Nov 5-26: | Kate & Ken Anderson: Collaborative Work Exhibit |
| Dec 2: | 56th Annual Frosted Window Panes |
| Dec 2: | 53rd Annual Christmas Parade |
| Dec 3-21: | Children's Christmas Card Design Competition |
| Dec 7-10: | Christmas Musical |
| Dec 9: | "The Nutcracker" |
| Jan 7-28: | 10th Annual Small Works on Paper |
| Jan 7-28: | Linda Palmer: Changing Seasons Exhibit |
| Feb 5-26: | The Lost Roads Project: A Walk-In Book of Arkansas |
| Feb 24: | Celebration of a Native Son Concert |

**Fountain Hill**

| | |
|---|---|
| Oct 20-21: | 5th Annual Frontier Days Festival |

## G

**Gassville**

| | |
|---|---|
| Oct 7: | 3rd Annual Frontier Festival |

**Glenwood:**

| | |
|---|---|
| Sep 29-Oct 1: | 8th Annual Caddo River Sawmill Days |

**Gosnell**

| | |
|---|---|
| Sep 29-30: | 5th Annual Cotton Pickin' Contest & Festival |

**Greenbrier (See Woolly Hollow State Park)**

**Greenwood**

| | |
|---|---|
| Dec 11: | Christmas Parade |

## H

**Hampton Museum State Park**

| | |
|---|---|
| Dec 2: | Dream Catcher Workshop |

**Hardy**

| | |
|---|---|
| Sep 2-3: | 12th Annual Pioneer Antique Auction |
| Sep 30-Oct 1: | 12th Annual Pioneer Antique Auction |
| Oct 13-14: | 2nd Annual Murder Mystery Weekend |
| Oct 21-22: | 13th Annual Old Hardy Town Arts & Crafts Show |
| Nov 4-5: | 12th Annual Pioneer Antique Auction |
| Nov 10-11: | 2nd Annual Murder Mystery Weekend |
| Dec 1-2: | 2nd Annual Murder Mystery Weekend |
| Dec 2-3: | 12th Annual Pioneer Antique Auction |
| Dec 9: | 13th Old Hardy Town Christmas Parade |
| Jan 6-7: | 12th Annual Pioneer Antique Auction |
| Jan 12-13: | 2nd Annual Murder Mystery Weekend |
| Feb 2-3: | 2nd Annual Murder Mystery Weekend |
| Feb 3-4: | 12th Annual Pioneer Antique Auction |

**Harrisburg**

| | |
|---|---|
| Oct 21-22: | 5th Annual Homestead Festival |

**Harrison**

| | |
|---|---|
| Sep 9-10: | 7th Annual Airshow of the Ozarks |
| Nov 28: | Christmas Parade |

**Hatfield**

| | |
|---|---|
| Oct 18-22: | Christian Motorcycle Assn. Changing of the Colors Rally |

**Heber Springs**

| | |
|---|---|
| Sep 5-9: | Cleburne County Fair |
| Sep 9: | 26th Annual Greers Ferry Lake/Little Red River Cleanup |
| Oct 13-15: | 30th Annual Ozark Frontier Trail & Trout Festival |
| Oct 14: | 10th Annual Greers Ferry Lake 5K Road Run |
| Dec 2: | Heber Under the Lights Christmas Celebration |

**Helena**

| | |
|---|---|
| Sep 11: | An Evening at the Operetta |
| Oct 6-7: | 10th Annual King Biscuit Blues Festival |
| Oct 11: | Warfield Concert |
| Nov 1: | Warfield Concert: The Kremlin Chamber Orchestra |
| Nov 28: | Warfield Concert: "A Christmas Carol" |
| Feb 11: | Warfield Concert: Zabava Russian Dance Group |

**Hindsville**

| | |
|---|---|
| Oct 19-22: | 42nd Annual War Eagle Fair |

**Hot Springs (See also Lake Catherine State Park)**

Thru Sep 3: 10th Season of "The Witness"
Thru Nov 25: Simulcast Racing Season at Oaklawn Jockey Club
Sep 9: 3rd Annual Jazz & Blues Fest
Sep 23: 9th Annual Hickory Hill Park Gospel Sing
Sep 28-Oct 1: 13th Annual Arkansas Senior Olympics
Oct 6-8: 27th Annual Arts & Crafts Fair
Oct 21: 12th Annual Volksmarsch
Oct 21-29: 21ST Annual Arkansas Oktoberfest
Nov 1-5: 6th Annual Arkansas Celebration of the Arts
Nov 7-12: 4th Annual Hot Springs Documentary Film Festival
Nov 11: 37th Annual South Arkansas Quartet Convention
Nov 17-18: 8th Annual Holiday Crafts Fair
Nov 17-19: 12th Annual Arkansas Healthfest
Nov 24-Jan 1: 4th Annual Holiday in the Park
Dec 10: 23rd Annual Christmas to Share
Dec 12-13: 4th Annual Live Nativity
Jan 12-Apr 13: 92nd Annual Live Thoroughbred Racing at Oaklawn Race Track

**Huntsville (See also Withrow Springs State Park)**
Dec 2-3: 4th Annual Christmas Arts & Crafts Fair

## J

**Jacksonville**
Sep 30-Oct 1: 8th Annual Mums, Music & Muscadines Festival
Dec 2: Christmas Parade
Dec 2-3: 20th Annual Holiday Crafts Sale

**Jasper**
Thru Sep 2: Newton County Fair & Rodeo
Oct 20: Fall Color Tour
Oct 20-22: 6th Annual North Scenic 7 Holiday Showcase
Dec 7-8: Newton County Christmas Festival

**Jonesboro**
Sep 2-3: 5th Annual Blues Fest
Oct 14: Airport Open House
Nov 10-12: 9th Annual Lit'l Bita Christmas Arts & Crafts Show
Nov 22-Jan 2: 2nd Annual Lights on the Ridge
Dec 7: 44th Annual Northeast Arkansas Christmas Parade
Dec 8-10: 12th Annual Living Christmas Tree

## L

**Lake Catherine State Park**
Sep 9: Starlight Concert
Sep 15-17: Family Wildlife Adventure Weekend

**Lake Chicot State Park**
Sep 1-24: 8th Annual Sunset Barge Tours
Oct 20-22: 9th Annual Civil War Weekend
Dec 19: 4th Annual Christmas Bird Count
Feb 2-4: 6th Annual Winter Wings Weekend

**Lake Fort Smith State Park**
Oct 13-15: 6th Annual Fall Splendor
Jan 19-21: 4th Annual Eagle Awareness

**Lake Ouachita State Park**
Sep-Oct: 4th Annual Fall Foliage Tours
Oct 14-15: Fall Foliage Weekend
Oct 31: 4th Annual Halloween Bonfire & Owl Prowl
Dec 2-3: 5th Annual Eagle Watch Weekend
Jan 13-14: 16th Annual Eagle Extravaganza Weekend

**Lake Village (See Lake Chicot State Park)**

**Leslie**
Oct 20-22: "Bone Chiller"
Dec 15-16: "Fruitcakes"

**Lincoln**
Oct 6-8: 20th Annual Arkansas Apple Festival

**Little Rock**
Thru Oct 10: Space: The Art of Robert McCall Exhibit
Thru Jun 1996: The Dream is Alive
Thru Sep 1,1996: Convergence in Space Exhibit
Thru Sep 1,1996: Russian Space Art Exhibit
Thru Sep 1,1996: Animated Rocket Launch Site
Sep 1-Feb: To Fly!
Sep 1-17: 38th Annual Delta Art Exhibition
Sep 1-Oct 1: Silver Holloware Exhibit
Sep 2-3: 2nd Annual World Fest
Sep 8-Nov 5: Alone in a Crowd: Prints by African-American Artists of the 1930s & 40s
Sep 15-Oct 1: "Alice in Wonderland"
Sep 15-Sep 15, 1996: Sweet Sounds: Arkansas Musical Contributions Exhibit
Sep 16-17: Masterworks Series
Sep 22-Nov 26: Hans Burkhardt: Drawings Exhibit
Sep 22-Nov 26: Driven to Create: The Anthony Petullo Collection of Self-Taught & Outsider Art
Sep 29-30: 34th Annual St. Mark's Antiques Show & Sale
Sep 30: Civil War Re-Enactment of the Occupation of the Old State House
Sep 30: Pops Live! Series
Oct 6-15: 56th Annual Arkansas State Fair & Livestock Show
Oct 12: Tales From the Crypt
Oct 15: Arkansas Symphony Orchestra Chamber Series
Oct 21-22: 5th Annual Arts & Crafts Fair at the Pumpkin Patch
Oct 21-22: Masterworks Concert Featuring Pianist James Dick
Oct 25-31: 4th Annual Boo at the Zoo
Oct 26: Happy Hour Concert
Oct 27: Museum Associates Annual Supper
Oct 27: Quapaw String Quartet in Concert
Oct 27-Nov 12: "The Hardy Boys in the Mystery of the Haunted House"
Nov 3: Opus XI
Nov 15-Dec 15: Aids Quilt Exhibit
Nov 17-19: 26th Annual West Pulaski Arts & Crafts Show
Nov 17-19: 10th Annual Ark. Antique Dealers Semi-Annual Show & Sale
Nov 18-19: Masterworks Series Featuring Violinist Zina Schiff
Nov 23-Jan 7: 23rd Annual Toys Designed by Artists Exhibition
Nov 25-28: 18th Annual Festival of Trees
Nov 30-Jan 31: The Pictographs of Adolph Gottlieb
Dec 1-3: 17th Annual Arkansas Craft Guild Christmas Showcase
Dec 1-17: "The Velveteen Rabbit"
Dec 1-31: 2nd Annual Zoo Luminations
Dec 2: Quapaw Quarter Christmas Tours & Holiday Potpoutti
Dec 2-3: 28th Annual Christmas Open House
Feb 17: 2nd Annual Mardi Gras at the Villa Marre
Jan 14-Feb 25: Visions: Quilts, Layers of Excellence Exhibit
Dec 10: Holiday Open House
Dec 10: 10th Annual Holiday Open House
Dec 13-17: 8th Annual Living Nativity
Dec 16: Pops Live! Concert: A Christmas Celebration
Jan 13-14: Masterworks Series Featuring Pianist Anthony Pattin

Jan 19-Feb 4: The Three Little Pigs & Three Billy Goats Gruff
Feb 2: Arkansas Symphony Orchestra Quapaw Quarter in Concert
Feb 9-11: African Tales
Feb 10: Broadway Showstoppers
Feb 16: Arkansas Symphony Orchestra Chamber Series
Feb 23-25: 5th Annual Arkansas Flower & Garden Show
Feb 24-25: 10th Annual Arkansas Glasshoppers Depression Glass Show & Sale

**Logoly State Park**
Sep 4: Labor Day Volleyball
Sep 16: 8th Annual Native American Day
Sep 23-24: 10th Annual Hunter Education Weekend
Oct 28-29: 10th Annual Hunter's Education Weekend
Oct 31: Haunted Trail Walk
Nov 4-5: 8th Annual Colors of Nature
Dec 1-Feb 28: 7th Annual Winter Bird Seed & Feeder Sale
Dec 2: Nature Crafts
Dec 16: Nature Crafts
Jan 13: Nature Crafts
Jan 14: 7th Annual Sunday Afternoon at the Movies
Feb 3: Nature Crafts
Feb 17: 7th Annual Sunday Afternoon at the Movies

**Lonoke**
Nov 26: 11th Annual Merry Thanks Open House
Sep 18-23: 55th Annual Lonoke County Fair & Rodeo

## M

**Magnolia**
Oct 29: Orchestral Fireworks with Guitarist Benjamin Verdery
Nov 22-Dec 31: 3rd Annual Lights Fantastic Festival
Dec 9: Holiday Celebration with Guest Artist, Louis Nabors
Feb 18: All Tchaikovsky Concert with Guest Artist Andreas Klein

**Malvern**
Dec 7: Christmas Parade & Festival of Lights & Carols

**Mammoth Spring (See Mammoth Spring State Park)**

**Mammoth Spring State Park**
Sep 1-2: 7th Annual Solemn Ol' Judge Days
Oct 7: Acoustical Concert by Bill Haymes

**Marked Tree**
Dec 2: 4th Annual Christmas Parade

**Marshall**
Sep 9-16: Searcy County Fair & Rodeo
Nov 18: 6th Annual Searcy County Christmas Fair
Dec 1-23: 6th Annual Christmas Open House
Feb 24: 12th Annual Searcy County Wild Turkey Calling Contest

**Maumelle**
Nov 11: 13th Annual American Red Cross Turkey Trot 7K Race

**Maynard**
Sep 10-16: 15th Annual Pioneer Days

**McNeil (See Logoly State Park)**

**Melbourne**
Sep 7-9: Izard County Fair

**Mena (See also Queen Wilhelmina State Park)**
Sep 1-Nov 11: Rich Mountain Fire Tower Open to the Public
Sep 6-9: Polk County Fair & Carnival
Oct 13-14: Polk County Arts & Crafts Fair
Oct 15-23: Christian Motorcycle Changing of Colors Rally
Oct 15-27: 50th Anniversary of Ouachita Expressions Fall Art Show
Dec 1-2: Christmas Craft Fair

**Monticello**
Sep 19: "Always...Patsy Cline"
Nov 28: "Babes in Toyland"
Feb 8: Dr. Rosephyne Powell in Concert

**Morrilton (See also Petit Jean State Park)**
Sep 29-30: Petit Jean Fall Antique Auto Show

**Mount Ida**
Oct 13-15: 12th Annual Quartz, Quiltz & Craftz Festival
Oct 13-15: 9th Annual World's Championship Quartz Crystal Dig

**Mountain Home**
Oct 19-21: We've Gotcha Covered Quilt Show & Sale
Nov 3-4: 20th Annual Crafts Fair
Nov 17-18: 9th Annual CraftsFest
Dec 8-9: Crafty Christmas

**Mountain Pine (See also Lake Ouachita State Park)**
Oct 15: 4th Annual Spillway 5K & Kids 1K Fun Run

**Mountain View (See also Ozark Folk Center State Park)**
Sep 6-Oct 31: Dripstone Trail Tour
Oct 26: 20th Annual Bean Fest & Great Arkansas
Nov 1-Feb 28: Dripstone Trail Tours
Nov 19: 10th Annual Photography Tour
Nov 30: Community Tree Lighting
Feb 25: 10th Annual Photography Tour

**Murfreesboro**
Sep 22-24: 8th Annual Gem Mineral & Jewelry Show

## N

**Nashville**
Oct 26: 2nd Annual Golden Gathering

**North Little Rock**
Sep 2-3: 15th Annual Summerset
Sep 4: 11th Annual Summerset Motocross Races
Sep 15-17: Tennis Tournament
Sep 23-24: 23rd Annual Burns Park Arts & Crafts Fair
Sep 29-30: 12th Annual Minuteman Days
Oct 6-7: 4th Annual North Heights Arts & Crafts Fair
Oct 14-15: 23rd Annual Rock & Mineral Swap
Nov 4: 12th Annual Christmas Arts & Crafts Extravaganza
Mid Nov (TBA): 23rd Annual Ozark Rugby Invitational Tournament
Early Dec (TBA): Willow House Christmas Bazaar
Dec 3: Annual Christmas Parade
Mid Feb (TBA): Southern Boys & Girls 16 & 18 Tennis Tournament

## O

**Old Washington Historic State Park**
Sep 9-10: 5th Annual Civil War Weekend
Oct 21-22: 19th Annual Frontier Days

**Osceola**

Dec 1: 17th Annual Winter Festival

**Ozark**

Sep (TBA): Great Arkansas Cleanup
Oct 7: 5th Annual Old-Fashioned Square Gathering Chili Cook-Off
Oct 7: Duck Derby
Oct 7: 23rd Annual Old-Fashioned Square Gathering
Dec 2: Christmas Parade

**Ozark Folk Center State Park**

Sep 8-9: Folk Dance Festival
Sep 22-23: Arkansas State Old-Time Fiddle Championships
Oct 5: Herb Harvest Fall Reception & Herbal Feast
Oct 6-8: Herb Harvest Fall Festival
Oct 13-14: 22nd Annual Fiddle & Dance Jamboree
Oct 13-28: 22nd Annual Harvest Festival
Oct 26: 20th Annual Bean Fest & Great Arkansas Championship Outhouse Race
Nov 3-5: SPBGMA National Bluegrass Fiddle Championships
Nov 18: 7th Annual Herbal Elves Holiday Workshop & Luncheon
Nov 23-25: 7th Annual Thanksgiving in the Ozarks
Dec 1-3: 16th Annual Ozark Christmas
Jan 27: 3rd Annual Organic Greenhouse Workshop
Feb 14: Romantic Valentine Day Dinner
Feb 17: 3rd Annual Organic Greenhouse Workshop

## P

**Paragould**

Nov 11: 5th Annual Art Manifest

**Paris**

Oct 7: 16th Annual Mt. Magazine Frontier Day

**Parkin (See Parkin Archeological State Park)**

**Parkin Archeological State Park**

Sep 16: 2nd Annual Visions of the Park Festival
Sep-Feb: Casqui Rediscovered
Thru Oct 31: Archeological Excavations

**Perryville**

Sep 29-30: 29th Annual Perry County Arts & Crafts Fair
Oct 7-8: 4th Annual Arkansas Traveller 100-Mile Ultra Run

**Petit Jean State Park**

Sep 2: Dr. T.W. Hardison Day
Oct 11-12: 13th Annual Fall Senior American Special
Oct 28: 7th Annual Halloween Party
Dec 9: 8th Annual Christmas Open House
Feb 3-4: 13th Annual Eagle Awareness Days
Feb 10-11: 9th Annual Hikes, Hearts & Hugs

**Plantation Agriculture Museum**

Sep 9-10: 4th Annual Antique Power Days
Feb 24: Plantation History Day

**Pine Bluff**

Sep 1-Oct 27: Arkansas Landscapes Exhibit
Sep 1-Dec 31: Make it Move Science Exhibit
Sep 23: SABBA Western Division Regional Bass Tournament
Oct 7: American Music Celebration
Oct 26-29: Razzle Dazzle Revue
Oct 28-29: 11th Annual Holiday Arts & Crafts Fair
Oct 29: 2nd Annual Steamboats Coming!
Nov 1-Dec 10: Honore Daumier Art Exhibit
Nov 2-4: 1996 BASSMASTER Central Invitational Tournament Trail
Nov 6: 2nd Annual Steamboats Coming!
Nov 28: "Babes in Toyland"
Nov 20-Jan 1: Celebration of Lights
Dec 2: Holiday Pops with the Pine Bluff Symphony
Dec 9-10: "The Best Christmas Pageant Ever"
Dec 14-Jan 31: Exhibit by Benini
Dec 16-17: "The Best Christmas Pageant Ever"
Jan 1-29: Mad Scientist's Lab
Feb 3-Apr 29: Body Tech Science Exhibit
Feb 29-Mar 3: "Ten Little Indians"

**Pinnacle Mountain State Park**

Sep 9: Recycle Cyclone Sale
Sep 9: 6th Annual Great Arkansas Cleanup
Sep 23-24: 6th Annual Fall Book Sale
Oct 1: 17th Annual Backpacking Basics
Oct 21-22: 4th Annual Pinnacle Mountain Rendezvous
Oct 28: 4th Annual Owl Prowl
Nov 12: Backyard Wildlife
Nov 18: Volunteer Hard Hat Day
Dec 2: 4th Annual Elf Encounter Christmas Bazaar
Dec 2: 4th Annual Christmas for Critters
Dec 2: Winter Bird Count
Dec 16: 6th Annual Caroling in the Forest
Jan 6: Winter Wandering
Jan 7: Volunteer Hard Hat Day
Jan 20-21: 6th Annual Eagle Watch Barge Tours
Jan 27: 2nd Annual Waterfowl Watch
Feb 10: Eagle Awareness
Feb 25: 17th Annual Backpacking Basics

**Pocahontas**

Thru Sep 2: Randolph County Fair
Oct 14: 7th Annual Good Earth Harvest Time
Oct 14: 16th Annual Indian Summer Arts & Crafts Show

**Ponca**

Sep 9: Ponca Days
Sep 15-17: 8th Annual Buffalo River Trail Ride
Sep 30: Forest Fest

**Powhatan (See Powhatan Courthouse State Park)**

**Powhatan Courthouse State Park**

Sep 30: 5th Annual Pearl Fest
Dec 14-30: 5th Annual Old-Time Christmas

**Prairie Grove (See Prairie Grove Battlefield State Park)**

**Prairie Grove Battlefield State Park**

Sep 2-4: 44th Annual Clothesline Fair
Dec 2-3: 4th Annual Christmas Open House

## Q

**Queen Wilhelmina State Park**

Dec 21-24: 11th Annual Christmas on the Mountain

## R

**Rector**
Sep 2-4: 54th Labor Day Picnic

**Rison**
Oct 7: 6th Annual Rison in the Fall

**Rogers**
Sep 10: Pops in the Park Concert
Sep 16: 11th Annual Frisco Festival
Sep 21-24: "The Farndale Avenue Housing Estate Townswomen's Guild Dramatic Society Murder Mystery"
Sep 29-Oct 1: "The Farndale Avenue Housing Estate Townswomen's Guild Dramatic Society Murder Mystery"
Oct 5-7: "The Farndale Avenue Housing Estate Townswomen's Guild Dramatic Society Murder Mystery"
Oct 19-22: 23rd Annual War Eagle Mill Arts & Crafts Fair
Oct 20-22: 26th Annual Antique Show & Sale
Oct 20-22: 13th Semi-Annual Quail Oaks Craft Fair
Nov 2-5: "Deathtrap"
Nov 7-Mar 31: Our Favorite Things
Nov 9-12: "Deathtrap"
Nov 16-18: "Deathtrap"
Dec 1-30: The Carols of Christmas Hawkins House Tours
Dec 2: 8th Annual Victorian Christmas Open House
Dec 2-Jun 1: The Sagers: Pioneer Cabinetmakers Exhibit
Dec 4: 11th Annual Community Christmas Parade
Jan 26-28: 3rd Annual Eagle Watch Weekend
Feb 15-18: "The Sensuous Senator"
Feb 22-25: "The Sensuous Senator"
Feb 29-Mar 2: "The Sensuous Senator"

**Roland (See Pinnacle Mountain State Park)**

**Russellville**
Oct 28: 4th Annual Downtown Fall Festival
Nov 10-12: 25th Annual Arkansas River Valley Arts & Crafts Show
Nov 26: 13th Annual Wrap up Your Holidays in Downtown Russellville

## S

**Salem**
Sep 2-30: 15th Annual Saturday Night Jamboree
Oct 7-28: Saturday Night Jamboree
Nov 4-25: Saturday Night Jamboree
Dec 2-16: Saturday Night Jamboree
Jan 6-27: Saturday Night Jamboree
Feb 3-24: Saturday Night Jamboree

**Scott (See Plantation Agriculture Museum & Toltec Mounds Archeological State Park)**

**Searcy**
Sep 1-29: Art Exhibit
Sep 11-16: 54th Annual White County Fair
Sep 28-Dec 29: Art Exhibit by Jo Patterson
Oct 1-27: Works by Nancy Patterson
Nov 1-30: The Art Room Art Exhibit
Nov 2-3: Ernie Kilman Oil Workshop
Nov 24-Jan 1: 6th Annual Holiday of Lights
Nov 30-Dec 29: Still Life Paintings Exhibit
Dec 1-18: 5th Annual Student Competition & Holiday Open House

**Sheridan**
Oct 6-8: 12th Annual Timberfest

**Sherwood**
Sep 16: 19th Annual Sherwood Fest
Oct 28: 2nd Annual Halloween Bash
Dec 10: 12th Annual Christmas Parade

**Siloam Springs**
Sep 16: Pops in the Park Concert
Oct 21: 2nd Annual Portabello Road
Oct 21-22: 2nd Annual International Fall Festival
Nov 5: The Faure Requiem
Nov 18: Miami String Quartet with Pianist Alan Chow
Dec 2: 11th Annual Light up Siloam
Dec 7-9: 55th Annual Candlelight Service
Feb 1-4: Opera Workshop
Feb 8-11: Opera Workshop

**Smackover (See Ark. Oil & Brine Museum)**

**Snowball**
Sep 21-23: 21st Annual Fall Fox Hunter

**Springdale**
Sep 8-10: "Picnic"
Sep 15-16: "Picnic"
Sep 16: Ozark Quilt Fair
Oct 5-6: 8th Annual Sheep to Shawl
Oct 19-21: 18th Annual Arts & Crafts Show
Oct 20-21: 4th Annual Fall Craft Fest
Oct 21: 4th Annual NW Ark. Barbershop Harmony Festival
Oct 21: Bird Seed Savings Day
Oct 27-29: "1940 Radio Hour"
Nov 2-4: "1940 Radio Hour"
Nov 17: Ever the River Runs by Mick Souter
Nov 24-25: 3rd Annual Holiday Craft Fest
Dec 1-2: Christmas Arts & Crafts Fair
Dec 2-3: "The Best Christmas Pageant Ever"
Dec 9-10: "The Best Christmas Pageant Ever"
Dec 10: Christmas Open House
Feb 9-11: "The Crucible"
Feb 16-17: "The Crucible"

**St. Paul**
Sep 8-9: 28th Annual Pioneer Day

**Stamps**
Oct 14: Timber Days

**Star City**
Sep 30: 2nd Annual Sportsman's Preview

**Stuttgart**
Sep 28-Oct 1: 39th Annual Grand Prairie Festival of the Arts
Nov 24-25: 60th Annual World's Championship Duck Calling Contest & Wings Over the Prairie Festival

## T

**Texarkana**
Thru Sep 3: 14th Annual Strange Family Bluegrass Festival
Sep 9-10: 14th Annual Quadrangle Festival
Sep 15-24: 51st Annual Four States Fair & Rodeo

Oct 1-May 31: Snakes, Saws & Skidders: The Forest Industry of Southwest Arkansas & Northeast Texas
Dec: 5th Annual Victorian Christmas
Feb 1-29: 3rd Annual Black History Month

**Toltec Mounds Archeological State Park**
Sep 2: Saturdays with the Native American Center for the Living Arts
Sep 4: Holiday Open House
Sep 23: Fall Equinox Sunset Tours
Sep 23: Flintknapping Day
Oct 7: Saturdays with the Native American Center for the Living Arts
Oct 21: Dream Catcher Workshop
Nov 4: Saturdays with the Native American Center for the Living Arts
Nov 5: Archeological Site Exploration Hikes
Nov 12: Archeological Site Exploration Hikes
Nov 18-19: A Thanksgiving Hero: The Legend of Squanto
Dec 2: Saturdays with the Native American Center for the Living Arts
Dec 16: Native American Stories
Dec 30: Native American Stories
Jan 2-Feb 29: Indian Portraits Exhibit
Jan 6: Saturdays with the Native American Center for the Living Arts
Jan 13: Introductory Flintknapping Workshop
Jan 20: Native American Stories
Feb 1-29: Henry Jackson Lewis Exhibit
Feb 3: Saturdays with the Native American Center for the Living Arts
Feb 10: Winter Lodge Stories
Feb 24: Winter Lodge Stories

**Trumann**
Sep 29-Oct 1: 13th Annual Wild Duck Festival

## V

**Van Buren**
Sep 2-4: 19th Annual Lake Lou Emma Arts & Crafts Fair
Sep 9: Old Town Cruisers Car Show
Sep 10: Exhibit Opening & Artists Reception
Sep 15-17: Watercolor Workshop
Oct 1: Exhibit Opening & Artists' Reception
Oct 6: Fall Festival Street Dance
Oct 7-8: 14th Annual Fall Festival
Nov 5: Exhibit Opening & Artists' Reception
Nov 5: Historic District Christmas Open House
Dec 2: 4th Annual Christmas Parade
Dec 3: 19th Annual Christmas Open House
Dec 16: Christmas Living Windows Display
Jan 13: Soup's On/Super Bowl Sunday on Saturday
Feb 10-11: Expressions of Love

**Village**
Sep 15-16: 8th Annual Deer Dog Festival

**Village Creek State Park**
Sep 9: 6th Annual Great Arkansas Cleanup
Oct 7: 4th Annual Fall Hay Rides
Oct 21: 7th Annual Fall Star Party
Oct 21-22: 19th Annual Fall Foliage Weekend
Oct 28: 3rd Annual Halloween Hay Rides & Other Surprises

## W

**Waldron**
Thru Sep 2: Scott County Fair & Livestock Show
Sep 28-30: 7th Annual Lakeview Bluegrass Music Festival
Oct 11-14: 18th Annual Turkey Track Harvest Time Bluegrass Music
Nov 24-25: 22nd Annual Scott County Arts & Crafts Christmas Show

**Walnut Ridge**
Oct 7: 11th Annual Gateway Funfest

**War Eagle**
Oct 19-22: 10th Annual Hillbilly Corner Arts, Crafts & Antiques Fair

**Warren**
Sep 13-17: Bradley County Fair
Dec 1: 2nd Annual Bradley County Christmas Parade

**Washington (See Old Washington Historic State Park)**

**West Fork (See Devil's Den State Park)**

**West Memphis**
Sep 16: Crittenden County March of Dimes Walk America
Oct 1: 7th Annual Southland 5K Run

**Wickes**
Sep 15-17: 2nd Annual Western Arkansas Arts & Crafts Festival

**Wilmar**
Oct 28: 11th Annual Possum Valley Fun Day

**Wilson (See Hampson Museum State Park)**

**Winslow**
Oct 21-22: 17th Annual Quilt Fair

**Withrow Springs State Park**
Oct 14-15: 41st Annual American Crossbow Tournament

**Woodlawn**
Dec 2-Jan 1: 9th Annual Christmas Road to Bethlehem

**Woolly Hollow State Park**
Sep 9: 3rd Annual Great Arkansas Cleanup
Sep 22-24: 8th Annual Lake Bennett Rendezvous
Nov 17-18: 3rd Annual Blue & Gray Civil War Day
Dec 9: 8th Annual Christmas in the Hollow

**Wynne (See Village Creek State Park)**

## Y

**Yellville**
Sep 2-4: 6th Annual Picnic in the Park
Oct 13-15: 50th Annual Turkey Trot Festival & National Wild Turkey Calling Contest

# SPRING and SUMMER

## A

**Adona**
Apr 4-6: 10th Annual Bluegrass Jammers Reunion
Jul 11-13: 16th Annual Bluegrass Music Show

**Altus**
Apr 7: Easter Celebration
May 4: 16th Annual Springtime Gala
Jul 4: 4th of July Celebration
Jul 26-27: Grape Festival

**Arkadelphia**
Jul 27: Dam Night Run 5K

**Arkansas Oil & Brine Museum**
Mar-Sep 22: Colonel T.H. Barton: The Lion Shared Exhibit
Thru Apr 6: Art Show by Charlotte Copeland
Apr 7-May 18: Art Show by Roy Rooks
Apr 20: 4th Annual Antique & Classic Car Show
May 19: 9th Annual Oral History Reunion
May 19-Jun 29: Watercolors by Gail Peppers Exhibit
Jun 8: "Boom Town"
Jun 30-Aug 10: Art Show by Dr. Barbara Teague
Aug 11-Sep 21: Porches Art Exhibit by Dee Ludwig

**Ash Flat**
Aug (TBA): 51st Annual Sharp County Fair

**Atkins**
May 17-18: 5th Annual Picklefest

## B

**Bald Knob**
May 3-5: 7th Annual Homefest

**Batesville**
Mar 29-30: 6th Annual Ozark Hawg Bar-B-Que
Apr 26-28: 16th Annual Ozark Scottish Festival
Jul 4: 4th Annual Boatmen' National Bank Fireworks
Jul 27-Aug 3: 53rd Annual White River Water Carnival
Aug 13-17: 76th Annual Independence County Fair

**Bauxite**
May 25: 15th Annual Bauxite Reunion

**Bee Branch**
Jun 6-8: 14th Annual Cadron Creek Bluegrass Spring Showcase
Aug 22-24: 14th Annual Cadron Creek Bluegrass Festival

**Bella Vista**
May 3-5: 2nd Annual Spring Arts & Crafts Festival

**Benton**
Mar 2: 21st Annual Arkansas Bluegrass Association Festival

**Bentonville**
May 3-5: 12th Annual Sugar Creek Arts & Crafts Fair
May 3-5: 10th Annual Spring Arts & Crafts Festival
Jun 21-23: 5th Annual Summer Arts & Crafts Festival
Aug 31-Sep 2: 5th Annual Labor Day Weekend Arts & Crafts Festival

**Berryville**
May 3-5: 23rd Annual Arkansas State Championship Muzzleshoot
Jun 14-15: 11th Annual Ice Cream Social & Handcrafters Show

**Bigelow**
Mid Mar (TBA): 18th Annual Wye Mountain Daffodil Festival

**Bismarck (See DeGray Lake Resort Lake State Park)**

**Bluff City (See White Oak Lake State Park)**

**Blytheville**
Apr 28: 16th Annual Springtime on the Mall

**Booneville**
Mar 1-10: National German Shorthaired Pointer Assn., Inc.
Jun (TBA): Rodeo
Jun 1: 4th Annual National Trails Day Equestrian Ride
Jun 8: 7th Annual Kids' Fishing Derby
Jul 4: July 4th Celebration & Fireworks Display
Aug 22-23: 124th Annual Logan County Gospel Music Convention
Sep (TBA): 49th Annual South Logan County Fair & Livestock Show
Sep (TBA): Arkansas Association for Morgan Horses

**Bradley (See Conway Cemetery State Park)**

**Bull Shoals State Park**
Apr 7: 8th Annual Easter Egg Hunt
Apr 12-14: 8th Annual Ozark Springtime Wildflower Weekend
May 10-12: 8th Annual Ozarks Birder's Springtime Retreat
Jun 14-16: 9th Annual Troutfest
Jun 16: 8th Annual Father's Day Trout Fishing Tournament
Jul 4: 9th Annual July 4th Tons of Fun

## C

**Cabot**
Apr 13-14: 11th Annual Old West Days

**Calico Rock**
May 11: 11th Annual Riverside Festival
Jun 13-15: 39th Annual Championship Rodeo
Jul 3: 10th Annual Lions Club 4th of July Fireworks Display
Aug 10: 2nd Annual Duck Round-Up

**Camden**
Mar 2-3: 2nd Annual Garden Tours
Mar 9-10: 2nd Annual Garden Tours

**Crater of Diamonds State Park**
Apr 6: 4th Annual Citizens with Disabilities Day
Jun 15: 13th Annual John Huddleston Day

**Cave City**
Aug 8-10: 17th Annual Watermelon Festival

**Cecil**
Sep (TBA): 16th Annual Talent Show & Womanless Beauty Pageant

**Cherokee Village**
May 4: 2nd Annual Spring Music Fest
May 18-19: 6th Annual Spring River Open Golf Tournament
May 25: 5th Annual Lions Club Parade
Jul 4: 5th Annual Boat Parade & Fireworks Display

**Chidester (See Poison Spring Battlefield State Park)**

**Clarendon**
Jun 28-29: 7th Annual Rollin on the River Festival

**Clarksville**
Mar 1-29: Theatre Students Design Exhibit
Mar 2-Dec 7: Southern Flames Music Show
Mar 28: The Naked Truth: Advertising's Image of Women
Mar 30-31: 14th Annual Peach Festival Spring Gala
Apr 1-30: Student Art Exhibit
Apr 9: University Band Concert
Apr 16: Handbell Choir Concert
Apr 18-19: "Godspell"
Apr 25: Spring Choral Concert
May 1-31: Senior Art Exhibit
Jul 4: 4th of July Celebration

Jul 12-13: Round-Up Club Rodeo
Jul 15-20: 6th Annual Quilts Downtown Exhibit
Jul 17: 4th Annual Barbecue
Jul 18-21: 55th Annual Johnson County Peach Festival
Jul 21: 20th Annual Peach Festival Horseshoe Pitching Tournament
Sep (TBA): Round-Up Club Junior Rodeo

**Clinton**
Aug 9-10: 12th Annual Bull Riding Spectacular
Aug 30-Sep 1: 11th Annual National Championship Chuckwagon Race

**Conway**
Mar 5: Spring Concert
Mar 23-24: 35th Annual State Daffodil Show
Apr 2: Foreign Film Series
Apr 18: Confucianism: Reshaping The Modern World
Apr 30: Foreign Film Series
May 1-5: "Two Gentlemen of Verona"
May 3-5: 15th Annual Toad Suck Daze
Aug 1-3: 84th Annual School Bazaar

**Conway Cemetery State Park**
May 29-31: 11th Annual Governor Conway Days

**Crossett**
May 25-26: 13th Annual Arkansas High School Rodeo Regional
Jun 1: 11th Annual Buddy Bass Tournament
Jul 5-7: 7th Annual Fun Run Car Show
Aug 10: 9th Annual Rodeo Round-Up Day
Aug 13-17: 48th Annual PRCA Rodeo & Parade

**Crowley's Ridge State Park**
Apr 6: 7th Annual Easter Egg Hunt
Apr 27: 12th Annual Junior & Senior Citizens Fishing Tournament
May 11: Wildflowers on Wheels Guided Wildflower Tour
May 27: 9th Annual Sock Hop
Jul 4: 14th Annual Old-Fashioned 4th of July Celebration
Jul 19-20: 4th Annual Bats Unlimited Weekend
Aug 9-11: 12th Annual Mosquito Awareness Weekend

## D

**Dardanelle (See also Mount Nebo State Park)**
May 10-11: 7th Annual Free State of Yell Fest

**Daisy State Park**
Apr 6: 7th Annual Easter Egg Hunt & Egg Toss
Jun 8: 8th Annual Volleyball Tournament
Jun 22: 6th Annual Junior Fishing Fest
Jul 28: 7th Annual Fun Day
Aug 24: 2nd Annual Horseshoe Tournament

**DeGray Lake Resort State Park**
Apr 3: 7th Annual Moonlight Cruises
Apr 5-7: 9th Annual Easter Ecstasy
Apr 20-21: Creepy, Crawly, Cold-Blooded Creatures
Apr 26-28: 7th Annual Beaks & Bills, Feathers & Quills
May 2-3: 7th Annual Moonlight Cruises
May 3-5: 7th Annual Wildflower Wanderings
May 31: 7th Annual Moonlight Cruises
Jun 1: 7th Annual Moonlight Cruises
Jun 8-9: 6th Annual 3-Person Scramble Golf Tournament
Jun 16: 7th Annual Jr. Fishing Fest
Jun 29-30: 7th Annual Moonlight Cruises
Jul 13-14: 16th Annual Men's Four-Ball Tournament
Jul 29-30: 7th Annual Moonlight Cruises
Aug 9-10: August Astronomy Weekend
Aug 27-28: 7th Annual Moonlight Cruises

**DeQueen**
Mar 1-31: 9th Annual Art Exhibition
Apr 18-20: Watercolor Energies Workshop
Apr 27-28: 8th Annual Spring Flower Show

**Decatur**
Aug 2: 43rd Annual Decatur Barbecue

**Deer**
Jul 4: VFD Fourth of July Celebration

**Dermott**
May 17-18: 13th Annual Crawfish Festival

**Des Arc (See also Prairie County Museum)**
Jun 6-8: 11th Annual Steamboat Days Festival

**Devil's Den State Park**
Apr 13-14: 14th Annual Wildflower Weekend
May 3-5: 14th Annual Birders Weekend
May 18: 15th Annual Camp-Out & Square Dance
Jun 14-16: 7th Annual Bat-O-Rama
Jul 4: 21st Annual Devil's Den Games
Jul 20: 2nd Annual Caller Fest

**Dierks**
Aug 2-3: 24th Annual Pine Tree Festival

**Doddridge**
Jun 1: 7th Annual Spring Bank Ferry Festival

**Dover**
May 3-5: 2nd Annual Mugwump Crazi Daze Craft Fair

**Dumas**
Jul 26-28: 16th Annual Ding Dong Days
Aug 17: 2nd Annual Shorebirds

## E

**El Dorado**
Apr 26: 4th Annual Mayhaw Festival
Apr 26: 5th Annual Office Olympics
Jul 4-6: 18th Annual Fantastic Fourth Celebration

**Emerson**
Jun 29: 7th Annual Purple Hull Pea Festival & World's Championship Rotary Tiller Race

**Eureka Springs**
Mar 9: Gallery Tour
Mar 16: 15th Annual Victorian Classic
Mar 17: 3rd Annual St. Patrick's Day Parade
Mar 23: 6th Annual Kite Festival
Mar 29-31: 23rd Annual Mystery Weekend
Mar 30: 26th Annual Cavalcade of Magic
Apr 6: 15th Annual Old-Fashioned Easter Egg Hunt
Apr 7: 30th Annual Easter Sunrise Service
Apr 12-14: 8th Annual Ozark UFO Conference
Apr 13: Gallery Tour
Mid Apr: Annual Dogwood & Redbud Review
Apr 26-Oct 26: 29th Season of The Great Passion Play
Apr 27: 6th Annual Taste of Eureka
Apr 27: 2nd Annual All-Mustang Car Show
Apr 27: "If You Give a Mouse a Cookie"
May 1-31: 9th Annual May Fine Arts Festival
May 4: Gallery Tour
May 10-11: 2nd Annual Classical Music Festival
May 11: Gallery Tour
May 11: Gallery Tour
May 17: 6th Annual Studio Walk
May 18: Gallery Tour
May 18: 14th Annual Doll & Toy Show
May 18: 12th Annual Spring Tour of Homes
May 18-19: 32nd Annual Sidewalk Arts & Crafts Show
May 25: Gallery Tour
May 30-Jun 2: 8th Annual Blues Festival
Jun 14-15: Bon Temps Cajun Festival

Jun 21-Jul 20: 46th Annual Opera in the Ozarks
Jun 22: 2nd Annual Rag Top Rally
Jun 24-28: 8th Annual Paint-Out with Sheila Parsons
Jul 4: 4th of July Fireworks
Jul 13: 2nd Annual Truckin' Show
Jul 19-21: 4th Annual Ozark Bridge Tournament
Jul 21-27: Vocal Jazz Camp
Jul 28-Aug 3: 5th Annual Piano & String Camp
Aug 2-3: 6th Annual Ark. Championship Wild Hog Barbecue Cook-off
Aug 4: 2nd Annual Carroll County 3-D Championship
Aug 17-18: 2nd Annual Yards & Yards of Yard Sales
Aug 17-18: 10th Annual Summer Village Crafters Show & Sale
Aug 19-23: 7th Annual Scootercade
Aug 23-25: 4th Annual Volkswagen Weekend
Sep 2-7: Carroll County Fair & Livestock Show

**Evening Shade**
Jul 6: 9th Annual Summerfest

## F

**Fairfield Bay**
Apr 13-May 10: 3rd Annual Spring Fine Arts Festival
Apr 15: 3rd Annual Starving Artist Sidewalk Sale & Exhibit
Apr 19: 3rd Annual An Evening of Readings
May 5-10: 4th Annual Watercolor Workshop
May 7-10: 3rd Annual Watercolor Magic with Sheila Parsons
May 27-31: Watercolor Fun with Sheila Parsons

**Fayetteville**
Apr 6-Oct 26: 21st Annual Farmers Market
Apr 27: 14th Annual Springfest
Jun 17-19: Paint with Sheila Parsons
Sep (TBA): Pops in the Park

**Felsenthal**
May 24-25: 11th Annual Bream Festival

**Fordyce**
Apr 22-28: 16th Annual Fordyce on the Cotton Belt Festival
Aug (TBA): Dallas County Fair

**Forrest City**
Jul 20: 13th Annual Mightymite Triathlon

**Fort Smith**
Feb 29-Mar 2: 29th Annual Red Stocking Review
Mar 3-24: 20th Annual Student Art Competition
Mar 14: Rosilee Walker in Concert
Apr 2-28: 46th Annual Art Competition
Apr 6: 3rd Annual Mid-South Beer Festival
Apr 9-10: Westark Spring Choral Concert
Apr 13: Tomorrow's Promise Concert
Mid Apr (TBA): 23rd Annual Young Women's Community Guild Benefit Golf Tournament
Apr 16: New York Voices & the Westark Jazz Band
Apr 18-20: 32nd Annual Ark. Federation of Porcelain Artists Show & Convention
May 2-26: African-American Artists Exhibit
May 2-26: Evan Lindquist: Arkansas Printmaker Exhibit
May 5: "42nd Street"
May 11: Western Gateway Concert
May 16-19: Strawberry Junction Arts & Crafts Show
May 23-25: 19th Annual Old Fort Days Barrel Racing Futurity
May 27-Jun 1: 53rd Annual Old Fort Days Rodeo
May 30-Jun 23: Gene Franks: Scenes of Arkansas Exhibit
Jun 13-15: 17th Annual Old Fort River Festival
Jun 13-15: Rubber Duck Race
Jun 30-Jul 28: Thomas Primm: Paintings & Mixed Media Work Exhibit
Jun 30-Jul 28: Liz Powers: Paintings & Drawings Exhibit
Jul 4: 2nd Annual Mayor's Fourth of July Celebration
Jul 26-28: 9th Annual Commissary Charity Hunter Jumper Show
Aug (TBA): 10th Annual Hanging Dice Kustom Kemp Car Show

## G

**Gentry**
Jul 4: Fourth of July Celebration

**Gillett**
May 19: 2nd Annual Eagle Watch

**Greenbrier (See also Woolly Hollow State Park)**
Jun 8-9: 12th Annual Brier Fest

**Greenwood**
Apr 20: 6th Annual Kristen Lowery Foundation Springfest
Jul 4: 18th Annual Freedom Fest

**Greers Ferry**
May 25-27: 2nd Annual Arts & Crafts Fair
Aug 10: 22nd Annual Pancake Breakfast

## H

**Hampson Museum State Park**
Apr (TBA): 12th Annual Indian Lore Days

**Hampton**
Apr 12-13: 5th Annual Hogskin Holidays

**Hardy**
Apr 20-21: 14th Annual Old Hardy Town Spring Arts & Crafts Show
May 25: 24th Annual Spring River Canoe Race & Picnic
May 25-26: 14th Annual Old Hardy Town Antique Festival
May 27-Sep 2: 28th Season of the Arkansaw Traveller Dinner Theatre
Jun 15: 5th Annual Homesteaders Day
Aug 31-Sep 1: 14th Annual Old Hardy Town Antique Festival

**Harrison**
Mar 21-24: 13th Annual Arkansas Fiddlers Convention
May 17-18: 6th Annual Crooked Creek Crawdad Days
Jun 9-15: 10th Annual Ozark Mountain Bicycle Challenge
Jul 4: 26th Annual Old-Fashioned 4th of July
Aug 15-17: 25th Annual Northwest Arkansas Bluegrass Festival

**Heber Springs**
Apr 19: 7th Annual Earth Day Celebration
Apr 26-28: 9th Annual Springfest
May 5-31: Have Brush Will Travel Watercolor Exhibit
Jul (TBA): July 4th Activities
Jul 19-20: 24th Annual Arkansas in Cleburne County Gospel Quartet Sing
Jul 20: Cardboard Boat Festival

**Helena**
Mar 22: Arrival of the Delta Queen Steamboat
Mar 26: Warfield Concert: the Incredible Acrobats of China
Apr 5: Arrival of the Delta Queen Steamboat
Apr 7: Arrival of the Mississippi Queen Steamboat
Apr 9: Arrival of the Mississippi Queen Steamboat
Apr 14: Arrival of the American Queen Steamboat
Apr 24: Arrival of the Mississippi Queen Steamboat
Apr 25: Arrival of the Delta Queen Steamboat
May 3: Warfield Concert: Multimedia Piano Recital by Christine Miller
May 4: Warfield Music Festival: "Sleeping Beauty"
May 5: Warfield Music Festival: Solid Brass in Concert
May 6: Warfield Music Festival: Brigham Young University Ballroom Dance Company
Jun 29: Arrival of the Delta Queen & the Mississippi Queen Steamboats
Sep 2: Arrival of the Delta Queen Steamboat

**Hindsville**

May 3-5: 35th Annual Springtime War Eagle Fair & Antique Show

**Hope**

Aug 15-18: 20th Annual Watermelon Festival

**Horseshoe Bend**

Apr 13-21: 9th Annual Dogwood Days Festival
Jul 4: 12th Annual Independence Day Celebration

**Hot Springs (See also Hot Springs National Park & Lake Catherine State Park)**

Thru Apr 13: Live Thoroughbred Racing Season
Apr 7: 4th Annual Easter in the Park
Apr 12-14: 5th Annual Holiday Craft Fair
May 18: Downtown Taste Festival
May 25: 6th Annual Memorial Day Cajun Crawfish Boil
May 26: 10th Annual Hickory Hill Park Gospel Music Sing
May 31-Sep 1: 11th Annual Season of "The Witness"
Jun 3-16: Hot Springs Music Festival
Jun 19-22: 39th Annual Miss Arkansas Pageant
Jun 22: 10th Annual Hickory Hill Park Gospel Music Sing
Jul 20-21: 12th Annual Good Ole Summertime Arts & Crafts Fair
Jul 25-27: 8th Annual Hickory Hill Park Homecoming Gospel Music Celebration
Aug 24: 10th Annual Hickory Hill Park Gospel Music Sing
Aug 24: 20th Annual Parade of Harmony

**Hot Springs National Park**

Mar-Dec: 2nd Annual Volksmarsch
Apr 19-21: Hiking & Canoeing with Outdoor Adventure Tours
Apr 26-28: Biking with Outdoor Adventure Tours
May 17-19: Hiking & Canoeing with Outdoor Adventure Tours
Jun 1: 2nd Annual National Trails Day Hike
Jul 12-14: 2nd Annual Civil War Weekend

**Huntsville (See Withrow Springs State Park)**

## J

**Jacksonport State Park**

May 31-Jun 1: 15th Annual Portfest Rollin' on the River

**Jasper**

Apr 19: Spring Dogwood Tour
May 3-4: Spring Fever Days

**Jersey (See Moro Bay State Park)**

**Jessieville**

Jun 1: 3rd Annual National Trails Day Celebration
Jun 1: 2nd Annual National Trails Day Celebration
Jun 8: 7th Annual Kids' Fishing Day

**Jonesboro**

Mar 8-9: 23rd Annual Mid-South Gospel Quartet Convention
Mar 10-Apr 14: Through a Child's Eyes X Exhibit
Apr 12-14: 5th Annual Spring 'N Arkansas Arts & Crafts Show
Apr 15: Lecture-Concert Series
Apr 18: 7th Annual Business Expo
Apr 22: Lecture-Concert Series
Apr 25-27: "I Ought to be in Pictures"
Apr 27: 9th Annual Northeast Arkansas Symphony Concert
May 4: 4th Annual Health & Fitness Expo
Aug 2-3: 11th Annual Sing America Sing
Aug 31-Sep 1: 6th Annual Blues Fest

**Judsonia**

May 10-11: 2nd Annual Bluegrass & Country Music Festival
Jun 15: Fishing Derby
Jul 4: Summer Blast

## K

**Kirby (See Daisy State Park)**

## L

**Lake Catherine State Park**

Jun 8: 10th Annual Possum Stampede
Jun 22: 7th Annual Jr. Naturalist Weekend
Jul 4-6: 4th of July Blowout
Aug 31-Sep 2: Labor Day Bonanza

**Lake Charles State Park**

Apr 6: 8th Annual Easter Egg Hunt
May 10-11: 2nd Annual Lakefest
Jun 8: 5th Annual Kids' Fishing Derby & Casting Contest
Aug 5-9: 2nd Annual Jr. Naturalist Day Camp

**Lake Chicot State Park**

Mar 16-17: 2nd Annual Primitive Ways
Apr 4-14: 7th Annual Night Life on Lake Chicot
May 11: 6th Annual Birding Big Day
Jun 7-9: 6th Annual Park Explorers Weekend
Aug 1-31: 9th Annual Sunset Barge Tours
Aug 24: 2nd Annual Stork Count
Sep 1-29: 9th Annual Sunset Barge Tours

**Lake Dardanelle State Park**

May 27: 7th Annual Mini-Golf Classic
Jul 4: 7th Annual Mini-Golf Classic
Sep 2: 7th Annual Mini-Golf Classic

**Lake Fort Smith State Park**

Mar 1-3: 3rd Annual Birding Weekend
Apr 7: 5th Annual Easter Egg Hunt
May 10-12: 4th Annual Back-to-Nature Weekend

**Lake Ouachita State Park**

Apr 7: 10th Annual Easter Egg Hunt
Apr 20: 12th Annual Wildflower Wonderful Weekend
Jul 4: 4th of July Ouachita Waterfest
Jul 15-Aug 2: 2nd Annual Discovery Week

**Lake Village (See also Lake Chicot State Park)**

Jun 28-30: 9th Annual Lake Chicot Water Festival

**Lakeview (See Bull Shoals State Park)**

**Langley**

Jun 1: 4th Annual National Trails Day

**Lavaca**

Jun 1: 5th Annual Berry Festival

**Leslie**

Mar 1-2: 5th Annual Hee Haw
Mar 14: Ozark Literary Society
Mar 29-31: "Deadly Earnest"
Apr 11: Ozark Literary Society
May 9: Ozark Literary Society
Jun 1: 7th Annual North Ark. Ancestor Fair
Jun 7-9: "Rest Assured"
Jun 13: Ozark Literary Society
Jun 13-15: 42nd Annual Homecoming
Jul 11: Ozark Literary Society
Aug 8: Ozark Literary Society
Aug 9-11: "Winnie The Pooh"

**Little Italy**

Mar 9-10: 7th Annual Little Italy Arts & Crafts Fair

**Little Rock**

Thru May 5: Tree Army: The Civilian Conservation Corps in Arkansas Exhibit
Thru May 31: The Dream is Alive IMAX Feature Film
Thru Jun 1: Blue Planet IMAX Feature Film
Thru Sep 1: To Fly! IMAX Feature Film
Thru Sep 1: Russian Space Art Exhibit
Thru Sep 1: Convergence in Space Exhibit
Feb 2-Apr 21: National Drawing Invitational

Mar-Aug 1996: Kidzibit
Mar 3-Apr 14: Regional Craft Biennial
Mar 7-Apr 7: 35th Annual Barrett Hamilton Young Arkansas Artists Competition & Exhibit
Mar 8-24: "Rapunzel"
Mar 10: "La Traviata"
Mar 16-17: Arkansas Symphony Orchestra Masterworks Concert V
Mar 25-Apr 19: Arkansas Landscapes Exhibit
Mar 25-May 2: Annual Student Competitive Exhibition
Apr 1-May 1: Spring Senior Exhibit
Apr 4-6: "This Man Called Jesus"
Apr 12-14: 27th Annual Arkansas Arabian Victory Challenge Horse Show
Apr 12-May 19: Adrian Brewer: Arkansas Artist Exhibit
Apr 19-May 5: "Wind in the Willows"
Apr 20: 4th Annual Big Bud Run
Apr 20-21: Arkansas Symphony Orchestra Masterworks Concert VI
Apr 21-Jun 2: Double Vision Exhibit
Apr 22-May 22: Exhibition by Toni Lowden
Apr 23: Asia Minor Ethnic Jazz Quartet
Apr 26-May 2: Hans Burkhardt: Drawings & Pastels Exhibit
Apr 26-Jul 21: The Astronomer's Dream: Installation & Objects Exhibit
Apr 28: 2nd Annual Solid Brass of Little Rock In Concert
Apr 30: St. Lawrence String Quartet In Concert
May 3: Quapaw Quartet Recital
May 4-5: 34th Annual Quapaw Quarter Spring Tour
May 6-31: Edwin Brewer Retrospective Exhibit
May 11: Pops Live! Series: Manhattan Rhythm Kings in Concert
May 11-12: 23rd Annual Crafts & Folk Music Festival
May 17-19: 12th Annual Greek Food Festival
May 23-Aug 18: Structural Foundations of Clarity: Permanent Collection
May 24-26: 19th Annual Riverfest
May-Nov: Political Exhibit
May-May 1997: Quilts by Arkansas African Americans
Jun 3-28: Laurie Weller & Gary Washmon Exhibit
Jun 7-Aug 18: Expressive Voices of the Meaningful Exhibit
Jun 9-Aug 5: International Lathe-Turned Objects: Challenge V
Jun 15: Arkansas's 160th Birthday Party
Jun 30: 2nd Annual Solid Brass of Little Rock in Concert
Jul 4: 8th Annual Frontier Fourth of July
Jul 4: Pops! on the Fourth
Jul 8-Aug 9: 3rd Annual Arkansas Artists Group Show
Jul 28: 2nd Annual Solid Brass of Little Rock in Concert
Aug 7-Sep 4: 10th Annual Small Works on Paper
Aug 19-Sep 20: The Darrell Walker Collection Exhibit
Aug 26: 2nd Annual Solid Brass of Little Rock in Concert

**Logoly State Park**
Mar 23-24: 9th Annual Spring Fling Weekend & Arbor Day
Apr 20: 4th Annual Earth Day Observance
Jun 8: 7th Annual Kids' Fishing Derby
Jun 8: 4th Annual Senior Fishing Derby
Jul 13: 14th Annual Fun Day
Jul 15-19: 6th Annual Discovery Day Camp I
Aug 3-4: 12th Annual Wild Orchid Hunt
Aug 5-9: 6th Annual Discovery Day Camp II
Aug 24-25: 11th Annual Hunters' Education Course

**Lonoke**
May 18: 4th Annual Courthouse Day

## M

**Magazine**
Apr 19-20: New Shiloh Arts & Crafts Fair

**Magnolia**
May 12-18: 8th Annual Magnolia Blossom Festival & World's Championship Steak Cook-off

**Malvern**
Jun 27-29: 16th Annual Brickfest

**Mammoth Spring State Park**
Mar 16: Bluebird Clinic
Apr 7: 5th Annual Easter Egg Hunt
May 4: 4th Annual Herbfest
May 25: Bluegrass Concert
Jun 8-9: Spike the Spring Sand Volleyball Tournament
Jun 19: Spring River Cleanup
Aug 5-10: 103rd Annual Old Soldiers Reunion
Aug 21: Spring River Cleanup

**Marion**
May 2-4: 4th Annual Esperanza Bonanza Festival

**Marked Tree**
Jul 6: 20th Annual Tree Spree

**Marks' Mill State Park**
Apr 20: 5th Annual Commemorative of the Battle of Marks' Mill

**Marmaduke**
May 3-4: 8th Annual Mayfest
Aug 24: 7th Annual City-Wide Yard Sale

**Marshall**
Jun 9-15: 10th Annual Ozark Mountain Bicycle Challenge
Aug 3: 5th Annual Junkfest

**McCrory**
Jun 14-15: 11th Annual Mosquitofest

**McGehee**
Jun 7-8: Natural Fest

**McNeil (See Logoly State Park)**

**Melbourne**
Apr 6: 5th Annual Citywide Yard Sale
May 4: 55th Annual Izard County Pioneer Day

**Mena (See also Queen Wilhelmina State Park)**
May 27: 8th Annual T. Texas Tyler Memorial Gospel
Jun 7-16: 20th Annual Lum 'N Abner Days
Aug 8-10: Polk County Rodeo Festival

**Monticello**
Apr 25: Arkansas Symphony Orchestra in Concert

**Moro Bay State Park**
May 11: 3rd Annual Tri-County Yard Sale
Jun 1: 4th Annual Perch Jerk Classic Fishing Tournament

**Morrilton (See also Petit Jean State Park)**
May 18: 13th Annual Cajun Night
May 25-27: 3rd Annual Petit Jean Honey Fest
Jun 12-16: 38th Annual Antique Auto Show & Swap Meet
Aug 1-3: 8th Annual Great Arkansas Pig-Out

**Mount Ida**
Jun 15: 7th Annual Charley Weaver Day

**Mount Nebo State Park**
Jul 19-20: 48th Annual Mount Nebo Chicken Fry

**Mountain Home**
Apr 14: 17th Annual North Arkansas Woodcarvers Show & Sale
Jun 9-15: 10th Annual Ozark Mountain Bicycle Challenge

**Mountain Pine (See also Lake Ouachita State Park)**
May 2-4: 3rd Annual Timberfest

**Mountain View (See also Ozark Folk Center State Park)**
Apr 19-21: 35th Annual Arkansas Folk Festival

Jul 4: 2nd Annual Old-Time Gathering on the Square & 4th of July Celebration
Mar 1-Apr 1: Dripstone Tour
Apr 1-May 26: Dripstone Tour
May 27-Sep 2: Dripstone Tour
May 27-Sep 2: Discovery Tour

**Mountainburg (See Lake Fort Smith Park)**

**Murfreesboro (See Crater of Diamonds State Park)**

## N

**Nashville**
Jul 4: 19th Annual Stand Up for America Celebration

**New Edinburg (See Marks' Mill State Park)**

**Newport (See also Jacksonport State Park)**
May 31-Jun 1: 15th Annual Portfest Rollin' on the River

**North Little Rock**
Mar 2: 6th Annual Spring Arts & Crafts Sale
Apr (TBA): Easter Egg Hunt
Mid Apr (TBA): 4th Annual U.S. Taekwondo Federation Grand Nationals
Mid Apr (TBA): Orchid Show
May (TBA): 3rd Annual Paws-in-the-Park
May-Oct: Spirit Riverboat Cruises
May 27: 11th Annual Fireworks Dinner Dance Cruise
Jul 4: 11th Annual Fireworks Cruise
Jul 4: 2nd Annual Silver City Silly Shenanigans
Aug 9-11: 4th Annual Summer Shakespeare Festival
Aug 16-18: 4th Annual Summer Shakespeare Festival
Aug 31-Sep 1: 16th Annual Summerset

## O

**Old Davidsonville State Park**
Apr 20: 5th Annual Earth Day Celebration & Five Rivers Car Show
May 18: Antique Flea Market
Jun 1: 2nd Annual Davidsonville Days
Jul 4: 5th Annual Fishing Tournament
Aug 10-11: 3rd Annual Jr. Naturalist Weekend

**Old Washington Historic State Park**
Mar 8-10: 29th Annual Jonquil Festival
Jun 1-2: 4th Annual Fiddle Fest & Barbecue Cook-off

**Ozark**
Mar (TBA): White Rock Classic 25K & 50K
Mar 2-3: 15th Annual Turner Bend Canoe Race
Apr (TBA): Easter Celebration
Apr (TBA): Bull Drop
Apr (TBA): Golf Tournament
Apr 5: Kelly-Miller Circus
May 25: Hickory Grove Old Timers' Reunion
Jun (TBA): 6th Annual Original Ozark Festival
Jun (TBA): Ozark Bass Club Benefit Tournament
Aug (TBA): North Franklin County Fair
Aug (TBA): Fair Air Hole In one

**Ozark Folk Center State Park**
Mar 16: 7th Annual Medicinal Herb Workshop & Luncheon
Mar 22-23: 3rd Annual Clog Dancing Workshops & Dance Extravaganza
Mar 30: 3rd Annual Organic Greenhouse Workshop
Apr 1-May 31: 8th Annual Young Pioneer Programs
Apr 5-6: 8th Annual Fiddle Fest
Apr 12-13: 9th Annual Gospel Jubilee
Apr 13: 3rd Annual Organic Greenhouse Workshop
Apr 26-28: 19th Annual Dulcimer Jamboree
May 9: 8th Annual Lavish Herbal Reception & Feast
May 10-11: 8th Annual Heritage Herb Spring Extravaganza
May 24-26: 18th Annual Tribute to Merle Travis
May 31-Jun 8: 7th Annual Garden Glory Days
Jun 1-Aug 31: 8th Annual Young Pioneer Programs
Jun 3-6: Autoharp Beginners Workshop
Jun 6: 4th Annual High Tea
Jun 10-13: White Oak Basket Workshop
Jun 10-13: Intermediate Autoharp Workshops
Jun 10-15: 15th Annual Youth Week Activities
Jun 13-15: 4th Annual Western Music & Film Festival
Jun 17-20: 17th Annual Mountain Dulcimer Workshops
Jul 1: Tartan Day
Jul 1-4: Dance Week Folk Dance Workshops
Jul 4: Children's Games & Races
Jul 11-13: Performance by the Great Smoky Mountain Cloggers
Jul 25: 5th Annual Christmas in July Herbal Workshop & Luncheon
Jul 26-27: Tribute to Elton Britt
Jul 29-Aug 1: Hammered Dulcimer Workshops
Jul 29-Aug 3: Youth Week
Aug 2-3: 9th Annual Jacky Christian & Country Kicks Concerts
Aug 8-10: 14th Annual Autoharp Jamboree
Aug 23-24: Ozark Humor & Storytelling Weekend
Aug 30-31: Tribute to Jimmie Rodgers Concerts

## P

**Paragould**
May 17-18: 7th Annual Loose Caboose Festival

**Paris**
Apr 27: 10th Annual Arkansas Amateur Wine Competition
May 4: Arkansas Wine Heritage Day
Jul 4: 7th Annual Freedom Fest
Aug 3: 17th Arkansas Championship Grape Stomp & Wine Fest

**Parkin Archeological State Park**
Feb 1-Mar 31: Fort Mose: Colonial America's Black Fortress of Freedom
Mar 10: 2nd Annual Second Sunday Lecture Series
Apr 14: 2nd Annual Second Sunday Lecture Series
May 1-31: Historic Arkansas Maps Exhibit
May 12: 2nd Annual Second Sunday Lecture Series
Jun 9: 2nd Annual Second Sunday Lecture Series
Jul 9-Oct 31: 6th Annual Field Season of the Arkansas Archeological Survey
Jul 14: 2nd Annual Second Sunday Lecture Series
Aug 11: 2nd Annual Second Sunday Lecture Series

**Petit Jean State Park**
Mar 24-29: 10th Annual Paint Springtime on the Mountain Workshop
Apr 5-7: 14th Annual Great Escape Weekend & Easter Egg Hunt
Apr 13-14: 10th Annual Wildflower Weekend
Apr 23-25: 14th Annual Spring Senior American Special
Jun 1: 3rd Annual Asphalt Art in the Park
Jun 8: 7th Annual Mountain Fishin' Derby
Jul 4: 7th Annual 4th of July Fun Day
Jul 26-27: 3rd Annual Civil War Encampment
Aug 3: 2nd Annual Dr. T.W. Hardison Day

**Pettigrew**
Apr 13: Pettigrew Day

**Pine Bluff**
May 25: Arrival of Delta Queen Steamboat
Jun 1: Arrival of Delta Queen Steamboat
Jun 23-29: National Amateur All-Star Baseball Tournament
Jul 19-21: Budweiser/King Cotton Bass Classic
Jul 20: Arrival of Delta Queen Steamboat
Jul 30: Arrival of Delta Queen Steamboat

**Pinnacle Mountain State Park**
Mar 9-10: 4th Annual Spring Book Sale
Mar 23: 12th Annual Canoe Day Floats
Apr 6: Spring Wildflower Walk
Apr 7: Wildflowers Presentation
Apr 20: 12th Annual Canoe Day Floats
Apr 20: 5th Annual Earth Day Hard Hat Day
Apr 27: 12th Annual Canoe Day Floats
May 11: Star Party
May 18: 12th Annual Campfire Program
May 18: 12th Annual Canoe Day Floats
May 18: 16th Annual Sierra Club Picnic
May 25: Chipmunks: Spirits of the Forest
Jun 2: 12th Annual Canoe Day Floats
Jun 8: 7th Annual Hook, Line & Sinker Kids' Fishing Derby
Jun 15: Star Party
Jun 22: 12th Annual Canoe Day Floats
Jul 6: 4th Annual Snake Snoop
Jul 13: Star Party
Aug 17: The Deer Dilemma

**Plantation Agriculture Museum**
Mar 8: 2nd Annual Blacksmithing Day
Apr 1-30: 2nd Annual Patchwork Bits & Pieces Exhibit
May 11: 2nd Annual Old-Time Fun & Games
Jun 1: 2nd Annual Antique Woodworking
Jul 6: 4th Annual Homespun Day

**Pocahontas (See also Old Davidsonville State Park)**
May 5: 10th Annual Randolph County Old-Fashioned Plowing Demonstration

**Poison Spring Battlefield State Park**
Mar 30-31: 8th Annual Battle of Poison Spring Re-enactment

**Powhatan (See Lake Charles State Park & Powhatan Courthouse State Park)**

**Powhatan Courthouse State Park**
May 5-31: 5th Annual Mother's Things Exhibit
Jun 6-30: 5th Annual Father's Day Exhibit
Aug 5-31: 5th Annual Back to School Exhibit

**Prairie County Museum**
Mar 15-17: Art Exhibition
May 1-31: Mother's Exhibit
Jun 6-8: Antique Tool Collection Display
Jul 12-14: Quilt Show
Aug 10: 2nd Annual Old-Fashioned Fun for Children
Aug 20: 2nd Annual Beautification Day

**Prairie Grove Battlefield State Park**
Apr 6: 15th Annual Battlefield Easter Egg Hunt
May 27: 4th Annual Memorial Day Tribute
Aug 31-Sep 2: 45th Annual Clothesline Fair

**Prescott**
Jul 19-20: 9th Annual Chicken & the Egg Festival

## Q

**Queen Wilhelmina State Park**
Aug 2-4: 8th Annual Mountainfest
Aug 30-Sep 1: 21st Annual Rod Run & Antique Car Show

**Quitman**
Jul 4-6: 11th Annual Arts & Crafts Fair

## R

**Rector**
Sep 2: 55th Annual Labor Day Picnic

**Redfield**
Jul 4: Redfield Day

**Rison**
Mar 16: 6th Annual Arkansas Dutch Oven Cook-off
Mar 16-17: 25th Annual Pioneer Craft Festival

**Rogers**
Mar 1-2: "The Sensuous Senator"
Mar 9-10: 2nd Annual Southwest Days
Mar 17: 5th Annual Saint Patrick's Day
Mar 30: 2nd Annual Wholegrain Bread Machine Workshop
Apr 7: 13th Annual War Eagle Easter Egg Hunt
Apr 20: 3rd Annual Bird & Wildlife Weekend
Apr 25-28: "Deathtrap"
Apr-May 1997: Founding Families Exhibit
May 2-5: "Deathtrap"
May 3-5: 14th Semi-Annual Quail Oaks Country Fair
May 3-5: 5th Annual Antique Show & Sale
May 3-5: 22nd Annual War Eagle Mill Spring Antique & Crafts Show
May 9-11: "Deathtrap"
Aug 1-Jan 30: Let's Play: Pastimes From America's Past
Aug 2-3: 41st Annual Crazy Days
Aug 2-4: "Fiddler on the Roof"
Aug 9-11: "Fiddler on the Roof"

**Roland (See Pinnacle Mountain State Park)**

**Russellville (See also Lake Dardanelle State Park)**
Apr 18: 4th Annual Taste of the Valley
Apr 19-20: 4th Annual Spring Gala
Apr 27: 3rd Annual Party in the Park
Jul 4: 2nd Annual Freedom Fest

## S

**Salem**
Mar 2-Sep 7: Saturday Night Jamboree

**Scott (See Plantation Agriculture Museum & Toltec Mounds Archeological State Park)**

**Shirley**
Mar 6: Herb Ellis & Group in Concert
Apr 21: An Afternoon of Classic Ballet
Apr 27: 2nd Annual Fine Arts Festival School Competition
May 5: 3rd Annual Combined High School Band Concert
Jun 2: Edenson Chorus in Concert

**Siloam Springs**
Apr 26-28: 22nd Annual Dogwood Festival
Mid-Jun (TBA): 38th Annual Rodeo

**Smackover (See also Arkansas Oil & Brine Museum)**
Jun 19-22: 25th Annual Oil Town Celebration

**Solgohachia**
May 25: 3rd Annual Solgohachia & Washington Township Day

**South Bend**
May 11: 20th Annual Birthday Party

**Springdale**
Mar 29: 3rd Annual History Day
May 3-4: Springtime Arts & Crafts Festival
May 17: Beans 'N Cornbread Lunch
Jul 1-4: 52nd Annual Rodeo of the Ozarks
Jul 5-6: 4th Annual Christmas in July Arts & Crafts Show
Jul 26-27: 3rd Annual 4-Corners Ancestor Fair
Aug 1-3: 28th Annual Albert E. Brumley Gospel Sing

**Star City**
May 4: 13th Annual Arts & Crafts Spring Festival

**Sulphur Springs**
Jul 6: 106th Annual Barbecue

## T

### Texarkana

Mar 1-31: Snakes, Saws & Skidders Exhibit
Mar 16: Joseph Holmes Chicago Dance Theatre in Concert
Mar 26-30: 14th Annual Strange Family Picking Around the Campfire
Apr 13: Kapelle Trio in Concert
Apr 23-27: 14th Annual Strange Family Picking Around the Campfire
May 23-26: 14th Annual Strange Family Bluegrass Festival
Jul 4: 12th Annual 4th of July Celebration
Aug 29-Sep 1: 14th Annual Strange Family Bluegrass Festival
Thru May 1997: All Systems Go Exhibit

### Toltec Mounds Archeological State Park

Mar 2: Native American Stories
Mar 2: Saturdays with the Arkansas Native American Center for the Living Arts
Mar 16: Pine Needle Basket Workshop
Mar 17-Apr 21: Archeology Lecture Series
Mar 23: Spring Equinox Program & Tour
Apr 6: Saturdays with the Arkansas Native American Center for the Living Arts
Apr 6: Native American Stories
Apr 20: 7th Annual Exploring Indian Life
Apr 20: Adult Archeology Workshop
May 4: 14th Annual Cub Scout Day
May 4: Saturdays with the Arkansas Native American Center for the Living Arts
May 4: Native American Stories
May 27: Memorial Day Open House
Jun 1: 11th Annual Girl Scout Day
Jun 1: Saturdays with the Arkansas Native American Center for the Living Arts
Jun 1: Native American Stories
Jun 22: Saturdays with the Arkansas Native American Center for the Living Arts
Jun 22-23: 16th Annual Sunfest Celebration
Jul 6: Saturdays with the Arkansas Native American Center for the Living Arts
Jul 6: Native American Stories
Jul 22-27: Youth Archeology Camp
Aug 3: Saturdays with the Arkansas Native American Center for the Living Arts
Aug 3: Native American Stories
Aug 10: 2nd Annual Native American Games
Aug 18-Nov 17: Special Speaker Series
Sep 2: Labor Day Open House

### Tontitown

Aug 13-17: 98th Annual Tontitown Grape Festival

### Tuckerman

May 10-11: 12th Annual Hometown Days

## V

### Van Buren

Mar 3-31: Art Exhibit
Apr 7-30: 20th Annual Jr. Juried Art Competition
May 3: Old Timer's Days Street Dance
May 3-5: 2nd Lake Lou Emma Spring Arts & Crafts Fair
May 4: 18th Annual Spring Fashion Show & Luncheon Cruise
May 4-5: 20th Annual Old Timer's Days Arts & Crafts Festival
May 5-31: Art Exhibit
May 25: Pioneer Day Parade
Jun 2-30: 20th Annual June in Van Buren Art Competition
Jun 29-30: 2nd Annual Cool Down in Downtown
Jul 7-31: Art Exhibit by Jane Ford-Young
Jul 8-12: 17th Annual Wonderful World of Art
Jul 15-19: 17th Annual Wonderful World of Art
Aug 4-31: 20th Annual Birthday Party & Members Exhibit
Aug 31-Sep 2: 20th Annual Labor Day Weekend Arts & Crafts Fair

### Village Creek State Park

Mar 30-31: 2nd Annual Living History Weekend
Apr 7: Easter Egg Extravaganza
Apr 9-13:: The Wonder of Wildflowers Week
Apr 27: Spring Fever Hay Rides
May 11: Star Party
May 11-12: Birdwatcher's Weekend
May 24-27: Memorial Weekend Activities
Aug 30-Sep 2: Labor Day Activities

### Vilonia

Apr 26-27: 9th Annual Jammers Jamboree
May 23-25: Bluegrass Gospel Festival
Jun 20-22: 15th Annual Bluegrass Festival
Aug 2-10: 14th Annual Southern Gospel Singing

## W

### Walcott (See Crowley's Ridge State Park)

### War Eagle

May 3-5: 10th Annual Hillbilly Corner Arts, Crafts & Antiques

### Warren

Jun 14-15: 40th Annual Bradley County Pink Tomato Festival

### Washington (See Old Washington Historic State Park)

### Watson

Aug 8-10: Homecoming Days Festival

### West Fork (See Devil's Den State Park)

### West Memphis

May 19: 7th Annual Southland Doggy Derby
Aug 23-24: 7th Annual Living on the Levee

### Wheatley

Mar 30: 15th Annual Springfest

### White Oak Lake State Park

May 4: 4th Annual Wildflower Walk in the Sandhills
May 11: 2nd Annual Heritage Day
May 31-Jun 1: 6th Annual Fishing Derby
Jun 29: 8th Annual Fun Day
Jul (TBA): 4th Annual Star Party

### Wilson (See Hampson Museum State Park)

### Withrow Springs State Park

Apr 6: 5th Annual Easter Egg Hunt
Jun 8: 5th Annual Kids Fishing Derby

### Woolly Hollow State Park

Jun 10-14: 6th Annual Cub Scout Day Camp
Jun 20: 13th Annual Fun Day
Jul 6: 5th Annual Kids' Fishing Derby
Aug 1: 3rd Annual Kid Fest

### Wynne (See also Village Creek State Park)

Apr-Sep: Railroad Caboose Museum
Jun 8: 21st Annual Farmfest

## Y

### Yellville

Apr 6: 4th Annual Buffalo National River Canoe & Kayak Race
May 4: 2nd Annual Marion County Music Jamboree
May 10-11: 2nd Annual Celebration of Shawnee Town
Jun 9-15: 10th Annual Ozark Mountain Bicycle Challenge
Aug 31-Sep 3: 8th Annual Picnic in the Park

## HEADSTONES AND HISTORY

You can't drive far on a rural road in Arkansas without, at some point, passing a local cemetery. I had cause to stop at one the other day. It was an interesting and enlightening experience, and I thought I'd share it with you.

As I walked across the manicured grass, punctuated by a rainbow of flowers, I studied the headstones around me. I was amazed by the insight I was given of those souls who had come to this land before me. It was an exercise in history and a lesson into the character of the Arkansan. I found testimonials to courage and faith, and kindness, memorials to teachers and preachers, to masons, doctors and soldiers, and the loving memory etched in the stone was nearly always the same: that they had served their nation, their God, and their fellow man, to the best of their ability.

Many a head stone reflected the pride they carried for their country, and the honor they felt having served when their name was called.

Floyd William Slatter, Airman First Class WWII. 1910-1984
Mary Beth Campbell, Lieutenant R.N. U.S. Army, WWII. 1913-1990
Terry Peterson, Captain, 101st Airborne, Vietnam. 1947-1970

I could almost see them in their crisply pressed uniforms, saluting from the train on that brilliant morning, as their wives and their girlfriends waved and cried, and whispered Godspeed home. The dates on the stones told that some returned. For others, their loved ones were left with only the memory of those proud, bright faces smiling back at them. . . . Americans, real Americans, one and all.

There was Fred Sanders, born in 1893. His wife Lydia was born in 1897. They found each other, fell in love, and raised a family, but Lydia died when she was forty-three. The dates on the single tombstone told the story of how he had waited forty more years to lie beside her once again.

William and Claudia Pellston were both seventeen when they were married in 1926. They spent the next sixty years together as man and wife, and when the sun rises each day now, the first rays that touch that little knoll still find them together.

In a time when marriages seem to last about as long as a head cold, when people rotate their mates like they do the tires on their car, and devotion to your country no longer seems to be in fashion, it was remarkably refreshing to discover loyalty and love that had lasted a lifetime, to be reminded of honor and courage, and pride in these United States.

Walking through that stone garden I was also reminded that the weave that has bound the tapestry of this land for so long is not technological achievement, nor grand edifices. It is not cultural autonomy nor even the independence of race and gender, but rather it is an amalgam of integrity, responsibility, and spirit, for without these qualities in its people, no nation can stand strong for long.

I recommend that each of us take pause at a rural, roadside cemetery and stroll through the headstones of history, so that we might remember that it is the individual character of the people within a nation that lend character to that land.

Hold fast to your faith and your honor Arkansans, as your forefathers did, for I have discovered what I suspected all along: that we are the pith and the marrow of America.

The Intrepid Arkansas Traveler

## WE ARE AMERICA!

I got up yesterday morning and looked out the window at the cold stillness of a frozen pasture, hemmed by trees whose barren branches reached upward in supplication, beseeching warmth from a sullen winter sky. I thought to myself that somewhere, perhaps two thousand miles away, someone was sitting on the veranda of a plush motel in Montego Bay, watching a warm sun rise off the ocean while being served croissants and coffee, and fresh tropical fruit.

It also occurred to me that at that same moment, someone was waking up from a not-so-good night's sleep inside a cardboard box in a New York City alleyway, with absolutely no idea where his next meal was coming from.

As I savored the aroma from the steaming cup of coffee in my hands, I was reminded that most of us fall somewhere in between those two destinies. I for one was pleased that I felt my cup half full rather than half empty. I realized that there was little chance this lifetime that I would end up with my permanent domicile being a Maytag washer box. Yet I felt the potential for making it to the veranda in Montego was still pretty good.

This faith and confidence in the future, coupled with persistence and determination is the cornerstone of the Arkansan and the basis of the American work ethic which has made this country a world leader. It also embodies the new culture emerging in rural America. We, in the plains states and the mountain communities of America are experiencing a metamorphosis. This change has, at its apex, a migration of people from the large coastal cities--individuals who have become dissatisfied with the quality of their lives or who recognize the disastrous consequences of our government's failed social programs and crippled judicial system, people who worry for the safety and the future of their offspring.

If I could wave a magic wand and stop it, preserving the Arkansas that I know and love, I probably would. But I'm not sure it would solve the problem; it might only exasperate it, for the changes that America faces in the future are dire and many.

This new influx of people, these Californians and Texans and Floridians, (not too many New Yorkers, apparently. It seems that going from the teeming streets of Manhattan to a place where you have to stop occasionally to let cows cross the road is just too great a transition, gives most of them hives.) bring with them a sophistication and an understanding of this new age that may well be necessary for the healthy growth of rural America. The important thing--the absolutely essential thing--is that we integrate these newcomers into our communities, patiently seeing that they adopt the philosophies and values that have served to maintain the integrity of rural America for so long, while firmly refusing to accept any of the aberrational baggage that some may have brought with them. It is absolutely essential that their children adopt the ideals of our children, not the other way around, or the cycle can be broken with dire consequences for the future of middle America.

Most of these people come here genuinely seeking refuge and a fresh start. Those who come for the fad of it will weed themselves out soon enough. Those that come with the thought of creating agitation and dissension may need a little help being weeded. Don't misunderstand; we must always be tolerant of the other man's view and religious philosophy, but we need not allow any circumstance that rends the fabric of our society. Our law enforcement must be decisive, our judicial process quick and sure. We cannot afford to make the same mistakes as those who already suffer with rampant crime and mayhem.

I understand all of this well because I was a part of the migration; I came from a place where society and the governing systems were out of control, and bars on our windows were the rule, not the exception. I will never live like that again, and I will do all I can to prevent an eventuality such as that from happening here, for I am an Arkansan now!

I have come to realize that this brave new world is upon us whether we want it or not. Our only hope is that we maintain a spiritual and social continuity within the communities of rural America. We must remember at all times that we as Arkansans, are now--maybe more than ever--the future of this country. I say again, hold fast to your faith and your virtue, Arkansans, for WE ARE AMERICA!

P.S. I know you read this whole article waiting for it to get funny, and it never did. I write humor so that every once in a while I can trick you into reading something important.

The Intrepid Arkansas Traveler

# *An Arkansas Fantasy*

By J. Breckenridge Ellis

HERE lived in the State of New York a little girl who had never traveled from her native town because her health had always been uncertain. Her mother had come from Arkansas on her honeymoon, and had remained in the East with the family of her husband. There remained, however, stamped upon her memory, the sunny hills, the billowing cottonfields, and the forests of fruit trees among which her youth had been spent. When the snows lay for weeks upon the ground and the sharp-cutting wind crept through crevices at door and window in spite of all one could do, the mother would take her delicate little daughter upon her lap and tell her how at that moment the flowers were blooming, and the peach trees were blossoming, down in Arkansas.

It became the dream of the child's life to visit that heaven-blessed land where the light frosts do not kill and where the snows vanish like white ghosts at touch of the warm earth. But in the rigorous climate of the North, the little one's strength wasted away, and death came before her dream could be realized.

Her soul rose to that heavenly abode set apart for children and for those who have become as one of them. She looked about her in wonder at the glorious splendors of heaven -- its hills of green and gold, its fields of flowers, its trees of life and knowledge. Too young to understand death, she thought she had awakened from a deep sleep. Saint Peter greeted her with an angelic smile and said:

"Do you know where you are, little one?"

With eyes still dancing with delight at the vision of surpassing loveliness, the child laughed with joy, and she cried with confidence, "Yes; *this must be Arkansas!*"

# THE TRAVELER'S DISCOUNT COUPON PAGES

## SAVE ON LODGING, FOOD, ENTERTAINMENT AND RECREATION

**Note: Do not tear coupons from book! Present book to retailer who will stamp or sign coupon for validation.**

| Evergreen Resort<br>10% off one nights stay<br>5 Evergreen Drive<br>Bull Shoals, AR<br>501-445-4440 | Top of the Hill Motel<br>10% off on lodging<br>401 S. Main<br>Harrison, AR<br>501-743-1000 |
|---|---|

Best Western Lime Tree
10% Discount on One
Nights Lodging
Hwy. 71 N., Mena, AR
1-800-528-1234

Lost Spur Guest Ranch
10% Discount on Three
Nights Lodging
Rt. 3 Box 93, Harrison, AR
501-743-7787

Smoke House BBQ
10% Off Any Meal
7th & Main
Heber Springs, AR
501-362-7732

Spillway Resort
10% Off T-Shirt or Gift Item
Mountain Pine, AR
501-767-2997

Aunt Shirley's Sleeping Loft
10% Off Lodging
Rt. 1 Box 84-D
Omaha, AR
501-426-5408

Trigger Gap Float Service
10% Discount on Any
Canoe Float Trip
Rockhouse Rd., Eureka Springs
501-253-2225

Scott Valley Resort
$50.00 Off 3 or more nights
with family of 4 +
P.O. Box 1447 IAT,
Mountain Home, AR
501-425-5136

Rivers Edge Bed & Breakfast

10% Discount
on 2 or More Nights
HC65 Box 5, Caddo Gap, AR
501-356-4864

El Matador Tex-Mex Cafe
10% off ElGrande Dinner
( all you can eat )

1901 E. Main, Russellville, AR

501-968-8226

Southfork Canoe Resort
10% Discount on Cabin Rental
With Canoe Rental
Hwy. 289, Saddle, AR
501-895-2803

Best Western Fiddler's Inn
10% Discount on Lodging
Sunday thru Wednesday
Hwys. 5,9,&14
Mountain Home, AR
501-269-2828

The Holland House Restaurant
10% Discount on Lunch
or Dinner
Hwy. 71 South, Mena, AR
501-394-6200

Norfork Trout Dock
10% Discount on Guided Trips
Weekdays Only
P.O. Box 129, Norfork, AR
501-499-5500

Arrowhead Cabin & Canoe
Rentals
10% Discount for Groups
Overnight Stay and Canoeing
HC65 Box 2, Caddo Gap, AR
1-800-538-6578

Little Switzerland Inn
10% Discount on Lodging
or Crafts
Scenic Byway 7, Jasper, AR
1-800-510-0691

The Belle of Hot Springs
$1.00 Off Adult Fare

5200 Central Ave.
Hot Springs, AR
501-525-4438

Ozark Heritage Gifts
15% Discount on All Craft
Merchandise
2711 N. Arkansas Ave.
Russellville, AR
501-968-3941

Whitewater Travel Park
25% Discount on One Day
of Camping!
(Not Valid During April or Oct.)
P.O. Box 446
Mountain View, AR
501-269-8047

Morning Star Retreat
10% Off Lodging on Any
Midweek Stay
Kings River, Eureka Springs, AR
1-800-298-5995

Fish & Game Guaranteed!!
25% Off Any Float /
Fishing Trip
Rt. 2 Box 247, Dover, AR
501-331-2712

M&M Canoe Rentals
$5.00 Off 1 Canoe Rental
HC64, Box 72
Pencil Bluff, AR
501-326-4617

The Captain's House
10% Off Lunch or Dinner!
301 W. Quitman
Heber Springs, AR
501-362-3963

Days Inn of Arkadelphia
10% Discount for One
Nights Lodging

Hwy.67N./ 7N.• I-30 exit 78
501-246-3031

Sun Bay Resort Hotel
1 Free Nights Lodging With
Time Share Tour -
(Some Restrictions Apply)
6110 Central Ave., Hot Springs
1-800-468-0055

Hot Springs Zoological Park
50¢ Off Admission
2179 Old Bear Road, Royal, AR

501-767-0478

Little Rock Cottage
Bed & Breakfast
10% off Lodging per night
512 Grandview Heights
Mena, AR
501-394-6310

Ridge Crest Resort
5% Off Lodging Up to 1 Week
RR1, Box 284, Midway, AR
1-800-828-5237

Clear Fork Canoeing
$1.00 Off Canoe Trip
3 Miles W. Hwy. 27
Murfreesboro, AR
501-285-2729

Olde StoneHouse
Bed & Breakfast
10% Off Lodging or Giftshop
511 Main St., Hardy, AR
1-800-514-2983

Red Bud Dock
10% Off All Rentals!!
Rt. 2, Box 541 Gassville, AR
501-435-6303

Self Creek Resort
10% Discount on One
Nights Lodging
HC-71 Box 100, Daisy, AR
501-398-4321

Woods Old Fashioned
Soda Fountain
Buy 1 Ice Cream Treat,
Receive 50¢ Off the Second
W. of Court House Square
Mountain View, AR
501-269-8304

Oak Tree Inn
10% Discount
on 2 Nights Lodging
1802 W. Main
Heber Springs, AR
501-362-7731

Arkatents USA!
5% Off Any In-Stock
Merchandise
3856 Hwy 88E., Ink, AR
501-394-7893

White Buffalo Resort
10% Off Lodging
and Boat Rental
Rt. 2 Box 438
Mountain Home, AR
501-425-8555

Circle G Western Wear
10% Discount on All
Merchandise!
Hwy. 71 S., Mena, AR
501-394-7777

Moore Outdoors
10% Discount on Canoe Rental
Hwy. 164 West
Dover, AR
501-331-3606

White Hole Resort
10% Off Guided Fishing Trip
HCR62, Box 100
Flippin, AR
501-453-2913

Riverwood Inn
10% Discount on one
Nights Stay
Hwy. 70 East, Glenwood, AR
501-356-4567

Arsenic & Old Lace B&B
15% Off 1 or More Nights
Sunday Thru Thursday
60 Hillside Avenue
Eureka Springs, AR
1800-243-Lace

Owl Hollow Inn
10% Off Minimum of 2
Nights Lodging
Hwy. 9 South
Mountain View, AR
501-269-8699

Rainbow Drive Resort
5% Discount on Professional
Guided Fishing Trip!
Rt. 1, Box 1185
Cotter, AR
501-430-5217

*Magee's Cafe*
10% Off Lunch or Dinner
362 Central Avenue
Hot Springs, AR
501-623-4091

The Ouachita Mountaineer

$5.00 off any
2 year subscription

501-285-2244

Riverview Hotel Bed & Breakfast
10% Off One Nights Lodging
One Block Off Main
Hot Springs, AR
501-297-8208

Swinging Bridge Resort
10% Off Lodging or
Boat Rental
100 Swinging Bridge Drive
Hot Springs, AR
501-362-3327

Ouachita Outdoor Mountain
Center
10% Off on Canoe Rentals
P.O. Box 65
Pencil Bluff, AR
1-800-748-3718

National Park Duck Tour
10 % Off Adult Duck Ticket!
418 Central
Hot Springs, AR
1-800-682-7044

Stetsons Resort
$10.00 Off on Lodging,
Boat, Guide Combo
HCR62 Box 102
Flippin, AR
501-453-8066

The Mustard Seed
10% Off on Any Dulcimer Tape
or CD
46 Spring
Eureka Springs, AR
501-253-7484

# The Traveler Thanks his Advertisers,
## Names you Can Rely on for Quality Service

M&M Canoe Rentals

LOST SPUR Dude Ranch

The Spillway Resort

ARROWHEAD

TRIGGER GAP
FLOAT SERVICE

MOORE OUTDOORS

WHITE HOLE RESORT

The Old Fashioned
SODA FOUNTAIN
Mountain View, Arkansas

Experience.............
LITTLE
SWITZERLAND

RESORT

Oak Tree INN

RIDGECREST
Resort

Rainbow Drive
RESORT

Red Bud Dock

River's Edge

Best Western
Limetree Inn

Join Us for Fun & Relaxation at
Self Creek Resort

Mountain View's
Best Western
Fiddler's Inn

OWL HOLLOW
INN
Bed & Breakfast

LOOKING GLASS
GRAPHICS

# TRAVEL NOTES